실전 1000제

KB074492

파고다
토익 LC
실전 1000제 개정판

초판　1쇄 인쇄　2020년　1월　2일
개정판 1쇄 발행　2023년　2월　3일

지 은 이 | 파고다교육그룹 언어교육연구소
펴 낸 이 | 박경실
펴 낸 곳 | **PAGODA Books** 파고다북스
출판등록 | 2005년 5월 27일 제 300-2005-90호
주　　소 | 06614 서울특별시 서초구 강남대로 419, 19층(서초동, 파고다타워)
전　　화 | (02) 6940-4070
팩　　스 | (02) 536-0660
홈페이지 | www.pagodabook.com

저작권자 | ⓒ 2023 파고다아카데미

ISBN 978-89-6281-895-6 (13740)

파고다북스　　　www.pagodabook.com
파고다 어학원　　www.pagoda21.com
파고다 인강　　　www.pagodastar.com
테스트 클리닉　　www.testclinic.com

▎낙장 및 파본은 구매처에서 교환해 드립니다.

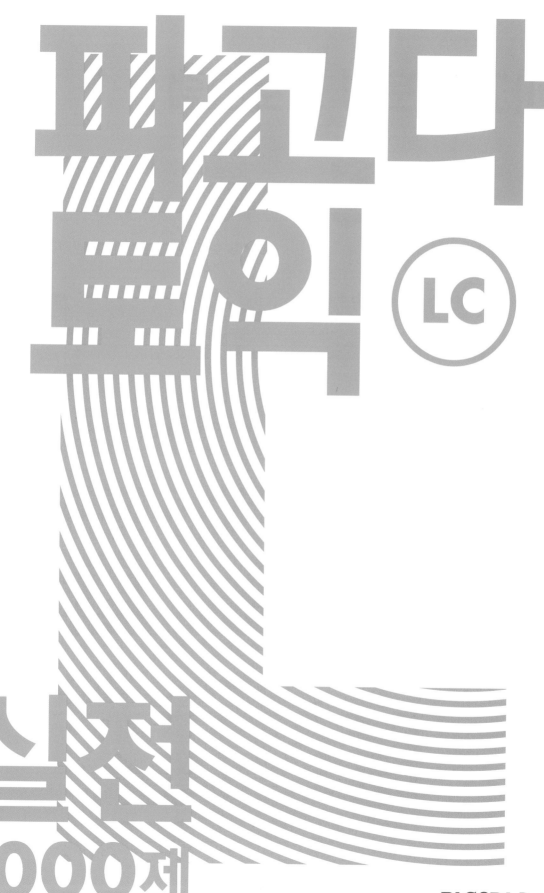

파고다
토익
LC

실전
1000제

PAGODA Books

파고다 토익 프로그램

독학자를 위한 다양하고 풍부한 학습 자료

세상 간편한 등업 신청으로 각종 학습
자료가 쏟아지는

파고다 토익 공식 온라인 카페
http://cafe.naver.com/pagodatoeicbooks

교재 Q&A	온라인 모의고사 2회분
교재 학습 자료	받아쓰기 훈련 자료
나의 학습 코칭	단어 암기장
정기 토익 분석 자료	단어 시험지
기출 분석 자료	MP3 기본 버전
예상 적중 특강	MP3 추가 버전(1.2배속 등)
논란 종결 총평	추가 연습 문제 등 각종 추가 자료

매회 업데이트! 토익 학습 센터

시험 전 적중 문제, 특강 제공
시험 직후 실시간 정답, 총평 특강, 분석 자료집 제공

토익에 풀! 빠져 풀TV

파고다 대표 강사진과 전문 연구원들의
다양한 무료 강의를 들으실 수 있습니다.

파고다 토익 기본 완성 LC/RC
토익 기초 입문서
토익 초보 학습자들이 단기간에 쉽게 접근할
수 있도록 토익의 필수 개념을 집약한 입문서

파고다 토익 실력 완성 LC/RC
토익 개념&실전 종합서
토익의 기본 개념을 확실히 다질 수 있는
풍부한 문제 유형과 실전형 연습 문제를 담은 훈련서

파고다 토익 고득점 완성 LC/RC
최상위권 토익 만점 전략서
기본기를 충분히 다진 토익 중상위권들의 고득점
완성을 위해 핵심 스킬만을 뽑아낸 토익 전략서

600+ 700+ 800+

파고다 토익 입문서 LC/RC
기초와 최신 경향 문제 완벽 적응 입문서
개념-핵심 스킬-집중 훈련의 반복을 통해 기초와
실전에서 유용한 전략을 동시에 익히는 입문서

파고다 토익 종합서 LC/RC
중상위권이 고득점으로 가는 도움 닫기 종합서
고득점 도약을 향한 한 끗 차이의 간격을 좁히는 종합서

이제는 인강도 밀착 관리!
체계적인 학습 관리와 목표 달성까지 가능한
파고다 토익 인생 점수반
www.pagodastar.com

성적 달성만 해도 100% 환급
인생 점수 달성하면 최대 300% 환급

최단기간 목표 달성 보장
X10배속 토익
현강으로 직접 듣는 1타 강사의 노하우
파고다 토익 점수 보장반
www.pagoda21.com

1개월 만에 2명 중 1명은 900점 달성!
파고다는 오직 결과로 증명합니다.

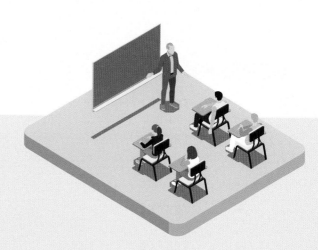

파고다 토익 적중 실전 LC/RC
최신 경향 실전 모의고사 10회분
끊임없이 변화하는 토익 트렌드에 대처하기 위해
적중률 높은 문제만을 엄선한 토익 실전서

900+ VOCA+

파고다 토익 실전 1000제 LC/RC
LC/RC 실전 모의고사 10회분(1000제)
문제 구성과 난이도까지 동일한 최신 경향 모의고사
와 200% 이해력 상승시키는 온라인 및 모바일 해설
서 구성의 실전서

파고다 토익 VOCA
LC, RC 목표 점수별 필수 어휘 30일 완성
600+, 700+, 800+, 900+ 목표 점수별,
우선 순위별 필수 어휘 1500

목차

이 책의 구성과 특징

깜짝 놀랄 정도로 실제 시험과 똑같은 10회분 모의고사 문제집

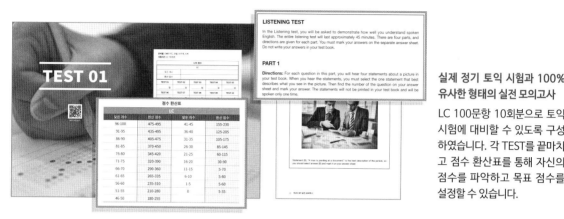

실제 정기 토익 시험과 100% 유사한 형태의 실전 모의고사

LC 100문항 10회분으로 토익 시험에 대비할 수 있도록 구성하였습니다. 각 TEST를 끝마치고 점수 환산표를 통해 자신의 점수를 파악하고 목표 점수를 설정할 수 있습니다.

두꺼운 해설서는 이제 No! 온라인 해설서 + 모바일 해설서 동시 제공!

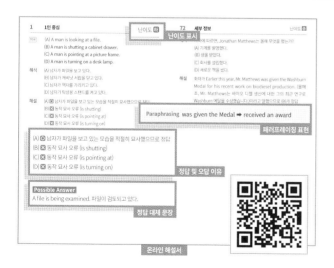

이해력을 200% 상승시키는 온라인 해설서

www.pagodabook.com

교재에 수록된 모든 문제의 답의 근거가 되는 문장을 함께 정리하였고, 정답과 오답의 근거를 쉽고 명확하게 파악하여 똑같은 실수를 반복하지 않도록 구성하였습니다. 또한, 정답을 대체할 수 있는 문장 및 패러프레이징 표현 등을 제시하여 정답 적중률을 한층 더 높일 수 있습니다.

언제 어디서나 쉽게 확인이 가능한 모바일 해설서

이동하면서 언제 어디서나 쉽게 궁금한 문제의 해설을 찾아볼 수 있도록 모바일 해설서를 제공해 드립니다. 모바일 해설서 QR코드를 인식하여 접속하면 별도의 로그인이나 회원 가입 없이 바로 해설을 확인하실 수 있습니다.

토익이란?

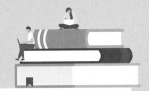

TOEIC(Test of English for International Communication)은 영어가 모국어가 아닌 사람들을 대상으로 일상생활 또는 국제 업무 등에 필요한 실용 영어 능력을 평가하는 시험입니다.

상대방과 '의사소통할 수 있는 능력(Communication ability)'을 평가하는 데 중점을 두고 있으므로 영어에 대한 '지식'이 아니라 영어의 실용적이고 기능적인 '사용법'을 묻는 문항들이 출제됩니다.

TOEIC은 1979년 미국 ETS(Educational Testing Service)에 의해 개발된 이래 전 세계 160개 이상의 국가 14,000여 개의 기관에서 승진 또는 해외 파견 인원 선발 등의 목적으로 널리 활용하고 있으며 우리나라에는 1982년 도입되었습니다. 해마다 전 세계적으로 약 700만 명 이상이 응시하고 있습니다.

▶ 토익 시험의 구성

	파트	시험 형태		문항 수	시간	배점
듣기 (LC)	1	사진 묘사		6	45분	495점
	2	질의응답		25		
	3	짧은 대화		39		
	4	짧은 담화		30		
읽기 (RC)	5	단문 공란 메우기 (문법/어휘)		30	75분	495점
	6	장문 공란 메우기		16		
	7	독해	단일 지문	29		
			이중 지문	10		
			삼중 지문	15		
계	7 Parts			200문항	120분	990점

1979 첫 토익

2006 NEW 토익

2016 신 토익

Present

토익 시험 접수와 성적 확인

토익 시험은 TOEIC 위원회 웹사이트(www.toeic.co.kr)에서 접수할 수 있습니다. 본인이 원하는 날짜와 장소를 지정하고 필수 기재 항목을 기재한 후 본인 사진을 업로드하면 간단하게 끝납니다.

보통은 두 달 후에 있는 시험일까지 접수 가능합니다. 각 시험일의 정기 접수는 시험일로부터 2주 전에 마감되지만, 시험일의 3일 전까지 추가 접수할 수 있는 특별 접수 기간이 있습니다. 그러나 특별 추가 접수 기간에는 응시료가 4,800원 더 비싸며, 희망하는 시험장을 선택할 수 없는 경우도 발생할 수 있습니다.

성적은 시험일로부터 12~15일 후에 인터넷이나 ARS(060-800-0515)를 통해 확인할 수 있습니다.

성적표는 우편이나 온라인으로 발급받을 수 있습니다. 우편으로 발급받을 경우는 성적 발표 후 대략 일주일이 소요되며, 온라인 발급을 선택하면 유효 기간 내에 홈페이지에서 본인이 직접 1회에 한해 무료 출력할 수 있습니다.

시험 당일 준비물

시험 당일 준비물은 규정 신분증, 연필, 지우개입니다. 허용되는 규정 신분증은 토익 공식 웹사이트에서 확인하시기 바랍니다. 필기구는 연필이나 샤프펜만 가능하고 볼펜이나 컴퓨터용 사인펜은 사용할 수 없습니다. 수험표는 출력해 가지 않아도 됩니다.

시험 진행 안내

시험 진행 일정은 시험 당일 고사장 사정에 따라 약간씩 다를 수 있지만 대부분 아래와 같이 진행됩니다.

▶ 시험 시간이 오전일 경우

AM 9:30~9:45	AM 9:45~9:50	AM 9:50~10:05	AM 10:05~10:10	AM 10:10~10:55	AM 10:55~12:10
15분	5분	15분	5분	45분	75분
답안지 작성에 관한 Orientation	수험자 휴식 시간	신분증 확인 (감독 교사)	문제지 배부, 파본 확인	듣기 평가(LC)	읽기 평가(RC) 2차 신분증 확인

* 주의: 오전 9시 50분 입실 통제

▶ 시험 시간이 오후일 경우

PM 2:30~2:45	PM 2:45~2:50	PM 2:50~3:05	PM 3:05~3:10	PM 3:10~3:55	PM 3:55~5:10
15분	5분	15분	5분	45분	75분
답안지 작성에 관한 Orientation	수험자 휴식 시간	신분증 확인 (감독 교사)	문제지 배부, 파본 확인	듣기 평가(LC)	읽기 평가(RC) 2차 신분증 확인

* 주의: 오후 2시 50분 입실 통제

파트별 토익 소개

PART 1

PHOTOGRAPHS
사진 묘사 문제

PART 1은 제시한 사진을 올바르게 묘사한 문장을 찾는 문제로, 방송으로 사진에 대한 4개의 짧은 설명문을 한번 들려준다. 4개의 설명문은 문제지에 인쇄되어 있지 않으며 4개의 설명문을 잘 듣고 그중에서 사진을 가장 정확하게 묘사하고 있는 문장을 답으로 선택한다.

문항 수	6문항(1번 ~ 6번에 해당합니다.)
Direction 소요 시간	약 1분 30초(LC 전체 Direction 약 25초 포함)
문제를 들려주는 시간	약 20초
다음 문제까지의 여유 시간	약 5초
문제 유형	1. 1인 중심 사진 2. 2인 이상 사진 3. 사물/풍경 사진

▶ 시험지에 인쇄되어 있는 모양

1.

▶ 스피커에서 들리는 음성

Number 1. Look at the picture marked number 1 in your test book.

(A) They're writing on a board.
(B) They're taking a file from a shelf.
(C) They're working at a desk.
(D) They're listening to a presentation.

정답 **1.** (C)

PART 2

QUESTION-RESPONSE
질의응답 문제

PART 2는 질문에 대한 올바른 답을 찾는 문제로, 방송을 통해 질문과 질문에 대한 3개의 응답문을 각 한 번씩 들려준다. 질문과 응답문은 문제지에 인쇄가 되어 있지 않으며 질문에 대한 가장 어울리는 응답문을 답으로 선택한다.

문항 수	25문항 (7번 ~ 31번에 해당합니다.)
Direction 소요 시간	약 25초
문제를 들려주는 시간	약 15초
다음 문제까지의 여유 시간	약 5초
문제 유형	1. 의문사 의문문 - Who/When/Where - What/Which - How/Why 2. 비의문사 의문문 - Be/Do/Will/Have/Should/May - 부정/부가/간접/선택 - 제안문·요청문/평서문

▶ **시험지에 인쇄되어 있는 모양**

7. Mark your answer on your answer sheet.

▶ **스피커에서 들리는 음성**

Number 7. How was the English test you took today?

(A) I took the bus home.
(B) I thought it was too difficult.
(C) I have two classes today.

정답 **7.**(B)

PART 3

SHORT CONVERSATIONS
짧은 대화 문제

PART 3는 짧은 대화문을 듣고 이에 대한 문제를 푸는 형식으로, 먼저 방송을 통해 짧은 대화를 들려준 뒤 이에 해당하는 질문을 들려준다. 문제지에는 질문과 4개의 보기가 인쇄되어 있으며 문제를 들은 뒤 제시된 보기 중 가장 적절한 것을 답으로 선택한다.

문항 수	13개 대화문, 39문항 (32번 ~ 70번에 해당합니다.)
Direction 소요 시간	약 30초
문제를 들려주는 시간	약 30~40초
다음 문제까지의 여유 시간	약 8초
지문 유형	- 회사 생활, 일상생활, 회사와 일상의 혼합 - 총 13개 대화문 중 '2인 대화문 11개, 3인 대화문 2개'로 고정 출제 - 주고받는 대화 수: 3~10번
질문 유형	- 일반 정보 문제: 주제·목적, 화자의 신분, 대화 장소 - 세부 정보 문제: 키워드, 제안·요청, 다음에 할 일/일어날 일 - 화자가 그렇게 말한 의도를 묻는 문제 (2문제 고정 출제) - 시각 자료 연계 문제 (62~70번 사이에서 3문제 고정 출제)

▶ 시험지에 인쇄되어 있는 모양

32. What is the conversation mainly about?
(A) Changes in business policies
(B) Sales of a company's products
(C) Expanding into a new market
(D) Recruiting temporary employees

33. Why does the woman say, "There you go"?
(A) She is happy to attend a meeting.
(B) She is frustrated with a coworker.
(C) She is offering encouragement.
(D) She is handing over something.

34. What do the men imply about the company?
(A) It has launched new merchandise.
(B) It is planning to relocate soon.
(C) It has clients in several countries.
(D) It is having financial difficulties.

▶ 스피커에서 들리는 음성

Questions 32 through 34 refer to the following conversation with three speakers.

M1: How have you two been doing with your sales lately?

W: Um, not too bad. My clients have been ordering about the same amount of promotional merchandise as before.

M2: I haven't been doing so well. But I do have a meeting with a potential new client tomorrow.

W: There you go. I'm sure things will turn around for you.

M1: Yeah, I hope it works out.

W: It's probably just temporary due to the recession.

M2: Maybe, but I heard that the company may downsize to try to save money.

M1: Actually, I heard that, too.

정답 **32.** (B) **33.** (C) **34.** (D)

PART 4

SHORT TALKS
짧은 담화 문제

PART 4는 짧은 담화문을 듣고 이에 대한 문제를 푸는 형식으로, 먼저 방송을 통해 짧은 담화를 들려준 뒤 이에 해당하는 질문을 들려준다. 문제지에는 질문과 4개의 보기가 인쇄되어 있으며 문제를 들은 뒤 제시된 보기 중 가장 적절한 것을 답으로 선택한다.

문항 수	10개 담화문, 30문항(71번 ~ 100번에 해당합니다.)
Direction 소요 시간	약 30초
문제를 들려주는 시간	약 30~40초
다음 문제까지의 여유 시간	약 8초
지문 유형	– 전화 메시지, 회의 발췌록, 안내 방송, 광고 방송, 뉴스 보도, 연설 등
질문 유형	– 일반 정보 문제: 주제·목적, 화자/청자의 신분, 담화 장소 – 세부 정보 문제: 키워드, 제안·요청, 다음에 할 일/일어날 일 – 화자가 그렇게 말한 의도를 묻는 문제(3문제 고정 출제) – 시각 자료 연계 문제(95~100번 사이에서 2문제 고정 출제)

▶ 시험지에 인쇄되어 있는 모양

71. Where most likely is the speaker?
(A) At a trade fair
(B) At a corporate banquet
(C) At a business seminar
(D) At an anniversary celebration

72. What are the listeners asked to do?
(A) Pick up programs for employees
(B) Arrive early for a presentation
(C) Turn off their mobile phones
(D) Carry their personal belongings

73. Why does the schedule have to be changed?
(A) A speaker has to leave early.
(B) A piece of equipment is not working.
(C) Lunch is not ready.
(D) Some speakers have not yet arrived.

▶ 스피커에서 들리는 음성

Questions 71 through 73 refer to the following talk.

I'd like to welcome all of you to today's employee training and development seminar for business owners. I'll briefly go over a few details before we get started. There will be a 15-minute break for coffee and snacks halfway through the program. This will be a good opportunity for you to mingle. If you need to leave the room during a talk, make sure to keep your wallet, phone, and … ah… any other valuable personal items with you. Also, please note that there will be a change in the order of the program. Um… Mr. Roland has to leave earlier than originally scheduled, so the last two speakers will be switched.

정답 **71.** (C) **72.** (D) **73.** (A)

TEST 01

MP3 바로 듣기

준비물: OMR 카드, 연필, 지우개, 시계
시험시간: LC 약 45분

나의 점수		
LC		
맞은 개수		
환산 점수		

TEST 01	TEST 02	TEST 03	TEST 04	TEST 05
_____점	_____점	_____점	_____점	_____점
TEST 06	**TEST 07**	**TEST 08**	**TEST 09**	**TEST 10**
_____점	_____점	_____점	_____점	_____점

점수 환산표

LC			
맞은 개수	환산 점수	맞은 개수	환산 점수
96-100	475-495	41-45	155-230
91-95	435-495	36-40	125-205
86-90	405-475	31-35	105-175
81-85	370-450	26-30	85-145
76-80	345-420	21-25	60-115
71-75	320-390	16-20	30-90
66-70	290-360	11-15	5-70
61-65	265-335	6-10	5-60
56-60	235-310	1-5	5-60
51-55	210-280	0	5-35
46-50	180-255		

LISTENING TEST

In the Listening test, you will be asked to demonstrate how well you understand spoken English. The entire listening test will last approximately 45 minutes. There are four parts, and directions are given for each part. You must mark your answers on the separate answer sheet. Do not write your answers in your test book.

PART 1

Directions: For each question in this part, you will hear four statements about a picture in your test book. When you hear the statements, you must select the one statement that best describes what you see in the picture. Then find the number of the question on your answer sheet and mark your answer. The statements will not be printed in your test book and will be spoken only one time.

Statement (B), "A man is pointing at a document," is the best description of the picture, so you should select answer (B) and mark it on your answer sheet.

1.

2.

GO ON TO THE NEXT PAGE

3.

4.

5.

6.

GO ON TO THE NEXT PAGE

PART 2

Directions: You will hear a question or statement and three responses spoken in English. They will not be printed in your test book and will be spoken only one time. Select the best response to the question or statement and mark the letter (A), (B), or (C) on your answer sheet.

7. Mark your answer on your answer sheet.

8. Mark your answer on your answer sheet.

9. Mark your answer on your answer sheet.

10. Mark your answer on your answer sheet.

11. Mark your answer on your answer sheet.

12. Mark your answer on your answer sheet.

13. Mark your answer on your answer sheet.

14. Mark your answer on your answer sheet.

15. Mark your answer on your answer sheet.

16. Mark your answer on your answer sheet.

17. Mark your answer on your answer sheet.

18. Mark your answer on your answer sheet.

19. Mark your answer on your answer sheet.

20. Mark your answer on your answer sheet.

21. Mark your answer on your answer sheet.

22. Mark your answer on your answer sheet.

23. Mark your answer on your answer sheet.

24. Mark your answer on your answer sheet.

25. Mark your answer on your answer sheet.

26. Mark your answer on your answer sheet.

27. Mark your answer on your answer sheet.

28. Mark your answer on your answer sheet.

29. Mark your answer on your answer sheet.

30. Mark your answer on your answer sheet.

31. Mark your answer on your answer sheet.

PART 3

Directions: You will hear some conversations between two or more people. You will be asked to answer three questions about what the speakers say in each conversation. Select the best response to each question and mark the letter (A), (B), (C), or (D) on your answer sheet. The conversations will not be printed in your test book and will be spoken only one time.

32. What is the man trying to submit?

(A) An evaluation report
(B) A financial statement
(C) A job application
(D) A rental lease

33. What does the woman say happened last week?

(A) Network security was tightened.
(B) Some work was outsourced.
(C) Risk assessments were revised.
(D) Mail services were suspended.

34. What will the man do next?

(A) Call a network engineer
(B) Organize a meeting
(C) Meet a client
(D) Read some e-mails

35. What is the conversation mainly about?

(A) A corporate health initiative
(B) A company fundraiser
(C) An industry convention
(D) A professional development program

36. What does the woman say about a seminar?

(A) It was well received.
(B) It was overpriced.
(C) It was conducted online.
(D) It was postponed.

37. What does the man suggest doing?

(A) Hiring a caterer for an event
(B) Sending out a pamphlet
(C) Looking for some volunteers
(D) Providing consultation sessions

38. What type of product are the speakers discussing?

(A) Exercise clothing
(B) Protective equipment
(C) Stationary bicycles
(D) Athletic footwear

39. What product feature does the woman say she is worried about?

(A) Weight
(B) Durability
(C) Design
(D) Functionality

40. What does the man offer to do?

(A) Write an online post
(B) Find a supplier
(C) Recruit new salespeople
(D) Submit some designs

41. What is June's job?

(A) Computer programmer
(B) Accounting clerk
(C) Office administrator
(D) Financial officer

42. What will June most likely do next?

(A) Complete an assignment
(B) Meet a manager
(C) Read an article
(D) Visit a website

43. What does June say about some software?

(A) It is widely used in the industry.
(B) She downloaded it on her computer.
(C) She is already familiar with it.
(D) It is from another country.

GO ON TO THE NEXT PAGE

44. Why will the woman be going to Chicago?

(A) To meet with potential clients
(B) To attend a conference
(C) To give a keynote speech
(D) To inspect a facility

45. What does the woman ask the man about?

(A) Whether an expense can be reimbursed
(B) Whether a trip can be rescheduled
(C) Whether she can get a seat upgrade
(D) Whether she can stay at a different hotel

46. What does the man say he will do?

(A) Consult a manager
(B) Check a request form
(C) Compose an e-mail
(D) Conduct some research

47. Why did the man contact the woman?

(A) To confirm travel arrangements
(B) To postpone a consultation
(C) To change a meeting place
(D) To request an invoice

48. What does the woman ask about?

(A) Completing some paperwork
(B) Conducting an interview
(C) Extending a deadline
(D) Meeting another lawyer

49. Why does the woman say a location is convenient?

(A) It is situated downtown.
(B) It is open late.
(C) It is close to a subway station.
(D) It is near her workplace.

50. What are the speakers discussing?

(A) A license clearance
(B) A corporate merger
(C) A new office procedure
(D) A business negotiation

51. What does Max say he will do?

(A) Write a press release
(B) Check with some coworkers
(C) Sign a contract
(D) Contact a client

52. What does the woman hope will happen next year?

(A) A new product will be released.
(B) A company's profits will increase.
(C) A global event will be organized.
(D) A company will open an overseas branch.

53. Where most likely are the speakers?

(A) At a vehicle rental agency
(B) At a conference hall
(C) At a tourist office
(D) At a city bus terminal

54. Why does the woman say, "I've never been to this city"?

(A) To request a tour guide
(B) To ask for a suggestion
(C) To describe a problem
(D) To inquire about transportation

55. Why does the man encourage the woman to order online?

(A) A discount will be available.
(B) There is no additional fee.
(C) There is no wait time.
(D) A website has more items.

56. What type of business do the speakers work at?

(A) A farm
(B) A bakery
(C) A coffee shop
(D) A food manufacturer

57. What does the man say a winner will receive?

(A) Some merchandise
(B) Some prize money
(C) A lifetime supply of products
(D) A gift voucher

58. Why does the man say, "The office next door is under renovation right now"?

(A) To propose rescheduling a discussion
(B) To suggest changing a venue
(C) To recommend a new office space
(D) To apologize for a delay

59. Where do the speakers work?

(A) At a supermarket
(B) At a café
(C) At a bank
(D) At a bottling plant

60. According to the man, what has recently happened?

(A) The price of a product has increased.
(B) A contract was terminated.
(C) The owner of a business has changed.
(D) A sales event was held.

61. What does the woman say she will do tomorrow?

(A) Call a new supplier
(B) Speak with an applicant
(C) Conduct a survey
(D) Hold a meeting

Wall Display

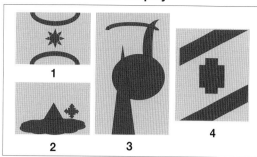

62. Who most likely is the woman?

(A) A gallery curator
(B) A university lecturer
(C) A Web designer
(D) An art teacher

63. Look at the graphic. Which painting does the man prefer?

(A) Painting 1
(B) Painting 2
(C) Painting 3
(D) Painting 4

64. What will the woman most likely do next?

(A) Produce an invoice
(B) Measure an artwork
(C) Make an introduction
(D) Purchase a portfolio

GO ON TO THE NEXT PAGE

Date	Location
October 8	Boston
October 15	New Haven
October 22	Hartford
October 29	Providence

65. Why does the woman think the exhibit looks great?

(A) It will feature artists from around the world.
(B) It will show a video by critics.
(C) It will display works by famous painters.
(D) It will include a lecture by artists.

66. Look at the graphic. Where do the speakers live?

(A) In Boston
(B) In New Haven
(C) In Hartford
(D) In Providence

67. What does the woman say she will do with the booklet?

(A) Share it with her family members
(B) Hand out some photocopies
(C) Send out an electronic copy
(D) Post it on a notice board

 Geller's Grocery Store
Recognizing Achievements

- 5 years rated as Top Small Business
- 20 years run by the current owner
- 50 years in the same location
- 80 years in operation

68. Where does the man most likely work?

(A) At a delivery company
(B) At a grocery store
(C) At a convention center
(D) At a printing business

69. Look at the graphic. Which achievement is the man amazed by?

(A) Years rated as Top Small Business
(B) Years run by the current owner
(C) Years in the same location
(D) Years in operation

70. What will the woman have to pay extra for?

(A) On-site installation
(B) Express shipping
(C) A rental vehicle
(D) Special supplies

PART 4

Directions: You will hear some talks given by a single speaker. You will be asked to answer three questions about what the speaker says in each talk. Select the best response to each question and mark the letter (A), (B), (C), or (D) on your answer sheet. The talks will not be printed in your test book and will be spoken only one time.

71. What is the topic of the convention?

(A) Renewable energy
(B) Computer engineering
(C) Waste recycling
(D) Textile production

72. According to the speaker, what did Jonathan Matthews do this year?

(A) He invented a machine.
(B) He received an award.
(C) He founded a company.
(D) He wrote a new book.

73. What does the speaker remind the listeners to do?

(A) Write down questions
(B) Sample a product
(C) Attend a demonstration
(D) Wear a name tag

74. What is the broadcast mainly about?

(A) Local businesses
(B) Current events
(C) Weather conditions
(D) Celebrity interviews

75. What are the listeners encouraged to do?

(A) Download an app
(B) Purchase a ticket
(C) Check a website
(D) Remain in the city center

76. What is taking place in the city center?

(A) A music festival
(B) A flea market
(C) A marathon
(D) A fundraising event

77. What kind of business is being advertised?

(A) A home landscaping company
(B) An interior design service
(C) A photography studio
(D) An art gallery

78. How can the listeners receive a complimentary gift?

(A) By mentioning an advertisement
(B) By posting a review
(C) By submitting a photo
(D) By completing a survey

79. What does the speaker say the listeners can do during a phone call?

(A) Order a picture frame
(B) Get some directions
(C) Schedule an appointment
(D) Receive some advice

80. What does the speaker's company produce?

(A) Energy drinks
(B) Health supplements
(C) Meal kits
(D) Cosmetic products

81. Why does the speaker want to partner with the department store?

(A) It has locations countrywide.
(B) It is trusted by most consumers.
(C) It has a strong international presence.
(D) It has access to key partners.

82. Why does the speaker say, "our products are completely organic"?

(A) To suggest a marketing strategy
(B) To indicate a potential problem
(C) To emphasize a point of difference
(D) To address a common question

GO ON TO THE NEXT PAGE

83. What kind of business do the listeners most likely work for?

(A) A staffing agency
(B) An auto repair shop
(C) An electronics store
(D) A marketing firm

84. What does the speaker mean when he says, "Now, we've added a section on our website"?

(A) A new product will be introduced.
(B) An employee has been hired.
(C) A layout will be changed.
(D) An issue has been resolved.

85. What does the speaker plan to do on Mondays?

(A) Compile some comments
(B) Talk to some customers
(C) Check some inventory
(D) Send some packages

86. Who most likely is the speaker?

(A) A sanitary worker
(B) An organic farmer
(C) A restaurant owner
(D) A nutrition scientist

87. What will be changing next week?

(A) A rental fee
(B) A hiring process
(C) A zoning law
(D) A supplies vendor

88. What will the speaker do next?

(A) Put up a notice
(B) Demonstrate a product
(C) Create an action plan
(D) Listen to some ideas

89. Where do the listeners most likely work?

(A) At a news station
(B) At a library
(C) At a bookstore
(D) At a publishing company

90. What was the questionnaire designed to find out?

(A) Security policies
(B) Newly launched products
(C) Reader satisfaction
(D) Subscription prices

91. What incentive was offered for completing the questionnaire?

(A) A service upgrade
(B) A discount voucher
(C) A complimentary bag
(D) A cash prize

92. What is the speaker helping the listener do?

(A) Organize a conference
(B) Schedule a flight
(C) Give a presentation
(D) Book a venue

93. What does the speaker imply when he says, "the less expensive option has received mixed reviews recently"?

(A) A budgeting change will be coming into place.
(B) A suggestion has been ignored in the past.
(C) The listener needs to narrow the list of requirements.
(D) The listener should not choose an inexpensive option.

94. Why does the speaker request to be contacted by phone?

(A) He is leaving the company.
(B) He does not wish to be recorded.
(C) He will be preoccupied.
(D) He requires an answer immediately.

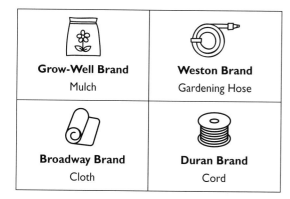

| **Grow-Well Brand**
Mulch | **Weston Brand**
Gardening Hose |
| **Broadway Brand**
Cloth | **Duran Brand**
Cord |

95. Who sponsors the podcast?

(A) An agricultural cooperative
(B) A plant nursery
(C) A hardware store
(D) A landscaping service

96. What does the speaker say the podcast is about?

(A) Protecting plants from the cold
(B) Cultivating healthy produce
(C) Choosing the best type of soil
(D) Transplanting seedlings outdoors

97. Look at the graphic. Which item is on sale?

(A) The mulch
(B) The gardening hose
(C) The cloth
(D) The cord

A-Z Commercial Cleaning Service

400 to 600 Square Feet = $45
600 to 800 Square Feet = $65
800 to 1,000 Square Feet = $85
1,000 to 1,200 Square Feet = $105

98. Where did the caller get the listener's phone number?

(A) From a television commercial
(B) From a neighbor
(C) From a newsletter
(D) From a city guide

99. Look at the graphic. How much will the service cost?

(A) $45
(B) $65
(C) $85
(D) $105

100. Why is the caller unavailable this morning?

(A) He is visiting a doctor's office.
(B) He is meeting with a client.
(C) He is presenting at a company workshop.
(D) He is going to the bank.

This is the end of the Listening test.

TEST 02

MP3 바로 듣기

준비물: OMR 카드, 연필, 지우개, 시계
시험시간: LC 약 45분

나의 점수		
LC		
맞은 개수		
환산 점수		

TEST 01	TEST 02	TEST 03	TEST 04	TEST 05
_____ 점	_____ 점	_____ 점	_____ 점	_____ 점
TEST 06	**TEST 07**	**TEST 08**	**TEST 09**	**TEST 10**
_____ 점	_____ 점	_____ 점	_____ 점	_____ 점

점수 환산표

LC			
맞은 개수	환산 점수	맞은 개수	환산 점수
96-100	475-495	41-45	155-230
91-95	435-495	36-40	125-205
86-90	405-475	31-35	105-175
81-85	370-450	26-30	85-145
76-80	345-420	21-25	60-115
71-75	320-390	16-20	30-90
66-70	290-360	11-15	5-70
61-65	265-335	6-10	5-60
56-60	235-310	1-5	5-60
51-55	210-280	0	5-35
46-50	180-255		

LISTENING TEST

In the Listening test, you will be asked to demonstrate how well you understand spoken English. The entire listening test will last approximately 45 minutes. There are four parts, and directions are given for each part. You must mark your answers on the separate answer sheet. Do not write your answers in your test book.

PART 1

Directions: For each question in this part, you will hear four statements about a picture in your test book. When you hear the statements, you must select the one statement that best describes what you see in the picture. Then find the number of the question on your answer sheet and mark your answer. The statements will not be printed in your test book and will be spoken only one time.

Statement (B), "A man is pointing at a document," is the best description of the picture, so you should select answer (B) and mark it on your answer sheet.

1.

2.

GO ON TO THE NEXT PAGE

3.

4.

5.

6.

GO ON TO THE NEXT PAGE

PART 2

Directions: You will hear a question or statement and three responses spoken in English. They will not be printed in your test book and will be spoken only one time. Select the best response to the question or statement and mark the letter (A), (B), or (C) on your answer sheet.

7. Mark your answer on your answer sheet.

8. Mark your answer on your answer sheet.

9. Mark your answer on your answer sheet.

10. Mark your answer on your answer sheet.

11. Mark your answer on your answer sheet.

12. Mark your answer on your answer sheet.

13. Mark your answer on your answer sheet.

14. Mark your answer on your answer sheet.

15. Mark your answer on your answer sheet.

16. Mark your answer on your answer sheet.

17. Mark your answer on your answer sheet.

18. Mark your answer on your answer sheet.

19. Mark your answer on your answer sheet.

20. Mark your answer on your answer sheet.

21. Mark your answer on your answer sheet.

22. Mark your answer on your answer sheet.

23. Mark your answer on your answer sheet.

24. Mark your answer on your answer sheet.

25. Mark your answer on your answer sheet.

26. Mark your answer on your answer sheet.

27. Mark your answer on your answer sheet.

28. Mark your answer on your answer sheet.

29. Mark your answer on your answer sheet.

30. Mark your answer on your answer sheet.

31. Mark your answer on your answer sheet.

PART 3

Directions: You will hear some conversations between two or more people. You will be asked to answer three questions about what the speakers say in each conversation. Select the best response to each question and mark the letter (A), (B), (C), or (D) on your answer sheet. The conversations will not be printed in your test book and will be spoken only one time.

32. Where does the woman work?

(A) At a public university
(B) At a travel agency
(C) At an art gallery
(D) At a newspaper company

33. Why is the woman calling?

(A) To request access to some equipment
(B) To file a complaint about a purchase
(C) To express interest in using a picture
(D) To order some copies of a publication

34. What does the man ask the woman for?

(A) A name of an item
(B) An e-mail address
(C) A proof of identification
(D) A product code

35. What are the speakers preparing to do?

(A) Record a video
(B) Attend a music festival
(C) Perform in a play
(D) Hold some rehearsals

36. What does the man say about the Deanville Cultural Center?

(A) It has poor acoustics.
(B) It is too small.
(C) It is over the budget.
(D) It is far from the city.

37. What will the woman most likely do next?

(A) Change a shipping address
(B) Reschedule an event
(C) Call a family member
(D) Visit a venue

38. What field do the speakers most likely work in?

(A) Journalism
(B) Technology
(C) Health
(D) Finance

39. Why are many people interested in attending the conference?

(A) It will be shown in a prominent magazine.
(B) It will be attended by industry leaders.
(C) It will include opportunities to network.
(D) It will feature a product announcement.

40. Who will be permitted to attend the conference?

(A) Employees who have the most experience
(B) Employees who are not currently out of the country
(C) Employees with the most knowledge of a product
(D) Employees who are willing to pay the entry fee

41. Who most likely is the woman?

(A) A hotel clerk
(B) A flight attendant
(C) A travel agent
(D) A fitness trainer

42. What do the men inquire about?

(A) Purchasing airplane tickets
(B) Enrolling in some classes
(C) Upgrading some equipment
(D) Touring a facility

43. What does the woman offer to do?

(A) Reduce a price
(B) Print out an invoice
(C) Contact a supervisor
(D) Provide a map

GO ON TO THE NEXT PAGE

44. What did the speakers' company do within the last week?

(A) It acquired a major international client.
(B) It appointed a new vice president.
(C) It relocated its headquarters.
(D) It went through organizational restructuring.

45. What problem do the speakers mention?

(A) A business trip must be postponed.
(B) Office renovation work is incomplete.
(C) Some of their colleagues have been let go.
(D) Some personal belongings are missing.

46. Where will the speakers go next?

(A) To a storage space
(B) To a reception desk
(C) To a building parking lot
(D) To a meeting room

47. What did the woman do over the weekend?

(A) She built a shed in the backyard.
(B) She learned a new recipe.
(C) She took photographs.
(D) She installed new wallpaper.

48. What will the woman send to the man this afternoon?

(A) A product
(B) An instruction manual
(C) A discount code
(D) A store address

49. What advantage does the woman mention?

(A) Custom designs
(B) Waterproof material
(C) Fast delivery
(D) Low costs

50. What feature of the shoes is the man pleased about?

(A) The comfortable soles
(B) The eco-friendly materials
(C) The cost
(D) The patterns

51. Why does the man say, "Tina told me not to make design changes to the boots"?

(A) To mention that a budget is limited
(B) To report that Tina will revise a sketch
(C) To point out that a product is selling well
(D) To give a reason for not doing a task

52. What will the woman send to Tina?

(A) Some sales data
(B) Some new designs
(C) A guest list
(D) A project proposal

53. What does the woman's company plan to offer?

(A) Expedited international shipment
(B) Free installation
(C) Online shopping
(D) Customized design service

54. What does the man suggest the woman do?

(A) Try another financing option
(B) Visit a different branch
(C) Open a new bank account
(D) Consult a tax advisor

55. What does the woman ask the man about?

(A) A payment schedule
(B) A membership form
(C) An employee handbook
(D) An application process

56. What industry do the speakers most likely work in?

(A) Finance
(B) Retail
(C) Hospitality
(D) Architecture

57. Why does the woman interrupt the men?

(A) To inquire about a location of a meeting
(B) To inform them about a revised schedule
(C) To rent some office equipment
(D) To provide assistance with a project

58. What will the men do next?

(A) Go out for a meal
(B) Visit a client's office
(C) Review an estimate
(D) Contact a coworker

59. Where are the speakers?

(A) At a ski resort
(B) At a hardware store
(C) At a manufacturing plant
(D) At a landscaping firm

60. Why does the man say, "it's going to be winter soon"?

(A) To point out an upcoming deadline
(B) To indicate that he is excited about traveling
(C) To show that he is interested in a service
(D) To order some new products

61. What does the woman give to the man?

(A) A project portfolio
(B) A work schedule
(C) A sample contract
(D) An information pamphlet

Ivy Dental Clinic Thursday Schedule				
	Dr. Sharp	Dr. Baker	Dr. Olson	Dr. Ross
10:00 A.M.	X	FREE	X	FREE
11:00 A.M.	X	X	X	X
12:00 P.M.	X	X	X	FREE
1:00 P.M.	FREE	X	FREE	X
2:00 P.M.	X	X	FREE	X

62. Where does the woman most likely work?

(A) At a dentist's office
(B) At a government agency
(C) At a theater
(D) At a factory

63. Why does an appointment need to be rescheduled?

(A) An appointment took longer than expected.
(B) A payment system was faulty.
(C) There was an unplanned outage.
(D) Several employees were late to work.

64. Look at the graphic. Who will the man most likely see?

(A) Dr. Sharp
(B) Dr. Baker
(C) Dr. Olson
(D) Dr. Ross

GO ON TO THE NEXT PAGE

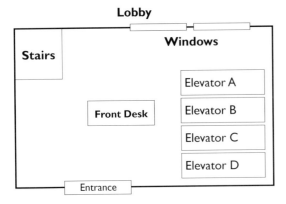

Lobby

Stairs

Windows

Front Desk

Elevator A
Elevator B
Elevator C
Elevator D

Entrance

Statesville Technology Convention				
[Morning Sessions]				
	Diamond Hall	Star Room	Emerald Lounge	Crystal Auditorium
7:30 A.M. – 9:30 A.M.	Using Social Media	Future of Internet		
9:40 A.M. – 11:40 A.M.		Tablets and Smartphones		Online Payment Platforms

65. Why is the woman visiting Lange and Associates?

(A) To repair some broken equipment
(B) To review some financial documents
(C) To attend a job interview
(D) To file for tax returns

66. Look at the graphic. Which elevator should the woman avoid?

(A) Elevator A
(B) Elevator B
(C) Elevator C
(D) Elevator D

67. What will the woman most likely do next?

(A) Show her identification
(B) Complete an application form
(C) Head back outside
(D) Contact an associate

68. What was the woman concerned about?

(A) Not bringing an ID
(B) Losing an important packet
(C) Being unable to sign up
(D) Going to an incorrect location

69. Look at the graphic. Where will Baymox, Inc. give its product demonstration?

(A) In the Diamond Hall
(B) In the Star Room
(C) In the Emerald Lounge
(D) In the Crystal Auditorium

70. Why does the man apologize?

(A) There are no more complimentary pens.
(B) A guide contains some wrong information.
(C) A presentation has been delayed.
(D) The woman's credit card cannot be processed.

PART 4

Directions: You will hear some talks given by a single speaker. You will be asked to answer three questions about what the speaker says in each talk. Select the best response to each question and mark the letter (A), (B), (C), or (D) on your answer sheet. The talks will not be printed in your test book and will be spoken only one time.

71. What most likely is being advertised?

(A) A convention hall
(B) A fitness center
(C) A retail store
(D) A café

72. According to the speaker, what has the business recently done?

(A) It hired additional managers.
(B) It expanded into a new area.
(C) It merged with a company.
(D) It won a prestigious award.

73. Why are the listeners encouraged to visit a website?

(A) To see some photographs
(B) To sign up as a member
(C) To win a prize
(D) To view a list of services

74. Why did the speaker leave the message?

(A) To explain a schedule
(B) To report a problem
(C) To arrange a meeting
(D) To apologize for an error

75. What has the speaker already done?

(A) Talked to a business owner
(B) Paid for a service
(C) Reserved some tables
(D) Checked some equipment

76. What does the speaker say she will do today?

(A) Conduct an inspection
(B) Send some photos
(C) Renovate a store
(D) Visit an office

77. Why does the speaker thank the listeners?

(A) For working extra hours
(B) For meeting a sales target
(C) For subscribing to a magazine
(D) For responding to a survey

78. What has the company decided to do?

(A) Update some software
(B) Postpone an event
(C) Revise a company policy
(D) Expand office space

79. According to the speaker, what will the listeners probably do next month?

(A) Participate in performance evaluations
(B) Work from other locations
(C) Meet new personnel
(D) Attend a trade show

80. What is being discussed?

(A) A high-tech sports watch
(B) A wireless audio device
(C) A digital camera
(D) A portable heater

81. According to the speaker, what is special about the item?

(A) It is energy efficient.
(B) It is wearable.
(C) It is water resistant.
(D) It is inexpensive.

82. What does the speaker recommend doing?

(A) Reserving a product online
(B) Watching a tutorial
(C) Purchasing an extended warranty
(D) Picking up a package in person

GO ON TO THE NEXT PAGE

83. Who most likely is the talk intended for?

(A) Automotive mechanics
(B) Factory employees
(C) Sales associates
(D) Computer technicians

84. What does the speaker imply when he says, "They probably have limited knowledge about it"?

(A) The listeners should explain a topic clearly.
(B) The listeners should show a video.
(C) The listeners should attend a seminar.
(D) The listeners should meet with an expert.

85. What does the speaker remind the listeners about?

(A) Hiring staff members
(B) Meeting a quota
(C) Printing out a document
(D) Cutting some costs

86. What most likely is the speaker's profession?

(A) Project manager
(B) Florist
(C) Carpenter
(D) Electrician

87. What does the speaker suggest doing first?

(A) Taking measurements
(B) Gathering some materials
(C) Cleaning some equipment
(D) Preparing a shopping list

88. What does the speaker thank the audience for doing?

(A) Asking questions
(B) Donating to a cause
(C) Promoting a channel
(D) Sending in photos

89. What will the listeners learn at the museum?

(A) The history of cinema
(B) The history of printing
(C) The history of languages
(D) The history of art

90. What does the speaker mean when she says, "We have a curator in every room"?

(A) The museum is crowded with visitors.
(B) The museum needs more funding.
(C) The artifacts are protected.
(D) The listeners may ask questions.

91. What does the speaker invite the listeners to do?

(A) Refer to an exhibit catalog
(B) Upload some photographs
(C) Make donations to the museum
(D) Purchase some souvenirs

92. What is the speaker's company planning to do this fall?

(A) Attend an exposition
(B) Conduct a seminar
(C) Hire some interns
(D) Launch a website

93. What does the speaker mean when he says, "it's completely different from what I've seen in the past"?

(A) He is upset with an outcome.
(B) He is satisfied with some designs.
(C) He needs help moving some tools and supplies.
(D) He is unsure about following a suggestion.

94. What does the speaker request?

(A) A cost estimate
(B) A phone number
(C) A size measurement
(D) A sample catalog

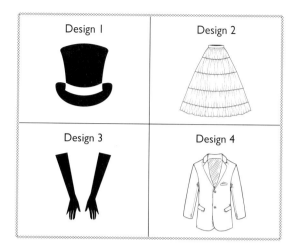

Design 1	Design 2
Design 3	Design 4

Location	Safety sign required
Freezer	Label opened containers
Stove	No cell phone use
Restaurant Floors	Mop any wet spots
Storage Room	Wear protective gloves

95. Why is the film special for the speaker?

(A) It was her first major production.
(B) It was written by a close friend.
(C) It was widely anticipated by the media.
(D) It was directed by someone she admires.

96. Look at the graphic. Which design does the speaker point out?

(A) Design 1
(B) Design 2
(C) Design 3
(D) Design 4

97. What will most likely happen next?

(A) A video will be shown.
(B) A short break will commence.
(C) Some questions will be answered.
(D) Some samples will be passed around.

98. Who is the speaker?

(A) A tour guide
(B) A restaurant manager
(C) A government official
(D) A lawyer

99. According to the speaker, what took place recently?

(A) An employee orientation
(B) A teambuilding workshop
(C) A facility renovation
(D) A health and safety inspection

100. Look at the graphic. Where will an additional sign be placed?

(A) Near a freezer
(B) Near a stove
(C) On the restaurant floors
(D) Outside a storage room

This is the end of the Listening test.

TEST 03

MP3 바로 듣기

준비물: OMR 카드, 연필, 지우개, 시계
시험시간: LC 약 45분

<table>
<tr><th colspan="5">나의 점수</th></tr>
<tr><td colspan="5">LC</td></tr>
<tr><td colspan="2">맞은 개수</td><td colspan="3"></td></tr>
<tr><td colspan="2">환산 점수</td><td colspan="3"></td></tr>
</table>

TEST 01	TEST 02	TEST 03	TEST 04	TEST 05
_____점	_____점	_____점	_____점	_____점
TEST 06	**TEST 07**	**TEST 08**	**TEST 09**	**TEST 10**
_____점	_____점	_____점	_____점	_____점

점수 환산표

LC			
맞은 개수	환산 점수	맞은 개수	환산 점수
96-100	475-495	41-45	155-230
91-95	435-495	36-40	125-205
86-90	405-475	31-35	105-175
81-85	370-450	26-30	85-145
76-80	345-420	21-25	60-115
71-75	320-390	16-20	30-90
66-70	290-360	11-15	5-70
61-65	265-335	6-10	5-60
56-60	235-310	1-5	5-60
51-55	210-280	0	5-35
46-50	180-255		

LISTENING TEST

In the Listening test, you will be asked to demonstrate how well you understand spoken English. The entire listening test will last approximately 45 minutes. There are four parts, and directions are given for each part. You must mark your answers on the separate answer sheet. Do not write your answers in your test book.

PART 1

Directions: For each question in this part, you will hear four statements about a picture in your test book. When you hear the statements, you must select the one statement that best describes what you see in the picture. Then find the number of the question on your answer sheet and mark your answer. The statements will not be printed in your test book and will be spoken only one time.

Statement (B), "A man is pointing at a document," is the best description of the picture, so you should select answer (B) and mark it on your answer sheet.

1.

2.

GO ON TO THE NEXT PAGE

3.

4.

5.

6.

GO ON TO THE NEXT PAGE

→

PART 2

Directions: You will hear a question or statement and three responses spoken in English. They will not be printed in your test book and will be spoken only one time. Select the best response to the question or statement and mark the letter (A), (B), or (C) on your answer sheet.

7. Mark your answer on your answer sheet.

8. Mark your answer on your answer sheet.

9. Mark your answer on your answer sheet.

10. Mark your answer on your answer sheet.

11. Mark your answer on your answer sheet.

12. Mark your answer on your answer sheet.

13. Mark your answer on your answer sheet.

14. Mark your answer on your answer sheet.

15. Mark your answer on your answer sheet.

16. Mark your answer on your answer sheet.

17. Mark your answer on your answer sheet.

18. Mark your answer on your answer sheet.

19. Mark your answer on your answer sheet.

20. Mark your answer on your answer sheet.

21. Mark your answer on your answer sheet.

22. Mark your answer on your answer sheet.

23. Mark your answer on your answer sheet.

24. Mark your answer on your answer sheet.

25. Mark your answer on your answer sheet.

26. Mark your answer on your answer sheet.

27. Mark your answer on your answer sheet.

28. Mark your answer on your answer sheet.

29. Mark your answer on your answer sheet.

30. Mark your answer on your answer sheet.

31. Mark your answer on your answer sheet.

PART 3

Directions: You will hear some conversations between two or more people. You will be asked to answer three questions about what the speakers say in each conversation. Select the best response to each question and mark the letter (A), (B), (C), or (D) on your answer sheet. The conversations will not be printed in your test book and will be spoken only one time.

32. What sort of merchandise are the speakers discussing?

(A) A vehicle
(B) A mobile phone
(C) Some fitness equipment
(D) Some office furniture

33. What still needs to be decided?

(A) A name
(B) A marketing campaign
(C) A launch date
(D) A price

34. What does the man recommend doing?

(A) Speaking with coworkers
(B) Scheduling a meeting
(C) Revising a deadline
(D) Modifying some features

35. Why is the man meeting with the woman?

(A) To check out available office space
(B) To participate in a job interview
(C) To inquire about a service
(D) To negotiate a contract

36. Why does the man mention his sister?

(A) To discuss a well-known author
(B) To explain where he learned a skill
(C) To request a special price
(D) To describe how he found out about a firm

37. What area does the man want to concentrate on?

(A) Software programming
(B) Book editing
(C) Client relations
(D) Web design

38. What most likely is the man's job?

(A) Artist
(B) Event planner
(C) Real estate agent
(D) Repair worker

39. What does the woman say will happen next Friday?

(A) A work conference
(B) A dinner party
(C) A promotional event
(D) A yard sale

40. What will the man do next?

(A) Tow a vehicle
(B) Check the building
(C) Order new equipment
(D) Install an air conditioner

41. What industry do the speakers probably work in?

(A) Appliance sales
(B) Automobile manufacturing
(C) Food production
(D) Computer programming

42. What problem is being discussed?

(A) Some equipment keeps turning off.
(B) A manager is not available.
(C) Some customers have made complaints.
(D) An inventory list is incorrect.

43. What does the man recommend?

(A) Choosing a new vendor
(B) Ordering a replacement part
(C) Offering a coupon
(D) Delaying a shipment

GO ON TO THE NEXT PAGE

44. What is Spencer congratulated for?

(A) Receiving an award
(B) Beating a record
(C) Graduating from college
(D) Getting a promotion

45. What will happen next month?

(A) A new promotion will take place.
(B) A training workshop will be held.
(C) Another branch will open.
(D) The salon will close.

46. What does the woman ask to do?

(A) Use a coupon
(B) Apply for a position
(C) Schedule an appointment
(D) Conduct a survey

47. Who most likely are the speakers?

(A) Laboratory scientists
(B) Graphic designers
(C) TV show writers
(D) Video editors

48. What do the clients want the speakers to do?

(A) Renew an agreement
(B) Change a project timeline
(C) Modify a commercial
(D) Update a quotation

49. Why does the man say, "the Vasquez account is due today"?

(A) To complain about lack of communication with the client
(B) To request that his colleague sign up for an account
(C) To show concern about a financial problem
(D) To explain that he cannot provide immediate assistance

50. Where are the speakers?

(A) At a bookstore
(B) At a university
(C) At a supermarket
(D) At a bank

51. What does the man confirm?

(A) The location of a store
(B) The availability of a product
(C) The delivery date of an order
(D) The viability of a suggestion

52. What does the man suggest the woman do?

(A) Sign up for a service
(B) Take a taxi downtown
(C) Speak to a manager
(D) Reserve an order

53. What will happen in the first week of August?

(A) Some new instructors will be recruited.
(B) An awards ceremony will take place.
(C) Some machines will be replaced.
(D) A director will visit the Chicago area.

54. What will be offered to the students?

(A) A free device
(B) A refund
(C) A discount
(D) An online consultation

55. What will the man most likely do next?

(A) Inspect some computers
(B) Teach a class
(C) Design a website
(D) Speak with some students

56. What does the woman ask for?

(A) A parking permit
(B) A local guide
(C) A bus pass
(D) A product catalog

57. What does the man say about an art gallery?

(A) It changed owners.
(B) It has free admission.
(C) It features famous paintings.
(D) It was recently renovated.

58. What event will be held on Sunday?

(A) A concert
(B) A park opening
(C) A sports competition
(D) A parade

59. Why does the man say, "Samantha, you've been here a long time, right"?

(A) To ask for assistance
(B) To compliment a colleague
(C) To accept a recommendation
(D) To request approval

60. What did the man do yesterday?

(A) He revised a document.
(B) He participated in a workshop.
(C) He downloaded an update.
(D) He met with a customer.

61. What will the man most likely do next?

(A) Sign up for a training session
(B) Check out a website
(C) Book a meeting room
(D) Contact the IT Department

Carlton Hotel

Bill

Valet Parking	$10
Room Service	$30
Breakfast	$7
Deluxe Suite	$250

62. Who most likely is the man?

(A) A retail worker
(B) A hotel receptionist
(C) A restaurant server
(D) An electrician

63. Look at the graphic. Which amount on the bill is incorrect?

(A) $7
(B) $10
(C) $30
(D) $250

64. What will the woman do at 2 P.M.?

(A) Attend a conference
(B) Make an appointment
(C) Visit a tourist site
(D) Go to the airport

GO ON TO THE NEXT PAGE

TEST 03

Macmore's Flooring

Special Discount Event!

(Offer Valid Until June 30)

Ceramic Tile Installation: 40% off

Porcelain Tile Installation: 30% off

Stone Tile Installation: 20% off

Marble Tile Installation: 10% off

65. Why does the man want to install new floor tiles?

(A) To replace old flooring
(B) To match the living room wallpaper
(C) To accommodate more floor space
(D) To sell his home

66. Look at the graphic. How much will most likely be discounted from the man's order?

(A) 10%
(B) 20%
(C) 30%
(D) 40%

67. What does the woman emphasize about the floor tiles?

(A) They are lightweight.
(B) They are durable.
(C) They are eco-friendly.
(D) They are affordable.

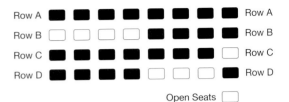

MAIN STAGE

(GOLD SECTION)

Open Seats

68. What has recently happened at the performing arts center?

(A) A new manager was hired.
(B) The dates of a show were changed.
(C) The renovation of a facility was finished.
(D) A parking lot was constructed.

69. Look at the graphic. Which row will the woman most likely buy tickets for?

(A) Row A
(B) Row B
(C) Row C
(D) Row D

70. What does the woman say she would like to do?

(A) Use a voucher
(B) Become a member
(C) Receive electronic tickets
(D) Upgrade her seats

PART 4

Directions: You will hear some talks given by a single speaker. You will be asked to answer three questions about what the speaker says in each talk. Select the best response to each question and mark the letter (A), (B), (C), or (D) on your answer sheet. The talks will not be printed in your test book and will be spoken only one time.

71. What type of businesses does the company own?

(A) Stationery stores
(B) Food services
(C) Wholesale markets
(D) Car rentals

72. What will the businesses begin doing?

(A) Arranging automatic payments
(B) Offering time-based discounts
(C) Extending their business hours
(D) Providing delivery of items

73. What does the speaker ask José Alvarez to do?

(A) Send out an e-mail
(B) Describe an action plan
(C) Pass out a schedule
(D) Call a caterer

74. Where does the speaker most likely work?

(A) At a computer manufacturer
(B) At an Internet service provider
(C) At a home repair company
(D) At a broadcasting station

75. What is the cause of the problem?

(A) There was a technical error.
(B) Some work was left unfinished.
(C) Some machines were damaged.
(D) There was severe weather.

76. What should the listeners do if the problem continues?

(A) Submit some paperwork
(B) Replace some equipment
(C) Call again later
(D) Visit a business

77. What is the theater celebrating?

(A) A film premiere
(B) A showroom opening
(C) A building renovation
(D) An anniversary

78. What will the listeners do first?

(A) Watch a video
(B) Go on a tour
(C) Take some pictures
(D) Answer some questions

79. What will the listeners receive?

(A) A concession stand voucher
(B) A movie display prop
(C) A free entrance ticket
(D) A show time schedule

80. What is the speaker preparing?

(A) A research presentation
(B) A client visit
(C) An anniversary party
(D) A holiday

81. Who most likely is the listener?

(A) A ship captain
(B) A travel agent
(C) A resort manager
(D) An exhibition coordinator

82. What does the speaker mean when she says, "I'm told that the Mediterranean is breathtaking during that season"?

(A) She is dissatisfied with a service.
(B) She agrees with a recommendation.
(C) She believes a purchase may be worth the price.
(D) She wants the listener to accompany her.

GO ON TO THE NEXT PAGE

83. What decision has Sunrise Avenue made?

(A) To allow employees to work from home
(B) To advertise positions overseas
(C) To release detailed plans to the public
(D) To start an internship program

84. According to the speaker, what can his company help the listeners manage?

(A) Securing office space
(B) Minimizing security risks
(C) Enhancing advertising
(D) Reducing wait times

85. What will be discussed next?

(A) Functionality
(B) Timelines
(C) Fees
(D) Reputation

86. What is the purpose of the meeting?

(A) To review some job candidates
(B) To organize an event
(C) To develop an evaluation form
(D) To introduce some employees

87. According to the speaker, what is an objective this year?

(A) To expand a business
(B) To improve productivity
(C) To combine teams
(D) To lower operating costs

88. What does the speaker instruct the listeners to do?

(A) Move to another room
(B) Turn on some laptops
(C) Hold group discussions
(D) Sign some paperwork

89. What is the speaker's job?

(A) Entrepreneur
(B) Aerospace engineer
(C) Risk analyst
(D) Product designer

90. Why does the speaker say, "but no two days will be the same"?

(A) To emphasize a common pitfall
(B) To commend her past employers
(C) To highlight the importance of education
(D) To mention a potential benefit

91. What aspect of the speaker's job surprised her?

(A) The chance for promotions
(B) The networking opportunities
(C) The high base remuneration
(D) The amount of travel required

92. Where do the listeners most likely work?

(A) At a shopping mall
(B) At a publishing house
(C) At a market research firm
(D) At a law office

93. What will Laurence Kim do after lunch?

(A) Visit another location
(B) Attend a tutorial
(C) Negotiate an agreement
(D) Hold meetings with staff

94. What does the speaker mean when he says, "it is rare for executives to dedicate entire days to meetings"?

(A) Managers should be aware of a conflicting appointment.
(B) The listeners should take advantage of an opportunity.
(C) The office may be unsuitable for visitors today.
(D) The listeners should prepare a presentation.

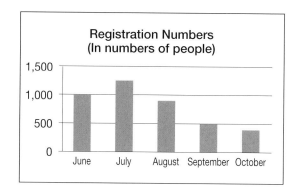

Registration Numbers
(In numbers of people)

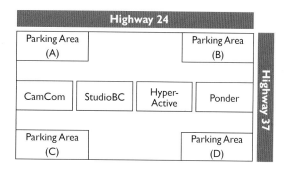

95. Where does the speaker most likely work?

(A) At an educational institute
(B) At a department store
(C) At a delivery company
(D) At a conference center

96. Look at the graphic. In what month did the online program start?

(A) June
(B) July
(C) August
(D) September

97. What will probably happen next?

(A) Listeners will access a website.
(B) Listeners will divide into groups.
(C) Some interviews will be conducted.
(D) Some questionnaire data will be presented.

98. What change is being announced?

(A) Higher parking rates
(B) Upcoming renovations
(C) An earlier closing time
(D) Updated sales events

99. Look at the graphic. Where does a shuttle depart from?

(A) Parking Area A
(B) Parking Area B
(C) Parking Area C
(D) Parking Area D

100. What event will happen next Saturday?

(A) A prize giveaway
(B) A holiday celebration
(C) A food fair
(D) A celebrity meeting

This is the end of the Listening test.

TEST 04

MP3 바로 듣기

준비물: OMR 카드, 연필, 지우개, 시계
시험시간: LC 약 45분

<table>
<tr><th colspan="5">나의 점수</th></tr>
<tr><td colspan="5">LC</td></tr>
<tr><td>맞은 개수</td><td colspan="4"></td></tr>
<tr><td>환산 점수</td><td colspan="4"></td></tr>
<tr><th>TEST 01</th><th>TEST 02</th><th>TEST 03</th><th>TEST 04</th><th>TEST 05</th></tr>
<tr><td>_____점</td><td>_____점</td><td>_____점</td><td>_____점</td><td>_____점</td></tr>
<tr><th>TEST 06</th><th>TEST 07</th><th>TEST 08</th><th>TEST 09</th><th>TEST 10</th></tr>
<tr><td>_____점</td><td>_____점</td><td>_____점</td><td>_____점</td><td>_____점</td></tr>
</table>

점수 환산표

LC			
맞은 개수	환산 점수	맞은 개수	환산 점수
96-100	475-495	41-45	155-230
91-95	435-495	36-40	125-205
86-90	405-475	31-35	105-175
81-85	370-450	26-30	85-145
76-80	345-420	21-25	60-115
71-75	320-390	16-20	30-90
66-70	290-360	11-15	5-70
61-65	265-335	6-10	5-60
56-60	235-310	1-5	5-60
51-55	210-280	0	5-35
46-50	180-255		

LISTENING TEST

In the Listening test, you will be asked to demonstrate how well you understand spoken English. The entire listening test will last approximately 45 minutes. There are four parts, and directions are given for each part. You must mark your answers on the separate answer sheet. Do not write your answers in your test book.

PART 1

Directions: For each question in this part, you will hear four statements about a picture in your test book. When you hear the statements, you must select the one statement that best describes what you see in the picture. Then find the number of the question on your answer sheet and mark your answer. The statements will not be printed in your test book and will be spoken only one time.

Statement (B), "A man is pointing at a document," is the best description of the picture, so you should select answer (B) and mark it on your answer sheet.

1.

2.

GO ON TO THE NEXT PAGE

3.

4.

5.

6.

GO ON TO THE NEXT PAGE

PART 2

Directions: You will hear a question or statement and three responses spoken in English. They will not be printed in your test book and will be spoken only one time. Select the best response to the question or statement and mark the letter (A), (B), or (C) on your answer sheet.

7. Mark your answer on your answer sheet.

8. Mark your answer on your answer sheet.

9. Mark your answer on your answer sheet.

10. Mark your answer on your answer sheet.

11. Mark your answer on your answer sheet.

12. Mark your answer on your answer sheet.

13. Mark your answer on your answer sheet.

14. Mark your answer on your answer sheet.

15. Mark your answer on your answer sheet.

16. Mark your answer on your answer sheet.

17. Mark your answer on your answer sheet.

18. Mark your answer on your answer sheet.

19. Mark your answer on your answer sheet.

20. Mark your answer on your answer sheet.

21. Mark your answer on your answer sheet.

22. Mark your answer on your answer sheet.

23. Mark your answer on your answer sheet.

24. Mark your answer on your answer sheet.

25. Mark your answer on your answer sheet.

26. Mark your answer on your answer sheet.

27. Mark your answer on your answer sheet.

28. Mark your answer on your answer sheet.

29. Mark your answer on your answer sheet.

30. Mark your answer on your answer sheet.

31. Mark your answer on your answer sheet.

PART 3

Directions: You will hear some conversations between two or more people. You will be asked to answer three questions about what the speakers say in each conversation. Select the best response to each question and mark the letter (A), (B), (C), or (D) on your answer sheet. The conversations will not be printed in your test book and will be spoken only one time.

32. What kind of business do the speakers work for?

(A) A clothing retailer
(B) An advertising agency
(C) A construction firm
(D) A grocery store

33. What does the man recommend?

(A) Providing a discount
(B) Displaying a sign
(C) Hiring a company
(D) Adjusting a budget

34. What does the man say Kay is skilled at?

(A) Selling products
(B) Designing graphics
(C) Making websites
(D) Training new employees

35. What is the subject of the conversation?

(A) The expansion of a business
(B) Responses to a questionnaire
(C) An annual budget
(D) Potential job candidates

36. What does the woman say is the main problem?

(A) An application is difficult to use.
(B) A team is understaffed.
(C) Some expenses are too high.
(D) Some employees are not motivated.

37. What does the man recommend doing?

(A) Upgrading some hardware
(B) Talking to a security officer
(C) Posting an explanation
(D) Redesigning a website

38. What type of business do the speakers most likely work for?

(A) A laundry service
(B) A law firm
(C) A retail company
(D) A restaurant

39. What concern does the woman mention?

(A) The plastic bags tear easily.
(B) The containers are not recyclable.
(C) The food gets cold quickly.
(D) The delivery service is too expensive.

40. Why does the woman say she likes the man's suggestion?

(A) It will increase profits.
(B) It will reduce delivery times.
(C) It will attract investors.
(D) It will appease customers.

41. Why is the man calling?

(A) To upgrade a seat
(B) To offer a recommendation
(C) To file a complaint
(D) To ask for directions

42. What information does the woman ask for?

(A) A phone number
(B) An ID card
(C) The duration of a trip
(D) The name of a station

43. What does the woman say is causing a delay?

(A) Traffic accident
(B) Inclement weather
(C) Equipment malfunction
(D) Roadside repair

GO ON TO THE NEXT PAGE

44. What type of event is being planned?

(A) A birthday celebration
(B) An art exhibition
(C) A company anniversary
(D) A seasonal promotion

45. Why does the man say, "I've ordered from The Baking Room for special occasions"?

(A) To agree with a statement
(B) To suggest an alternate option
(C) To turn down an offer
(D) To make a complaint

46. What will the speakers most likely do next?

(A) Browse some products
(B) Book a venue
(C) Call a client
(D) Request for an invoice

47. Where does the conversation most likely take place?

(A) At a clothing accessory store
(B) At an antique shop
(C) At a sporting goods retailer
(D) At a football stadium

48. What is Baton Co. known for?

(A) Selling affordable products
(B) Hiring qualified employees
(C) Operating for a long time
(D) Receiving a prize

49. What additional benefit does an item have?

(A) It includes a cleaning tool.
(B) It comes with a large carrying bag.
(C) It includes a 10-year warranty.
(D) It comes with an online discount voucher.

50. What does the woman point out about her flight?

(A) Her luggage was lost.
(B) The flight was noisy.
(C) The flight was canceled.
(D) Her seat was uncomfortable.

51. What does the man say about room 710?

(A) It has an ocean view.
(B) It has high-speed internet.
(C) It has an extra bed.
(D) It has a balcony.

52. What additional service does the man offer the woman?

(A) Laundry service
(B) Complimentary breakfast
(C) A room discount
(D) A chauffeur

53. Where does the man work?

(A) At a talent agency
(B) At a private school
(C) At a gallery
(D) At a hospital

54. What does the man ask about?

(A) The location of a venue
(B) The availability of a service
(C) The date of an event
(D) The terms of an agreement

55. What does the woman say she will do?

(A) Send some menus
(B) Deliver a product
(C) Determine a cost
(D) Hire entertainment

56. What is the main topic of the conversation?

(A) A landscaping project
(B) A price estimate
(C) A vacant property
(D) A gardening tool

57. What does the man mention about some fountains?

(A) They are not working properly.
(B) They will be installed tomorrow.
(C) They are too heavy.
(D) They look outdated.

58. What does the man imply when he says, "This patio area is larger than I thought"?

(A) It will take a while to finish a task.
(B) A manager's approval is required.
(C) Additional supplies need to be ordered.
(D) He would like to request more workers.

59. Where are the speakers?

(A) At a press conference
(B) At a professional convention
(C) At a product demonstration
(D) At an employee seminar

60. What does the woman say about Lester?

(A) He is in a probationary period.
(B) He transferred to a different department.
(C) He recently switched jobs.
(D) He recently received a promotion.

61. What will the speakers do next?

(A) Sign up for some sessions
(B) Check into an event
(C) Pick up some documents
(D) Complete a registration form

Gasoline Type	Price Per Gallon
Unleaded	$1.10
Super	$1.20
Supreme	$1.35
Diesel	$1.55

62. What does the man ask for?

(A) A password
(B) A receipt
(C) A guide
(D) A refund

63. Look at the graphic. Which type of gasoline did the man select?

(A) Unleaded
(B) Super
(C) Supreme
(D) Diesel

64. What will the man receive with his fuel purchase?

(A) A movie ticket
(B) A beverage
(C) A gift certificate
(D) A car accessory

GO ON TO THE NEXT PAGE

Invoice	
Work Description	Price
Oil change	$30
Windshield repair	$70
Battery replacement	$120
Tire installation	$600

65. Why is the woman calling?

(A) To set up a maintenance inspection
(B) To inquire about a special deal
(C) To purchase some supplies
(D) To receive help with a program

66. Look at the graphic. Which price will be changed?

(A) $30
(B) $70
(C) $120
(D) $600

67. What does the man recommend that the woman do next time?

(A) Pay with a credit card
(B) Use an online communication service
(C) View a video tutorial
(D) Check some customer testimonials

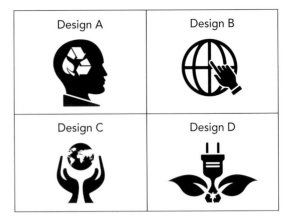

68. What are the speakers planning?

(A) A business convention
(B) A city festival
(C) A fundraising campaign
(D) An international congress

69. Look at the graphic. Which design does the man like?

(A) Design A
(B) Design B
(C) Design C
(D) Design D

70. What does the woman ask the man to send?

(A) An address of an editing room
(B) A name of a crew member
(C) Some filming equipment
(D) Some video files

PART 4

Directions: You will hear some talks given by a single speaker. You will be asked to answer three questions about what the speaker says in each talk. Select the best response to each question and mark the letter (A), (B), (C), or (D) on your answer sheet. The talks will not be printed in your test book and will be spoken only one time.

71. Where does the speaker probably work?

(A) At a clothing manufacturer
(B) At a sports stadium
(C) At a marketing firm
(D) At an accounting company

72. What is the speaker mainly discussing?

(A) A service fee
(B) A new company policy
(C) An event venue
(D) A schedule change

73. What does the speaker ask the listeners to do?

(A) Arrange a delivery
(B) Submit a report
(C) Work additional hours
(D) Contact their clients

74. Who most likely are the listeners?

(A) Professional architects
(B) Internet advertisers
(C) Business consultants
(D) Corporate accountants

75. What is the main purpose of the program?

(A) To expand a company's profile
(B) To explain new guidelines
(C) To recruit prospective employees
(D) To plan an end-of-year event

76. What does the speaker say the listeners will do on the last day?

(A) Visit a company
(B) Watch a demonstration
(C) Evaluate the program
(D) Listen to a talk

77. What type of business did the woman most likely call?

(A) A furniture store
(B) A café
(C) A painting company
(D) A library

78. Why did the woman call?

(A) To inquire about a missing item
(B) To look into operating hours
(C) To request a discount
(D) To reschedule an appointment

79. What does the woman say she will do tonight?

(A) Pick up a client
(B) Call another location
(C) Work extra hours
(D) Check out a business

80. What is the speaker enthusiastic about?

(A) A garden wall
(B) An escalator system
(C) An art installation
(D) A window design

81. Why does the speaker say, "this is a unique space"?

(A) To persuade a prospective investor
(B) To justify a project duration
(C) To express gratitude to the employees
(D) To demand a higher budget

82. What will the speaker most likely do next?

(A) Photograph a structure
(B) Eat a meal
(C) Take a tour
(D) Lead a presentation

GO ON TO THE NEXT PAGE

83. What does the speaker explain about a trail?

(A) When it was discovered
(B) Where it takes the group
(C) Why it is closed sometimes
(D) What wildlife can be found

84. What does the speaker suggest the listeners do while they wait?

(A) Do some exercises
(B) Enjoy the scenery
(C) Purchase some gifts
(D) Read a guidebook

85. Why does the speaker say he will be stopping?

(A) To view periodic weather updates
(B) To take a group photograph
(C) To conduct some activities
(D) To explain safety precautions

86. What department does the speaker most likely work in?

(A) Payroll
(B) Information Technology
(C) Sales
(D) Research and Development

87. What does the speaker mean when she says, "we already have your information from the last job you did for us"?

(A) The listener was able to recover a file.
(B) The listener does not have to make a visit.
(C) The speaker has another assignment.
(D) The speaker does not have a phone number.

88. What does the speaker recommend the listener do soon?

(A) Create a new account
(B) Retrieve some documents
(C) Inquire about another job
(D) Email a résumé

89. What industry does the speaker most likely work in?

(A) Technology
(B) Video games
(C) Film
(D) Education

90. According to the speaker, who developed the Garden Path Program?

(A) A recruitment consultant
(B) A designer
(C) A professor
(D) An administrative assistant

91. What does the speaker say will happen next week?

(A) A new manager will be appointed.
(B) A partnership will be announced.
(C) A student will be selected.
(D) A project will be finalized.

92. Who most likely is the speaker?

(A) A marketing assistant
(B) A product designer
(C) A movie producer
(D) A storekeeper

93. What type of product is being discussed?

(A) A beverage
(B) A blender
(C) A laptop
(D) An office chair

94. Why does the speaker say, "We made the product, after all"?

(A) To request opinions
(B) To provide an update
(C) To reject a suggestion
(D) To celebrate a milestone

COURSE MAP

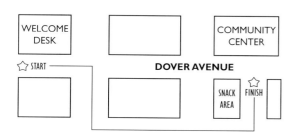

Membership Application

Name: _____ Date: _____
Address: _____

Adult $50 ____   Youth $25 ____
Senior $30 ____   Family $90 ____

95. What event are the listeners probably attending?

(A) A guided tour
(B) A clean-up initiative
(C) An athletic contest
(D) A street parade

96. According to the speaker, what should the listeners pick up?

(A) A permit
(B) A drink
(C) A towel
(D) A hat

97. Look at the graphic. Where will the listeners take a group photo?

(A) At the welcome desk
(B) At the starting line
(C) At the snack area
(D) At the community center

98. Where most likely is the meeting taking place?

(A) At a community center
(B) At an amusement park
(C) At a department store
(D) At a health club

99. Why does the speaker thank the listeners?

(A) For assisting with a task
(B) For signing up for a magazine
(C) For attending an orientation session
(D) For purchasing a membership

100. Look at the graphic. Which amount has changed?

(A) $25
(B) $30
(C) $50
(D) $90

This is the end of the Listening test.

TEST 05

MP3 바로 듣기

준비물: OMR 카드, 연필, 지우개, 시계
시험시간: LC 약 45분

나의 점수	
LC	
맞은 개수	
환산 점수	

TEST 01	TEST 02	TEST 03	TEST 04	TEST 05
_____점	_____점	_____점	_____점	_____점
TEST 06	TEST 07	TEST 08	TEST 09	TEST 10
_____점	_____점	_____점	_____점	_____점

점수 환산표

LC			
맞은 개수	환산 점수	맞은 개수	환산 점수
96-100	475-495	41-45	155-230
91-95	435-495	36-40	125-205
86-90	405-475	31-35	105-175
81-85	370-450	26-30	85-145
76-80	345-420	21-25	60-115
71-75	320-390	16-20	30-90
66-70	290-360	11-15	5-70
61-65	265-335	6-10	5-60
56-60	235-310	1-5	5-60
51-55	210-280	0	5-35
46-50	180-255		

LISTENING TEST

In the Listening test, you will be asked to demonstrate how well you understand spoken English. The entire listening test will last approximately 45 minutes. There are four parts, and directions are given for each part. You must mark your answers on the separate answer sheet. Do not write your answers in your test book.

PART 1

Directions: For each question in this part, you will hear four statements about a picture in your test book. When you hear the statements, you must select the one statement that best describes what you see in the picture. Then find the number of the question on your answer sheet and mark your answer. The statements will not be printed in your test book and will be spoken only one time.

Statement (B), "A man is pointing at a document," is the best description of the picture, so you should select answer (B) and mark it on your answer sheet.

1.

2.

GO ON TO THE NEXT PAGE

3.

4.

5.

6.

GO ON TO THE NEXT PAGE

PART 2

Directions: You will hear a question or statement and three responses spoken in English. They will not be printed in your test book and will be spoken only one time. Select the best response to the question or statement and mark the letter (A), (B), or (C) on your answer sheet.

7. Mark your answer on your answer sheet.

8. Mark your answer on your answer sheet.

9. Mark your answer on your answer sheet.

10. Mark your answer on your answer sheet.

11. Mark your answer on your answer sheet.

12. Mark your answer on your answer sheet.

13. Mark your answer on your answer sheet.

14. Mark your answer on your answer sheet.

15. Mark your answer on your answer sheet.

16. Mark your answer on your answer sheet.

17. Mark your answer on your answer sheet.

18. Mark your answer on your answer sheet.

19. Mark your answer on your answer sheet.

20. Mark your answer on your answer sheet.

21. Mark your answer on your answer sheet.

22. Mark your answer on your answer sheet.

23. Mark your answer on your answer sheet.

24. Mark your answer on your answer sheet.

25. Mark your answer on your answer sheet.

26. Mark your answer on your answer sheet.

27. Mark your answer on your answer sheet.

28. Mark your answer on your answer sheet.

29. Mark your answer on your answer sheet.

30. Mark your answer on your answer sheet.

31. Mark your answer on your answer sheet.

PART 3

Directions: You will hear some conversations between two or more people. You will be asked to answer three questions about what the speakers say in each conversation. Select the best response to each question and mark the letter (A), (B), (C), or (D) on your answer sheet. The conversations will not be printed in your test book and will be spoken only one time.

32. What type of product are the speakers discussing?

(A) Cooling fans
(B) Computer monitors
(C) Handheld radios
(D) Rice cookers

33. What does the woman say she likes about the product?

(A) It is sturdily built.
(B) It is highly energy efficient.
(C) It is intuitive to use.
(D) It is easier to store.

34. What does the woman suggest doing?

(A) Designing some prototypes
(B) Producing a cost estimate
(C) Finding an investor
(D) Gathering some feedback

35. What does the man say he did?

(A) Moved a meeting time
(B) Visited a client's office
(C) Arranged a delivery
(D) Revised a presentation

36. What does the woman decide to do?

(A) Go on a business trip
(B) Order more supplies for a lounge
(C) Change a catering menu
(D) Allow employees to leave early

37. According to the man, what will happen in the evening?

(A) A parking lot will close.
(B) A machine will be fixed.
(C) An area will be renovated.
(D) A system will restart.

38. What is the man trying to do?

(A) Book a table
(B) Purchase a train ticket
(C) Check into a room
(D) Submit a cover letter

39. What is the man missing?

(A) His photo ID
(B) His discount voucher
(C) His mobile phone
(D) His confirmation code

40. What does the woman offer to do?

(A) Call a colleague
(B) Browse a system
(C) Send a work request
(D) Review an invoice

41. Who most likely is the man?

(A) A movie director
(B) A singer
(C) An actor
(D) A TV show host

42. What is the purpose of the meeting?

(A) To prepare for a performance
(B) To confirm a shooting schedule
(C) To review some photographs
(D) To discuss an advertising campaign

43. What does the man say about the products?

(A) They are affordable.
(B) They are in great demand.
(C) They have been effective for him.
(D) They have been reformulated.

GO ON TO THE NEXT PAGE

44. What are the speakers mainly discussing?

(A) A county event
(B) A recent transaction
(C) Monthly salaries
(D) New laws

45. What does the woman suggest?

(A) Contacting a government worker
(B) Providing some training
(C) Working extra hours
(D) Reviewing some forms

46. What does the woman say some accountants will be doing on Friday?

(A) Visiting some banks
(B) Participating in a convention
(C) Going to another branch
(D) Meeting with some clients

47. Where does the conversation take place?

(A) At a warehouse
(B) At a grocery store
(C) At a post office
(D) At a pharmacy

48. What does the woman imply when she says, "My delivery tracker app says two"?

(A) She will be able to help the man.
(B) She believes the man is mistaken.
(C) She needs additional work assignments.
(D) She is almost done with work.

49. What does the man recommend the woman do?

(A) Contact her colleague
(B) Take another route
(C) Check the inventory
(D) Review a document

50. Where does the man most likely work?

(A) At a fashion boutique
(B) At a theater
(C) At an antique shop
(D) At a bookstore

51. What is the woman responsible for?

(A) Script editing
(B) Musical scores
(C) Stage lighting
(D) Costume design

52. What does the man remind the woman about?

(A) Some items are fragile.
(B) Some items are costly.
(C) Some items are rare.
(D) Some items are too big.

53. Where most likely do the speakers work?

(A) At a hotel
(B) At a landscaping firm
(C) At a magazine publisher
(D) At a construction company

54. Why does the man say, "She won it last year"?

(A) To express admiration
(B) To confirm a detail
(C) To refuse a recommendation
(D) To suggest a solution

55. What do the speakers decide to do?

(A) To cancel a meeting
(B) To ask for staff opinions
(C) To extend working hours
(D) To take a training course

56. What industry do the speakers work in?

    (A) Manufacturing
    (B) Hospitality
    (C) Education
    (D) Retail

57. Why did the man stop working at his previous job?

    (A) He relocated to a different city.
    (B) He wanted a higher position.
    (C) He needed more free time.
    (D) He wanted to explore other industries.

58. What will the woman most likely discuss next?

    (A) Submitting additional paperwork
    (B) Negotiating contract terms
    (C) Working with the headquarters
    (D) Adjusting the work start date

---

59. What product are the speakers discussing?

    (A) A laptop
    (B) A charging device
    (C) A wireless earphone
    (D) A phone

60. Why is a prototype being changed?

    (A) To lower the price
    (B) To increase the battery life
    (C) To add a noise-canceling feature
    (D) To improve the fit

61. What does the man ask Fatima to do?

    (A) Request an extension
    (B) Send a report
    (C) Revise a schedule
    (D) Hire a consultant

16-MILE MINI-MARATHON MAP

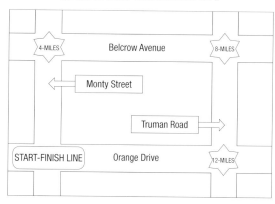

62. What will the woman do at the marathon?

    (A) Take some pictures
    (B) Direct some traffic
    (C) Provide some beverages
    (D) Interview some participants

63. Look at the graphic. Which intersection will the woman go to?

    (A) Monty Street and Belcrow Avenue
    (B) Belcrow Avenue and Truman Road
    (C) Truman Road and Orange Drive
    (D) Orange Drive and Monty Street

64. What is the woman instructed to do after the marathon?

    (A) Clean up an area
    (B) Hand out some prizes
    (C) Fill out a survey
    (D) Share some photos

GO ON TO THE NEXT PAGE

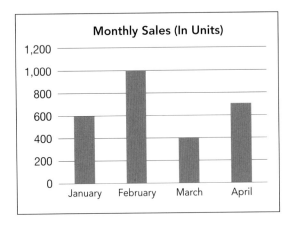

Monthly Sales (In Units)

Available Units	
Apartment	**Rate**
213	$1,296
275	$1,341
348	$1,396
425	$1,195

65. What kind of business do the speakers most likely work for?

(A) An office supply store
(B) A car dealership
(C) An electronics producer
(D) A sporting goods retailer

66. Look at the graphic. Which sales number is the man surprised about?

(A) 400
(B) 600
(C) 700
(D) 1,000

67. Who is Catherine Burke?

(A) A marketing specialist
(B) A financial consultant
(C) An IT supervisor
(D) A HR recruiter

68. What does the man say he likes about the apartments?

(A) It allows pets to live inside the units.
(B) It was recently renovated.
(C) It is conveniently located.
(D) It is priced cheaper than others.

69. Look at the graphic. How much will the man pay in monthly rent?

(A) $1,195
(B) $1,296
(C) $1,341
(D) $1,396

70. What does the woman say is required?

(A) Some references letters
(B) Some proof of income
(C) A signed lease
(D) An insurance policy

PART 4

Directions: You will hear some talks given by a single speaker. You will be asked to answer three questions about what the speaker says in each talk. Select the best response to each question and mark the letter (A), (B), (C), or (D) on your answer sheet. The talks will not be printed in your test book and will be spoken only one time.

71. Where does the talk most likely take place?

(A) At a warehouse
(B) At a clothing store
(C) At a restaurant
(D) At a train station

72. What will the listeners do this morning?

(A) Complete a training program
(B) Conduct a safety inspection
(C) Sign a contract
(D) Restock some shelves

73. What does the speaker ask the listeners to wear?

(A) Headsets
(B) Work gloves
(C) Name tags
(D) Uniforms

74. What does the speaker's company sell?

(A) Used books
(B) Vehicle parts
(C) Exercise equipment
(D) Kitchen appliances

75. What does Rick recommend?

(A) Reducing a price
(B) Hiring an expert
(C) Increasing advertising
(D) Optimizing costs

76. What will the listeners most likely do next?

(A) Research a store
(B) Check their inboxes
(C) Schedule a meeting
(D) Listen to a speaker

77. Why is the speaker unavailable until 11 o'clock on Saturday?

(A) He is meeting a colleague.
(B) He will be traveling from out of town.
(C) He has to retrieve some equipment.
(D) He has to attend a course.

78. What does the speaker say about a mutual friend?

(A) He will be moving overseas.
(B) He appeared on television.
(C) He received a promotion.
(D) He started a new job.

79. Why does the speaker say, "I have to see why everyone waits in lines"?

(A) To justify a suggestion
(B) To comment on a trend
(C) To reject an offer
(D) To argue a point

80. Where is the introduction being held?

(A) At an awards ceremony
(B) At an international convention
(C) At an anniversary party
(D) At an employee luncheon

81. What does the speaker say Benedict Freeman is known for?

(A) His travel books
(B) His work for endangered species
(C) His problem-solving skills
(D) His illustrated guides of plants

82. What are the listeners encouraged to do?

(A) Welcome a guest speaker
(B) Fill out a questionnaire
(C) Go on a tour
(D) Make a donation

GO ON TO THE NEXT PAGE

83. Why is the speaker calling?

(A) To request an updated schedule
(B) To invite the listener to an event
(C) To ask the listener for a reference
(D) To express interest in a new role

84. What did the speaker do in Luton?

(A) She visited her parents.
(B) She started a company.
(C) She worked on a project.
(D) She attended university.

85. What does the speaker say she is excited about?

(A) Delivering a speech
(B) Featuring on television
(C) Meeting with businesspeople
(D) Receiving an award

86. What does the speaker's company sell?

(A) Construction equipment
(B) Computer software
(C) Outdoor advertising
(D) Automotive parts

87. What does the speaker mean when she says, "we are manufacturing overseas"?

(A) She would like to hear some feedback.
(B) She is aware of a likely reason.
(C) The listeners did not pay attention to a point.
(D) The competitors did not provide any useful information.

88. What event will be held next month?

(A) A company anniversary
(B) A holiday break
(C) An internal audit
(D) An industry trade show

89. What is the message mainly about?

(A) Springtime programs
(B) Roadside construction
(C) A sports competition
(D) A location change

90. According to the speaker, what can be accessed on a website?

(A) Directions
(B) Photographs
(C) A registration form
(D) An events calendar

91. How can listeners borrow some sports equipment?

(A) By submitting an ID card
(B) By completing an application
(C) By paying a fee
(D) By reserving it online

92. What will a mobile application allow users to do?

(A) Find businesses
(B) Play games
(C) Upload pictures
(D) Bank online

93. What does the speaker mean when she says, "it has over 25,000 downloads"?

(A) A program is popular.
(B) A marketing campaign is needed.
(C) A server needs to be upgraded.
(D) A site is malfunctioning.

94. What can some users participate in?

(A) A raffle contest
(B) A trial period
(C) A research study
(D) An athletic race

Table Arrangements

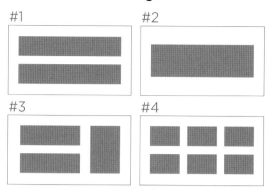

#1   #2

#3   #4

Product #75 Chocolate Box ($25)	Product #82 Wallet ($55)
Product #79 Sunglasses ($70)	Product #95 Wireless Charger ($40)

95. What event are the listeners preparing for?

(A) A post-seminar dinner
(B) A company anniversary celebration
(C) A networking event
(D) An employee retirement party

96. Look at the graphic. Which table arrangement will be used?

(A) Arrangement #1
(B) Arrangement #2
(C) Arrangement #3
(D) Arrangement #4

97. According to the speaker, why is a ladder needed?

(A) To replace a light
(B) To place some speakers
(C) To clean the ceiling
(D) To hang a banner

98. Who most likely are the listeners?

(A) Airline passengers
(B) Concert attendees
(C) Resort customers
(D) Shopping mall visitors

99. What does the speaker offer to do?

(A) Provide a beverage
(B) Turn off the lights
(C) Store some belongings
(D) Refund some money

100. Look at the graphic. Which item is no longer available?

(A) The chocolate box
(B) The wallet
(C) The sunglasses
(D) The wireless charger

This is the end of the Listening test.

TEST 06

MP3 바로 듣기

준비물: OMR 카드, 연필, 지우개, 시계
시험시간: LC 약 45분

나의 점수	
LC	
맞은 개수	
환산 점수	

TEST 01	TEST 02	TEST 03	TEST 04	TEST 05
_____점	_____점	_____점	_____점	_____점
TEST 06	**TEST 07**	**TEST 08**	**TEST 09**	**TEST 10**
_____점	_____점	_____점	_____점	_____점

점수 환산표

LC			
맞은 개수	환산 점수	맞은 개수	환산 점수
96-100	475-495	41-45	155-230
91-95	435-495	36-40	125-205
86-90	405-475	31-35	105-175
81-85	370-450	26-30	85-145
76-80	345-420	21-25	60-115
71-75	320-390	16-20	30-90
66-70	290-360	11-15	5-70
61-65	265-335	6-10	5-60
56-60	235-310	1-5	5-60
51-55	210-280	0	5-35
46-50	180-255		

LISTENING TEST

In the Listening test, you will be asked to demonstrate how well you understand spoken English. The entire listening test will last approximately 45 minutes. There are four parts, and directions are given for each part. You must mark your answers on the separate answer sheet. Do not write your answers in your test book.

PART 1

Directions: For each question in this part, you will hear four statements about a picture in your test book. When you hear the statements, you must select the one statement that best describes what you see in the picture. Then find the number of the question on your answer sheet and mark your answer. The statements will not be printed in your test book and will be spoken only one time.

Statement (B), "A man is pointing at a document," is the best description of the picture, so you should select answer (B) and mark it on your answer sheet.

1.

2.

GO ON TO THE NEXT PAGE

➡

3.

4.

5.

6.

GO ON TO THE NEXT PAGE ➡

PART 2

Directions: You will hear a question or statement and three responses spoken in English. They will not be printed in your test book and will be spoken only one time. Select the best response to the question or statement and mark the letter (A), (B), or (C) on your answer sheet.

7. Mark your answer on your answer sheet.

8. Mark your answer on your answer sheet.

9. Mark your answer on your answer sheet.

10. Mark your answer on your answer sheet.

11. Mark your answer on your answer sheet.

12. Mark your answer on your answer sheet.

13. Mark your answer on your answer sheet.

14. Mark your answer on your answer sheet.

15. Mark your answer on your answer sheet.

16. Mark your answer on your answer sheet.

17. Mark your answer on your answer sheet.

18. Mark your answer on your answer sheet.

19. Mark your answer on your answer sheet.

20. Mark your answer on your answer sheet.

21. Mark your answer on your answer sheet.

22. Mark your answer on your answer sheet.

23. Mark your answer on your answer sheet.

24. Mark your answer on your answer sheet.

25. Mark your answer on your answer sheet.

26. Mark your answer on your answer sheet.

27. Mark your answer on your answer sheet.

28. Mark your answer on your answer sheet.

29. Mark your answer on your answer sheet.

30. Mark your answer on your answer sheet.

31. Mark your answer on your answer sheet.

PART 3

Directions: You will hear some conversations between two or more people. You will be asked to answer three questions about what the speakers say in each conversation. Select the best response to each question and mark the letter (A), (B), (C), or (D) on your answer sheet. The conversations will not be printed in your test book and will be spoken only one time.

32. What does the man need assistance with?

(A) Exchanging a product
(B) Unloading some packages
(C) Renewing a store membership
(D) Finding some merchandise

33. What is the cause of the problem?

(A) A warehouse closed early.
(B) A manager is not available.
(C) A shipment was damaged.
(D) A price tag was incorrect.

34. Where does the woman instruct the man to go?

(A) To the cashier
(B) To the help desk
(C) To a different aisle
(D) To a storage room

35. What activity is scheduled for the morning?

(A) A mediation process
(B) A retirement party
(C) A product demonstration
(D) An orientation session

36. What do the women say they would like to do?

(A) Cancel a plan
(B) Send some e-mails
(C) Place an order
(D) Take some notes

37. What does the man say will happen after lunch?

(A) Some documents will be signed.
(B) Some desks will be assigned.
(C) An exam will be given.
(D) A meeting will take place.

38. What did the woman recently do?

(A) She delivered a package.
(B) She met with a supervisor.
(C) She moved to a new home.
(D) She bought some supplies.

39. What is the reason for the woman's call?

(A) To submit a payment
(B) To make a complaint
(C) To purchase extra items
(D) To schedule a consultation

40. What does the man request?

(A) Some personal information
(B) A coupon code
(C) A store map
(D) Some product samples

41. What did the man recently find out?

(A) The date of a CEO's visit has changed.
(B) An employee has been promoted.
(C) The location of a meeting has been moved.
(D) A magazine will report on the company.

42. What do the speakers have to do?

(A) Update some software
(B) Meet with some candidates
(C) Finish a report
(D) Respond to a customer

43. What does the woman suggest to the man?

(A) Revising a sales report
(B) Taking a break for lunch
(C) Participating in a conference call
(D) Letting a coworker handle a task

GO ON TO THE NEXT PAGE

44. What kind of business does the man own?

(A) A restaurant
(B) A trading corporation
(C) An IT firm
(D) A taxi service

45. What do the speakers like about the auditorium?

(A) It has a place to buy food.
(B) It has plenty of space.
(C) It is convenient for travelers.
(D) It is in a scenic location.

46. How is the computer network used at the man's business?

(A) To calculate expenses
(B) To process orders
(C) To create schedules
(D) To inspect merchandise

47. What are the speakers mainly discussing?

(A) A malfunctioning machine
(B) An upcoming conference
(C) A room reservation
(D) A delivery fee

48. Why does the woman say, "We use this room frequently for meetings"?

(A) To describe why a request is important
(B) To change the location of a meeting
(C) To recommend purchasing more furniture
(D) To indicate that an area is too small

49. What will the man do next?

(A) Explain a process
(B) Issue a refund
(C) Revise a report
(D) Contact a store

50. What will the listeners learn about?

(A) Entering customer data
(B) Uploading expense reports
(C) Installing a program
(D) Repairing a device

51. What does the woman offer to do?

(A) Find a different seat
(B) Bring new equipment
(C) Provide her notes
(D) Give a presentation

52. What will the listeners probably do next?

(A) Complete a survey
(B) Test a product
(C) Download an update
(D) Review a file

53. What are the speakers mainly discussing?

(A) A marketing campaign
(B) An investor meeting
(C) A company audit
(D) A budget proposal

54. Which aspect of an agency is the most important to the speakers?

(A) Its service is timely.
(B) Its costs are cheap.
(C) It is recognized worldwide.
(D) It has related experience.

55. What does the man say he forgot to mention?

(A) A deadline
(B) A financial constraint
(C) A location
(D) A business trip

56. Who most likely is the woman?

(A) A realtor
(B) An engineer
(C) An office manager
(D) A maintenance worker

57. Why is the man disappointed?

(A) A schedule cannot be adjusted.
(B) Some locations are too pricey.
(C) Some fixtures are broken.
(D) An employee is not available.

58. What will the speakers do on Thursday?

(A) View a property
(B) Set a deadline
(C) Review a budget
(D) Attend a conference

59. How did the man hear about a company?

(A) From a neighbor
(B) From a coworker
(C) From a family member
(D) From an online advertisement

60. What does the woman mean when she says, "We've handled five projects like that this year"?

(A) Some work may be time-consuming.
(B) The particular project is popular.
(C) The business has expertise.
(D) They have a full schedule this year.

61. What does the woman offer to send?

(A) A website link
(B) Some images
(C) A quotation
(D) Some references

Business Proposal

Section 1	Description of Business
Section 2	Location and Facilities
Section 3	Industry Trends
Section 4	Profit Forecast
Section 5	Marketing

62. What type of business does the woman want to start?

(A) A travel agency
(B) A fitness center
(C) A market research company
(D) A financial planning firm

63. According to the woman, what did she learn from her last business?

(A) How to choose an ideal location
(B) How to design effective ads
(C) How to establish a loyal customer base
(D) How to obtain a business license

64. Look at the graphic. According to the man, which section of the business proposal should be revised?

(A) Section 2
(B) Section 3
(C) Section 4
(D) Section 5

GO ON TO THE NEXT PAGE

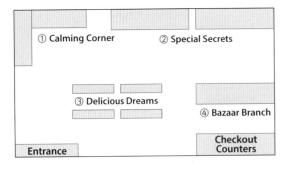

65. What type of product are the speakers mainly discussing?

(A) Towels
(B) Shoes
(C) Books
(D) Candles

66. Look at the graphic. Where will the products be placed?

(A) Display 1
(B) Display 2
(C) Display 3
(D) Display 4

67. Why does the man say a staff meeting will be held?

(A) To revise a contract
(B) To confirm some dates
(C) To request a payment
(D) To fill out a form

Company Survey

1. Employment Status:
   ☐ Full-time   ☐ Part-time

2. Department: _____

3. Preference regarding proposed change:
   ☐ Same hours ☐ Earlier start ☐ Later start

4. Comments: _____

---

68. What change is the company considering?

(A) Changing working hours
(B) Updating the software
(C) Relocating to a new office
(D) Opening a new branch

69. What is the man concerned about?

(A) Missing files
(B) A new manager
(C) Unproductive meetings
(D) A crowded commute

70. Look at the graphic. Which survey item does the man mention?

(A) Item 1
(B) Item 2
(C) Item 3
(D) Item 4

PART 4

Directions: You will hear some talks given by a single speaker. You will be asked to answer three questions about what the speaker says in each talk. Select the best response to each question and mark the letter (A), (B), (C), or (D) on your answer sheet. The talks will not be printed in your test book and will be spoken only one time.

71. Where will the tour take place?

(A) At a crafts workshop
(B) At a research laboratory
(C) At an art gallery
(D) At a photo studio

72. What should the listeners avoid doing?

(A) Talking to the designers
(B) Using their mobile phones
(C) Bringing food with them
(D) Wandering away from the group

73. What does the speaker request the listeners to do?

(A) Provide some feedback
(B) Browse a souvenir store
(C) Sign up for a membership
(D) Enter a competition

74. Who most likely are the listeners?

(A) International clients
(B) Plant supervisors
(C) Landscaping workers
(D) Furniture designers

75. According to the speaker, what will the listeners be able to do with their employee number?

(A) Open a safe
(B) Register for a seminar
(C) Enter an office
(D) Update a website

76. What will happen next week?

(A) Some clients will visit a facility.
(B) Some devices will be delivered.
(C) A company will relocate.
(D) An employee questionnaire will be submitted.

77. Where does the talk most likely take place?

(A) At a construction site
(B) At an office
(C) At a grocery store
(D) At a laboratory

78. What complaint does the speaker mention?

(A) Some orders are not being fulfilled.
(B) Some tools are not being put back in the case.
(C) Some safety rules are not being followed correctly.
(D) Some people are not turning up on time.

79. What will the listeners now be required to do?

(A) Complete a training course
(B) Receive official approval
(C) Pay a fine
(D) Record their details

80. Who is Mr. Barnes?

(A) A school teacher
(B) A journalist
(C) A government worker
(D) An artist

81. What will happen in the summer?

(A) A museum will be renovated.
(B) An internship program will be held.
(C) Local officials will be elected.
(D) Award winners will be announced.

82. According to the speaker, what will be distributed in August?

(A) Some survey forms
(B) Some parking passes
(C) Some concert tickets
(D) Some cash payments

GO ON TO THE NEXT PAGE

83. Where does the speaker most likely work?

(A) At a supermarket
(B) At a pharmacy
(C) At an architecture firm
(D) At a bank

84. Where were some advertisements placed?

(A) On newspapers
(B) On the Internet
(C) On billboards
(D) On television

85. What does the speaker imply when he says, "we haven't had to sit through many interviews at all"?

(A) The city is lacking people.
(B) A change was beneficial.
(C) Some employees should work overtime.
(D) More suggestions are needed.

86. What does the speaker say she received from the listener?

(A) A draft of an article
(B) A purchase order
(C) A credit card number
(D) A job application

87. What impressed the listener about a product?

(A) It is customizable.
(B) It comes with an extended warranty.
(C) It can be easily assembled.
(D) It is budget-friendly.

88. Why does the speaker say, "that is a feature of the premium model"?

(A) To decline an offer
(B) To compliment the listener
(C) To correct a mistake
(D) To make a recommendation

89. Who does the speaker work for?

(A) A news agency
(B) A construction company
(C) A government office
(D) A consultancy firm

90. What is the speaker talking about?

(A) The expansion of an apartment complex
(B) The opening of a shopping center
(C) The partnership with a neighboring city
(D) The induction of a new city mayor

91. What is the purpose of the project?

(A) To create additional jobs
(B) To promote recycling
(C) To save the city money
(D) To increase tourism

92. Where do the listeners work?

(A) At a dairy farm
(B) At a grocery store
(C) At a bakery
(D) At a restaurant

93. How did the company find out about Web Maestros?

(A) From a TV commercial
(B) From a current employee
(C) From a former client
(D) From a newspaper advertisement

94. Why does the speaker say, "Web Maestros will designate a qualified technician to us"?

(A) A project will be delayed.
(B) A contract needs to be reviewed.
(C) The listeners do not have to be concerned.
(D) The listeners should interview a job applicant.

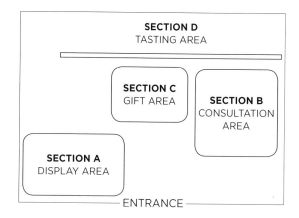

Event Schedule	
10 A.M.	Technology and its Place
11 A.M.	Analytics and Scores
12 P.M.	Lunch
2 P.M.	Best Practice Competition
3 P.M.	Authentic Assessments
4 P.M.	Going Online

95. What most likely is the speaker's occupation?

(A) Event planner
(B) Head chef
(C) Interior designer
(D) Computer technician

96. What does the speaker say about the pasta sauces?

(A) They must be stored in a cool area.
(B) They can be sold at reduced prices.
(C) They are going to be distributed as gifts.
(D) They will be located in the front.

97. Look at the graphic. Which section was added?

(A) Section A
(B) Section B
(C) Section C
(D) Section D

98. According to the speaker, which field has had a lot of innovation recently?

(A) Education
(B) Fashion
(C) Technology
(D) Finance

99. What does the speaker remind the listeners to do?

(A) Answer a survey
(B) Register their details
(C) Distribute business cards
(D) Sign up for a study

100. Look at the graphic. Which session has been canceled?

(A) Analytics and Scores
(B) Best Practice Competition
(C) Authentic Assessments
(D) Going Online

This is the end of the Listening test.

TEST 07

MP3 바로 듣기

준비물: OMR 카드, 연필, 지우개, 시계
시험시간: LC 약 45분

나의 점수	
LC	
맞은 개수	
환산 점수	

TEST 01	TEST 02	TEST 03	TEST 04	TEST 05
_____ 점	_____ 점	_____ 점	_____ 점	_____ 점
TEST 06	**TEST 07**	**TEST 08**	**TEST 09**	**TEST 10**
_____ 점	_____ 점	_____ 점	_____ 점	_____ 점

점수 환산표

LC			
맞은 개수	환산 점수	맞은 개수	환산 점수
96-100	475-495	41-45	155-230
91-95	435-495	36-40	125-205
86-90	405-475	31-35	105-175
81-85	370-450	26-30	85-145
76-80	345-420	21-25	60-115
71-75	320-390	16-20	30-90
66-70	290-360	11-15	5-70
61-65	265-335	6-10	5-60
56-60	235-310	1-5	5-60
51-55	210-280	0	5-35
46-50	180-255		

LISTENING TEST

In the Listening test, you will be asked to demonstrate how well you understand spoken English. The entire listening test will last approximately 45 minutes. There are four parts, and directions are given for each part. You must mark your answers on the separate answer sheet. Do not write your answers in your test book.

PART 1

Directions: For each question in this part, you will hear four statements about a picture in your test book. When you hear the statements, you must select the one statement that best describes what you see in the picture. Then find the number of the question on your answer sheet and mark your answer. The statements will not be printed in your test book and will be spoken only one time.

Statement (B), "A man is pointing at a document," is the best description of the picture, so you should select answer (B) and mark it on your answer sheet.

1.

2.

GO ON TO THE NEXT PAGE

3.

4.

5.

6.

GO ON TO THE NEXT PAGE

PART 2

Directions: You will hear a question or statement and three responses spoken in English. They will not be printed in your test book and will be spoken only one time. Select the best response to the question or statement and mark the letter (A), (B), or (C) on your answer sheet.

7. Mark your answer on your answer sheet.

8. Mark your answer on your answer sheet.

9. Mark your answer on your answer sheet.

10. Mark your answer on your answer sheet.

11. Mark your answer on your answer sheet.

12. Mark your answer on your answer sheet.

13. Mark your answer on your answer sheet.

14. Mark your answer on your answer sheet.

15. Mark your answer on your answer sheet.

16. Mark your answer on your answer sheet.

17. Mark your answer on your answer sheet.

18. Mark your answer on your answer sheet.

19. Mark your answer on your answer sheet.

20. Mark your answer on your answer sheet.

21. Mark your answer on your answer sheet.

22. Mark your answer on your answer sheet.

23. Mark your answer on your answer sheet.

24. Mark your answer on your answer sheet.

25. Mark your answer on your answer sheet.

26. Mark your answer on your answer sheet.

27. Mark your answer on your answer sheet.

28. Mark your answer on your answer sheet.

29. Mark your answer on your answer sheet.

30. Mark your answer on your answer sheet.

31. Mark your answer on your answer sheet.

PART 3

Directions: You will hear some conversations between two or more people. You will be asked to answer three questions about what the speakers say in each conversation. Select the best response to each question and mark the letter (A), (B), (C), or (D) on your answer sheet. The conversations will not be printed in your test book and will be spoken only one time.

32. Why did the woman visit Roy's room?

(A) To return an item
(B) To fix some equipment
(C) To discuss a budget proposal
(D) To submit some documents

33. Why is Roy unavailable?

(A) He is meeting with an executive.
(B) He is leaving for the airport soon.
(C) He is conducting a customer survey.
(D) He is participating in a convention.

34. What will the woman do next?

(A) Contact a manager
(B) Read a user guide
(C) Give an office tour
(D) Download a program

35. Who most likely are the women?

(A) Librarians
(B) Curators
(C) Magazine editors
(D) Construction workers

36. Why is the man unable to enter an area?

(A) It is being relocated.
(B) The elevator is being repaired.
(C) It is going through renovation.
(D) The workers are taking a lunch break.

37. How can Joanne help the man?

(A) By signing into an online database
(B) By making an appointment
(C) By locating some journals
(D) By contacting a publisher

38. Why is the man calling?

(A) To discuss an extra charge
(B) To purchase some supplies
(C) To register for a business conference
(D) To follow up on a renovation project

39. What did the woman recently do?

(A) She sold her company.
(B) She published a book.
(C) She came back from a trip.
(D) She designed a new product.

40. What will happen in the first week of March?

(A) Some prices will be finalized.
(B) Some interviews will take place.
(C) A workshop will be held.
(D) A client will visit.

41. What most likely is the woman's job?

(A) Personnel manager
(B) Computer programmer
(C) Mathematician
(D) Translator

42. Why is the woman concerned?

(A) She will have to take a pay cut.
(B) She needs a recommendation letter.
(C) She is inexperienced.
(D) She was late for her first interview.

43. What does the man ask the woman about?

(A) Whether she heard back from the company
(B) Whether she will telecommute
(C) Whether she will take a screening test
(D) Whether she submitted her resignation letter

GO ON TO THE NEXT PAGE

44. What did the man receive a reward for?

(A) Designing a successful product
(B) Cutting operating expenses
(C) Overseeing a project overseas
(D) Attracting many customers

45. What does the man plan to do next week?

(A) Participate in a sports competition
(B) Meet some family members
(C) Attend a performance
(D) Host a company banquet

46. What does the man say he might do with his reward?

(A) Give it to a colleague
(B) Sell it online
(C) Use it later
(D) Put it in a frame

47. Where are the speakers?

(A) At a clothing retailer
(B) At a department store
(C) At a construction firm
(D) At an elementary school

48. What does the woman say has happened?

(A) A building has been remodeled.
(B) A marketing campaign has been launched.
(C) Some new workers have been hired.
(D) Some new policies have been adopted.

49. What does the woman imply when she says, "I know we adjusted some of the brands that we carry"?

(A) The man will like some merchandise.
(B) The man should speak to a team manager.
(C) The man needs to walk to another building.
(D) The man might not find what he is looking for.

50. What is the purpose of the man's call?

(A) To apply for a position
(B) To ask for a refund
(C) To report a problem
(D) To extend a membership

51. Why does the woman apologize?

(A) The man was given incorrect instructions.
(B) An invoice included an extra charge.
(C) The man does not qualify for a discount.
(D) A credit card cannot be processed.

52. What does the woman offer to do?

(A) Update some contact information
(B) Revise an order
(C) Provide a free item
(D) Call another branch

53. Where do the speakers probably work?

(A) At a law firm
(B) At a publishing company
(C) At a high school
(D) At a broadcasting agency

54. What is the main topic of the conversation?

(A) A revised contract
(B) Some award nominees
(C) A retiring employee
(D) Some budget figures

55. Why is the man relieved?

(A) A project will get additional funding.
(B) A client is pleased with some work.
(C) He will receive more help with an assignment.
(D) He has enough time to make a selection.

56. What is the man working on?

(A) Planning a business trip
(B) Analyzing sales figures
(C) Updating an employee handbook
(D) Making a customer satisfaction survey

57. Why does the woman say, "the presentation is this Friday"?

(A) To extend gratitude
(B) To make an amendment
(C) To show concern
(D) To provide some context

58. What does the woman say she will do?

(A) Conduct a training session
(B) Talk with the board of directors
(C) Recruit additional employees
(D) Contact a travel agency

59. What type of products do the speakers sell?

(A) Food
(B) Cookware
(C) Apparel
(D) Appliance

60. How does the woman suggest changing the packaging?

(A) By rewording the text
(B) By using more colors
(C) By changing the font
(D) By resizing the logo

61. Why did the man choose the computer program?

(A) It can be used on multiple devices.
(B) It comes with free online resources.
(C) It supports more file types.
(D) It is most commonly used.

Leon's Wednesday Schedule	
8:00 A.M.	Department Meeting
9:00 A.M.	
10:00 A.M.	Videoconference Session
11:00 A.M.	
12:00 P.M.	Team Luncheon
1:00 P.M.	
2:00 – 5:00 P.M.	Client Meetings

62. According to the woman, what will happen on Thursday?

(A) She will leave for vacation.
(B) Some clients will visit an office.
(C) She will record a video.
(D) Some software will be installed.

63. Look at the graphic. What time will the speakers probably meet?

(A) 8:00 A.M.
(B) 10:00 A.M.
(C) 11:00 A.M.
(D) 1:00 P.M.

64. What does the man say he will do next?

(A) Update a system
(B) Edit a document
(C) Email a coworker
(D) Reserve a room

GO ON TO THE NEXT PAGE

Front of Bus

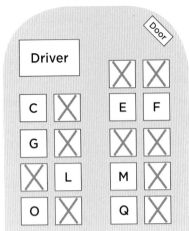

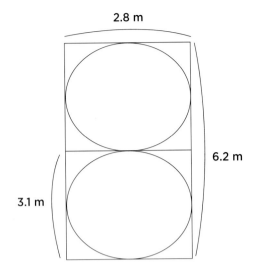

2.8 m

6.2 m

3.1 m

65. What event are the speakers preparing for?

(A) A networking event
(B) An exhibition
(C) A trade fair
(D) A company retreat

66. What does the man ask the woman to help with?

(A) Printing a pamphlet
(B) Updating emergency contacts
(C) Packing a suitcase
(D) Making a schedule

67. Look at the graphic. Which seats will the speakers choose?

(A) Seats E and F
(B) Seats C and G
(C) Seats L and M
(D) Seats O and Q

68. What kind of business does the man own?

(A) A storage facility
(B) A coffee shop
(C) An employment agency
(D) An art gallery

69. Look at the graphic. Which dimension does the man want to change?

(A) 2.8 meters
(B) 3.1 meters
(C) 4.3 meters
(D) 6.2 meters

70. What will the woman probably do next?

(A) Calculate a price
(B) Measure some material
(C) Provide a sample
(D) Contact a manufacturer

PART 4

Directions: You will hear some talks given by a single speaker. You will be asked to answer three questions about what the speaker says in each talk. Select the best response to each question and mark the letter (A), (B), (C), or (D) on your answer sheet. The talks will not be printed in your test book and will be spoken only one time.

71. Who most likely are the listeners?

(A) Professional athletes
(B) Construction workers
(C) Market researchers
(D) Computer programmers

72. What will the membership allow the listeners to do?

(A) Receive meal plans
(B) Rent a facility
(C) Borrow fitness equipment
(D) Access to the parking lot

73. What will the listeners do next?

(A) Tour a facility
(B) Enroll in a course
(C) Watch a video
(D) Speak to a representative

74. What business most likely created the message?

(A) An employment agency
(B) An insurance company
(C) A doctor's office
(D) A law firm

75. What is mentioned about the business?

(A) It is being remodeled.
(B) It will be relocating.
(C) It will have new business hours.
(D) It is closed due to a holiday.

76. What does the speaker instruct the listeners to do?

(A) Go to a website
(B) Leave a message
(C) Call at another time
(D) Submit some forms

77. What is the main topic of the broadcast?

(A) An automotive conference
(B) A corporate merger
(C) Current shopping trends
(D) Revised hiring procedures

78. According to the speaker, who is Terry Logan?

(A) A Web designer
(B) A news reporter
(C) A construction supervisor
(D) An executive officer

79. According to the speaker, what will WIE Motors do next year?

(A) Move its headquarters
(B) Build a manufacturing facility
(C) Launch a new product
(D) Make financial donations

80. Why is the speaker meeting with the listeners?

(A) To suggest staff training
(B) To present an investment opportunity
(C) To advertise a service
(D) To share some research findings

81. According to the speaker, what benefit is suggested by research?

(A) Increased productivity
(B) Faster delivery time
(C) Higher annual earnings
(D) Improved employee retention

82. What does the speaker show the listeners?

(A) An event schedule
(B) A marketing report
(C) An instruction manual
(D) A pricing list

GO ON TO THE NEXT PAGE

83. What is the subject of the convention?

(A) Hiring qualified employees
(B) Developing better products
(C) Reducing operating expenses
(D) Building brand awareness

84. What does the speaker imply when he says, "we invite experts from across the world"?

(A) The listeners will learn from a variety of speakers.
(B) The listeners will have to pay a bigger fee this year.
(C) He thinks convention tickets will sell out fast.
(D) He believes more translators are needed for an event.

85. How can the listeners receive a discount?

(A) By recommending a presenter
(B) By organizing a group package
(C) By contacting a coordinator
(D) By registering early

86. According to the speaker, what has just arrived today?

(A) An air conditioner
(B) A laptop
(C) A photocopier
(D) A label maker

87. What does the speaker emphasize about the product?

(A) It is easy to use.
(B) It is the best-selling model.
(C) It is long-lasting.
(D) It is environmentally friendly.

88. Why does the speaker say, "But keep in mind that they're pretty busy this time of year"?

(A) To ask that listeners be patient
(B) To request that more employees be recruited
(C) To point out an unreasonable project timeline
(D) To recommend contacting a manufacturer

89. Who most likely are the listeners?

(A) Security officers
(B) Real estate agents
(C) Insurance workers
(D) Electrical engineers

90. What type of product is the speaker discussing?

(A) A phone accessory
(B) A Bluetooth speaker
(C) A security system
(D) A wireless printer

91. What will the listeners do after lunch?

(A) Visit an office
(B) Install devices
(C) Make a payment
(D) Update a software program

92. What kind of construction project is the speaker discussing?

(A) A town hall
(B) A school gymnasium
(C) A community center
(D) A sports stadium

93. What feature does the speaker describe?

(A) A storage shed
(B) A parking area
(C) A security system
(D) An additional toilet

94. Why does the speaker say, "Melissa Richardson is your best bet"?

(A) To acknowledge one of his colleagues
(B) To refer the listeners to the correct person
(C) To request clarification from an expert
(D) To explain a discrepancy in some documents

AA Driver Licenses	
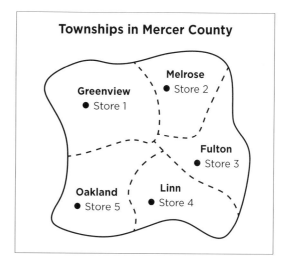	
Driver License Test Bookings	Counter 1
Driver License Renewals	Counter 2
Online Applications	Counter 3
Vehicle Registrations	Counter 4

Townships in Mercer County

Greenview
● Store 1

Melrose
● Store 2

Fulton
● Store 3

Oakland
● Store 5

Linn
● Store 4

95. What does the speaker say has happened recently?

(A) The management team has changed.
(B) Some services are no longer available.
(C) There have been budget cutbacks.
(D) A building has been repurposed.

96. Look at the graphic. Which counter are some listeners allowed to go to immediately?

(A) Counter 1
(B) Counter 2
(C) Counter 3
(D) Counter 4

97. According to the speaker, what should the listeners consider doing?

(A) Using a new application
(B) Paying using a credit card
(C) Consulting an expert
(D) Coming in earlier

98. Why does the speaker congratulate Maddie Apodaca?

(A) Her store has outstanding customer service.
(B) Her store made the highest profit last year.
(C) She was promoted to store manager.
(D) She will be featured in a magazine article.

99. Look at the graphic. Which store does Maddie Apodaca manage?

(A) Store 1
(B) Store 2
(C) Store 3
(D) Store 4

100. What will be discussed next?

(A) An upgrade
(B) An expansion
(C) A relocation
(D) A workshop

This is the end of the Listening test.

TEST 07

TEST 08

MP3 바로 듣기

준비물: OMR 카드, 연필, 지우개, 시계
시험시간: LC 약 45분

나의 점수		
LC		
맞은 개수		
환산 점수		

TEST 01	TEST 02	TEST 03	TEST 04	TEST 05
_____점	_____점	_____점	_____점	_____점
TEST 06	**TEST 07**	**TEST 08**	**TEST 09**	**TEST 10**
_____점	_____점	_____점	_____점	_____점

점수 환산표

LC			
맞은 개수	환산 점수	맞은 개수	환산 점수
96-100	475-495	41-45	155-230
91-95	435-495	36-40	125-205
86-90	405-475	31-35	105-175
81-85	370-450	26-30	85-145
76-80	345-420	21-25	60-115
71-75	320-390	16-20	30-90
66-70	290-360	11-15	5-70
61-65	265-335	6-10	5-60
56-60	235-310	1-5	5-60
51-55	210-280	0	5-35
46-50	180-255		

LISTENING TEST

In the Listening test, you will be asked to demonstrate how well you understand spoken English. The entire listening test will last approximately 45 minutes. There are four parts, and directions are given for each part. You must mark your answers on the separate answer sheet. Do not write your answers in your test book.

PART 1

Directions: For each question in this part, you will hear four statements about a picture in your test book. When you hear the statements, you must select the one statement that best describes what you see in the picture. Then find the number of the question on your answer sheet and mark your answer. The statements will not be printed in your test book and will be spoken only one time.

Statement (B), "A man is pointing at a document," is the best description of the picture, so you should select answer (B) and mark it on your answer sheet.

1.

2.

GO ON TO THE NEXT PAGE

3.

4.

5.

6.

GO ON TO THE NEXT PAGE

PART 2

Directions: You will hear a question or statement and three responses spoken in English. They will not be printed in your test book and will be spoken only one time. Select the best response to the question or statement and mark the letter (A), (B), or (C) on your answer sheet.

7. Mark your answer on your answer sheet.

8. Mark your answer on your answer sheet.

9. Mark your answer on your answer sheet.

10. Mark your answer on your answer sheet.

11. Mark your answer on your answer sheet.

12. Mark your answer on your answer sheet.

13. Mark your answer on your answer sheet.

14. Mark your answer on your answer sheet.

15. Mark your answer on your answer sheet.

16. Mark your answer on your answer sheet.

17. Mark your answer on your answer sheet.

18. Mark your answer on your answer sheet.

19. Mark your answer on your answer sheet.

20. Mark your answer on your answer sheet.

21. Mark your answer on your answer sheet.

22. Mark your answer on your answer sheet.

23. Mark your answer on your answer sheet.

24. Mark your answer on your answer sheet.

25. Mark your answer on your answer sheet.

26. Mark your answer on your answer sheet.

27. Mark your answer on your answer sheet.

28. Mark your answer on your answer sheet.

29. Mark your answer on your answer sheet.

30. Mark your answer on your answer sheet.

31. Mark your answer on your answer sheet.

PART 3

Directions: You will hear some conversations between two or more people. You will be asked to answer three questions about what the speakers say in each conversation. Select the best response to each question and mark the letter (A), (B), (C), or (D) on your answer sheet. The conversations will not be printed in your test book and will be spoken only one time.

32. What type of event are the speakers discussing?

(A) A sports competition
(B) A musical performance
(C) A craft festival
(D) A local election

33. Where do the speakers most likely work?

(A) At a travel agency
(B) At a publishing company
(C) At a broadcasting network
(D) At a police station

34. What problem does the man mention?

(A) Some equipment has been misplaced.
(B) There is insufficient seating.
(C) An order has not been delivered.
(D) A staff member is unavailable.

35. Where do the speakers probably work?

(A) At a fabric store
(B) At a newspaper company
(C) At a library
(D) At a factory

36. What do the speakers believe is most important?

(A) Hiring knowledgeable employees
(B) Expanding product lines
(C) Maintaining good client relations
(D) Creating high-quality materials

37. What will the man send the woman?

(A) A bonus payment
(B) A sample contract
(C) A job summary
(D) A product list

38. What did the woman buy online?

(A) A computer
(B) A television
(C) A camera
(D) A phone

39. What error did the woman make?

(A) She provided an incorrect phone number.
(B) She did not submit the entire payment.
(C) She chose the wrong size.
(D) She forgot to apply a discount.

40. What does the man inform the woman about?

(A) A promotional event
(B) A product feature
(C) A delivery service
(D) An extra charge

41. In which department does the man work?

(A) Design
(B) Sales
(C) Finance
(D) Editorial

42. What does the man say is the cause for a change in consumer habits?

(A) The availability of better technology
(B) Improved economic conditions
(C) The need for a cleaner environment
(D) Increased fuel costs

43. What do the speakers agree on?

(A) Hosting an online workshop
(B) Discontinuing a service
(C) Hiring a new marketing agency
(D) Renovating an office

GO ON TO THE NEXT PAGE

44. What did the man recently approve?

(A) A website
(B) A blueprint
(C) A manual
(D) A bank guide

45. What good news does the woman share?

(A) The security has been upgraded.
(B) The client has expressed satisfaction.
(C) The business has received new orders.
(D) The profit has been increased.

46. Why did the man reassign staff?

(A) To meet with a client
(B) To process payments
(C) To diagnose a problem
(D) To organize new projects

47. What is the man calling about?

(A) Completing an order
(B) Recruiting temporary workers
(C) Arranging some furniture
(D) Finding a bigger venue

48. What does the woman imply when she says, "the client made a specific request for this"?

(A) The man should contact the client.
(B) A price has already been set.
(C) A modification cannot be made.
(D) The man has to fix an error.

49. What does the man offer to do?

(A) Contact local businesses
(B) Provide a discount
(C) Expedite a delivery
(D) Set up some equipment

50. Where is the conversation taking place?

(A) At a train station
(B) At a bus terminal
(C) At an airport gate
(D) At a ferry port

51. What problem does the woman mention?

(A) A payment cannot be processed.
(B) A computer is not working.
(C) Some seats are unavailable.
(D) Some documents are missing.

52. What does the woman suggest that the man do?

(A) Download an application
(B) Purchase a membership
(C) Go to a restaurant
(D) Print out a voucher

53. Where does the conversation take place?

(A) At a public library
(B) At a coworking space
(C) At a fitness club
(D) At an art gallery

54. Why does the woman say, "You won't find many facilities that offer this many services"?

(A) To justify a price
(B) To express concern about a facility
(C) To recommend starting a business
(D) To disagree with a decision

55. What does the woman give to the man?

(A) A business card
(B) A membership ID
(C) A day pass
(D) A discount voucher

56. What are the speakers discussing?

(A) Staff retention strategies
(B) Customer feedback implementation
(C) Additional income sources
(D) Social media marketing

57. What does the man think about the idea of selling dairy products?

(A) Similar products are sold elsewhere.
(B) More employees need to be hired to produce those products.
(C) The farm does not have a license to manufacture food.
(D) There is not enough space to create a store.

58. What does the man plan to do?

(A) Conduct some research
(B) Find out a recipe
(C) Post an online advertisement
(D) Speak with some suppliers

59. Why is the man at Watscorp Publishers?

(A) To discuss a new book project
(B) To lead a company workshop
(C) To conduct an inspection
(D) To interview for a position

60. According to the man, what is his biggest accomplishment?

(A) Making educational materials
(B) Starting his own business
(C) Receiving a national award
(D) Becoming an R&D manager

61. What does the man like about Watscorp?

(A) It publishes famous novels.
(B) It cares about its workers.
(C) It is an industry leader.
(D) It recently expanded its offices.

Train Number	Destination	Departure Time / Status
230	Rochester	8:20 A.M. On Schedule
231	Buffalo	9:15 A.M. Delayed 60 minutes
232	Albany	10:30 A.M. On Schedule
233	Syracuse	11:00 A.M. Delayed 45 minutes

62. What is the man's problem?

(A) He will arrive late.
(B) He could not reserve a ticket.
(C) He left his notes at home.
(D) He is unable to find a parking space.

63. Look at the graphic. Which train will the speakers board?

(A) 230
(B) 231
(C) 232
(D) 233

64. What does the man request the woman do?

(A) Give a speech
(B) Send a message
(C) Review a presentation
(D) Make a payment

GO ON TO THE NEXT PAGE

Upcoming Spring Seminars

March 12	Eating for Energy
March 29	Starting Yoga
April 3	Creating a Jogging Program
April 16	Keeping a Training Journal

65. Why is the woman able to participate in free seminars?

(A) She is a local resident.
(B) She is a fitness trainer.
(C) She purchased a membership.
(D) She completed early registration.

66. Look at the graphic. On which date will the woman attend an event?

(A) March 12
(B) March 29
(C) April 3
(D) April 16

67. What will Brianne Pyle introduce?

(A) A nutrition plan
(B) A fitness machine
(C) An exercise routine
(D) A health book

Coffee and Tea
Shelf 1

Cupcakes
Shelf 2

Fruit Cups
Shelf 3

Orange Juice
Shelf 4

68. Where is the conversation most likely taking place?

(A) At a convention center
(B) At a grocery store
(C) At a coffee shop
(D) At an airport lounge

69. Look at the graphic. Which shelf does the man direct the woman to?

(A) Shelf 1
(B) Shelf 2
(C) Shelf 3
(D) Shelf 4

70. What does the woman ask the man to do?

(A) Update a menu
(B) Inquire about an order
(C) Exchange some items
(D) Revise an inventory list

PART 4

Directions: You will hear some talks given by a single speaker. You will be asked to answer three questions about what the speaker says in each talk. Select the best response to each question and mark the letter (A), (B), (C), or (D) on your answer sheet. The talks will not be printed in your test book and will be spoken only one time.

71. What service is being advertised?

(A) Event planning
(B) Interior designing
(C) Digital marketing
(D) Product packaging

72. What advantage does the advertisement mention?

(A) Express delivery
(B) Quality merchandise
(C) Affordable pricing
(D) Flexible hours

73. Why should the listeners check a website?

(A) To contact a representative
(B) To view previous projects
(C) To download a program
(D) To complete a registration form

74. Who most likely are the listeners?

(A) Management consultants
(B) Customer service staff
(C) Computer scientists
(D) Corporate trainers

75. What will Traci Soto talk about?

(A) Client management
(B) Time management
(C) Data storage
(D) Business opportunities

76. What does the speaker ask the listeners to do?

(A) Respond to an e-mail
(B) Organize a meeting
(C) Meet with a manager
(D) Suggest some ideas

77. What product has the speaker's company developed?

(A) A thermometer
(B) A cooking table
(C) A microwave
(D) A refrigerator

78. What does the speaker say was important to her?

(A) Inexpensiveness
(B) Aesthetics
(C) Sturdiness
(D) Simplicity

79. What will the speaker do next?

(A) Conduct a demonstration
(B) Pass around a flyer
(C) Show a video
(D) Refer to some data

80. Why was the listener's application most likely rejected?

(A) She does not have enough work experience.
(B) She does not know a specific language.
(C) She is not able to work on weekends.
(D) She is not able to move to another city.

81. What does the speaker imply when he says, "they've already started interviewing people"?

(A) Action should be taken soon.
(B) Interviews cannot be rescheduled.
(C) A department has already hired someone.
(D) A job is more difficult than expected.

82. What does the speaker offer to do?

(A) Book a room
(B) Forward a document
(C) Visit an office
(D) Call an applicant

GO ON TO THE NEXT PAGE

83. Where does the speaker most likely work?

(A) At an Internet provider
(B) At a science laboratory
(C) At an electronics manufacturer
(D) At a broadcasting network

84. What is the speaker concerned about?

(A) Loss of business
(B) Increased cost of materials
(C) A shipment delay
(D) A safety inspection

85. What does the speaker say he will do?

(A) Provide a financial incentive to staff
(B) Assign more employees to a project
(C) Approve requests to work overtime
(D) Work over the holidays

86. What is the talk mainly about?

(A) Safety procedures
(B) Training schedules
(C) Employee benefits
(D) Vacation policies

87. According to the speaker, what can the listeners get discounts on?

(A) Medicine
(B) Airfare
(C) Phone plans
(D) Office supplies

88. What will the speaker do next?

(A) Answer some questions
(B) Hand out some information
(C) Introduce some guests
(D) Demonstrate some equipment

89. What is the speaker preparing for?

(A) An anniversary event
(B) A training session
(C) A sales conference
(D) A charity fundraiser

90. What does the speaker imply when he says, "the employees from the overseas branch are also coming"?

(A) More food should be ordered.
(B) A bigger venue will be required.
(C) A guest list should be updated.
(D) Some documents will be translated.

91. Why does the speaker want to meet with the woman?

(A) To select menu options
(B) To discuss a budget
(C) To review a contract
(D) To choose a speaker

92. What does the speaker announce?

(A) A company has won an award.
(B) A new location will open soon.
(C) A project has been delayed.
(D) A partnership has been finalized.

93. Who does the speaker say the company will hire?

(A) Photographers
(B) Web designers
(C) Caterers
(D) Reporters

94. What does the speaker imply when she says, "We're going to need a new office for the team at this rate"?

(A) A location is ideal.
(B) A contract has been received.
(C) A suggestion has been noted.
(D) A team has grown rapidly.

Reward Tier	Amount of Sales	Reward
Tier A	Over $3,000	Free round-trip airfare
Tier B	$2,000 to $3,000	$300 Gift Certificate
Tier C	$1,000 to $2,000	Set of Steak Knives
Tier D	Under $1,000	Pair of Headphones

95. What kind of business does the speaker most likely work for?

(A) A mobile phone company
(B) A car dealership
(C) A clothing store
(D) An advertising agency

96. Look at the graphic. Which reward tier did most of the staff members achieve?

(A) Tier A
(B) Tier B
(C) Tier C
(D) Tier D

97. Why does the speaker say Henry Manning will travel to Vermont next month?

(A) To see his family
(B) To attend a marketing seminar
(C) To receive a prize
(D) To compete in a contest

Five-Alarm Chili Recipe

2 onions
5 red peppers
6 tomatoes
7 cloves of garlic
1 cup of shredded cheese
1 can of beans
500g beef

98. What event did the speaker attend last Monday?

(A) A culinary competition
(B) A corporate anniversary party
(C) A new employee luncheon
(D) A store opening

99. Look at the graphic. Which amount does the speaker suggest changing?

(A) 2
(B) 5
(C) 6
(D) 7

100. Where did the speaker get the recipe from?

(A) An article
(B) A friend
(C) A TV show
(D) A cookbook

This is the end of the Listening test.

TEST 09

MP3 바로 듣기

준비물: OMR 카드, 연필, 지우개, 시계
시험시간: LC 약 45분

나의 점수		
LC		
맞은 개수		
환산 점수		

TEST 01	TEST 02	TEST 03	TEST 04	TEST 05
_____점	_____점	_____점	_____점	_____점
TEST 06	TEST 07	TEST 08	TEST 09	TEST 10
_____점	_____점	_____점	_____점	_____점

점수 환산표

LC			
맞은 개수	환산 점수	맞은 개수	환산 점수
96-100	475-495	41-45	155-230
91-95	435-495	36-40	125-205
86-90	405-475	31-35	105-175
81-85	370-450	26-30	85-145
76-80	345-420	21-25	60-115
71-75	320-390	16-20	30-90
66-70	290-360	11-15	5-70
61-65	265-335	6-10	5-60
56-60	235-310	1-5	5-60
51-55	210-280	0	5-35
46-50	180-255		

LISTENING TEST

In the Listening test, you will be asked to demonstrate how well you understand spoken English. The entire listening test will last approximately 45 minutes. There are four parts, and directions are given for each part. You must mark your answers on the separate answer sheet. Do not write your answers in your test book.

PART 1

Directions: For each question in this part, you will hear four statements about a picture in your test book. When you hear the statements, you must select the one statement that best describes what you see in the picture. Then find the number of the question on your answer sheet and mark your answer. The statements will not be printed in your test book and will be spoken only one time.

Statement (B), "A man is pointing at a document," is the best description of the picture, so you should select answer (B) and mark it on your answer sheet.

1.

2.

GO ON TO THE NEXT PAGE

3.

4.

5.

6.

GO ON TO THE NEXT PAGE

PART 2

Directions: You will hear a question or statement and three responses spoken in English. They will not be printed in your test book and will be spoken only one time. Select the best response to the question or statement and mark the letter (A), (B), or (C) on your answer sheet.

7. Mark your answer on your answer sheet.

8. Mark your answer on your answer sheet.

9. Mark your answer on your answer sheet.

10. Mark your answer on your answer sheet.

11. Mark your answer on your answer sheet.

12. Mark your answer on your answer sheet.

13. Mark your answer on your answer sheet.

14. Mark your answer on your answer sheet.

15. Mark your answer on your answer sheet.

16. Mark your answer on your answer sheet.

17. Mark your answer on your answer sheet.

18. Mark your answer on your answer sheet.

19. Mark your answer on your answer sheet.

20. Mark your answer on your answer sheet.

21. Mark your answer on your answer sheet.

22. Mark your answer on your answer sheet.

23. Mark your answer on your answer sheet.

24. Mark your answer on your answer sheet.

25. Mark your answer on your answer sheet.

26. Mark your answer on your answer sheet.

27. Mark your answer on your answer sheet.

28. Mark your answer on your answer sheet.

29. Mark your answer on your answer sheet.

30. Mark your answer on your answer sheet.

31. Mark your answer on your answer sheet.

PART 3

Directions: You will hear some conversations between two or more people. You will be asked to answer three questions about what the speakers say in each conversation. Select the best response to each question and mark the letter (A), (B), (C), or (D) on your answer sheet. The conversations will not be printed in your test book and will be spoken only one time.

32. Where does the conversation most likely take place?

(A) On an airplane
(B) On a bus
(C) On a train
(D) On a ferry

33. What task does the woman ask the man to do?

(A) Assist a passenger
(B) Make an announcement
(C) Play a safety video
(D) Secure some cargo

34. What does the woman say she will be doing?

(A) Checking some tickets
(B) Inspecting some bags
(C) Preparing for a meal
(D) Contacting a control center

35. Who most likely is the man?

(A) A business consultant
(B) A factory worker
(C) An assistant
(D) A golf instructor

36. Why do the speakers move to a different location?

(A) To assist other workers
(B) To avoid stormy weather
(C) To finish a project
(D) To serve a patron

37. What does the man recommend doing?

(A) Wearing appropriate gear
(B) Running outside
(C) Eating sufficient protein
(D) Carrying an extra bag

38. Who most likely is the man?

(A) A university professor
(B) A museum manager
(C) A famous artist
(D) A conference organizer

39. What is the main topic of the conversation?

(A) Sculpture exhibits
(B) Traffic conditions
(C) Membership benefits
(D) Photo submissions

40. What does the woman ask about?

(A) Buying a gift
(B) Renting a device
(C) Storing a bag
(D) Paying a fee

41. Why is the woman at the theater?

(A) To interview an actor
(B) To celebrate an anniversary
(C) To apply for a job
(D) To perform an inspection

42. Why is the woman disappointed?

(A) An entrance fee has increased.
(B) She could not find parking.
(C) A performance was canceled.
(D) The lead actor has retired.

43. What does the man offer the woman?

(A) Some headphones
(B) A program guide
(C) A business card
(D) Reduced rates

GO ON TO THE NEXT PAGE

44. What are the speakers discussing?

(A) Painting a mural
(B) Evacuating an area
(C) Preserving a tree
(D) Cleaning some walls

45. What does Anthony give to the woman?

(A) A list of employees
(B) A cost estimate
(C) A business proposal
(D) A city permit

46. What does the woman say she needs to do?

(A) Make more bids
(B) Clean some equipment
(C) Assess a budget
(D) Receive approval

47. What did the speakers apply for?

(A) A scholarship
(B) A grant
(C) A loan
(D) A permit

48. What does the woman mean when she says, "I sent it in right before the final due date"?

(A) An overdue fine will not be charged.
(B) A process needs to be updated.
(C) A coworker is out of the office.
(D) An update cannot be made.

49. What technology do the speakers hope to use?

(A) Renewable energy
(B) LED lighting
(C) Electric vehicles
(D) Solar panels

50. Where do the women work?

(A) At a formal clothing retailer
(B) At a textile factory
(C) At a fashion magazine publisher
(D) At a laundry business

51. Why is the man visiting the business?

(A) To sign an agreement
(B) To receive a refund
(C) To apply for a job
(D) To pick up an item

52. What does the man agree to do?

(A) Return at another time
(B) Provide some comments
(C) Take a special tour
(D) Pay in cash

53. Who most likely is the man?

(A) A travel agent
(B) A journalist
(C) A performer
(D) A food caterer

54. What problem does the man mention?

(A) Certain expenses are not covered.
(B) Some documents were not delivered.
(C) A flight has been canceled.
(D) An event has been postponed.

55. What will the woman most likely do next?

(A) Interview some additional staff
(B) Consult with a supervisor
(C) Reserve a hotel room
(D) Reissue an invoice

56. Where do the speakers most likely work?

(A) At a marketing firm
(B) At a clothing retailer
(C) At a legal office
(D) At a production agency

57. What does the woman suggest?

(A) Moving to a bigger location
(B) Signing up for a seminar
(C) Consulting with a lawyer
(D) Working additional hours

58. What does the man offer to do?

(A) Process some payments
(B) Schedule a meeting
(C) Pick up a client
(D) Review some job applications

59. Where is the conversation taking place?

(A) At a bakery
(B) At a restaurant
(C) At a farm
(D) At a supermarket

60. What does the man imply when he says, "I came at the right time, then"?

(A) He was able to arrive at an event on time.
(B) He is eager to sample some items.
(C) He is available to help the woman.
(D) He was able to meet a project deadline.

61. What is the woman looking forward to?

(A) A revised packaging process
(B) The hiring of more employees
(C) A seasonal sales event
(D) The addition of a produce section

#1121 Rectangular Steel Legs	#1124 Round Three Legs
#1127 Rectangular Crossed Legs	#1129 Round Bar Table

62. According to the woman, what is happening in August?

(A) She is renovating her office.
(B) She is organizing a company dinner.
(C) She is relocating to a different city.
(D) She is starting a new business.

63. Look at the graphic. Which product will the woman order?

(A) #1121
(B) #1124
(C) #1127
(D) #1129

64. What offer does the man tell the woman about?

(A) The products can be shipped express.
(B) The purchase includes some free gifts.
(C) A product warranty can be extended.
(D) A payment may be made in installments.

GO ON TO THE NEXT PAGE

Trail Name	Trail Length
Housatonic Trail	10 miles
Naugatuck Trail	4 miles
Pistapaug Trail	2.5 miles
Pattaconk Trail	5 miles

65. Where do the speakers most likely work?

(A) At a real estate company
(B) At a government facility
(C) At an accounting firm
(D) At a public relations agency

66. Why is the man concerned?

(A) He wants to arrive early for an event.
(B) He has to respond to an urgent e-mail.
(C) He was unable to complete a document.
(D) He may have given a manager the wrong information.

67. Look at the graphic. Which trail are the speakers walking on?

(A) Housatonic Trail
(B) Naugatuck Trail
(C) Pistapaug Trail
(D) Pattaconk Trail

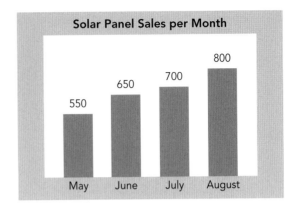

68. What is the purpose of the conversation?

(A) To discuss the sales of an item
(B) To review new safety protocols
(C) To highlight an issue
(D) To present a budget proposal

69. Look at the graphic. Which month does the man mention?

(A) May
(B) June
(C) July
(D) August

70. What does the man suggest doing?

(A) Advertising on television
(B) Hiring a consultant
(C) Reducing the budget
(D) Selling door to door

PART 4

Directions: You will hear some talks given by a single speaker. You will be asked to answer three questions about what the speaker says in each talk. Select the best response to each question and mark the letter (A), (B), (C), or (D) on your answer sheet. The talks will not be printed in your test book and will be spoken only one time.

71. What does the speaker say is prohibited on the tour?
(A) Running around
(B) Taking photographs
(C) Talking loudly
(D) Handling pottery

72. What does the speaker say happened last month?
(A) A community volunteered for an event.
(B) Some artists were featured in a documentary.
(C) A piece of art was sold for a large sum of money.
(D) Some new facilities were opened to the public.

73. What does the speaker say the listeners can do on weekends?
(A) Join a new tour
(B) Interact with the artists
(C) Purchase a gift
(D) Attend some classes

74. Where does the listener most likely work?
(A) At a software development firm
(B) At a bookstore
(C) At a publishing company
(D) At a graphic design agency

75. What is the speaker's supervisor worried about?
(A) A publication deadline
(B) A shipment date
(C) A local law
(D) A price estimate

76. What does the speaker imply when he says, "Ms. Yoon needs to review it by the end of the day"?
(A) A document contains some errors.
(B) His manager is going on vacation.
(C) He is unable to complete a task alone.
(D) A request should be handled quickly.

77. What does the speaker say will happen today?
(A) A seasonal sale will begin.
(B) A new product will arrive.
(C) A rewards program will launch.
(D) A new manager will start working.

78. What category of products does the business sell?
(A) Office supplies
(B) Indoor furniture
(C) Exercise equipment
(D) Electronic goods

79. What is the reason for the business's good reputation?
(A) Its location
(B) Its experienced staff
(C) Its product range
(D) Its low prices

80. What is the main purpose of the announcement?
(A) To update information about a showing
(B) To advertise a new offering at the snack bar
(C) To remind attendees of some common etiquettes
(D) To introduce a new restriction

81. What does the speaker say about the 1 P.M. movie tomorrow?
(A) It may be canceled on the day.
(B) It will be its first showing.
(C) Its director will be in attendance.
(D) Its prices will be reduced.

82. What will the listeners receive if they purchase tickets online?
(A) A soundtrack
(B) A free beverage
(C) A raffle ticket
(D) A movie souvenir

GO ON TO THE NEXT PAGE

83. What is the speaker's department working on?

(A) Client questionnaire replies
(B) A customer service process
(C) A new mobile phone
(D) Some computer software

84. Why did Tony recommend the listener?

(A) She has technical knowledge.
(B) She has worked with a company before.
(C) She can lead a training workshop.
(D) She can recommend an outside vendor.

85. Why does the speaker say, "Most of my teammates are at a seminar until Friday"?

(A) To ask that an event be postponed
(B) To explain the need for assistance
(C) To suggest a deadline extension
(D) To order some more supplies

86. What type of food does the radio program focus on?

(A) A meat
(B) A fruit
(C) A vegetable
(D) A nut

87. What aspect of the food will Jodi Ray discuss?

(A) Its seasonality
(B) Its health benefits
(C) Its various uses
(D) Its availability

88. Why should the listeners call the station?

(A) To claim a prize
(B) To speak to the guest
(C) To make a suggestion
(D) To answer a question

89. What is the main topic of the talk?

(A) Ingredients of some dishes
(B) Changes to a menu
(C) Renovations to a restaurant
(D) Locations of some food

90. What special event is probably being held?

(A) A welcome reception
(B) An awards dinner
(C) A grand opening
(D) A retirement party

91. What will the speaker check?

(A) The sizes of some tables
(B) The details of a reservation
(C) The availability of a room
(D) The prices of some items

92. What is the main topic of the program?

(A) A town parade
(B) A street construction project
(C) A public transit service
(D) A job opportunity

93. What does the speaker mean when she says, "this kind of thing takes a lot of time"?

(A) A deadline is difficult to meet.
(B) The results of a project are impressive.
(C) A budget should be increased.
(D) More volunteers are needed for an assignment.

94. According to the speaker, what will Mr. Rames do?

(A) Read some reviews
(B) Interview a resident
(C) Introduce a director
(D) Give some advice

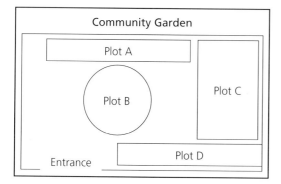

95. What does the speaker thank DMG Partners for?

(A) Providing funding
(B) Filming the event
(C) Creating brochures
(D) Designing the garden

96. Look at the graphic. According to the speaker, where will flowers be grown?

(A) In Garden Plot A
(B) In Garden Plot B
(C) In Garden Plot C
(D) In Garden Plot D

97. What will happen next?

(A) Some trees will be planted.
(B) Tools will be distributed.
(C) The listeners will tour the garden.
(D) A city official will give a speech.

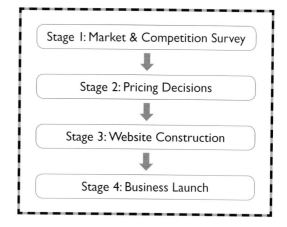

98. What industry do the listeners work in?

(A) Information Technology
(B) Food Service
(C) Healthcare
(D) Tourism

99. Look at the graphic. Which stage will a guest speaker discuss?

(A) Stage 1
(B) Stage 2
(C) Stage 3
(D) Stage 4

100. According to the speaker, what can the listeners do on the first floor?

(A) Attend another seminar
(B) Address some concerns
(C) Access a computer program
(D) Check out a map

This is the end of the Listening test.

TEST 10

MP3 바로 듣기

준비물: OMR 카드, 연필, 지우개, 시계
시험시간: LC 약 45분

나의 점수		
LC		
맞은 개수		
환산 점수		

TEST 01	TEST 02	TEST 03	TEST 04	TEST 05
_____점	_____점	_____점	_____점	_____점
TEST 06	**TEST 07**	**TEST 08**	**TEST 09**	**TEST 10**
_____점	_____점	_____점	_____점	_____점

점수 환산표

LC			
맞은 개수	환산 점수	맞은 개수	환산 점수
96-100	475-495	41-45	155-230
91-95	435-495	36-40	125-205
86-90	405-475	31-35	105-175
81-85	370-450	26-30	85-145
76-80	345-420	21-25	60-115
71-75	320-390	16-20	30-90
66-70	290-360	11-15	5-70
61-65	265-335	6-10	5-60
56-60	235-310	1-5	5-60
51-55	210-280	0	5-35
46-50	180-255		

LISTENING TEST

In the Listening test, you will be asked to demonstrate how well you understand spoken English. The entire listening test will last approximately 45 minutes. There are four parts, and directions are given for each part. You must mark your answers on the separate answer sheet. Do not write your answers in your test book.

PART 1

Directions: For each question in this part, you will hear four statements about a picture in your test book. When you hear the statements, you must select the one statement that best describes what you see in the picture. Then find the number of the question on your answer sheet and mark your answer. The statements will not be printed in your test book and will be spoken only one time.

Statement (B), "A man is pointing at a document," is the best description of the picture, so you should select answer (B) and mark it on your answer sheet.

1.

2.

GO ON TO THE NEXT PAGE

3.

4.

5.

6.

GO ON TO THE NEXT PAGE

PART 2

Directions: You will hear a question or statement and three responses spoken in English. They will not be printed in your test book and will be spoken only one time. Select the best response to the question or statement and mark the letter (A), (B), or (C) on your answer sheet.

7. Mark your answer on your answer sheet.

8. Mark your answer on your answer sheet.

9. Mark your answer on your answer sheet.

10. Mark your answer on your answer sheet.

11. Mark your answer on your answer sheet.

12. Mark your answer on your answer sheet.

13. Mark your answer on your answer sheet.

14. Mark your answer on your answer sheet.

15. Mark your answer on your answer sheet.

16. Mark your answer on your answer sheet.

17. Mark your answer on your answer sheet.

18. Mark your answer on your answer sheet.

19. Mark your answer on your answer sheet.

20. Mark your answer on your answer sheet.

21. Mark your answer on your answer sheet.

22. Mark your answer on your answer sheet.

23. Mark your answer on your answer sheet.

24. Mark your answer on your answer sheet.

25. Mark your answer on your answer sheet.

26. Mark your answer on your answer sheet.

27. Mark your answer on your answer sheet.

28. Mark your answer on your answer sheet.

29. Mark your answer on your answer sheet.

30. Mark your answer on your answer sheet.

31. Mark your answer on your answer sheet.

PART 3

Directions: You will hear some conversations between two or more people. You will be asked to answer three questions about what the speakers say in each conversation. Select the best response to each question and mark the letter (A), (B), (C), or (D) on your answer sheet. The conversations will not be printed in your test book and will be spoken only one time.

32. Why is the man calling the woman?

(A) To confirm an appointment
(B) To explain a process
(C) To discuss payment options
(D) To request a signature

33. What does the woman want to know?

(A) Where to find more information
(B) When to sign up for an exam
(C) Whether some forms were received
(D) How to file a complaint

34. What does the man say he will provide?

(A) A discount code
(B) A parking permit
(C) A phone number
(D) A guarantee

35. What does the woman say she would like to do?

(A) Meet some colleagues
(B) Take a trip abroad
(C) Acquire a new skill
(D) Learn a new language

36. What type of event does the man mention?

(A) A theatrical performance
(B) A band tour
(C) A film festival
(D) A sports competition

37. What does the man explain to the woman?

(A) Which office to visit
(B) How to get certified
(C) Where to register
(D) How to set up some equipment

38. Who most likely are the speakers?

(A) Airport engineers
(B) Cargo supervisors
(C) Immigration officers
(D) Aircraft pilots

39. What is causing a delay?

(A) Traffic congestion
(B) Adverse weather
(C) Security clearance
(D) Technical issues

40. What will the woman do next?

(A) Check passenger information
(B) Make a broadcast
(C) Monitor safety procedures
(D) Contact an airport employee

41. What are the speakers mainly discussing?

(A) Developing a website
(B) Improving user experience
(C) Communicating with clients
(D) Purchasing an office equipment

42. What does the woman imply when she says, "Did you see our annual budget"?

(A) She wants to revise a financial report.
(B) She warns the man about a delayed deadline.
(C) She has access to a classified document.
(D) She has reservations about a suggestion.

43. What will the woman do next?

(A) Find out about some companies
(B) Resend an e-mail
(C) Clean her workspace
(D) Update a work schedule

GO ON TO THE NEXT PAGE

TEST 10

44. What are the speakers planning to do next month?

(A) Visit a client
(B) Start a new project
(C) Go on vacation
(D) Attend a conference

45. Why has Brad NOT booked accommodations yet?

(A) There are no affordable hotels available.
(B) A corporate credit card must be used.
(C) He would like to get some feedback.
(D) A promotion begins next week.

46. What does the woman offer to do?

(A) Call a vehicle rental agency
(B) Install an application
(C) Print a restaurant menu
(D) Order some tickets

47. How do the speakers know each other?

(A) They are related to each other.
(B) They live in the same neighborhood.
(C) They work in the same office.
(D) They went to college together.

48. What career is the man pursuing?

(A) A guidance counselor
(B) A banker
(C) A lawyer
(D) A professor

49. What does the man mean when he says, "I haven't passed the bar yet"?

(A) He is not qualified to advise the woman yet.
(B) He has to buy new equipment.
(C) He is not training for a competition.
(D) He would have to ask his supervisor.

50. Where do the speakers most likely work?

(A) At a government agency
(B) At a local restaurant
(C) At a grocery store
(D) At a dairy farm

51. What does the man want to do?

(A) Recruit experienced labor
(B) Change a technique
(C) Follow a regulation
(D) Purchase more equipment

52. What does the woman say she will do today?

(A) Speak with an industry expert
(B) Compile a list of possible clients
(C) Arrange an annual inspection
(D) Submit a business proposal

53. Who most likely is the woman?

(A) An event organizer
(B) A professional photographer
(C) A news reporter
(D) A computer technician

54. What does the man's friend make?

(A) Speakers
(B) Laptops
(C) Digital cameras
(D) Mobile programs

55. What does the man give to the woman?

(A) A conference schedule
(B) A visitor's badge
(C) Some application forms
(D) Some contact information

56. What are the speakers discussing?

(A) Creating a financial plan
(B) Completing a company merger
(C) Attending a musical performance
(D) Organizing a retirement party

57. What information does Chelsea need?

(A) A list of food preferences
(B) An approval of a budget proposal
(C) A supplier's contact information
(D) An agenda for a presentation

58. What does the man suggest doing as soon as possible?

(A) Changing a reservation
(B) Confirming some responses
(C) Placing an order
(D) Sending a payment

59. Where do the speakers most likely work?

(A) At a manufacturing plant
(B) At a shipping warehouse
(C) At a machine repair shop
(D) At a customer service center

60. What problem does the woman mention?

(A) A delivery has not arrived.
(B) An employee is sick.
(C) Some machinery is out of service.
(D) Some documents have been misplaced.

61. What will the man most likely do next?

(A) Reissue an invoice
(B) Find a new supplier
(C) Participate in a conference call
(D) Write a complaint letter

Broadcasting Date	Clip
March 21	Tourists Visit the Local Zoo
March 22	Grand Opening of Reyes Theater
March 23	New Exhibit at the Art Museum
March 24	Music Performance at the Westville Urban Park

62. Why will a TV station broadcast some newsclips?

(A) To promote a community event
(B) To profile a local business
(C) To showcase urban architecture
(D) To celebrate an anniversary

63. Look at the graphic. Which clip does the woman mention?

(A) Tourists Visit the Local Zoo
(B) Grand Opening of Reyes Theater
(C) New Exhibit at the Art Museum
(D) Music Performance at the Westville Urban Park

64. What does the man say he will do?

(A) Verify some information
(B) Contact some colleagues
(C) Watch some video clips
(D) Interview some residents

GO ON TO THE NEXT PAGE

TEST 10

Rack 1	Apples
Rack 2	Oranges
Rack 3	Peaches
Rack 4	Strawberries

65. What problem does the man report?

(A) A storage room has to be cleaned.
(B) Some items must be restocked.
(C) Some food has expired.
(D) A delivery was damaged.

66. Look at the graphic. Which rack is the woman working on?

(A) Rack 1
(B) Rack 2
(C) Rack 3
(D) Rack 4

67. What does the man instruct the woman to do?

(A) Discard some boxes
(B) Repair a device
(C) Call a business
(D) Handle a customer inquiry

Mayertown Cooking Contest

May 25 Schedule

Time / Location	Cuisine
2:00 P.M. / Elk Arena	Chinese
3:00 P.M. / Elk Arena	Italian
4:00 P.M. / Remo Arena	Mexican
5:00 P.M. / Remo Arena	Greek

68. What does the woman suggest doing?

(A) Exchanging seats
(B) Meeting early
(C) Sharing a ride
(D) Ordering a meal

69. Look at the graphic. What is the man's favorite kind of food?

(A) Chinese
(B) Italian
(C) Mexican
(D) Greek

70. What does the woman remind the man to do?

(A) Reserve a table
(B) Wear warm clothing
(C) Submit a form
(D) Bring an umbrella

PART 4

Directions: You will hear some talks given by a single speaker. You will be asked to answer three questions about what the speaker says in each talk. Select the best response to each question and mark the letter (A), (B), (C), or (D) on your answer sheet. The talks will not be printed in your test book and will be spoken only one time.

71. Who most likely is the speaker?

(A) A construction worker
(B) A city official
(C) A building manager
(D) A property developer

72. What does the speaker like about a location?

(A) It is in a major residential area.
(B) It is conveniently located.
(C) It has easy access to the beach.
(D) It has plenty of parking space.

73. Why will the speaker miss a meeting?

(A) He will be attending a ceremony.
(B) He will be leading an open house.
(C) His car broke down.
(D) His train was delayed.

74. What most likely is being advertised?

(A) A job recruitment agency
(B) An interior design firm
(C) A storage warehouse
(D) An online advertising service

75. What does the speaker encourage the listeners to do?

(A) Read over a document
(B) Interview a candidate
(C) Write a customer review
(D) Apply for a consultation

76. What will first-time clients receive this week?

(A) A ticket to a concert
(B) A personalized mug
(C) A gift card for a store
(D) A magazine subscription

77. What does the speaker say she is concerned about?

(A) Employee turnover
(B) Sales projections
(C) Store security
(D) Late deliveries

78. What project will begin next month?

(A) A rewards system
(B) An overseas expansion
(C) A store renovation
(D) A leadership workshop

79. Why does the speaker say, "some of the best feedback actually comes from the users"?

(A) To disagree with a point
(B) To highlight a problem
(C) To encourage employees
(D) To suggest a different idea

80. Where is the announcement probably being heard?

(A) On a train
(B) On a bus
(C) On an airplane
(D) On a ferry

81. What problem does the speaker mention?

(A) Inclement weather
(B) A shortage of staff
(C) A faulty system
(D) Roadwork

82. What are the listeners instructed to do?

(A) Remain in their seats
(B) Pick up a discount voucher
(C) Take their belongings
(D) Contact their family members

GO ON TO THE NEXT PAGE

TEST 10

83. Why is the speaker interested in the Glenmoore community?

(A) It is near a recreation center.
(B) It has a security gate.
(C) It has a good school district.
(D) It is affordable.

84. What does the speaker want in his home?

(A) A home theater
(B) A garden area
(C) A furnished living room
(D) A large basement

85. What does the speaker say he will do tonight?

(A) Purchase some instruments
(B) Meet with a band
(C) Speak to his landlord
(D) Go on a business trip

86. What is the speaker excited to report?

(A) A sponsorship deal was confirmed.
(B) A new facility manager was hired.
(C) A project was completed ahead of time.
(D) A store opening was successful.

87. What would the speaker like the listener to do at an event?

(A) Collect feedback
(B) Distribute business cards
(C) Give a presentation
(D) Meet the management team

88. Why does the speaker say, "After that is generally when we expect things to pick up dramatically"?

(A) To indicate unavailability
(B) To ask for assistance
(C) To express frustration
(D) To disagree with a suggestion

89. Who most likely is the speaker?

(A) A repair technician
(B) A plant supervisor
(C) A program developer
(D) A car salesperson

90. According to the speaker, what is being replaced this week?

(A) Some software
(B) Some machinery
(C) Some name tags
(D) Some storage units

91. What are the listeners asked to do?

(A) Register for a training session
(B) Wear safety gear
(C) Prepare for an upcoming inspection
(D) Suggest some ideas

92. What does the speaker emphasize about the museum?

(A) Its staff
(B) Its history
(C) Its size
(D) Its location

93. Why does the speaker say, "the museum does rely on financial donations from our guests"?

(A) To respond to guest complaints
(B) To explain a membership plan
(C) To ask for contributions
(D) To announce a revised policy

94. According to the speaker, what is prohibited?

(A) Taking photographs
(B) Leaving a group
(C) Bringing a bag
(D) Touching artifacts

Productivity Challenge	
WEEK 1	Organize your life and your work
WEEK 2	Energize with physical activity
WEEK 3	Update your technical skills
WEEK 4	Improve your public speaking

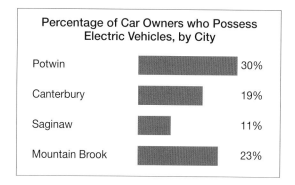

Percentage of Car Owners who Possess Electric Vehicles, by City

Potwin — 30%
Canterbury — 19%
Saginaw — 11%
Mountain Brook — 23%

95. What reward will some staff members receive?

(A) A cash prize
(B) An extra vacation day
(C) A discount voucher
(D) A free meal

96. Look at the graphic. When will a seminar take place?

(A) Week 1
(B) Week 2
(C) Week 3
(D) Week 4

97. What should listeners who want to attend a seminar do?

(A) Contact an event organizer
(B) Go to an information session
(C) Pay a deposit
(D) Fill out a registration form

98. Why does the speaker congratulate Mayor Wagner?

(A) The mayor is investing her own money into new initiatives.
(B) The mayor currently owns an electric vehicle.
(C) The mayor was recently re-elected.
(D) The mayor undertook an important project.

99. Look at the graphic. Where does the talk take place?

(A) In Potwin
(B) In Canterbury
(C) In Saginaw
(D) In Mountain Brook

100. What will the speaker do next?

(A) Distribute some information
(B) Introduce the next speaker
(C) Answer a question
(D) Show a variety of products

This is the end of the Listening test.

ANSWER SHEET

TEST 02

LISTENING (Part I-IV)

NO.	ANSWER	NO.	ANSWER	NO.	ANSWER	NO.	ANSWER	NO.	ANSWER
	A B C D		A B C D		A B C D		A B C D		A B C D
1	Ⓐ Ⓑ Ⓒ	21	Ⓐ Ⓑ Ⓒ	41	Ⓐ Ⓑ Ⓒ Ⓓ	61	Ⓐ Ⓑ Ⓒ Ⓓ	81	Ⓐ Ⓑ Ⓒ Ⓓ
2	Ⓐ Ⓑ Ⓒ Ⓓ	22	Ⓐ Ⓑ Ⓒ	42	Ⓐ Ⓑ Ⓒ Ⓓ	62	Ⓐ Ⓑ Ⓒ Ⓓ	82	Ⓐ Ⓑ Ⓒ Ⓓ
3	Ⓐ Ⓑ Ⓒ Ⓓ	23	Ⓐ Ⓑ Ⓒ	43	Ⓐ Ⓑ Ⓒ Ⓓ	63	Ⓐ Ⓑ Ⓒ Ⓓ	83	Ⓐ Ⓑ Ⓒ Ⓓ
4	Ⓐ Ⓑ Ⓒ Ⓓ	24	Ⓐ Ⓑ Ⓒ	44	Ⓐ Ⓑ Ⓒ Ⓓ	64	Ⓐ Ⓑ Ⓒ Ⓓ	84	Ⓐ Ⓑ Ⓒ Ⓓ
5	Ⓐ Ⓑ Ⓒ Ⓓ	25	Ⓐ Ⓑ Ⓒ	45	Ⓐ Ⓑ Ⓒ Ⓓ	65	Ⓐ Ⓑ Ⓒ Ⓓ	85	Ⓐ Ⓑ Ⓒ Ⓓ
6	Ⓐ Ⓑ Ⓒ Ⓓ	26	Ⓐ Ⓑ Ⓒ	46	Ⓐ Ⓑ Ⓒ Ⓓ	66	Ⓐ Ⓑ Ⓒ Ⓓ	86	Ⓐ Ⓑ Ⓒ Ⓓ
7	Ⓐ Ⓑ Ⓒ Ⓓ	27	Ⓐ Ⓑ Ⓒ	47	Ⓐ Ⓑ Ⓒ Ⓓ	67	Ⓐ Ⓑ Ⓒ Ⓓ	87	Ⓐ Ⓑ Ⓒ Ⓓ
8	Ⓐ Ⓑ Ⓒ	28	Ⓐ Ⓑ Ⓒ	48	Ⓐ Ⓑ Ⓒ Ⓓ	68	Ⓐ Ⓑ Ⓒ Ⓓ	88	Ⓐ Ⓑ Ⓒ Ⓓ
9	Ⓐ Ⓑ Ⓒ	29	Ⓐ Ⓑ Ⓒ	49	Ⓐ Ⓑ Ⓒ Ⓓ	69	Ⓐ Ⓑ Ⓒ Ⓓ	89	Ⓐ Ⓑ Ⓒ Ⓓ
10	Ⓐ Ⓑ Ⓒ	30	Ⓐ Ⓑ Ⓒ	50	Ⓐ Ⓑ Ⓒ Ⓓ	70	Ⓐ Ⓑ Ⓒ Ⓓ	90	Ⓐ Ⓑ Ⓒ Ⓓ
11	Ⓐ Ⓑ Ⓒ	31	Ⓐ Ⓑ Ⓒ	51	Ⓐ Ⓑ Ⓒ Ⓓ	71	Ⓐ Ⓑ Ⓒ Ⓓ	91	Ⓐ Ⓑ Ⓒ Ⓓ
12	Ⓐ Ⓑ Ⓒ	32	Ⓐ Ⓑ Ⓒ	52	Ⓐ Ⓑ Ⓒ Ⓓ	72	Ⓐ Ⓑ Ⓒ Ⓓ	92	Ⓐ Ⓑ Ⓒ Ⓓ
13	Ⓐ Ⓑ Ⓒ	33	Ⓐ Ⓑ Ⓒ	53	Ⓐ Ⓑ Ⓒ Ⓓ	73	Ⓐ Ⓑ Ⓒ Ⓓ	93	Ⓐ Ⓑ Ⓒ Ⓓ
14	Ⓐ Ⓑ Ⓒ	34	Ⓐ Ⓑ Ⓒ	54	Ⓐ Ⓑ Ⓒ Ⓓ	74	Ⓐ Ⓑ Ⓒ Ⓓ	94	Ⓐ Ⓑ Ⓒ Ⓓ
15	Ⓐ Ⓑ Ⓒ	35	Ⓐ Ⓑ Ⓒ	55	Ⓐ Ⓑ Ⓒ Ⓓ	75	Ⓐ Ⓑ Ⓒ Ⓓ	95	Ⓐ Ⓑ Ⓒ Ⓓ
16	Ⓐ Ⓑ Ⓒ	36	Ⓐ Ⓑ Ⓒ	56	Ⓐ Ⓑ Ⓒ Ⓓ	76	Ⓐ Ⓑ Ⓒ Ⓓ	96	Ⓐ Ⓑ Ⓒ Ⓓ
17	Ⓐ Ⓑ Ⓒ	37	Ⓐ Ⓑ Ⓒ	57	Ⓐ Ⓑ Ⓒ Ⓓ	77	Ⓐ Ⓑ Ⓒ Ⓓ	97	Ⓐ Ⓑ Ⓒ Ⓓ
18	Ⓐ Ⓑ Ⓒ	38	Ⓐ Ⓑ Ⓒ	58	Ⓐ Ⓑ Ⓒ Ⓓ	78	Ⓐ Ⓑ Ⓒ Ⓓ	98	Ⓐ Ⓑ Ⓒ Ⓓ
19	Ⓐ Ⓑ Ⓒ	39	Ⓐ Ⓑ Ⓒ	59	Ⓐ Ⓑ Ⓒ Ⓓ	79	Ⓐ Ⓑ Ⓒ Ⓓ	99	Ⓐ Ⓑ Ⓒ Ⓓ
20	Ⓐ Ⓑ Ⓒ	40	Ⓐ Ⓑ Ⓒ	60	Ⓐ Ⓑ Ⓒ Ⓓ	80	Ⓐ Ⓑ Ⓒ Ⓓ	100	Ⓐ Ⓑ Ⓒ Ⓓ

ANSWER SHEET

TEST 01

LISTENING (Part I-IV)

NO.	ANSWER	NO.	ANSWER	NO.	ANSWER	NO.	ANSWER	NO.	ANSWER
	A B C D		A B C D		A B C D		A B C D		A B C D
1	Ⓐ Ⓑ Ⓒ	21	Ⓐ Ⓑ Ⓒ Ⓓ	41	Ⓐ Ⓑ Ⓒ Ⓓ	61	Ⓐ Ⓑ Ⓒ Ⓓ	81	Ⓐ Ⓑ Ⓒ Ⓓ
2	Ⓐ Ⓑ Ⓒ	22	Ⓐ Ⓑ Ⓒ Ⓓ	42	Ⓐ Ⓑ Ⓒ Ⓓ	62	Ⓐ Ⓑ Ⓒ Ⓓ	82	Ⓐ Ⓑ Ⓒ Ⓓ
3	Ⓐ Ⓑ Ⓒ	23	Ⓐ Ⓑ Ⓒ Ⓓ	43	Ⓐ Ⓑ Ⓒ Ⓓ	63	Ⓐ Ⓑ Ⓒ Ⓓ	83	Ⓐ Ⓑ Ⓒ Ⓓ
4	Ⓐ Ⓑ Ⓒ	24	Ⓐ Ⓑ Ⓒ Ⓓ	44	Ⓐ Ⓑ Ⓒ Ⓓ	64	Ⓐ Ⓑ Ⓒ Ⓓ	84	Ⓐ Ⓑ Ⓒ Ⓓ
5	Ⓐ Ⓑ Ⓒ	25	Ⓐ Ⓑ Ⓒ Ⓓ	45	Ⓐ Ⓑ Ⓒ Ⓓ	65	Ⓐ Ⓑ Ⓒ Ⓓ	85	Ⓐ Ⓑ Ⓒ Ⓓ
6	Ⓐ Ⓑ Ⓒ	26	Ⓐ Ⓑ Ⓒ Ⓓ	46	Ⓐ Ⓑ Ⓒ Ⓓ	66	Ⓐ Ⓑ Ⓒ Ⓓ	86	Ⓐ Ⓑ Ⓒ Ⓓ
7	Ⓐ Ⓑ Ⓒ	27	Ⓐ Ⓑ Ⓒ Ⓓ	47	Ⓐ Ⓑ Ⓒ Ⓓ	67	Ⓐ Ⓑ Ⓒ Ⓓ	87	Ⓐ Ⓑ Ⓒ Ⓓ
8	Ⓐ Ⓑ Ⓒ	28	Ⓐ Ⓑ Ⓒ Ⓓ	48	Ⓐ Ⓑ Ⓒ Ⓓ	68	Ⓐ Ⓑ Ⓒ Ⓓ	88	Ⓐ Ⓑ Ⓒ Ⓓ
9	Ⓐ Ⓑ Ⓒ	29	Ⓐ Ⓑ Ⓒ Ⓓ	49	Ⓐ Ⓑ Ⓒ Ⓓ	69	Ⓐ Ⓑ Ⓒ Ⓓ	89	Ⓐ Ⓑ Ⓒ Ⓓ
10	Ⓐ Ⓑ Ⓒ	30	Ⓐ Ⓑ Ⓒ Ⓓ	50	Ⓐ Ⓑ Ⓒ Ⓓ	70	Ⓐ Ⓑ Ⓒ Ⓓ	90	Ⓐ Ⓑ Ⓒ Ⓓ
11	Ⓐ Ⓑ Ⓒ	31	Ⓐ Ⓑ Ⓒ Ⓓ	51	Ⓐ Ⓑ Ⓒ Ⓓ	71	Ⓐ Ⓑ Ⓒ Ⓓ	91	Ⓐ Ⓑ Ⓒ Ⓓ
12	Ⓐ Ⓑ Ⓒ Ⓓ	32	Ⓐ Ⓑ Ⓒ Ⓓ	52	Ⓐ Ⓑ Ⓒ Ⓓ	72	Ⓐ Ⓑ Ⓒ Ⓓ	92	Ⓐ Ⓑ Ⓒ Ⓓ
13	Ⓐ Ⓑ Ⓒ Ⓓ	33	Ⓐ Ⓑ Ⓒ Ⓓ	53	Ⓐ Ⓑ Ⓒ Ⓓ	73	Ⓐ Ⓑ Ⓒ Ⓓ	93	Ⓐ Ⓑ Ⓒ Ⓓ
14	Ⓐ Ⓑ Ⓒ Ⓓ	34	Ⓐ Ⓑ Ⓒ Ⓓ	54	Ⓐ Ⓑ Ⓒ Ⓓ	74	Ⓐ Ⓑ Ⓒ Ⓓ	94	Ⓐ Ⓑ Ⓒ Ⓓ
15	Ⓐ Ⓑ Ⓒ Ⓓ	35	Ⓐ Ⓑ Ⓒ Ⓓ	55	Ⓐ Ⓑ Ⓒ Ⓓ	75	Ⓐ Ⓑ Ⓒ Ⓓ	95	Ⓐ Ⓑ Ⓒ Ⓓ
16	Ⓐ Ⓑ Ⓒ Ⓓ	36	Ⓐ Ⓑ Ⓒ Ⓓ	56	Ⓐ Ⓑ Ⓒ Ⓓ	76	Ⓐ Ⓑ Ⓒ Ⓓ	96	Ⓐ Ⓑ Ⓒ Ⓓ
17	Ⓐ Ⓑ Ⓒ Ⓓ	37	Ⓐ Ⓑ Ⓒ Ⓓ	57	Ⓐ Ⓑ Ⓒ Ⓓ	77	Ⓐ Ⓑ Ⓒ Ⓓ	97	Ⓐ Ⓑ Ⓒ Ⓓ
18	Ⓐ Ⓑ Ⓒ Ⓓ	38	Ⓐ Ⓑ Ⓒ Ⓓ	58	Ⓐ Ⓑ Ⓒ Ⓓ	78	Ⓐ Ⓑ Ⓒ Ⓓ	98	Ⓐ Ⓑ Ⓒ Ⓓ
19	Ⓐ Ⓑ Ⓒ	39	Ⓐ Ⓑ Ⓒ Ⓓ	59	Ⓐ Ⓑ Ⓒ Ⓓ	79	Ⓐ Ⓑ Ⓒ Ⓓ	99	Ⓐ Ⓑ Ⓒ Ⓓ
20	Ⓐ Ⓑ Ⓒ	40	Ⓐ Ⓑ Ⓒ Ⓓ	60	Ⓐ Ⓑ Ⓒ Ⓓ	80	Ⓐ Ⓑ Ⓒ Ⓓ	100	Ⓐ Ⓑ Ⓒ Ⓓ

ANSWER SHEET

TEST 04

LISTENING (Part I-IV)

NO.	ANSWER	NO.	ANSWER	NO.	ANSWER	NO.	ANSWER	NO.	ANSWER
	A B C D		A B C D		A B C D		A B C D		A B C D
1	Ⓐ Ⓑ Ⓒ	21	Ⓐ Ⓑ Ⓒ	41	Ⓐ Ⓑ Ⓒ Ⓓ	61	Ⓐ Ⓑ Ⓒ Ⓓ	81	Ⓐ Ⓑ Ⓒ Ⓓ
2	Ⓐ Ⓑ Ⓒ	22	Ⓐ Ⓑ Ⓒ	42	Ⓐ Ⓑ Ⓒ Ⓓ	62	Ⓐ Ⓑ Ⓒ Ⓓ	82	Ⓐ Ⓑ Ⓒ Ⓓ
3	Ⓐ Ⓑ Ⓒ	23	Ⓐ Ⓑ Ⓒ	43	Ⓐ Ⓑ Ⓒ Ⓓ	63	Ⓐ Ⓑ Ⓒ Ⓓ	83	Ⓐ Ⓑ Ⓒ Ⓓ
4	Ⓐ Ⓑ Ⓒ	24	Ⓐ Ⓑ Ⓒ	44	Ⓐ Ⓑ Ⓒ Ⓓ	64	Ⓐ Ⓑ Ⓒ Ⓓ	84	Ⓐ Ⓑ Ⓒ Ⓓ
5	Ⓐ Ⓑ Ⓒ	25	Ⓐ Ⓑ Ⓒ	45	Ⓐ Ⓑ Ⓒ Ⓓ	65	Ⓐ Ⓑ Ⓒ Ⓓ	85	Ⓐ Ⓑ Ⓒ Ⓓ
6	Ⓐ Ⓑ Ⓒ	26	Ⓐ Ⓑ Ⓒ	46	Ⓐ Ⓑ Ⓒ Ⓓ	66	Ⓐ Ⓑ Ⓒ Ⓓ	86	Ⓐ Ⓑ Ⓒ Ⓓ
7	Ⓐ Ⓑ Ⓒ	27	Ⓐ Ⓑ Ⓒ	47	Ⓐ Ⓑ Ⓒ Ⓓ	67	Ⓐ Ⓑ Ⓒ Ⓓ	87	Ⓐ Ⓑ Ⓒ Ⓓ
8	Ⓐ Ⓑ Ⓒ	28	Ⓐ Ⓑ Ⓒ	48	Ⓐ Ⓑ Ⓒ Ⓓ	68	Ⓐ Ⓑ Ⓒ Ⓓ	88	Ⓐ Ⓑ Ⓒ Ⓓ
9	Ⓐ Ⓑ Ⓒ	29	Ⓐ Ⓑ Ⓒ	49	Ⓐ Ⓑ Ⓒ Ⓓ	69	Ⓐ Ⓑ Ⓒ Ⓓ	89	Ⓐ Ⓑ Ⓒ Ⓓ
10	Ⓐ Ⓑ Ⓒ	30	Ⓐ Ⓑ Ⓒ	50	Ⓐ Ⓑ Ⓒ Ⓓ	70	Ⓐ Ⓑ Ⓒ Ⓓ	90	Ⓐ Ⓑ Ⓒ Ⓓ
11	Ⓐ Ⓑ Ⓒ	31	Ⓐ Ⓑ Ⓒ	51	Ⓐ Ⓑ Ⓒ Ⓓ	71	Ⓐ Ⓑ Ⓒ Ⓓ	91	Ⓐ Ⓑ Ⓒ Ⓓ
12	Ⓐ Ⓑ Ⓒ	32	Ⓐ Ⓑ Ⓒ Ⓓ	52	Ⓐ Ⓑ Ⓒ Ⓓ	72	Ⓐ Ⓑ Ⓒ Ⓓ	92	Ⓐ Ⓑ Ⓒ Ⓓ
13	Ⓐ Ⓑ Ⓒ	33	Ⓐ Ⓑ Ⓒ Ⓓ	53	Ⓐ Ⓑ Ⓒ Ⓓ	73	Ⓐ Ⓑ Ⓒ Ⓓ	93	Ⓐ Ⓑ Ⓒ Ⓓ
14	Ⓐ Ⓑ Ⓒ	34	Ⓐ Ⓑ Ⓒ Ⓓ	54	Ⓐ Ⓑ Ⓒ Ⓓ	74	Ⓐ Ⓑ Ⓒ Ⓓ	94	Ⓐ Ⓑ Ⓒ Ⓓ
15	Ⓐ Ⓑ Ⓒ	35	Ⓐ Ⓑ Ⓒ Ⓓ	55	Ⓐ Ⓑ Ⓒ Ⓓ	75	Ⓐ Ⓑ Ⓒ Ⓓ	95	Ⓐ Ⓑ Ⓒ Ⓓ
16	Ⓐ Ⓑ Ⓒ	36	Ⓐ Ⓑ Ⓒ Ⓓ	56	Ⓐ Ⓑ Ⓒ Ⓓ	76	Ⓐ Ⓑ Ⓒ Ⓓ	96	Ⓐ Ⓑ Ⓒ Ⓓ
17	Ⓐ Ⓑ Ⓒ	37	Ⓐ Ⓑ Ⓒ Ⓓ	57	Ⓐ Ⓑ Ⓒ Ⓓ	77	Ⓐ Ⓑ Ⓒ Ⓓ	97	Ⓐ Ⓑ Ⓒ Ⓓ
18	Ⓐ Ⓑ Ⓒ	38	Ⓐ Ⓑ Ⓒ Ⓓ	58	Ⓐ Ⓑ Ⓒ Ⓓ	78	Ⓐ Ⓑ Ⓒ Ⓓ	98	Ⓐ Ⓑ Ⓒ Ⓓ
19	Ⓐ Ⓑ Ⓒ	39	Ⓐ Ⓑ Ⓒ Ⓓ	59	Ⓐ Ⓑ Ⓒ Ⓓ	79	Ⓐ Ⓑ Ⓒ Ⓓ	99	Ⓐ Ⓑ Ⓒ Ⓓ
20	Ⓐ Ⓑ Ⓒ	40	Ⓐ Ⓑ Ⓒ Ⓓ	60	Ⓐ Ⓑ Ⓒ Ⓓ	80	Ⓐ Ⓑ Ⓒ Ⓓ	100	Ⓐ Ⓑ Ⓒ Ⓓ

ANSWER SHEET

TEST 03

LISTENING (Part I-IV)

NO.	ANSWER	NO.	ANSWER	NO.	ANSWER	NO.	ANSWER	NO.	ANSWER
	A B C D		A B C D		A B C D		A B C D		A B C D
1	Ⓐ Ⓑ Ⓒ	21	Ⓐ Ⓑ Ⓒ Ⓓ	41	Ⓐ Ⓑ Ⓒ Ⓓ	61	Ⓐ Ⓑ Ⓒ Ⓓ	81	Ⓐ Ⓑ Ⓒ Ⓓ
2	Ⓐ Ⓑ Ⓒ	22	Ⓐ Ⓑ Ⓒ Ⓓ	42	Ⓐ Ⓑ Ⓒ Ⓓ	62	Ⓐ Ⓑ Ⓒ Ⓓ	82	Ⓐ Ⓑ Ⓒ Ⓓ
3	Ⓐ Ⓑ Ⓒ	23	Ⓐ Ⓑ Ⓒ Ⓓ	43	Ⓐ Ⓑ Ⓒ Ⓓ	63	Ⓐ Ⓑ Ⓒ Ⓓ	83	Ⓐ Ⓑ Ⓒ Ⓓ
4	Ⓐ Ⓑ Ⓒ	24	Ⓐ Ⓑ Ⓒ Ⓓ	44	Ⓐ Ⓑ Ⓒ Ⓓ	64	Ⓐ Ⓑ Ⓒ Ⓓ	84	Ⓐ Ⓑ Ⓒ Ⓓ
5	Ⓐ Ⓑ Ⓒ	25	Ⓐ Ⓑ Ⓒ Ⓓ	45	Ⓐ Ⓑ Ⓒ Ⓓ	65	Ⓐ Ⓑ Ⓒ Ⓓ	85	Ⓐ Ⓑ Ⓒ Ⓓ
6	Ⓐ Ⓑ Ⓒ	26	Ⓐ Ⓑ Ⓒ Ⓓ	46	Ⓐ Ⓑ Ⓒ Ⓓ	66	Ⓐ Ⓑ Ⓒ Ⓓ	86	Ⓐ Ⓑ Ⓒ Ⓓ
7	Ⓐ Ⓑ Ⓒ	27	Ⓐ Ⓑ Ⓒ Ⓓ	47	Ⓐ Ⓑ Ⓒ Ⓓ	67	Ⓐ Ⓑ Ⓒ Ⓓ	87	Ⓐ Ⓑ Ⓒ Ⓓ
8	Ⓐ Ⓑ Ⓒ	28	Ⓐ Ⓑ Ⓒ Ⓓ	48	Ⓐ Ⓑ Ⓒ Ⓓ	68	Ⓐ Ⓑ Ⓒ Ⓓ	88	Ⓐ Ⓑ Ⓒ Ⓓ
9	Ⓐ Ⓑ Ⓒ	29	Ⓐ Ⓑ Ⓒ Ⓓ	49	Ⓐ Ⓑ Ⓒ Ⓓ	69	Ⓐ Ⓑ Ⓒ Ⓓ	89	Ⓐ Ⓑ Ⓒ Ⓓ
10	Ⓐ Ⓑ Ⓒ	30	Ⓐ Ⓑ Ⓒ Ⓓ	50	Ⓐ Ⓑ Ⓒ Ⓓ	70	Ⓐ Ⓑ Ⓒ Ⓓ	90	Ⓐ Ⓑ Ⓒ Ⓓ
11	Ⓐ Ⓑ Ⓒ	31	Ⓐ Ⓑ Ⓒ Ⓓ	51	Ⓐ Ⓑ Ⓒ Ⓓ	71	Ⓐ Ⓑ Ⓒ Ⓓ	91	Ⓐ Ⓑ Ⓒ Ⓓ
12	Ⓐ Ⓑ Ⓒ	32	Ⓐ Ⓑ Ⓒ Ⓓ	52	Ⓐ Ⓑ Ⓒ Ⓓ	72	Ⓐ Ⓑ Ⓒ Ⓓ	92	Ⓐ Ⓑ Ⓒ Ⓓ
13	Ⓐ Ⓑ Ⓒ	33	Ⓐ Ⓑ Ⓒ Ⓓ	53	Ⓐ Ⓑ Ⓒ Ⓓ	73	Ⓐ Ⓑ Ⓒ Ⓓ	93	Ⓐ Ⓑ Ⓒ Ⓓ
14	Ⓐ Ⓑ Ⓒ	34	Ⓐ Ⓑ Ⓒ Ⓓ	54	Ⓐ Ⓑ Ⓒ Ⓓ	74	Ⓐ Ⓑ Ⓒ Ⓓ	94	Ⓐ Ⓑ Ⓒ Ⓓ
15	Ⓐ Ⓑ Ⓒ	35	Ⓐ Ⓑ Ⓒ Ⓓ	55	Ⓐ Ⓑ Ⓒ Ⓓ	75	Ⓐ Ⓑ Ⓒ Ⓓ	95	Ⓐ Ⓑ Ⓒ Ⓓ
16	Ⓐ Ⓑ Ⓒ	36	Ⓐ Ⓑ Ⓒ Ⓓ	56	Ⓐ Ⓑ Ⓒ Ⓓ	76	Ⓐ Ⓑ Ⓒ Ⓓ	96	Ⓐ Ⓑ Ⓒ Ⓓ
17	Ⓐ Ⓑ Ⓒ	37	Ⓐ Ⓑ Ⓒ Ⓓ	57	Ⓐ Ⓑ Ⓒ Ⓓ	77	Ⓐ Ⓑ Ⓒ Ⓓ	97	Ⓐ Ⓑ Ⓒ Ⓓ
18	Ⓐ Ⓑ Ⓒ	38	Ⓐ Ⓑ Ⓒ Ⓓ	58	Ⓐ Ⓑ Ⓒ Ⓓ	78	Ⓐ Ⓑ Ⓒ Ⓓ	98	Ⓐ Ⓑ Ⓒ Ⓓ
19	Ⓐ Ⓑ Ⓒ	39	Ⓐ Ⓑ Ⓒ Ⓓ	59	Ⓐ Ⓑ Ⓒ Ⓓ	79	Ⓐ Ⓑ Ⓒ Ⓓ	99	Ⓐ Ⓑ Ⓒ Ⓓ
20	Ⓐ Ⓑ Ⓒ	40	Ⓐ Ⓑ Ⓒ Ⓓ	60	Ⓐ Ⓑ Ⓒ Ⓓ	80	Ⓐ Ⓑ Ⓒ Ⓓ	100	Ⓐ Ⓑ Ⓒ Ⓓ

ANSWER SHEET

TEST 05

LISTENING (Part I-IV)

NO.	ANSWER	NO.	ANSWER	NO.	ANSWER	NO.	ANSWER	NO.	ANSWER
	A B C D		A B C D		A B C D		A B C D		A B C D
1	Ⓐ Ⓑ Ⓒ	21	Ⓐ Ⓑ Ⓒ Ⓓ	41	Ⓐ Ⓑ Ⓒ Ⓓ	61	Ⓐ Ⓑ Ⓒ Ⓓ	81	Ⓐ Ⓑ Ⓒ Ⓓ
2	Ⓐ Ⓑ Ⓒ	22	Ⓐ Ⓑ Ⓒ Ⓓ	42	Ⓐ Ⓑ Ⓒ Ⓓ	62	Ⓐ Ⓑ Ⓒ Ⓓ	82	Ⓐ Ⓑ Ⓒ Ⓓ
3	Ⓐ Ⓑ Ⓒ	23	Ⓐ Ⓑ Ⓒ Ⓓ	43	Ⓐ Ⓑ Ⓒ Ⓓ	63	Ⓐ Ⓑ Ⓒ Ⓓ	83	Ⓐ Ⓑ Ⓒ Ⓓ
4	Ⓐ Ⓑ Ⓒ	24	Ⓐ Ⓑ Ⓒ Ⓓ	44	Ⓐ Ⓑ Ⓒ Ⓓ	64	Ⓐ Ⓑ Ⓒ Ⓓ	84	Ⓐ Ⓑ Ⓒ Ⓓ
5	Ⓐ Ⓑ Ⓒ	25	Ⓐ Ⓑ Ⓒ Ⓓ	45	Ⓐ Ⓑ Ⓒ Ⓓ	65	Ⓐ Ⓑ Ⓒ Ⓓ	85	Ⓐ Ⓑ Ⓒ Ⓓ
6	Ⓐ Ⓑ Ⓒ	26	Ⓐ Ⓑ Ⓒ Ⓓ	46	Ⓐ Ⓑ Ⓒ Ⓓ	66	Ⓐ Ⓑ Ⓒ Ⓓ	86	Ⓐ Ⓑ Ⓒ Ⓓ
7	Ⓐ Ⓑ Ⓒ	27	Ⓐ Ⓑ Ⓒ	47	Ⓐ Ⓑ Ⓒ Ⓓ	67	Ⓐ Ⓑ Ⓒ Ⓓ	87	Ⓐ Ⓑ Ⓒ Ⓓ
8	Ⓐ Ⓑ Ⓒ	28	Ⓐ Ⓑ Ⓒ	48	Ⓐ Ⓑ Ⓒ Ⓓ	68	Ⓐ Ⓑ Ⓒ Ⓓ	88	Ⓐ Ⓑ Ⓒ Ⓓ
9	Ⓐ Ⓑ Ⓒ	29	Ⓐ Ⓑ Ⓒ	49	Ⓐ Ⓑ Ⓒ Ⓓ	69	Ⓐ Ⓑ Ⓒ Ⓓ	89	Ⓐ Ⓑ Ⓒ Ⓓ
10	Ⓐ Ⓑ Ⓒ	30	Ⓐ Ⓑ Ⓒ	50	Ⓐ Ⓑ Ⓒ Ⓓ	70	Ⓐ Ⓑ Ⓒ Ⓓ	90	Ⓐ Ⓑ Ⓒ Ⓓ
11	Ⓐ Ⓑ Ⓒ	31	Ⓐ Ⓑ Ⓒ	51	Ⓐ Ⓑ Ⓒ Ⓓ	71	Ⓐ Ⓑ Ⓒ Ⓓ	91	Ⓐ Ⓑ Ⓒ Ⓓ
12	Ⓐ Ⓑ Ⓒ	32	Ⓐ Ⓑ Ⓒ	52	Ⓐ Ⓑ Ⓒ Ⓓ	72	Ⓐ Ⓑ Ⓒ Ⓓ	92	Ⓐ Ⓑ Ⓒ Ⓓ
13	Ⓐ Ⓑ Ⓒ	33	Ⓐ Ⓑ Ⓒ	53	Ⓐ Ⓑ Ⓒ Ⓓ	73	Ⓐ Ⓑ Ⓒ Ⓓ	93	Ⓐ Ⓑ Ⓒ Ⓓ
14	Ⓐ Ⓑ Ⓒ	34	Ⓐ Ⓑ Ⓒ	54	Ⓐ Ⓑ Ⓒ Ⓓ	74	Ⓐ Ⓑ Ⓒ Ⓓ	94	Ⓐ Ⓑ Ⓒ Ⓓ
15	Ⓐ Ⓑ Ⓒ	35	Ⓐ Ⓑ Ⓒ	55	Ⓐ Ⓑ Ⓒ Ⓓ	75	Ⓐ Ⓑ Ⓒ Ⓓ	95	Ⓐ Ⓑ Ⓒ Ⓓ
16	Ⓐ Ⓑ Ⓒ	36	Ⓐ Ⓑ Ⓒ	56	Ⓐ Ⓑ Ⓒ Ⓓ	76	Ⓐ Ⓑ Ⓒ Ⓓ	96	Ⓐ Ⓑ Ⓒ Ⓓ
17	Ⓐ Ⓑ Ⓒ	37	Ⓐ Ⓑ Ⓒ	57	Ⓐ Ⓑ Ⓒ Ⓓ	77	Ⓐ Ⓑ Ⓒ Ⓓ	97	Ⓐ Ⓑ Ⓒ Ⓓ
18	Ⓐ Ⓑ Ⓒ	38	Ⓐ Ⓑ Ⓒ	58	Ⓐ Ⓑ Ⓒ Ⓓ	78	Ⓐ Ⓑ Ⓒ Ⓓ	98	Ⓐ Ⓑ Ⓒ Ⓓ
19	Ⓐ Ⓑ Ⓒ	39	Ⓐ Ⓑ Ⓒ	59	Ⓐ Ⓑ Ⓒ Ⓓ	79	Ⓐ Ⓑ Ⓒ Ⓓ	99	Ⓐ Ⓑ Ⓒ Ⓓ
20	Ⓐ Ⓑ Ⓒ	40	Ⓐ Ⓑ Ⓒ	60	Ⓐ Ⓑ Ⓒ Ⓓ	80	Ⓐ Ⓑ Ⓒ Ⓓ	100	Ⓐ Ⓑ Ⓒ Ⓓ

ANSWER SHEET

TEST 06

LISTENING (Part I-IV)

NO.	ANSWER	NO.	ANSWER	NO.	ANSWER	NO.	ANSWER	NO.	ANSWER
	A B C D		A B C D		A B C D		A B C D		A B C D
1	Ⓐ Ⓑ Ⓒ	21	Ⓐ Ⓑ Ⓒ Ⓓ	41	Ⓐ Ⓑ Ⓒ Ⓓ	61	Ⓐ Ⓑ Ⓒ Ⓓ	81	Ⓐ Ⓑ Ⓒ Ⓓ
2	Ⓐ Ⓑ Ⓒ	22	Ⓐ Ⓑ Ⓒ	42	Ⓐ Ⓑ Ⓒ Ⓓ	62	Ⓐ Ⓑ Ⓒ Ⓓ	82	Ⓐ Ⓑ Ⓒ Ⓓ
3	Ⓐ Ⓑ Ⓒ	23	Ⓐ Ⓑ Ⓒ	43	Ⓐ Ⓑ Ⓒ Ⓓ	63	Ⓐ Ⓑ Ⓒ Ⓓ	83	Ⓐ Ⓑ Ⓒ Ⓓ
4	Ⓐ Ⓑ Ⓒ	24	Ⓐ Ⓑ Ⓒ	44	Ⓐ Ⓑ Ⓒ Ⓓ	64	Ⓐ Ⓑ Ⓒ Ⓓ	84	Ⓐ Ⓑ Ⓒ Ⓓ
5	Ⓐ Ⓑ Ⓒ	25	Ⓐ Ⓑ Ⓒ	45	Ⓐ Ⓑ Ⓒ Ⓓ	65	Ⓐ Ⓑ Ⓒ Ⓓ	85	Ⓐ Ⓑ Ⓒ Ⓓ
6	Ⓐ Ⓑ Ⓒ	26	Ⓐ Ⓑ Ⓒ	46	Ⓐ Ⓑ Ⓒ Ⓓ	66	Ⓐ Ⓑ Ⓒ Ⓓ	86	Ⓐ Ⓑ Ⓒ Ⓓ
7	Ⓐ Ⓑ Ⓒ	27	Ⓐ Ⓑ Ⓒ	47	Ⓐ Ⓑ Ⓒ Ⓓ	67	Ⓐ Ⓑ Ⓒ Ⓓ	87	Ⓐ Ⓑ Ⓒ Ⓓ
8	Ⓐ Ⓑ Ⓒ	28	Ⓐ Ⓑ Ⓒ	48	Ⓐ Ⓑ Ⓒ Ⓓ	68	Ⓐ Ⓑ Ⓒ Ⓓ	88	Ⓐ Ⓑ Ⓒ Ⓓ
9	Ⓐ Ⓑ Ⓒ	29	Ⓐ Ⓑ Ⓒ	49	Ⓐ Ⓑ Ⓒ Ⓓ	69	Ⓐ Ⓑ Ⓒ Ⓓ	89	Ⓐ Ⓑ Ⓒ Ⓓ
10	Ⓐ Ⓑ Ⓒ	30	Ⓐ Ⓑ Ⓒ	50	Ⓐ Ⓑ Ⓒ Ⓓ	70	Ⓐ Ⓑ Ⓒ Ⓓ	90	Ⓐ Ⓑ Ⓒ Ⓓ
11	Ⓐ Ⓑ Ⓒ	31	Ⓐ Ⓑ Ⓒ	51	Ⓐ Ⓑ Ⓒ Ⓓ	71	Ⓐ Ⓑ Ⓒ Ⓓ	91	Ⓐ Ⓑ Ⓒ Ⓓ
12	Ⓐ Ⓑ Ⓒ	32	Ⓐ Ⓑ Ⓒ	52	Ⓐ Ⓑ Ⓒ Ⓓ	72	Ⓐ Ⓑ Ⓒ Ⓓ	92	Ⓐ Ⓑ Ⓒ Ⓓ
13	Ⓐ Ⓑ Ⓒ	33	Ⓐ Ⓑ Ⓒ	53	Ⓐ Ⓑ Ⓒ Ⓓ	73	Ⓐ Ⓑ Ⓒ Ⓓ	93	Ⓐ Ⓑ Ⓒ Ⓓ
14	Ⓐ Ⓑ Ⓒ	34	Ⓐ Ⓑ Ⓒ	54	Ⓐ Ⓑ Ⓒ Ⓓ	74	Ⓐ Ⓑ Ⓒ Ⓓ	94	Ⓐ Ⓑ Ⓒ Ⓓ
15	Ⓐ Ⓑ Ⓒ	35	Ⓐ Ⓑ Ⓒ	55	Ⓐ Ⓑ Ⓒ Ⓓ	75	Ⓐ Ⓑ Ⓒ Ⓓ	95	Ⓐ Ⓑ Ⓒ Ⓓ
16	Ⓐ Ⓑ Ⓒ	36	Ⓐ Ⓑ Ⓒ	56	Ⓐ Ⓑ Ⓒ Ⓓ	76	Ⓐ Ⓑ Ⓒ Ⓓ	96	Ⓐ Ⓑ Ⓒ Ⓓ
17	Ⓐ Ⓑ Ⓒ	37	Ⓐ Ⓑ Ⓒ	57	Ⓐ Ⓑ Ⓒ Ⓓ	77	Ⓐ Ⓑ Ⓒ Ⓓ	97	Ⓐ Ⓑ Ⓒ Ⓓ
18	Ⓐ Ⓑ Ⓒ	38	Ⓐ Ⓑ Ⓒ	58	Ⓐ Ⓑ Ⓒ Ⓓ	78	Ⓐ Ⓑ Ⓒ Ⓓ	98	Ⓐ Ⓑ Ⓒ Ⓓ
19	Ⓐ Ⓑ Ⓒ	39	Ⓐ Ⓑ Ⓒ	59	Ⓐ Ⓑ Ⓒ Ⓓ	79	Ⓐ Ⓑ Ⓒ Ⓓ	99	Ⓐ Ⓑ Ⓒ Ⓓ
20	Ⓐ Ⓑ Ⓒ	40	Ⓐ Ⓑ Ⓒ	60	Ⓐ Ⓑ Ⓒ Ⓓ	80	Ⓐ Ⓑ Ⓒ Ⓓ	100	Ⓐ Ⓑ Ⓒ Ⓓ

ANSWER SHEET

TEST 07

LISTENING (Part I-IV)

NO.	ANSWER	NO.	ANSWER	NO.	ANSWER	NO.	ANSWER	NO.	ANSWER
1	Ⓐ Ⓑ Ⓒ Ⓓ	21	Ⓐ Ⓑ Ⓒ	41	Ⓐ Ⓑ Ⓒ Ⓓ	61	Ⓐ Ⓑ Ⓒ Ⓓ	81	Ⓐ Ⓑ Ⓒ Ⓓ
2	Ⓐ Ⓑ Ⓒ Ⓓ	22	Ⓐ Ⓑ Ⓒ	42	Ⓐ Ⓑ Ⓒ Ⓓ	62	Ⓐ Ⓑ Ⓒ Ⓓ	82	Ⓐ Ⓑ Ⓒ Ⓓ
3	Ⓐ Ⓑ Ⓒ Ⓓ	23	Ⓐ Ⓑ Ⓒ	43	Ⓐ Ⓑ Ⓒ Ⓓ	63	Ⓐ Ⓑ Ⓒ Ⓓ	83	Ⓐ Ⓑ Ⓒ Ⓓ
4	Ⓐ Ⓑ Ⓒ Ⓓ	24	Ⓐ Ⓑ Ⓒ	44	Ⓐ Ⓑ Ⓒ Ⓓ	64	Ⓐ Ⓑ Ⓒ Ⓓ	84	Ⓐ Ⓑ Ⓒ Ⓓ
5	Ⓐ Ⓑ Ⓒ Ⓓ	25	Ⓐ Ⓑ Ⓒ	45	Ⓐ Ⓑ Ⓒ Ⓓ	65	Ⓐ Ⓑ Ⓒ Ⓓ	85	Ⓐ Ⓑ Ⓒ Ⓓ
6	Ⓐ Ⓑ Ⓒ Ⓓ	26	Ⓐ Ⓑ Ⓒ	46	Ⓐ Ⓑ Ⓒ Ⓓ	66	Ⓐ Ⓑ Ⓒ Ⓓ	86	Ⓐ Ⓑ Ⓒ Ⓓ
7	Ⓐ Ⓑ Ⓒ	27	Ⓐ Ⓑ Ⓒ	47	Ⓐ Ⓑ Ⓒ Ⓓ	67	Ⓐ Ⓑ Ⓒ Ⓓ	87	Ⓐ Ⓑ Ⓒ Ⓓ
8	Ⓐ Ⓑ Ⓒ	28	Ⓐ Ⓑ Ⓒ	48	Ⓐ Ⓑ Ⓒ Ⓓ	68	Ⓐ Ⓑ Ⓒ Ⓓ	88	Ⓐ Ⓑ Ⓒ Ⓓ
9	Ⓐ Ⓑ Ⓒ	29	Ⓐ Ⓑ Ⓒ	49	Ⓐ Ⓑ Ⓒ Ⓓ	69	Ⓐ Ⓑ Ⓒ Ⓓ	89	Ⓐ Ⓑ Ⓒ Ⓓ
10	Ⓐ Ⓑ Ⓒ	30	Ⓐ Ⓑ Ⓒ	50	Ⓐ Ⓑ Ⓒ Ⓓ	70	Ⓐ Ⓑ Ⓒ Ⓓ	90	Ⓐ Ⓑ Ⓒ Ⓓ
11	Ⓐ Ⓑ Ⓒ	31	Ⓐ Ⓑ Ⓒ	51	Ⓐ Ⓑ Ⓒ Ⓓ	71	Ⓐ Ⓑ Ⓒ Ⓓ	91	Ⓐ Ⓑ Ⓒ Ⓓ
12	Ⓐ Ⓑ Ⓒ	32	Ⓐ Ⓑ Ⓒ Ⓓ	52	Ⓐ Ⓑ Ⓒ Ⓓ	72	Ⓐ Ⓑ Ⓒ Ⓓ	92	Ⓐ Ⓑ Ⓒ Ⓓ
13	Ⓐ Ⓑ Ⓒ	33	Ⓐ Ⓑ Ⓒ Ⓓ	53	Ⓐ Ⓑ Ⓒ Ⓓ	73	Ⓐ Ⓑ Ⓒ Ⓓ	93	Ⓐ Ⓑ Ⓒ Ⓓ
14	Ⓐ Ⓑ Ⓒ	34	Ⓐ Ⓑ Ⓒ Ⓓ	54	Ⓐ Ⓑ Ⓒ Ⓓ	74	Ⓐ Ⓑ Ⓒ Ⓓ	94	Ⓐ Ⓑ Ⓒ Ⓓ
15	Ⓐ Ⓑ Ⓒ	35	Ⓐ Ⓑ Ⓒ Ⓓ	55	Ⓐ Ⓑ Ⓒ Ⓓ	75	Ⓐ Ⓑ Ⓒ Ⓓ	95	Ⓐ Ⓑ Ⓒ Ⓓ
16	Ⓐ Ⓑ Ⓒ	36	Ⓐ Ⓑ Ⓒ Ⓓ	56	Ⓐ Ⓑ Ⓒ Ⓓ	76	Ⓐ Ⓑ Ⓒ Ⓓ	96	Ⓐ Ⓑ Ⓒ Ⓓ
17	Ⓐ Ⓑ Ⓒ	37	Ⓐ Ⓑ Ⓒ Ⓓ	57	Ⓐ Ⓑ Ⓒ Ⓓ	77	Ⓐ Ⓑ Ⓒ Ⓓ	97	Ⓐ Ⓑ Ⓒ Ⓓ
18	Ⓐ Ⓑ Ⓒ	38	Ⓐ Ⓑ Ⓒ Ⓓ	58	Ⓐ Ⓑ Ⓒ Ⓓ	78	Ⓐ Ⓑ Ⓒ Ⓓ	98	Ⓐ Ⓑ Ⓒ Ⓓ
19	Ⓐ Ⓑ Ⓒ	39	Ⓐ Ⓑ Ⓒ Ⓓ	59	Ⓐ Ⓑ Ⓒ Ⓓ	79	Ⓐ Ⓑ Ⓒ Ⓓ	99	Ⓐ Ⓑ Ⓒ Ⓓ
20	Ⓐ Ⓑ Ⓒ	40	Ⓐ Ⓑ Ⓒ Ⓓ	60	Ⓐ Ⓑ Ⓒ Ⓓ	80	Ⓐ Ⓑ Ⓒ Ⓓ	100	Ⓐ Ⓑ Ⓒ Ⓓ

ANSWER SHEET

TEST 08

LISTENING (Part I-IV)

NO.	ANSWER	NO.	ANSWER	NO.	ANSWER	NO.	ANSWER	NO.	ANSWER
1	Ⓐ Ⓑ Ⓒ Ⓓ	21	Ⓐ Ⓑ Ⓒ	41	Ⓐ Ⓑ Ⓒ Ⓓ	61	Ⓐ Ⓑ Ⓒ Ⓓ	81	Ⓐ Ⓑ Ⓒ Ⓓ
2	Ⓐ Ⓑ Ⓒ Ⓓ	22	Ⓐ Ⓑ Ⓒ	42	Ⓐ Ⓑ Ⓒ Ⓓ	62	Ⓐ Ⓑ Ⓒ Ⓓ	82	Ⓐ Ⓑ Ⓒ Ⓓ
3	Ⓐ Ⓑ Ⓒ Ⓓ	23	Ⓐ Ⓑ Ⓒ	43	Ⓐ Ⓑ Ⓒ Ⓓ	63	Ⓐ Ⓑ Ⓒ Ⓓ	83	Ⓐ Ⓑ Ⓒ Ⓓ
4	Ⓐ Ⓑ Ⓒ Ⓓ	24	Ⓐ Ⓑ Ⓒ	44	Ⓐ Ⓑ Ⓒ Ⓓ	64	Ⓐ Ⓑ Ⓒ Ⓓ	84	Ⓐ Ⓑ Ⓒ Ⓓ
5	Ⓐ Ⓑ Ⓒ Ⓓ	25	Ⓐ Ⓑ Ⓒ	45	Ⓐ Ⓑ Ⓒ Ⓓ	65	Ⓐ Ⓑ Ⓒ Ⓓ	85	Ⓐ Ⓑ Ⓒ Ⓓ
6	Ⓐ Ⓑ Ⓒ Ⓓ	26	Ⓐ Ⓑ Ⓒ	46	Ⓐ Ⓑ Ⓒ Ⓓ	66	Ⓐ Ⓑ Ⓒ Ⓓ	86	Ⓐ Ⓑ Ⓒ Ⓓ
7	Ⓐ Ⓑ Ⓒ	27	Ⓐ Ⓑ Ⓒ	47	Ⓐ Ⓑ Ⓒ Ⓓ	67	Ⓐ Ⓑ Ⓒ Ⓓ	87	Ⓐ Ⓑ Ⓒ Ⓓ
8	Ⓐ Ⓑ Ⓒ	28	Ⓐ Ⓑ Ⓒ	48	Ⓐ Ⓑ Ⓒ Ⓓ	68	Ⓐ Ⓑ Ⓒ Ⓓ	88	Ⓐ Ⓑ Ⓒ Ⓓ
9	Ⓐ Ⓑ Ⓒ	29	Ⓐ Ⓑ Ⓒ	49	Ⓐ Ⓑ Ⓒ Ⓓ	69	Ⓐ Ⓑ Ⓒ Ⓓ	89	Ⓐ Ⓑ Ⓒ Ⓓ
10	Ⓐ Ⓑ Ⓒ	30	Ⓐ Ⓑ Ⓒ	50	Ⓐ Ⓑ Ⓒ Ⓓ	70	Ⓐ Ⓑ Ⓒ Ⓓ	90	Ⓐ Ⓑ Ⓒ Ⓓ
11	Ⓐ Ⓑ Ⓒ	31	Ⓐ Ⓑ Ⓒ	51	Ⓐ Ⓑ Ⓒ Ⓓ	71	Ⓐ Ⓑ Ⓒ Ⓓ	91	Ⓐ Ⓑ Ⓒ Ⓓ
12	Ⓐ Ⓑ Ⓒ	32	Ⓐ Ⓑ Ⓒ Ⓓ	52	Ⓐ Ⓑ Ⓒ Ⓓ	72	Ⓐ Ⓑ Ⓒ Ⓓ	92	Ⓐ Ⓑ Ⓒ Ⓓ
13	Ⓐ Ⓑ Ⓒ	33	Ⓐ Ⓑ Ⓒ Ⓓ	53	Ⓐ Ⓑ Ⓒ Ⓓ	73	Ⓐ Ⓑ Ⓒ Ⓓ	93	Ⓐ Ⓑ Ⓒ Ⓓ
14	Ⓐ Ⓑ Ⓒ	34	Ⓐ Ⓑ Ⓒ Ⓓ	54	Ⓐ Ⓑ Ⓒ Ⓓ	74	Ⓐ Ⓑ Ⓒ Ⓓ	94	Ⓐ Ⓑ Ⓒ Ⓓ
15	Ⓐ Ⓑ Ⓒ	35	Ⓐ Ⓑ Ⓒ Ⓓ	55	Ⓐ Ⓑ Ⓒ Ⓓ	75	Ⓐ Ⓑ Ⓒ Ⓓ	95	Ⓐ Ⓑ Ⓒ Ⓓ
16	Ⓐ Ⓑ Ⓒ	36	Ⓐ Ⓑ Ⓒ Ⓓ	56	Ⓐ Ⓑ Ⓒ Ⓓ	76	Ⓐ Ⓑ Ⓒ Ⓓ	96	Ⓐ Ⓑ Ⓒ Ⓓ
17	Ⓐ Ⓑ Ⓒ	37	Ⓐ Ⓑ Ⓒ Ⓓ	57	Ⓐ Ⓑ Ⓒ Ⓓ	77	Ⓐ Ⓑ Ⓒ Ⓓ	97	Ⓐ Ⓑ Ⓒ Ⓓ
18	Ⓐ Ⓑ Ⓒ	38	Ⓐ Ⓑ Ⓒ Ⓓ	58	Ⓐ Ⓑ Ⓒ Ⓓ	78	Ⓐ Ⓑ Ⓒ Ⓓ	98	Ⓐ Ⓑ Ⓒ Ⓓ
19	Ⓐ Ⓑ Ⓒ	39	Ⓐ Ⓑ Ⓒ Ⓓ	59	Ⓐ Ⓑ Ⓒ Ⓓ	79	Ⓐ Ⓑ Ⓒ Ⓓ	99	Ⓐ Ⓑ Ⓒ Ⓓ
20	Ⓐ Ⓑ Ⓒ	40	Ⓐ Ⓑ Ⓒ Ⓓ	60	Ⓐ Ⓑ Ⓒ Ⓓ	80	Ⓐ Ⓑ Ⓒ Ⓓ	100	Ⓐ Ⓑ Ⓒ Ⓓ

LISTENING (Part I-IV)

NO.	ANSWER	NO.	ANSWER	NO.	ANSWER	NO.	ANSWER	NO.	ANSWER
	A B C D		A B C D		A B C D		A B C D		A B C D
1	Ⓐ Ⓑ Ⓒ Ⓓ	21	Ⓐ Ⓑ Ⓒ	41	Ⓐ Ⓑ Ⓒ Ⓓ	61	Ⓐ Ⓑ Ⓒ Ⓓ	81	Ⓐ Ⓑ Ⓒ Ⓓ
2	Ⓐ Ⓑ Ⓒ Ⓓ	22	Ⓐ Ⓑ Ⓒ	42	Ⓐ Ⓑ Ⓒ Ⓓ	62	Ⓐ Ⓑ Ⓒ Ⓓ	82	Ⓐ Ⓑ Ⓒ Ⓓ
3	Ⓐ Ⓑ Ⓒ Ⓓ	23	Ⓐ Ⓑ Ⓒ	43	Ⓐ Ⓑ Ⓒ Ⓓ	63	Ⓐ Ⓑ Ⓒ Ⓓ	83	Ⓐ Ⓑ Ⓒ Ⓓ
4	Ⓐ Ⓑ Ⓒ Ⓓ	24	Ⓐ Ⓑ Ⓒ	44	Ⓐ Ⓑ Ⓒ Ⓓ	64	Ⓐ Ⓑ Ⓒ Ⓓ	84	Ⓐ Ⓑ Ⓒ Ⓓ
5	Ⓐ Ⓑ Ⓒ Ⓓ	25	Ⓐ Ⓑ Ⓒ	45	Ⓐ Ⓑ Ⓒ Ⓓ	65	Ⓐ Ⓑ Ⓒ Ⓓ	85	Ⓐ Ⓑ Ⓒ Ⓓ
6	Ⓐ Ⓑ Ⓒ Ⓓ	26	Ⓐ Ⓑ Ⓒ	46	Ⓐ Ⓑ Ⓒ Ⓓ	66	Ⓐ Ⓑ Ⓒ Ⓓ	86	Ⓐ Ⓑ Ⓒ Ⓓ
7	Ⓐ Ⓑ Ⓒ	27	Ⓐ Ⓑ Ⓒ	47	Ⓐ Ⓑ Ⓒ Ⓓ	67	Ⓐ Ⓑ Ⓒ Ⓓ	87	Ⓐ Ⓑ Ⓒ Ⓓ
8	Ⓐ Ⓑ Ⓒ	28	Ⓐ Ⓑ Ⓒ	48	Ⓐ Ⓑ Ⓒ Ⓓ	68	Ⓐ Ⓑ Ⓒ Ⓓ	88	Ⓐ Ⓑ Ⓒ Ⓓ
9	Ⓐ Ⓑ Ⓒ	29	Ⓐ Ⓑ Ⓒ	49	Ⓐ Ⓑ Ⓒ Ⓓ	69	Ⓐ Ⓑ Ⓒ Ⓓ	89	Ⓐ Ⓑ Ⓒ Ⓓ
10	Ⓐ Ⓑ Ⓒ	30	Ⓐ Ⓑ Ⓒ	50	Ⓐ Ⓑ Ⓒ Ⓓ	70	Ⓐ Ⓑ Ⓒ Ⓓ	90	Ⓐ Ⓑ Ⓒ Ⓓ
11	Ⓐ Ⓑ Ⓒ	31	Ⓐ Ⓑ Ⓒ	51	Ⓐ Ⓑ Ⓒ Ⓓ	71	Ⓐ Ⓑ Ⓒ Ⓓ	91	Ⓐ Ⓑ Ⓒ Ⓓ
12	Ⓐ Ⓑ Ⓒ	32	Ⓐ Ⓑ Ⓒ	52	Ⓐ Ⓑ Ⓒ Ⓓ	72	Ⓐ Ⓑ Ⓒ Ⓓ	92	Ⓐ Ⓑ Ⓒ Ⓓ
13	Ⓐ Ⓑ Ⓒ	33	Ⓐ Ⓑ Ⓒ	53	Ⓐ Ⓑ Ⓒ Ⓓ	73	Ⓐ Ⓑ Ⓒ Ⓓ	93	Ⓐ Ⓑ Ⓒ Ⓓ
14	Ⓐ Ⓑ Ⓒ	34	Ⓐ Ⓑ Ⓒ	54	Ⓐ Ⓑ Ⓒ Ⓓ	74	Ⓐ Ⓑ Ⓒ Ⓓ	94	Ⓐ Ⓑ Ⓒ Ⓓ
15	Ⓐ Ⓑ Ⓒ	35	Ⓐ Ⓑ Ⓒ	55	Ⓐ Ⓑ Ⓒ Ⓓ	75	Ⓐ Ⓑ Ⓒ Ⓓ	95	Ⓐ Ⓑ Ⓒ Ⓓ
16	Ⓐ Ⓑ Ⓒ	36	Ⓐ Ⓑ Ⓒ	56	Ⓐ Ⓑ Ⓒ Ⓓ	76	Ⓐ Ⓑ Ⓒ Ⓓ	96	Ⓐ Ⓑ Ⓒ Ⓓ
17	Ⓐ Ⓑ Ⓒ	37	Ⓐ Ⓑ Ⓒ	57	Ⓐ Ⓑ Ⓒ Ⓓ	77	Ⓐ Ⓑ Ⓒ Ⓓ	97	Ⓐ Ⓑ Ⓒ Ⓓ
18	Ⓐ Ⓑ Ⓒ	38	Ⓐ Ⓑ Ⓒ	58	Ⓐ Ⓑ Ⓒ Ⓓ	78	Ⓐ Ⓑ Ⓒ Ⓓ	98	Ⓐ Ⓑ Ⓒ Ⓓ
19	Ⓐ Ⓑ Ⓒ	39	Ⓐ Ⓑ Ⓒ	59	Ⓐ Ⓑ Ⓒ Ⓓ	79	Ⓐ Ⓑ Ⓒ Ⓓ	99	Ⓐ Ⓑ Ⓒ Ⓓ
20	Ⓐ Ⓑ Ⓒ	40	Ⓐ Ⓑ Ⓒ	60	Ⓐ Ⓑ Ⓒ Ⓓ	80	Ⓐ Ⓑ Ⓒ Ⓓ	100	Ⓐ Ⓑ Ⓒ Ⓓ

LISTENING (Part I-IV)

NO.	ANSWER	NO.	ANSWER	NO.	ANSWER	NO.	ANSWER	NO.	ANSWER
	A B C D		A B C D		A B C D		A B C D		A B C D
1	Ⓐ Ⓑ Ⓒ Ⓓ	21	Ⓐ Ⓑ Ⓒ Ⓓ	41	Ⓐ Ⓑ Ⓒ Ⓓ	61	Ⓐ Ⓑ Ⓒ Ⓓ	81	Ⓐ Ⓑ Ⓒ Ⓓ
2	Ⓐ Ⓑ Ⓒ Ⓓ	22	Ⓐ Ⓑ Ⓒ Ⓓ	42	Ⓐ Ⓑ Ⓒ Ⓓ	62	Ⓐ Ⓑ Ⓒ Ⓓ	82	Ⓐ Ⓑ Ⓒ Ⓓ
3	Ⓐ Ⓑ Ⓒ Ⓓ	23	Ⓐ Ⓑ Ⓒ Ⓓ	43	Ⓐ Ⓑ Ⓒ Ⓓ	63	Ⓐ Ⓑ Ⓒ Ⓓ	83	Ⓐ Ⓑ Ⓒ Ⓓ
4	Ⓐ Ⓑ Ⓒ Ⓓ	24	Ⓐ Ⓑ Ⓒ Ⓓ	44	Ⓐ Ⓑ Ⓒ Ⓓ	64	Ⓐ Ⓑ Ⓒ Ⓓ	84	Ⓐ Ⓑ Ⓒ Ⓓ
5	Ⓐ Ⓑ Ⓒ Ⓓ	25	Ⓐ Ⓑ Ⓒ Ⓓ	45	Ⓐ Ⓑ Ⓒ Ⓓ	65	Ⓐ Ⓑ Ⓒ Ⓓ	85	Ⓐ Ⓑ Ⓒ Ⓓ
6	Ⓐ Ⓑ Ⓒ Ⓓ	26	Ⓐ Ⓑ Ⓒ Ⓓ	46	Ⓐ Ⓑ Ⓒ Ⓓ	66	Ⓐ Ⓑ Ⓒ Ⓓ	86	Ⓐ Ⓑ Ⓒ Ⓓ
7	Ⓐ Ⓑ Ⓒ	27	Ⓐ Ⓑ Ⓒ	47	Ⓐ Ⓑ Ⓒ Ⓓ	67	Ⓐ Ⓑ Ⓒ Ⓓ	87	Ⓐ Ⓑ Ⓒ Ⓓ
8	Ⓐ Ⓑ Ⓒ	28	Ⓐ Ⓑ Ⓒ	48	Ⓐ Ⓑ Ⓒ Ⓓ	68	Ⓐ Ⓑ Ⓒ Ⓓ	88	Ⓐ Ⓑ Ⓒ Ⓓ
9	Ⓐ Ⓑ Ⓒ	29	Ⓐ Ⓑ Ⓒ	49	Ⓐ Ⓑ Ⓒ Ⓓ	69	Ⓐ Ⓑ Ⓒ Ⓓ	89	Ⓐ Ⓑ Ⓒ Ⓓ
10	Ⓐ Ⓑ Ⓒ	30	Ⓐ Ⓑ Ⓒ	50	Ⓐ Ⓑ Ⓒ Ⓓ	70	Ⓐ Ⓑ Ⓒ Ⓓ	90	Ⓐ Ⓑ Ⓒ Ⓓ
11	Ⓐ Ⓑ Ⓒ	31	Ⓐ Ⓑ Ⓒ	51	Ⓐ Ⓑ Ⓒ Ⓓ	71	Ⓐ Ⓑ Ⓒ Ⓓ	91	Ⓐ Ⓑ Ⓒ Ⓓ
12	Ⓐ Ⓑ Ⓒ	32	Ⓐ Ⓑ Ⓒ	52	Ⓐ Ⓑ Ⓒ Ⓓ	72	Ⓐ Ⓑ Ⓒ Ⓓ	92	Ⓐ Ⓑ Ⓒ Ⓓ
13	Ⓐ Ⓑ Ⓒ	33	Ⓐ Ⓑ Ⓒ	53	Ⓐ Ⓑ Ⓒ Ⓓ	73	Ⓐ Ⓑ Ⓒ Ⓓ	93	Ⓐ Ⓑ Ⓒ Ⓓ
14	Ⓐ Ⓑ Ⓒ	34	Ⓐ Ⓑ Ⓒ	54	Ⓐ Ⓑ Ⓒ Ⓓ	74	Ⓐ Ⓑ Ⓒ Ⓓ	94	Ⓐ Ⓑ Ⓒ Ⓓ
15	Ⓐ Ⓑ Ⓒ	35	Ⓐ Ⓑ Ⓒ	55	Ⓐ Ⓑ Ⓒ Ⓓ	75	Ⓐ Ⓑ Ⓒ Ⓓ	95	Ⓐ Ⓑ Ⓒ Ⓓ
16	Ⓐ Ⓑ Ⓒ	36	Ⓐ Ⓑ Ⓒ	56	Ⓐ Ⓑ Ⓒ Ⓓ	76	Ⓐ Ⓑ Ⓒ Ⓓ	96	Ⓐ Ⓑ Ⓒ Ⓓ
17	Ⓐ Ⓑ Ⓒ	37	Ⓐ Ⓑ Ⓒ	57	Ⓐ Ⓑ Ⓒ Ⓓ	77	Ⓐ Ⓑ Ⓒ Ⓓ	97	Ⓐ Ⓑ Ⓒ Ⓓ
18	Ⓐ Ⓑ Ⓒ	38	Ⓐ Ⓑ Ⓒ	58	Ⓐ Ⓑ Ⓒ Ⓓ	78	Ⓐ Ⓑ Ⓒ Ⓓ	98	Ⓐ Ⓑ Ⓒ Ⓓ
19	Ⓐ Ⓑ Ⓒ	39	Ⓐ Ⓑ Ⓒ	59	Ⓐ Ⓑ Ⓒ Ⓓ	79	Ⓐ Ⓑ Ⓒ Ⓓ	99	Ⓐ Ⓑ Ⓒ Ⓓ
20	Ⓐ Ⓑ Ⓒ	40	Ⓐ Ⓑ Ⓒ	60	Ⓐ Ⓑ Ⓒ Ⓓ	80	Ⓐ Ⓑ Ⓒ Ⓓ	100	Ⓐ Ⓑ Ⓒ Ⓓ

파고다 토익 실전 1000제 LC

실전 1000제 | 정답·해석

PAGODA Books

파고다 토익 LC

실전

1000제 | 정답·해석

TEST 01

PART 1
P. 16

1 (A) **2** (A) **3** (A) **4** (B) **5** (C) **6** (C)

PART 2
P. 20

7 (B) **8** (B) **9** (A) **10** (C) **11** (B) **12** (B)
13 (A) **14** (A) **15** (A) **16** (A) **17** (A) **18** (C)
19 (C) **20** (C) **21** (C) **22** (C) **23** (C) **24** (C)
25 (B) **26** (C) **27** (C) **28** (B) **29** (A) **30** (A)
31 (A)

PART 3
P. 21

32 (A) **33** (A) **34** (D) **35** (A) **36** (A) **37** (D)
38 (D) **39** (D) **40** (A) **41** (C) **42** (A) **43** (C)
44 (B) **45** (A) **46** (D) **47** (B) **48** (D) **49** (D)
50 (D) **51** (B) **52** (C) **53** (A) **54** (B) **55** (A)
56 (D) **57** (C) **58** (A) **59** (B) **60** (A) **61** (D)
62 (A) **63** (A) **64** (C) **65** (D) **66** (B) **67** (D)
68 (D) **69** (D) **70** (D)

PART 4
P. 25

71 (A) **72** (B) **73** (D) **74** (C) **75** (D) **76** (A)
77 (B) **78** (A) **79** (C) **80** (B) **81** (A) **82** (C)
83 (B) **84** (D) **85** (A) **86** (C) **87** (D) **88** (D)
89 (D) **90** (C) **91** (B) **92** (D) **93** (D) **94** (C)
95 (C) **96** (A) **97** (C) **98** (B) **99** (C) **100** (B)

PART 1
P. 16

1 미국
(A) A man is looking at a file.
(B) A man is shutting a cabinet drawer.
(C) A man is pointing at a picture frame.
(D) A man is turning on a desk lamp.

(A) 남자가 파일을 보고 있다.
(B) 남자가 캐비닛 서랍을 닫고 있다.
(C) 남자가 액자를 가리키고 있다.
(D) 남자가 탁상용 스탠드를 켜고 있다.

2 호주
(A) She's removing a product from a refrigerated shelf.
(B) She's placing some fresh produce into a basket.
(C) She's picking up a shopping bag.
(D) She's lined up to make a purchase at a supermarket.

(A) 여자가 냉장 선반에서 제품을 꺼내고 있다.
(B) 여자가 신선한 농산물을 바구니 안에 놓고 있다.
(C) 여자가 쇼핑백을 집어 들고 있다.
(D) 여자가 슈퍼마켓에서 구매하려고 줄을 서 있다.

3 미국
(A) Beverages have been placed on a table.
(B) Shopping bags are piled on the floor.
(C) A woman is picking up a drink.
(D) A man is plugging in a laptop computer.

(A) 음료가 테이블 위에 놓여 있다.
(B) 쇼핑백이 바닥에 쌓여 있다.
(C) 여자가 음료를 집어 들고 있다.
(D) 남자가 노트북의 전원을 연결하고 있다.

4 호주
(A) A woman is adjusting a shelf.
(B) A woman is hanging up a skirt.
(C) A woman is trying on a shirt.
(D) A woman is opening a closet door.

(A) 여자가 선반을 조절하고 있다.
(B) 여자가 치마를 걸고 있다.
(C) 여자가 셔츠를 입어보고 있다.
(D) 여자가 벽장 문을 열고 있다.

5 영국
(A) One of the people is opening a suitcase.
(B) Some people are boarding an aircraft.
(C) Some travelers are waiting in a line.
(D) Some travelers are checking a departure screen.

(A) 사람들 중 한 명이 여행 가방을 열고 있다.
(B) 몇몇 사람들이 비행기에 탑승하고 있다.
(C) 몇몇 여행객들이 줄을 서 있다.
(D) 몇몇 여행객들이 출발 화면을 확인하고 있다.

6 미국
(A) Some lights have been hung across a bridge.
(B) Some smoke is rising from the buildings.
(C) A brige extends over a waterway.
(D) A boat is floating in a harbor.

(A) 몇몇 전등들이 다리를 가로질러 걸려 있다.
(B) 건물들에서 연기가 피어오르고 있다.
(C) 수로 위로 다리가 나 있다.
(D) 항구에 보트 한 척이 떠 있다.

PART 2
P. 20

7 미국 ⇄ 호주
Why wasn't the company newsletter sent out this month?
(A) That's great news!
(B) We had some mechanical issues.
(C) The last Friday of every month.

이번 달에는 왜 사보가 발송되지 않았나요?
(A) 그거 희소식이네요!
(B) 기계적인 문제가 좀 있었어요.
(C) 매월 마지막 금요일이요.

8 영국 ⇄ 미국

What time is the next shuttle to San Francisco departing?
(A) At the downtown terminal.
(B) In 30 minutes.
(C) More than 10 dollars.

San Francisco로 가는 다음 셔틀은 몇 시에 출발하나요?
(A) 시내 터미널에서요.
(B) 30분 후에요.
(C) 10달러 이상입니다.

9 미국 ⇄ 호주

When will we leave from the convention center?
(A) In an hour.
(B) We'll be at the arrival hall.
(C) The lectures were very informative.

컨벤션 센터에서 언제 출발하나요?
(A) 한 시간 뒤에요.
(B) 입국장에 있을게요.
(C) 강연은 아주 유익했어요.

10 미국 ⇄ 영국

Did you see your doctor this morning?
(A) Some hospital employees.
(B) Can you pick up my prescription?
(C) No, I had to run some other errands.

오늘 오전에 진찰받으셨어요?
(A) 몇몇 병원 직원들이요.
(B) 제 처방전 좀 받아 주시겠어요?
(C) 아니요, 다른 볼일이 좀 있었거든요.

11 미국 ⇄ 호주

Can you send me Mr. Rashid's updated contact information?
(A) Here's my business card.
(B) Sure. I'll take care of it right away.
(C) He's been there too.

Mr. Rashid의 최신 연락처를 보내 주시겠어요?
(A) 여기 제 명함이요.
(B) 물론이죠. 지금 바로 드릴게요.
(C) 그분도 거기 가 보셨어요.

12 호주 ⇄ 영국

When can I make a dental appointment with Dr. Price?
(A) For about half an hour.
(B) She's fully booked until next Thursday.
(C) Yes, I read about it this afternoon.

Dr. Price의 치과 진료 예약을 언제로 할 수 있나요?
(A) 약 30분 동안이요.
(B) 다음 주 목요일까지 예약이 다 찼어요.
(C) 네, 오늘 오후에 그걸 읽었어요.

13 미국 ⇄ 미국

Have you seen Warren from the Legal Department?
(A) Yes, but he's gone for the day.
(B) The corporate merger.
(C) Thanks for letting me know.

법무부 Warren 보셨어요?
(A) 네, 근데 퇴근하셨어요.
(B) 기업 합병요.
(C) 알려줘서 고마워요.

14 미국 ⇄ 영국

Ms. Rosa's presentation has been postponed to this afternoon.
(A) I see. I'll let everyone know.
(B) Please refer to the poster.
(C) Yes, the director is present.

Ms. Rosa의 프레젠테이션이 오늘 오후로 연기되었어요.
(A) 알겠어요. 제가 모두에게 알릴게요.
(B) 포스터를 참조해 주세요.
(C) 네, 이사님께서 참석하세요.

15 호주 ⇄ 미국

Will the office move take place before next month?
(A) The memo was just sent.
(B) I'll order more supplies this week.
(C) No, the Maintenance Department.

다음 달 전에 사무실 이전이 진행되나요?
(A) 메모가 방금 발송됐어요.
(B) 이번 주에 물품을 더 주문할게요.
(C) 아니요, 유지보수부서요.

16 미국 ⇄ 미국

Where are we celebrating Barbara's retirement this Friday?
(A) At an Italian restaurant nearby.
(B) To celebrate her birthday.
(C) For 25 years.

이번 주 금요일에 어디에서 Barbara의 은퇴를 축하해줄 건가요?
(A) 인근 이탈리아 식당에서요.
(B) 그녀의 생일을 축하해 주려고요.
(C) 25년 동안이요.

17 영국 ⇄ 호주

Are the subscription payments made monthly or yearly?
(A) On the first of every month.
(B) No, a weekly delivery.
(C) Cash or credit cards only.

구독료 납부는 한 달에 한 번 하나요, 일 년에 한 번 하나요?
(A) 매달 1일에요.
(B) 아니요, 매주 배송이요.
(C) 현금이나 신용카드만요.

18 미국 ⇄ 미국

Your company's looking to hire more employees, isn't it?
(A) She'm the Human Resources manager.
(B) The online job posting.
(C) Not at the moment.

당신 회사에서 직원을 추가로 채용할 예정인 거 맞죠?
(A) 그녀는 인사부 과장이에요.
(B) 온라인 채용 공고요.
(C) 지금 당장은 아니에요.

19 미국 ⇄ 영국

The jazz performance was entertaining.
(A) No, I can't play any instruments.
(B) It was at Lee Theater.
(C) Yes, the songs were very enjoyable.

재즈 공연이 재미있었어요.
(A) 아니요, 저는 악기를 전혀 다룰 줄 몰라요.
(B) Lee 극장에서 있었어요.
(C) 맞아요, 곡들이 매우 즐거웠어요.

20 미국 ⇄ 호주

I'm not sure how to get to the conference hall from the hotel.
(A) We'll be staying for three nights.
(B) The room has a great view.
(C) **Carl will send you the directions.**

호텔에서 회의장까지 어떻게 가는지 잘 모르겠어요.
(A) 저희는 3박을 할 거예요.
(B) 그 방은 전망이 아주 좋아요.
(C) Carl이 당신에게 약도를 보내줄 거예요.

21 영국 ⇄ 미국

Weren't you supposed to speak with the IT Department?
(A) The company's website.
(B) Yes, a keynote speaker.
(C) **The manager is too busy.**

IT 부서와 이야기하기로 하지 않았어요?
(A) 회사 웹사이트요.
(B) 네, 기조연설자요.
(C) 관리자가 너무 바빠요.

22 미국 ⇄ 미국

Who can drive Ms. Edwards to the bus terminal?
(A) To see a live performance.
(B) A three-hour ride.
(C) **I don't have a license.**

누가 Ms. Edwards를 버스 터미널까지 태워 주실 수 있으세요?
(A) 라이브 공연을 보려고요.
(B) 세 시간 거리예요.
(C) 저는 면허가 없어요.

23 미국 ⇄ 영국

Have you watched the new documentary film?
(A) A movie theater.
(B) OK. Let's have some.
(C) **Yes, it was very informative.**

새 다큐멘터리 영화 보셨나요?
(A) 극장이요.
(B) 좋아요. 좀 갖죠.
(C) 네, 아주 유익했어요.

24 호주 ⇄ 미국

When are the temporary workers coming to help?
(A) The subway station is temporarily closed.
(B) Sure, I can lend you a hand.
(C) **The staff budget was cut.**

임시직 근로자들이 도와주러 언제 나오나요?
(A) 지하철역이 임시 폐쇄됐어요.
(B) 네, 제가 도와드릴 수 있어요.
(C) 직원 예산이 삭감됐어요.

25 미국 ⇄ 미국

Which coffee shop do you usually go to?
(A) It opens at 8 A.M.
(B) **I use the company's machine.**
(C) No, I don't need a drink right now.

주로 어느 커피숍으로 가세요?
(A) 오전 8시에 문을 열어요.
(B) 전 회사 기계를 이용해요.
(C) 아니요, 전 지금 안 마셔도 됩니다.

26 영국 ⇄ 호주

Why is this window a circle instead of a rectangle?
(A) By taking measurements at all locations.
(B) No, they hired an architect last year.
(C) **That was the client's request.**

왜 이 창문은 직사각형 대신에 원형인가요?
(A) 모든 지점에서 치수를 재서요.
(B) 아니요, 작년에 건축가를 고용했어요.
(C) 그건 고객 요청 사항이었어요.

27 미국 ⇄ 미국

How long will it take you to prepare for the half marathon?
(A) It is a little over 21 kilometers.
(B) The route goes through Newton Park.
(C) **I'll have to ask my personal trainer.**

하프 마라톤 준비하는 데 얼마나 걸릴까요?
(A) 21킬로미터를 조금 넘어요.
(B) Newton 공원을 통과하는 경로예요.
(C) 제 개인 트레이너한테 물어봐야 해요.

28 미국 ⇄ 미국

How does this streaming service work?
(A) Your promotion is wonderful news.
(B) **The subscription renews automatically every month.**
(C) Yes, the service was outstanding.

이 스트리밍 서비스는 어떻게 이뤄지나요?
(A) 당신의 승진은 굉장한 소식이에요.
(B) 구독은 매달 자동 갱신됩니다.
(C) 네, 서비스가 훌륭했어요.

29 영국 ⇄ 미국

Would you like some help going through those applications?
(A) **No, there are only four left.**
(B) Incentive for the quarterly review.
(C) The office administrator position.

지원서 검토를 도와드릴까요?
(A) 아니요, 4개밖에 안 남았어요.
(B) 분기별 보고에 대한 인센티브요.
(C) 사무 행정직이요.

30 호주 ⇄ 미국

Did you like Adelyn's suggestion at the workshop?
(A) **Oh, that was today.**
(B) The workshop was mandatory for all employees.
(C) Great, I'll see you there.

워크숍 때 Adelyn의 의견은 마음에 들었어요?
(A) 아, 그게 오늘이었군요.
(B) 워크숍은 전 직원에게 의무입니다.
(C) 잘됐네요, 거기서 봐요.

31 미국 ⇄ 미국

I could help organize our filing system more efficiently.
(A) **Riley is in charge of document management.**
(B) The network system allows data sharing.
(C) Sorry, but those filing cabinets are currently unavailable.

저희 문서 정리 시스템을 더 효율적으로 조직할 수 있게 제가 도와드릴 수 있어요.
(A) Riley가 문서 관리를 담당하고 있어요.
(B) 네트워크 시스템으로 데이터를 공유할 수 있어요.
(C) 죄송하지만, 그 서류 캐비닛은 현재 이용할 수 없어요.

PART 3

P. 21

미국 ⇄ 미국

Questions 32-34 refer to the following conversation.

M: Madeleine, I need to access our personnel records so that I can submit our team's evaluation report.(32) However, the system is not letting me log in. Are you having the same issue?

W: I was in the system earlier today. The IT team did send out an e-mail last week mentioning some security changes. If you haven't linked up your phone to your account, you won't be able to log in.(33)

M: I suppose I should go through my e-mails and set that up now.(34)

W: Let me know if you need help setting it up. In the meantime, I can print out any records you need.

32-34번은 다음 대화에 관한 문제입니다.

남: Madeleine, 제가 부서 평가 보고서를 제출하려면 인사 기록에 접속해야 해요.(32) 그런데, 시스템에 로그인이 안 돼요. 당신도 그런가요?

여: 저는 아까 시스템에 들어갔어요. 지난주에 IT 부서에서 보안 변경 사항에 관한 이메일을 보내긴 했어요. 핸드폰을 계정에 연결 안 하셨으면, 로그인이 안 될 거예요.(33)

남: 지금 이메일을 보면서 설치해야겠네요.(34)

여: 설치하는 데 도움 필요하시면 알려주세요. 그러는 동안, 필요하신 기록은 제가 출력해드릴 수 있어요.

32 남자는 무엇을 제출하려고 하는가?
(A) 평가 보고서
(B) 재무제표
(C) 입사 지원서
(D) 임대 계약서

33 여자는 지난주 무슨 일이 있었다고 말하는가?
(A) 네트워크 보안이 강화되었다.
(B) 일부 작업이 외부로 위탁되었다.
(C) 리스크 평가가 개정되었다.
(D) 메일 서비스가 중단되었다.

34 남자는 다음에 무엇을 할 것인가?
(A) 네트워크 기술자에게 전화할 것이다
(B) 회의를 준비할 것이다
(C) 고객을 만날 것이다
(D) 이메일을 읽을 것이다

미국 ⇄ 영국

Questions 35-37 refer to the following conversation.

M: Fran, you're responsible for our company's staff health and wellness program,(35) right?

W: Yes. Last week I arranged for a physical therapist to come in and conduct a seminar on occupational safety. She discussed proper posture our employees should maintain to avoid injuries. Many people joined, and it was quite popular.(36)

M: That's great to hear. How about setting up private consultations for each employee?(37) They could learn some stretches or workouts they could do at the office.

W: Won't those sessions be too costly for our budget?

M: We could hold group sessions instead. Those tend to be cheaper than private ones.

35-37번은 다음 대화에 관한 문제입니다.

남: Fran, 우리 회사 직원 건강 관리 프로그램을 담당하고 계시죠,(35) 그렇죠?

여: 맞아요. 지난주에 제가 물리치료사를 모셔 와 직업 안전에 관한 세미나를 실시했어요. 직원들이 부상을 피하기 위해 유지해야 할 올바른 자세에 대해 알려주셨죠. 많은 분이 참여했고, 인기가 좋았어요.(36)

남: 너무 좋은 소식이네요. 직원 개개인을 위한 개인 상담 시간을 마련하는 건 어떨까요?(37) 사무실에서 할 수 있는 스트레칭이나 운동을 배울 수 있을 거예요.

여: 그런 세션은 저희 예산에 너무 비싸지 않을까요?

남: 그룹 세션을 마련할 수도 있어요. 개인 세션보다는 좀 더 저렴한 편이에요.

35 대화는 주로 무엇에 관한 것인가?
(A) 회사 건강 계획
(B) 회사 기금모금 행사
(C) 산업 컨벤션
(D) 직업 개발 프로그램

36 여자는 세미나에 관하여 뭐라고 말하는가?
(A) 좋은 평가를 받았다.
(B) 가격이 너무 비쌌다.
(C) 온라인으로 실시됐다.
(D) 연기됐다.

37 남자는 무엇을 하자고 제안하는가?
(A) 행사에 출장 연회 업체를 고용하자고
(B) 팸플릿을 발송하자고
(C) 자원자를 찾아보자고
(D) 상담 세션을 제공하자고

미국 ⇄ 미국

Questions 38-40 refer to the following conversation.

M: Beatrice, I have great hopes for our new line of sports shoes.(38) I think they'll be a huge success, and the samples turned out great.

W: I agree. But it'd be best to conduct some marketing research before we begin mass production. We need to make sure that the shoes function properly.(39) It's especially important that the shock absorption feature is effective.

M: That's a good point. How about we find some runners for a focus group? They could try using our product and give us feedback. I'll make a posting on our website to let our customers know about the opportunity.(40)

38-40번은 다음 대화에 관한 문제입니다.

남: Beatrice, 저는 저희 운동화 신제품에 기대가 아주 커요.(38) 크게 성공할 것 같아요, 샘플도 아주 잘 나왔고요.

여: 같은 의견이에요. 하지만 대량 생산에 들어가기 전에 마케팅 조사를 하면 아주 좋을 거예요. 신발이 제대로 기능하는지 확실히 할 필요가 있어요.(39) 충격 흡수 기능이 효과적인지 특히 중요해요.

남: 좋은 지적이에요. 포커스 그룹에 육상선수를 찾아보는 건 어떨까요? 저희 제품을 사용해보고 피드백을 줄 수도 있어요. 제가 웹사이트에 글을 올려서 고객들이 이러한 기회를 알 수 있게 할게요.(40)

38 화자들은 어떤 종류의 제품에 관해 이야기하고 있는가?
(A) 운동복
(B) 보호 장비
(C) 실내 자전거
(D) 운동화

39 여자는 어떤 제품 특성이 우려된다고 말하는가?
(A) 무게
(B) 내구성
(C) 디자인
(D) 기능성

40 남자는 무엇을 하겠다고 제안하는가?
(A) 온라인에 글을 쓰겠다고
(B) 공급업체를 찾겠다고
(C) 새로운 영업사원을 채용하겠다고
(D) 몇몇 디자인을 제출하겠다고

호주 ⇄ 영국 ⇄ 미국

Questions 41-43 refer to the following conversation with three speakers.

M: Hi, June, my name's Alex. I'm glad you've decided to join us here at Ottimo Accounting. **I'll be in charge of your training as the office administrator.**[41]

W1: It's great to meet you, Alex!

M: This is Tanya. Tanya, meet June, our new office administrator.

W2: Welcome, June. I look forward to working with you.

M: This is June's orientation manual. **Tanya, could you help her work through the first training assignment?**[42]

W2: I'd be glad to help.

M: OK. Once she's finished with that, bring her up to my office, and I'll show her how to use the AccountMaster 2000 software.

W1: Oh, I also used AccountMaster 2000 at the office where I did my internship.[43]

41-43번은 다음 세 화자의 대화에 관한 문제입니다.

남: 안녕하세요, June, 제 이름은 Alex입니다. 이곳 Ottimo Accounting에서 저희와 함께하기로 하셔서 기쁩니다. **제가 당신의 사무 관리자 교육을 담당할 거예요.**[41]

여1: 만나서 반갑습니다, Alex!

남: 이분은 Tanya예요. Tanya, 새로 오신 저희 사무 관리자이신 June이에요.

여2: 환영해요, June. 당신과 함께 일하기를 고대하고 있어요.

남: 이건 June의 오리엔테이션 설명서예요. **Tanya, 첫 번째 교육 과제를 수행하도록 도와주시겠어요?**[42]

여2: 기꺼이 도울게요.

남: 좋아요. 그녀가 그 일을 마치는 대로, 제 사무실로 데려와 주시면, 제가 그녀에게 AccountMaster 2000 소프트웨어 사용법을 알려 드릴게요.

여1: 아, 저도 제가 인턴으로 일했던 회사에서 AccountMaster 2000을 사용했어요.[43]

41 June의 직업은 무엇인가?
(A) 컴퓨터 프로그래머
(B) 회계 직원
(C) 사무 관리자
(D) 재무 책임자

42 June은 다음에 무엇을 하겠는가?
(A) 과제를 완료할 것이다
(B) 관리자를 만날 것이다
(C) 기사를 읽을 것이다
(D) 웹사이트를 방문할 것이다

43 June은 소프트웨어에 관하여 뭐라고 말하는가?
(A) 업계에서 널리 쓰인다.
(B) 자신의 컴퓨터에 다운로드했다.
(C) 이미 그것에 익숙하다.
(D) 다른 나라에서 온 것이다.

영국 ⇄ 호주

Questions 44-46 refer to the following conversation.

W: Hey, Edward. It's Carrie. Do you have some time right now? **I want to ask you a question about my business trip next month.**[44]

M: Yes. **You're traveling to Chicago for the business convention, right?**[44]

W: Right. The company always pays for the flight ticket, hotel accommodations, and three meals per day. **But do you know if the company will cover my mobile phone plan?**[45] I'll need to use data roaming while I'm in the United States.

M: Umm... That's a good question. We don't usually reimburse phone plans, but it seems like you'd definitely need to use your phone while you're there. OK. Why don't we make an exception this time?

W: Thank you for being understanding.

M: **I'll look up the most comprehensive international phone plan for you.**[46]

44-46번은 다음 대화에 관한 문제입니다.

여: 안녕하세요, Edward. 저는 Carrie예요. 지금 시간 있으세요? **다음 달 있을 제 출장 관련해서 문의드릴 게 있어요.**[44]

남: 네. **비즈니스 컨벤션 차 Chicago로 출장 가시는 거죠, 맞죠?**[44]

여: 맞아요. 회사에서 항공권, 호텔 숙박료, 일당 세 끼 식사를 항상 지불해주잖아요. 그런데 **회사에서 제 핸드폰 요금도 부담해주는지 혹시 아시나요?**[45] 제가 미국에 있는 동안 데이터 로밍을 사용해야 해서요.

남: 음... 좋은 질문이에요. 보통은 저희가 핸드폰 요금을 환급드리지는 않는데, 거기 계신 동안 핸드폰을 반드시 사용하셔야 할 것 같네요. 알았어요. 이번엔 예외로 할까요?

여: 이해해 주셔서 감사해요.

남: **제가 가장 포괄적인 국제 요금제로 알아볼게요.**[46]

44 여자는 왜 Chicago에 갈 것인가?
(A) 잠재 고객을 만나기 위해
(B) 콘퍼런스에 참석하기 위해
(C) 기조연설을 하기 위해
(D) 시설을 점검하기 위해

45 여자는 남자에게 무엇에 관하여 물어보는가?
(A) 비용을 상환받을 수 있을지
(B) 출장 일정을 다시 잡을 수 있을지
(C) 좌석 업그레이드를 받을 수 있을지
(D) 다른 호텔에서 투숙할 수 있을지

46 남자는 무엇을 하겠다고 말하는가?
   (A) 매니저와 상의하겠다고
   (B) 요청서를 확인하겠다고
   (C) 이메일을 작성하겠다고
   (D) 조사를 실시하겠다고

미국 ⇄ 영국

Questions 47-49 refer to the following conversation.
M: Hi, I'm Sal Guberman's assistant, and I'm calling regarding your consultation on Thursday. Something has come up, and Mr. Guberman will have to be out of town for the rest of the week. If you're available next week, we'd like to arrange a new appointment for you.(47)
W: Ah, well… My schedule is tight next week with meetings and projects. Can I just meet with a different lawyer on Thursday?(48)
M: Hmm… Violet Wakers is available at 5 P.M., but she works in our Belford branch.(49)
W: Oh, my office is in Belford so that should actually be less of a drive for me.(49) I'll do that.

47-49번은 다음 대화에 관한 문제입니다.
남: 안녕하세요, 저는 Sal Guberman의 비서인데요, 목요일에 있을 귀하의 상담과 관련하여 전화 드립니다. 일이 좀 생겨서, Mr. Guberman이 이번 주 내내 출장을 가셔야 합니다. 다음 주에 시간 괜찮으시면, 새로 예약을 잡아드렸으면 합니다.(47)
여: 아, 음… 저는 다음 주에 회의와 프로젝트들로 일정이 빡빡해요. 그냥 목요일에 다른 변호사와 만날 수 있을까요?(48)
남: 음… Violet Wakers가 오후 5시에 시간이 되시는데, Belford 지점에 계세요.(49)
여: 아, 제 사무실이 Belford에 있어서, 사실상 저로서는 운전을 덜 해도 되겠네요.(49) 그렇게 할게요.

47 남자는 왜 여자에게 연락했는가?
   (A) 여행 준비를 확인하기 위해
   (B) 상담을 연기하기 위해
   (C) 회의 장소를 변경하기 위해
   (D) 청구서를 요청하기 위해

48 여자는 무엇에 관하여 물어보는가?
   (A) 서류 작업을 완료하는 것
   (B) 면접을 진행하는 것
   (C) 마감 기한을 연장하는 것
   (D) 다른 변호사를 만나는 것

49 여자는 왜 장소가 편리하다고 말하는가?
   (A) 시내에 위치해 있다.
   (B) 늦게까지 문을 연다.
   (C) 지하철역에서 가깝다.
   (D) 자신의 직장 근처에 있다.

영국 ⇄ 미국 ⇄ 호주

Questions 50-52 refer to the following conversation with three speakers.
W: Before we go, I'd like to hear a status report on our efforts to sign the recording artist Essie Walton. Where are we with the negotiations?(50)

M1: Our lawyers are working closely with her legal team to draft the terms and conditions that favor both parties.
M2: I'm certain we'll be able to successfully close the contract within the next two weeks. We're just ironing out the final details at this point.
W: When do you think we can alert the press, Max?(51)
M2: By next Friday, but let me confirm with our Public Relations Department after the meeting.(51)
W: OK. Keep me in the loop. Once we sign Essie Walton on, we can start planning her international tour next year(52) riding on the popularity of her latest album.

50-52번은 다음 세 화자의 대화에 관한 문제입니다.
여: 가기 전에, 음반 가수 Essie Walton과의 계약 진행 현황에 관한 보고를 듣고 싶네요. 협상 상황은 어떤가요?(50)
남1: 저희 변호사들이 그쪽 법무팀과 긴밀히 협력하며 양측에 유리한 계약 조건 초안을 작성하고 있습니다.
남2: 앞으로 2주 안에 계약을 성공적으로 마무리할 수 있다고 봅니다. 현재 최종 세부 사항을 조율하고 있습니다.
여: 우리가 언론에는 언제 알릴 수 있을 것 같나요, Max?(51)
남2: 다음 주 금요일입니다만, 회의 후에 제가 홍보팀에 확인하겠습니다.(51)
여: 알았어요. 계속 알려주세요. 우리가 Essie Walton과 계약하고 나면, 그녀의 최신 앨범의 인기에 힘입어 내년 해외 투어 계획을 세우기 시작할 수 있어요.(52)

50 화자들은 무엇에 관해 논의하고 있는가?
   (A) 면허 승인
   (B) 기업 합병
   (C) 신규 사무 절차
   (D) 사업 협상

51 Max는 무엇을 하겠다고 말하는가?
   (A) 보도 자료를 작성하겠다고
   (B) 몇몇 동료들과 확인하겠다고
   (C) 계약서에 서명하겠다고
   (D) 고객에게 연락하겠다고

52 여자는 내년에 무슨 일이 있기를 바라는가?
   (A) 신제품이 출시될 것이다.
   (B) 회사 수익이 증가할 것이다.
   (C) 세계적인 행사가 마련될 것이다.
   (D) 회사가 해외 지점을 열 것이다.

호주 ⇄ 영국

Questions 53-55 refer to the following conversation.
M: OK, here are your keys. Just make sure to return the car this Friday before noon.(53) Are you here on business?
W: Yes, that's right. I'm attending the local sales conference, but I'm free all afternoon today. I've never been to this city.(54)
M: Well then, I suggest checking out Merkville National Park.(54) It has some of the most beautiful hiking trails.
W: Thank you. I do enjoy outdoor activities.
M: You should purchase your entrance pass through the park's website. Doing that can save you $10.(55)
W: I appreciate the tip!

53-55번은 다음 대화에 관한 문제입니다.

남: 자, 열쇠 여기 있습니다. 이번 주 금요일 정오 전에 차를 꼭 반납해 주세요.(53) 업무차 오신 건가요?

여: 네, 맞아요. 제가 이 지역에서 열리는 영업 콘퍼런스에 참석하는데, 오늘 오후 내내 자유시간이라서요. 제가 이 도시에는 처음이에요.(54)

남: 음, 그러면, Merkville 국립공원에 가보시는 걸 추천 드려요.(54) 정말 아름다운 등산로가 몇 군데가 있어요.

여: 감사해요. 제가 야외활동을 정말 좋아하거든요.

남: 공원 웹사이트에서 입장권을 구입하도록 하세요. 그렇게 하시면 10달러를 절약하실 수 있어요.(55)

여: 조언 감사해요!

53 화자들은 어디에 있겠는가?
(A) 차량 대여점에
(B) 콘퍼런스 홀에
(C) 관광 안내소에
(D) 도시 버스 터미널에

54 여자는 왜 "제가 이 도시에는 처음이에요"라고 말하는가?
(A) 여행 가이드를 요청하기 위해
(B) 제안을 요청하기 위해
(C) 문제를 설명하기 위해
(D) 교통수단에 대해 문의하기 위해

55 남자는 여자에게 왜 온라인으로 주문하라고 권하는가?
(A) 할인을 받을 수 있다.
(B) 추가 비용이 없다.
(C) 대기시간이 없다.
(D) 웹사이트에 제품이 더 많다.

미국 ⇌ 미국

Questions 56-58 refer to the following conversation.

W: Hi, Randall. I called to ask about the submissions for the naming contest. **Were our customers excited about our new cereal?**(56)

M: We had a great turnout. We got around 500 entries in total, and some of them are quite good.

W: I'm glad to hear. Our contest went viral online. What a great way to promote our new product!

M: I agree. **And the winner will really appreciate getting a lifetime supply of our breakfast cereals.**(57)

W: For sure. **Could you share some submissions with me now?**(58)

M: Sorry. **The office next door is under renovation right now.** (58)

W: Ah, OK. **Call me when you can then.**(58)

56-58번은 다음 대화에 관한 문제입니다.

여: 안녕하세요, Randall. 이름 공모전 출품작에 관해 물어보려고 연락드렸어요. **고객들이 저희 새로운 시리얼에 관심 있어 하나요?**(56)

남: 참가자 수가 어마어마해요. 총 500개 정도 들어왔는데, 일부는 아주 훌륭해요.

여: 좋은 소식이네요. 저희 공모전이 온라인에서 인기가 많았어요. 신제품 홍보로 최고의 방법이죠!

남: 맞아요. 그리고 우승자는 저희 아침용 시리얼을 평생 공급받게 돼요.(57)

여: 맞아요. 지금 출품작을 몇 개 저한테 보내주실 수 있으세요?(58)

남: 죄송해요. 옆 사무실이 지금 보수 중이에요.(58)

여: 아, 그렇군요. 그럼 가능하실 때 연락해주세요.(58)

56 화자들은 어떤 종류의 사업체에서 일하는가?
(A) 농장
(B) 빵집
(C) 카페
(D) 식품 제조업체

57 남자는 우승자가 무엇을 받을 거라고 말하는가?
(A) 제품
(B) 상금
(C) 제품 평생 이용권
(D) 상품권

58 남자는 왜 "옆 사무실이 지금 보수 중이에요"라고 말하는가?
(A) 논의 일정 변경을 제안하기 위해
(B) 행사장 변경을 제안하기 위해
(C) 신규 사무실 공간을 추천하기 위해
(D) 지연에 사과하기 위해

호주 ⇌ 미국

Questions 59-61 refer to the following conversation.

M: Janice, I wanted to talk to you about our café's produce supplier.(59)

W: Sure. What is it?

M: They just started charging 10 percent more for their strawberries.(60) This means that we'll have to charge more for our strawberry-based items.

W: Hmm... I wonder if this will lead to lower sales.

M: I don't think so. Our strawberry drinks and desserts sell pretty well, and we still have a variety of other items that won't be affected by this change.

W: All right. I'll get everyone together for a brief meeting tomorrow morning, and I'll explain what's going on.(61)

59-61번은 다음 대화에 관한 문제입니다.

남: Janice, 우리 카페의 농산물 납품 업체에 관해 말씀드리고 싶었어요.(59)

여: 그래요. 무슨 얘기인가요?

남: 그쪽에서 최근에 딸기 가격에 10퍼센트를 더 청구하기 시작했어요.(60) 이건 우리가 딸기를 원료로 한 제품의 가격을 올려야 한다는 걸 의미해요.

여: 음... 이게 판매량 하락으로 이어질지 궁금하군요.

남: 그렇지는 않을 거예요. 딸기 음료와 디저트는 꽤 잘 팔리고 있고, 이런 변화에 영향을 받지 않을 다른 다양한 제품들도 있으니까요.

여: 알았어요. 제가 내일 오전에 모두 모아 간단한 회의를 열고, 상황을 설명할게요.(61)

59 화자들은 어디서 일하는가?
(A) 슈퍼마켓에서
(B) 카페에서
(C) 은행에서
(D) 병 음료 공장에서

60 남자에 따르면, 최근에 무슨 일이 있었는가?
(A) 제품 가격이 인상되었다.
(B) 계약이 종료되었다.
(C) 사업주가 변경되었다.
(D) 할인 행사가 열렸다.

61 여자는 내일 무엇을 하겠다고 말하는가?
(A) 새 납품업체에 전화하겠다고
(B) 지원자 면접을 보겠다고
(C) 설문조사를 실시하겠다고
(D) 회의를 열겠다고

미국 ⇄ 미국

Questions 62-64 refer to the following conversation and wall display.

M: This was a fantastic event. I really enjoyed all of the paintings you selected for this show.(62)

W: Thank you. I got to work with such talented artists this year. The show today seemed very popular with the young crowd. I'm glad we reached a new demographic.

M: Yes, I can see why it was so popular. I was actually looking to add a painting to my collection. I normally prefer larger paintings. However, the symmetry on this smaller one is absolutely stunning.(63) I'm seriously considering purchasing it.

W: Excellent choice. The artist Todd Chung is young but extremely talented. Would you like to meet him? He's right over there. Come with me.(64)

62-64번은 다음 대화와 벽면 전시에 관한 문제입니다.

남: 엄청난 행사였어요. 이번 쇼에 선정하신 그림 모두 너무 좋았어요.(62)

여: 감사해요. 올해 정말 재능 있는 예술가와 함께 작업하게 됐어요. 오늘 쇼는 젊은 층에 인기가 아주 많았던 것 같아요. 저희가 새로운 계층에 닿게 돼 기쁩니다.

남: 네, 왜 인기가 많은지 알겠어요. 실은 제가 제 수집품에 그림을 하나 추가하려고 생각 중이었어요. 저는 보통 큰 그림을 선호하거든요. 그런데 이 작은 그림 속 대칭이 정말 놀라워요.(63) 이 작품 구입을 진지하게 고려 중이에요.

여: 탁월한 선택이세요. 예술가 Todd Chung은 젊지만 재능이 아주 대단해요. 그를 만나보실래요? 바로 저쪽에 있어요. 따라오세요.(64)

벽면 전시

62 여자는 누구겠는가?
(A) 미술관 큐레이터
(B) 대학 강사
(C) 웹 디자이너
(D) 미술 교사

63 시각 자료를 보시오. 남자는 어떤 그림을 선호하는가?
(A) 그림 1
(B) 그림 2
(C) 그림 3
(D) 그림 4

64 여자는 다음에 무엇을 하겠는가?
(A) 청구서를 발행할 것이다
(B) 예술품을 측정할 것이다
(C) 소개할 것이다
(D) 포트폴리오를 구입할 것이다

영국 ⇄ 미국

Questions 65-67 refer to the following conversation and schedule.

W: Rafael, did you read about the National Contemporary Art Gallery's traveling exhibit? I got this booklet from Jeff.

M: No, I haven't.

W: Well, it looks great. The artists will be traveling with the exhibit to give talks about their works.(65)

M: That does sound like fun. Is the exhibit coming to our city?(66)

W: Yes, it looks like it will get here on 15th of October.(66)

M: OK, I'll be sure to visit. We should share this information with our colleagues. How about putting up the booklet on the notice board in our break room?(67) I'm sure our colleagues and their families will enjoy the exhibit, too.

W: Good idea. I'll do that this afternoon.(67)

65-67번은 다음 대화와 일정에 관한 문제입니다.

여: Rafael, 현대 국립 미술관 순회 전시회 소식 읽었어요? 제가 Jeff 한테 이 팸플릿을 받았어요.

남: 아니요, 아직요.

여: 음, 아주 좋아 보여요. 예술가들이 전시회와 함께 순회하며 자기 작품에 대해 강연할 예정이에요.(65)

남: 재미있을 것 같네요. 전시가 우리 도시에 오나요?(66)

여: 네, 여기는 10월 15일에 오는 것 같아요.(66)

남: 알았어요, 꼭 가 볼게요. 동료들한테 이 정보를 알려야 해요. 휴게실 게시판에 팸플릿을 놓는 게 어때요?(67) 우리 동료들과 그들의 가족들도 그 전시를 좋아할 거예요.

여: 좋은 생각이에요. 오늘 오후에 할게요.(67)

날짜	장소
10월 8일	Boston
10월 15일	New Haven(66)
10월 22일	Hartford
10월 29일	Providence

65 여자는 전시회가 왜 아주 좋아 보인다고 생각하는가?
(A) 전 세계 예술가들을 다룰 것이다.
(B) 비평 영상을 선보일 것이다.
(C) 유명 화가의 작품을 전시할 것이다.
(D) 예술가의 강연을 포함할 것이다.

66 시각 자료를 보시오. 화자들은 어디에 사는가?
(A) Boston에
(B) New Haven에
(C) Hartford에
(D) Providence에

67 여자는 팸플릿으로 무엇을 하겠다고 말하는가?
(A) 가족과 공유하겠다고
(B) 사본을 나눠주겠다고
(C) 전자 사본을 발송하겠다고
(D) 게시판에 올리겠다고

호주 ⇄ 미국

Questions 68-70 refer to the following conversation and sign.

M: Hello, Ms. Harkins. I've been expecting you. **Is that the sign you'd like to make prints of?(68)**

W: It is. I want to print this on a big banner. You can do that, right?

M: Yes. Can you show me the sign? **Oh, wow... 80 years, huh? That's amazing for a small grocery store.(69)**

W: It's all thanks to our loyal customers and hardworking employees. By the way, **we're planning to attach the banner to a fence, so we'll need some ties to hold it in place.(70)**

M: **There'll be an additional fee for that,(70)** but it's not much.

68-70번은 다음 대화와 표지판에 관한 문제입니다.

남: 안녕하세요, Ms. Harkins. 기다리고 있었습니다. 그게 인화하시려는 게시물인가요?(68)

여: 맞아요. 이걸 큰 현수막에 인쇄하고 싶어요. 하실 수 있죠, 맞죠?

남: 네. 게시물을 좀 보여주시겠어요? 오, 와... 80년이라고요? 소규모 식료품점으로서 대단하네요.(69)

여: 전부 단골고객분들과 성실한 직원들 덕분이에요. 그런데 저희가 현수막을 울타리에 붙일 거라서 자리에 고정할 끈이 좀 필요해요.(70)

남: 그러려면 추가 요금이 들긴 하지만(70) 큰 금액은 아니에요.

Geller 식료품점
그 동안의 성과를 기념합니다

- 5년간 최우수 소규모 사업체로 선정
- 20년간 현 소유주가 운영
- 50년간 현 위치에서 운영
- **80년간 영업(69)**

68 남자는 어디에서 일하겠는가?
(A) 택배회사에서
(B) 식료품점에서
(C) 컨벤션 센터에서
(D) 인쇄업체에서

69 시각 자료를 보시오. 남자는 어떤 성과에 놀라는가?
(A) 최우수 소규모 사업체로 선정된 햇수
(B) 현 소유주가 운영한 햇수
(C) 현 위치에서 영업한 햇수
(D) 영업한 햇수

70 여자는 무엇에 추가 요금을 지불해야 하는가?
(A) 현장 설치
(B) 빠른 배송
(C) 임대 차량
(D) 특별 비품

PART 4

미국

Questions 71-73 refer to the following introduction.

W: Hello, and welcome to the 10th Annual Renewable Energy Convention.**(71)** Our first speaker is the renowned scholar Jonathan Matthews, who all of us know quite well. He has been one of the strongest advocates of our industry for the past decade. **Earlier this year, Mr. Matthews was given the Washburn Medal for his recent work on biodiesel production.(72)** Mr. Matthews will share with us the latest on his research. But before he takes the stage, **I want to remind you to keep your name badge on at all times.(73)**

71-73번은 다음 소개에 관한 문제입니다.

여: 안녕하세요, 제10회 연례 재생 가능 에너지 컨벤션에 오신 것을 환영합니다.(71) 첫 번째 연사는 우리 모두가 잘 아는 분이죠, 저명한 학자이신 Jonathan Matthews이십니다. 그분은 지난 10년간 우리 업계의 가장 강력한 지지자 중 한 분이셨습니다. 올해 초, Mr. Matthews는 바이오 디젤 생산에 대한 그의 최근 연구로 Washburn 메달을 수상했습니다.(72) Mr. Matthews는 그의 가장 최근 연구들을 우리에게 공유해 주실 겁니다. 하지만, 그를 무대로 모시기 전에 여러분께 다시 한번 말씀드리면 명찰을 항시 착용해 주시길 바랍니다.(73)

71 컨벤션의 주제는 무엇인가?
(A) 재생 가능 에너지
(B) 컴퓨터 공학 기술
(C) 쓰레기 재활용
(D) 직물 생산

72 화자에 따르면, Jonathan Matthews는 올해 무엇을 했는가?
(A) 기계를 발명했다.
(B) 상을 받았다.
(C) 회사를 설립했다.
(D) 새로운 책을 썼다.

73 화자는 청자들에게 무엇을 하라고 상기시키는가?
(A) 질문거리를 적으라고
(B) 제품을 써보라고
(C) 시연회에 참석하라고
(D) 명찰을 착용하라고

호주

Questions 74-76 refer to the following broadcast.

M: This is Radio 92.3, bringing you an update on the pending storm. It is expected to be quite severe, and the government has made the preemptive decision to close off the Harbor Bridge completely.**(74)** This has caused a buildup of traffic along the alternative route out of the city center. **For those of you currently in the city, I suggest hanging tight and leaving a little later when the traffic clears up.(75)** In other news, the annual music festival will be in town next week. It will be a weekend full of music of all genres, and it all takes place in the city center. **(76)** We have some interviews coming up with some of the bands after the break.

74-76번은 다음 방송에 관한 문제입니다.

남: 92.3 라디오에서 다가오는 폭풍에 관한 새로운 소식을 전해 드립니다. 상당히 강력할 것으로 예상되어, 정부에서는 예방 차원에서 Harbor 교를 전면 통제하기로 결정했습니다.(74) 이로 인해 도심을 빠져나가는 대체 경로에 교통량이 증가했습니다. 현재 도시에 계신 분들은 잠시 기다렸다가 교통 정체가 풀리면 나서시길 권해 드립니다.(75) 다른 소식으로는, 다음 주 연례 음악 축제가 열립니다. 온갖 장르의 음악으로 가득한 주말이 될 예정이며, 모두 도심에서 열립니다.(76) 잠시 후에는 몇몇 밴드와 인터뷰가 마련되어 있습니다.

74 방송은 주로 무엇에 관한 것인가?
(A) 현지 사업체
(B) 현안
(C) 기상 상황
(D) 유명인 인터뷰

75 청자들은 무엇을 하도록 권고받는가?
(A) 앱을 다운받으라고
(B) 티켓을 구입하라고
(C) 웹사이트를 확인하라고
(D) 도심에 머무르라고

76 도심에서 무슨 일이 있을 예정인가?
(A) 음악 축제
(B) 벼룩시장
(C) 육상 경주
(D) 모금 행사

미국

Questions 77-79 refer to the following advertisement.

W: Have you been wanting to remodel the rooms in your house, but thought it was too expensive? Michelle's Design is your solution.(77) Working with our creative team, you'll be able to create a modern design for any space, from your kitchen to your bathroom. **Stop by our office for a consultation and mention this advertisement, and we'll give you a complimentary picture frame.(78)** This beautiful frame is available in several colors to match any casual space you have in your home. Give your house the makeover it deserves. **Give us a call at 555-3426 to set up an appointment today.(79)**

77-79번은 다음 광고에 관한 문제입니다.

여: 집의 방들을 리모델링하고 싶었는데 너무 비싸다고 생각하셨나요? Michelle 디자인이 해결책입니다.(77) 저희 창의적인 팀과 함께하시면 주방부터 욕실까지 어떤 공간에든 현대적인 디자인을 만들어내실 수 있을 겁니다. 저희 사무실에 들러서 상담을 받으시고 이 광고를 보고 오셨다고 말씀하시면 무료 액자를 드립니다.(78) 이 아름다운 액자는 여러 가지 색상이 있어서 가정의 모든 편한 공간에 잘 어울립니다. 당신의 집에 마땅히 해야 할 단장을 해주세요. 오늘 555-3426으로 전화 주셔서 예약하시기 바랍니다.(79)

77 어떤 종류의 사업체가 광고되고 있는가?
(A) 가정 조경 회사
(B) 인테리어 디자인 서비스
(C) 사진 스튜디오
(D) 미술관

78 청자들은 어떻게 무료 선물을 받을 수 있는가?
(A) 광고를 언급함으로써
(B) 후기를 게재함으로써
(C) 사진을 제출함으로써
(D) 설문조사를 작성함으로써

79 화자는 청자들이 전화 통화로 무엇을 할 수 있다고 말하는가?
(A) 액자를 주문할 수 있다고
(B) 길 안내를 받을 수 있다고
(C) 시간 약속을 잡을 수 있다고
(D) 조언을 받을 수 있다고

영국

Questions 80-82 refer to the following talk.

W: Thank you for the opportunity to speak to you today. I am the owner of Prima You, and **our expertise is in producing supplements to keep everyone feeling young and healthy.(80)** We are making a name for ourselves locally, but we'd like to reach a wider audience. **Since your department store has locations throughout the country, I would love to discuss the potential for you to distribute our products.(81)** I understand you already carry similar products, and this category is extremely competitive. However, our products are completely organic.(82)

80-82번은 다음 담화에 관한 문제입니다.

여: 오늘 당신께 말할 기회를 주셔서 감사합니다. 저는 Prima You의 소유주이고, 저희는 모든 사람이 계속해서 젊음과 건강을 느끼게 하는 건강 보조제를 전문으로 생산합니다.(80) 저희는 인근 지역에서 이름이 많이 알려져 있으나, 보다 많은 사람에게 다가가고 싶습니다. 귀하의 백화점은 전국에 지점이 있기에, 귀사에서 저희 제품을 유통할 가능성에 대해 논의하고 싶습니다.(81) 이미 유사 제품을 취급하고 계시고, 이 부문의 경쟁이 아주 치열한 걸로 알고 있습니다. 하지만, 저희 제품은 완전 유기농입니다.(82)

80 화자의 회사에서는 무엇을 생산하는가?
(A) 에너지 음료
(B) 건강 보충제
(C) 밀키트
(D) 화장품

81 화자는 왜 백화점과 제휴를 맺고 싶어 하는가?
(A) 전국에 지점이 있다.
(B) 대다수 소비자가 신뢰한다.
(C) 국제적 위상이 막강하다.
(D) 주요 협력사에 접근할 수 있다.

82 화자는 왜 "저희 제품은 완전 유기농입니다"라고 말하는가?
(A) 마케팅 전략을 제안하기 위해
(B) 잠재 문제를 내비치기 위해
(C) 차이점을 강조하기 위해
(D) 공통 질문을 다루기 위해

미국

Questions 83-85 refer to the following announcement.

M: Hello, everybody. Good to see you all. **I know that we've got quite a few vehicles to fix today,(83)** so I'll make this quick. Before we start work for the day, I want to inform you about the new process for handling staff complaints and concerns. Employee feedback is very important to us, but it has been difficult getting your opinions on certain issues. **We realize that it's not always easy to speak up at work,**(84) even when you think something needs our attention. **Now, we've added a section on our website, and every Monday morning, I will make a compilation of all the feedback provided in that section so that it can be reviewed by the supervisors.**(84)/(85)

83-85번은 다음 공지에 관한 문제입니다.

남: 안녕하세요, 여러분. 모두 뵙게 되어 좋군요. **오늘 상당히 많은 차량을 수리해야 한다는 것을 알기에,**(83) 빨리하도록 하겠습니다. 오늘 근무를 시작하기 전에, 새로운 직원 불만 및 고충 처리 절차에 대해 알려드리고자 합니다. 직원 의견은 우리에게 매우 중요하지만, 특정 사안에 대한 의견을 듣는 건 어려웠습니다. 주목해야 할 부분이 있다고 생각하더라도, **직장에서 목소리를 내는 게 늘 쉽지만은 않다는 것을 알고 있습니다.**(84) 이제, 웹사이트에 게시판을 하나 추가했습니다, 그리고 제가 매주 월요일 아침에 그 게시판에 올라온 의견을 모두 취합해서 관리자들이 검토할 수 있도록 할 것입니다.(84)/(85)

83 청자들은 어떤 사업체에서 일하겠는가?
(A) 채용 업체
(B) 자동차 정비소
(C) 전자제품 매장
(D) 마케팅 회사

84 화자가 "이제, 웹사이트에 게시판을 하나 추가했습니다"라고 말할 때 무엇을 의미하는가?
(A) 신제품이 소개될 것이다.
(B) 직원 한 명이 채용되었다.
(C) 배치가 변경될 것이다.
(D) 문제가 해결되었다.

85 화자는 월요일마다 무엇을 할 계획인가?
(A) 의견을 취합할 것이다
(B) 고객과 대화할 것이다
(C) 재고를 점검할 것이다
(D) 상품을 발송할 것이다

[영국]

Questions 86-88 refer to the following talk.

W: As you may be aware, I've always wanted our restaurant to be environmentally conscious. This is a goal I had since the day I opened the business.(86) We recently began offering takeout service to our customers. However, the plastic containers that we currently use aren't good for the environment. **So, next week, we'll be working with a different vendor that supplies biodegradable paper containers.**(87) We will also offer discount to customers who bring their own reusable containers. Now, I'd like to invite all of you to make suggestions to help our restaurant stay environmentally friendly. Any ideas are welcome, so please feel free to share them.(88)

86-88번은 다음 담화에 관한 문제입니다.

여: 알고 계시겠지만, 전 항상 우리 식당이 환경친화적이기를 바라왔습니다. 제가 사업을 시작한 첫날부터 가졌던 목표예요.(86) 저희가 최근에 고객에게 테이크아웃 서비스를 제공하기 시작했죠. 그런데,

현재 사용하는 플라스틱 용기가 환경에 좋지 않아요. 그래서 다음 주부터 생산되는 종이 용기를 납품하는 다른 업체와 함께합니다.(87) 재사용 용기를 직접 가져오는 고객에게는 할인도 제공합니다. 이제, 우리 식당을 환경친화적으로 유지하는 데 도움이 되는 의견을 여러분 모두에게 들어보고 싶습니다. 어떤 의견이든지 환영하니, 자유롭게 말씀해 주세요.(88)

86 화자는 누구겠는가?
(A) 환경미화원
(B) 유기농 농장주
(C) 식당 주인
(D) 영양 과학자

87 다음 주에 무엇이 변경되는가?
(A) 대여료
(B) 채용 과정
(C) 토지 사용 제한법
(D) 납품 업체

88 화자는 다음에 무엇을 할 것인가?
(A) 공지를 올릴 것이다
(B) 제품을 시연할 것이다
(C) 실행 계획을 만들 것이다
(D) 의견을 들을 것이다

[미국]

Questions 89-91 refer to the following excerpt from a meeting.

W: As many of you know, **we included a questionnaire in the last issue of our magazine.**(89)/(90) We asked subscribers to rate our articles according to how much they enjoyed reading them and to write down any suggestions they have.(90) It's only been two weeks since our last issue went out, but we've already received over a thousand responses. This is quite an accomplishment. I am not surprised, however, because we did offer discount vouchers to those who filled out the questionnaire.(91) This was a great idea by our market research team, and something we should remember if we ever need to collect information about our consumers again.

89-91번은 다음 회의 발췌록에 관한 문제입니다.

여: 많은 분들이 아시다시피, 우리 잡지의 지난 호에 설문지를 포함했습니다.(89)/(90) 구독자에게 기사를 얼마나 즐겁게 읽었는지 평점을 매기고 의견이 있으면 적어달라고 요청했습니다.(90) 지난 호가 나간 지 2주밖에 안 됐지만, 이미 천 개가 넘는 회신을 받았습니다. 이건 꽤 큰 성과입니다. 하지만 설문지를 작성해주신 분께 할인권을 제공했기에 놀랍지는 않습니다.(91) 이건 우리 시장 조사팀의 좋은 아이디어였고, 우리가 소비자들에 대한 정보를 다시 취합해야 할 때 이를 기억하는 게 좋겠습니다.

89 청자들은 어디에서 일하겠는가?
(A) 방송국에서
(B) 도서관에서
(C) 서점에서
(D) 출판사에서

90 설문지는 무엇에 관해 알아보려고 고안되었는가?
(A) 보안 정책
(B) 새로 출시된 제품
(C) 독자 만족도
(D) 구독료

91 설문지 작성을 장려하기 위해 무엇이 제공됐는가?
(A) 서비스 업그레이드
(B) 할인권
(C) 무료 가방
(D) 상금

호주

Questions 92-94 refer to the following telephone message.

M: Hi, Brittany. This is Alex from the Events Department. **I have an update for you regarding the venues you can rent out for your event.** (92) We already had a pre-screened list, and I went through which ones met your requirements. Due to the size of your event, there were only two that had a large enough venue. **I will say that unless you are under a tight budget, the less expensive option has received mixed reviews recently.** (93) Also, **when you get this message, could you give me a call instead of sending me a text? I'll be driving to the airport so I won't be able to check my messages until later this evening.** (94)

92-94번은 다음 전화 메시지에 관한 문제입니다.

남: 안녕하세요, Brittany. 행사 부서의 Alex입니다. **임대하실 수 있는 행사용 장소와 관련하여 새로 알려드릴 정보가 있습니다.** (92) 저희가 이미 선별한 명단을 가지고 있어서, 어떤 것이 귀하의 요건을 충족하는지 살펴봤습니다. 행사 규모로 인해, 공간이 충분히 큰 장소를 가진 곳은 두 곳뿐이었습니다. **알려드리자면, 예산이 빠듯한 게 아니라면, 덜 비싼 쪽은 최근 엇갈리는 평을 받았습니다.** (93) 그리고 **이 메시지를 받으시면, 저한테 문자 대신 전화해 주시겠어요? 제가 공항까지 운전해서 갈 예정이라서, 이따 저녁까지는 메시지를 확인할 수 없을 거예요.** (94)

92 화자는 청자가 무엇을 하는 것을 도와주고 있는가?
(A) 콘퍼런스를 준비하는 것
(B) 항공편을 예약하는 것
(C) 프레젠테이션하는 것
(D) **장소를 예약하는 것**

93 화자가 "덜 비싼 쪽은 최근 엇갈리는 평을 받았습니다"라고 말할 때 무엇을 내비치는가?
(A) 예산 변경이 시행될 예정이다.
(B) 과거에 의견이 무시된 적 있다.
(C) 청자가 요건 목록을 좁혀야 한다.
(D) **청자가 비싸지 않은 옵션을 선택하지 않아야 한다.**

94 화자는 왜 전화로 연락해 달라고 요청하는가?
(A) 회사를 그만둘 것이다.
(B) 기록되는 것을 원치 않는다.
(C) **다른 일로 바쁠 것이다.**
(D) 답변을 즉시 요구한다.

미국

Questions 95-97 refer to the following podcast and store shelf.

W: Thank you for tuning into another episode of our gardening podcast brought to you by Couper Hardware Store. (95) Today, we will talk about how to protect the plants in your outdoor garden from the cold winter weather. (96) The most important step is to add an extra layer of mulch for insulation. You can also use some cloth to cover large plants and shrubs. And don't forget to tie the cloth with some cords for optimal protection. Did you know that some plants need more water in winter? At any Couper Hardware location nationwide, you will be able to find everything you need. **Broadway brand products are now on sale for a limited time only, so don't miss out.** (97)

95-97번은 다음 팟캐스트와 매장 선반에 관한 문제입니다.

여: 오늘도 Couper 철물점에서 제공하는 원예 팟캐스트 방송을 청취해 주셔서 감사합니다. (95) 오늘은 추운 겨울 날씨에 야외 정원에 있는 식물을 보호하는 방법에 관해 이야기를 나눠 보겠습니다. (96) 가장 중요한 조치는 단열을 위해 뿌리 덮개 층을 추가로 덧대주는 것입니다. 크기가 큰 식물과 관목에는 천을 이용해 덮어줄 수도 있습니다. 최적의 보호를 위해 끈으로 옷감을 묶어주는 것을 잊지 마세요. 어떤 식물은 겨울에 수분을 더 필요로 한다는 걸 알고 계셨나요? 전국의 Couper 철물점 매장에서 필요로 하시는 모든 것을 구할 수 있습니다. **Broadway 브랜드 제품이 현재 기간 한정 할인판매 중이니 기회를 놓치지 마세요.** (97)

Grow-Well 브랜드 뿌리 덮개	Weston 브랜드 원예용 호스
Broadway 브랜드 천(97)	Duran 브랜드 끈

95 누가 팟캐스트를 후원하는가?
(A) 농업 협동조합
(B) 식물 묘목장
(C) **철물점**
(D) 조경 서비스

96 화자는 팟캐스트가 무엇에 관한 내용이라고 말하는가?
(A) **추위로부터 식물을 보호하는 것**
(B) 건강한 농산물을 재배하는 것
(C) 최상의 흙 종류를 선택하는 것
(D) 야외에서 묘목을 옮겨 심는 것

97 시각 자료를 보시오. 어떤 제품이 할인판매 중인가?
(A) 뿌리 덮개
(B) 원예용 호스
(C) **천**
(D) 끈

Questions 98-100 refer to the following telephone message and sign.

M: Good morning. My name is Hans Kanter. I own an accounting firm on Yosemite Road, and I need to have the place cleaned for an event I'm holding this weekend. **My neighbor gave me your number–he said he really liked your service.** **(98)** My office is about 900 square feet,**(99)** and I need it cleaned as soon as possible. **I'll be in a client meeting all morning today, so please contact me in the afternoon.** **(100)** You can reach me at 555-8234. Thank you.

98-100번은 다음 전화 메시지와 표지판에 관한 문제입니다.

남: 안녕하세요. 제 이름은 Hans Kanter입니다. Yosemite로에 회계 사무소를 하나 갖고 있는데, 이번 주말에 주최하는 행사 때문에 청소가 필요합니다. 제 이웃이 그쪽 번호를 알려줬는데, 서비스가 정말 좋았다고 하더군요.**(98)** 제 사무실은 약 900제곱피트 정도 되고**(99)** 되도록 빨리 청소를 해야 합니다. 오늘은 제가 오전 내내 고객과 회의가 있어서 오후에 연락하셨으면 좋겠습니다.**(100)** 555-8234로 전화하시면 됩니다. 고맙습니다.

A-Z 기업 청소서비스

400 - 600제곱피트 = 45달러
600 - 800제곱피트 = 65달러
800 - 1,000제곱피트 = 85달러(99)
1,000 - 1,200제곱피트 = 105달러

---

98 발신인은 청자의 전화번호를 어디서 구했는가?
(A) 텔레비전 광고에서
(B) 이웃에게서
(C) 소식지에서
(D) 시 안내 책자에서

99 시각 자료를 보시오. 서비스 비용은 얼마나 들 것인가?
(A) 45달러
(B) 65달러
(C) 85달러
(D) 105달러

100 발신인은 왜 오늘 오전에 시간이 없는가?
(A) 병원에 간다.
(B) 고객과 만난다.
(C) 회사 워크숍에서 발표를 한다.
(D) 은행에 간다.

TEST 02

PART 1
P. 30

1 (D) **2** (D) **3** (C) **4** (C) **5** (D) **6** (D)

PART 2
P. 34

7 (C) **8** (C) **9** (C) **10** (B) **11** (C) **12** (B)

13 (A) **14** (B) **15** (A) **16** (A) **17** (B) **18** (B)

19 (A) **20** (A) **21** (C) **22** (C) **23** (A) **24** (A)

25 (A) **26** (A) **27** (A) **28** (C) **29** (B) **30** (C)

31 (C)

PART 3
P. 35

32 (D) **33** (C) **34** (A) **35** (D) **36** (D) **37** (C)

38 (A) **39** (D) **40** (A) **41** (A) **42** (C) **43** (C)

44 (C) **45** (D) **46** (B) **47** (D) **48** (A) **49** (C)

50 (D) **51** (D) **52** (A) **53** (C) **54** (A) **55** (D)

56 (D) **57** (B) **58** (A) **59** (D) **60** (C) **61** (D)

62 (A) **63** (C) **64** (D) **65** (C) **66** (D) **67** (A)

68 (C) **69** (B) **70** (A)

PART 4
P. 39

71 (D) **72** (B) **73** (A) **74** (B) **75** (A) **76** (B)

77 (D) **78** (D) **79** (B) **80** (B) **81** (C) **82** (A)

83 (C) **84** (A) **85** (B) **86** (C) **87** (B) **88** (A)

89 (A) **90** (D) **91** (B) **92** (A) **93** (B) **94** (A)

95 (D) **96** (C) **97** (A) **98** (B) **99** (D) **100** (D)

PART 1
P. 30

1 미국
(A) She's holding a dish.
(B) She's setting the table for a meal.
(C) He's sipping from a mug.
(D) He's speaking to a server.

(A) 여자가 접시를 들고 있다.
(B) 여자가 식사를 위해 식탁을 차리고 있다.
(C) 남자가 머그잔으로 조금씩 마시고 있다.
(D) 남자가 종업원과 대화하고 있다.

2 영국
(A) A man is processing a payment.
(B) A man is bending over to put down an item.
(C) Some customers are lined up to make a payment.
(D) Some patrons are seated in a restaurant.

(A) 남자가 결제를 처리하고 있다.
(B) 남자가 물건을 내려놓으려고 몸을 굽히고 있다.
(C) 몇몇 고객들이 결제하려고 줄을 서 있다.
(D) 몇몇 고객들이 식당에 앉아 있다.

3 미국
(A) The man is heating some ingredients on a stove.
(B) The man is weighing some items for a dish.
(C) The man is arranging some food on a plate.
(D) The man is peeling some vegetables.

(A) 남자가 가스레인지에 재료를 익히고 있다.
(B) 남자가 요리용 물품의 무게를 재고 있다.
(C) 남자가 접시 위에 음식을 배열하고 있다.
(D) 남자가 몇몇 야채의 껍질을 벗기고 있다.

4 호주
(A) A rug has been rolled up against the wall.
(B) A plant is being placed on a windowsill.
(C) Some tables have been set up for a meal.
(D) Some curtains are being draped across the window.

(A) 깔개가 둥글게 말려 벽에 기대어져 있다.
(B) 화분이 창턱에 놓이고 있다.
(C) 몇몇 테이블이 식사를 위해 준비되어 있다.
(D) 창문에 커튼이 드리워지고 있다.

5 미국
(A) A man is writing on a clipboard with a pen.
(B) A man is pushing a cart in a factory.
(C) A man is placing an item on a display shelf.
(D) A man is pressing a button on a panel.

(A) 남자가 펜으로 클립보드에 쓰고 있다.
(B) 남자가 공장에서 카트를 밀고 있다.
(C) 남자가 진열 칸에 물건을 놓고 있다.
(D) 남자가 패널에 있는 버튼을 누르고 있다.

6 미국
(A) A woman is putting on a winter jacket.
(B) A woman is washing a vehicle.
(C) Some snow is being cleaned off from a fence.
(D) Some tree branches are covered with snow.

(A) 여자가 겨울 점퍼를 입고 있다.
(B) 여자가 세차를 하고 있다.
(C) 눈이 담장에서 치워지고 있다.
(D) 몇몇 나뭇가지들이 눈으로 덮여 있다.

PART 2
P. 34

7 미국 ⇄ 영국
How do you recommend getting to your hotel?
(A) Yes, they're working properly.
(B) I had a great stay here.
(C) I suggest you take a cab.

호텔까지 어떻게 가는 걸 추천하시나요?
(A) 네, 제대로 작동하는 중이에요.
(B) 여기 숙박이 아주 좋았어요.
(C) 택시 타는 걸 추천해 드립니다.

8 영국 ⇄ 호주

Should I book the venue for the anniversary dinner?
(A) A guest list.
(B) Tomorrow afternoon around 2.
(C) The HR Department is in charge of that.

제가 기념일 만찬 장소를 예약할까요?
(A) 초대 손님 명단이요.
(B) 내일 오후 2시쯤이요.
(C) 그건 인사부가 담당해요.

9 미국 ⇄ 미국

Which radio program should we advertise our new product in?
(A) A 30-second commercial.
(B) I heard it at the broadcasting station.
(C) How about The Morning Show?

우리 신제품을 어느 라디오 프로그램에서 광고할까요?
(A) 30초짜리 광고요.
(B) 방송국에서 들었어요.
(C) <The Morning Show>는 어때요?

10 영국 ⇄ 호주

Would you like a ride to the company dinner?
(A) The main dish will be served in five minutes.
(B) Thanks, that'd be great.
(C) The bike ride this Saturday.

회식 장소까지 태워 드릴까요?
(A) 메인 요리는 5분 후에 나옵니다.
(B) 고마워요, 그게 좋겠어요.
(C) 이번 주 토요일에 자전거 타러 가요.

11 미국 ⇄ 미국

Why was the meeting postponed today?
(A) To tomorrow morning.
(B) I already went to the post office.
(C) Because the rooms are fully booked.

오늘 회의가 왜 연기되었나요?
(A) 내일 아침으로요.
(B) 제가 이미 우체국에 다녀왔어요.
(C) 방들이 모두 예약됐기 때문이에요.

12 미국 ⇄ 호주

Do you enjoy working as a computer engineer?
(A) No, I set up the software yesterday.
(B) Well, my pay is pretty competitive.
(C) The newest engine.

컴퓨터 기술자로 일하는 걸 즐기시나요?
(A) 아니요, 어제 소프트웨어를 설치했어요.
(B) 음, 급여가 꽤 높거든요.
(C) 최신 엔진이요.

13 호주 ⇄ 미국

Are you a resident of the city or a visitor?
(A) I'm from out of town.
(B) The vice president.
(C) I've never visited there.

시 주민이신가요 아니면 방문객이신가요?
(A) 저는 타지에서 왔어요.
(B) 부사장님이요.
(C) 저는 그곳을 가본 적이 없어요.

14 영국 ⇄ 미국

Didn't a new grocery store open nearby?
(A) For some fruits and vegetables.
(B) Not that I know of.
(C) A seven-percent growth.

인근에 새 식료품점이 문을 열지 않았나요?
(A) 과일과 채소 때문에요.
(B) 제가 알기로는 아니에요.
(C) 7퍼센트 성장이요.

15 미국 ⇄ 영국

This printer is on sale, right?
(A) No, but that one is.
(B) Yes, I repaired it yesterday.
(C) I'll print more labels.

이 프린터가 할인판매 중이죠, 그렇죠?
(A) 아니요, 하지만 저건 하고 있어요.
(B) 네, 제가 어제 수리했어요.
(C) 제가 라벨을 더 출력할게요.

16 미국 ⇄ 호주

Why isn't the new color photocopier being used?
(A) It hasn't been installed yet.
(B) Let's place the copies on the desk.
(C) No, we don't have the ink cartridge.

새로운 컬러복사기가 왜 사용되지 않나요?
(A) 아직 설치되지 않았어요.
(B) 복사본을 책상 위에 놓읍시다.
(C) 아니요, 잉크 카트리지가 없어요.

17 영국 ⇄ 미국

The air conditioner won't turn on.
(A) It was almost 30 degrees.
(B) I see. I'll have someone assist you.
(C) Some terms and conditions.

에어컨이 켜지지 않네요.
(A) 거의 30도였어요.
(B) 알겠습니다. 도와드릴 사람을 보내드리겠습니다.
(C) 일부 약관이요.

18 미국 ⇄ 호주

How long does it take to become a pharmacist?
(A) A new medicine for colds.
(B) Do you want to pursue a career in that field?
(C) Since the hospital was founded.

약사가 되는 데 시간이 얼마나 걸리나요?
(A) 감기 신약이요.
(B) 그 분야에서 경력을 쌓고 싶으세요?
(C) 병원이 설립된 후부터요.

19 미국 ⇄ 영국

The company dinner will start in ten minutes.
(A) I'm almost done with setting the tables.
(B) Yes, the seating chart.
(C) At the hotel downtown.

회사 만찬이 10분 후에 시작해요.
(A) 테이블 세팅이 거의 마무리됐어요.
(B) 네, 좌석 배치도요.
(C) 시내 호텔에서요.

20 호주 ⇄ 미국

You didn't bring your laptop with you, did you?
(A) No, but Sam brought his.
(B) Around two thousand dollars.
(C) Many high-tech features.

노트북 안 가져오셨죠, 그렇죠?
(A) 네, 그런데 Sam은 가져왔어요.
(B) 2,000달러 정도요.
(C) 여러 가지 첨단 기능이요.

21 미국 ⇄ 미국

Who has the list of attendees for the annual conference?
(A) Around 200 people are scheduled to attend.
(B) In Conference Hall D.
(C) Natsumi has them.

누가 연례 콘퍼런스 참석자 명단을 가지고 있나요?
(A) 200명 정도 참석할 예정이에요.
(B) 콘퍼런스 홀 D에서요.
(C) Natsumi가 가지고 있어요.

22 영국 ⇄ 호주

Didn't you hire the candidates you met with last week?
(A) Yes, the fee was much higher.
(B) Please confirm the date.
(C) They didn't have enough experience.

지난주에 만난 지원자들은 채용하지 않으셨나요?
(A) 네, 비용이 훨씬 더 비쌌어요.
(B) 날짜를 확인해 주세요.
(C) 그들은 경력이 부족했어요.

23 미국 ⇄ 영국

When can I buy tickets to the jazz concert?
(A) They go on sale tomorrow.
(B) At the box office.
(C) Yes, I heard about it last week.

재즈 콘서트 티켓들을 언제 살 수 있나요?
(A) 내일 판매를 시작해요.
(B) 매표소에서요.
(C) 네, 지난주에 이야기 들었어요.

24 미국 ⇄ 미국

What do you think is the problem with the engine?
(A) It's important to use good motor oil.
(B) You're right. That's exactly it.
(C) OK. I'll call the repairperson right away.

엔진에 어떤 문제가 있는 것 같으세요?
(A) 좋은 엔진 오일을 쓰는 게 중요해요.
(B) 맞아요. 바로 그거예요.
(C) 알았어요. 제가 바로 수리공을 부를게요.

25 미국 ⇄ 미국

Where did Brian save the article draft?
(A) It's in the online shared folder.
(B) On the third Monday of the month.
(C) Probably as early as next week.

Brian이 기사 초안을 어디에 저장했어요?
(A) 온라인 공유 폴더에 있어요.
(B) 셋째 주 월요일이요.
(C) 이르면 다음 주일 거예요.

26 호주 ⇄ 미국

The factory plans to stop manufacturing this TV model soon.
(A) That's because of low sales.
(B) The inspector will visit the factory today.
(C) I watch the news on TV every morning.

공장에서 이 TV 모델 생산을 조만간 중단할 예정이에요.
(A) 판매가 저조해서 그렇군요.
(B) 오늘 검사관이 공장을 방문할 거예요.
(C) 저는 매일 아침 TV로 뉴스를 시청해요.

27 미국 ⇄ 미국

May I help you place your bags in the overhead compartment?
(A) There's plenty of room under my seat.
(B) I've unlocked my suitcases.
(C) I don't like to wear hats.

가방을 짐칸에 올리는 걸 도와드릴까요?
(A) 제 자리 밑에 공간이 많아요.
(B) 제가 여행 가방 잠금을 풀었어요.
(C) 전 모자 쓰는 걸 안 좋아해요.

28 영국 ⇄ 미국

Would you rather go to an art gallery or a sports game this weekend?
(A) A modern art collection.
(B) I believe it's the following weekend.
(C) There's a game I want to watch.

이번 주말에 미술관에 갈래요, 아니면 스포츠 경기 보러 갈래요?
(A) 현대 미술 컬렉션이요.
(B) 다음 주말인 걸로 알고 있어요.
(C) 제가 보고 싶은 경기가 있어요.

29 호주 ⇄ 영국

When is the board of directors meeting?
(A) Sorry. I misplaced mine.
(B) They already cast their votes.
(C) That's a generous offer.

이사회 회의가 언제죠?
(A) 죄송해요. 제 걸 잃어버렸어요.
(B) 이미 투표하셨어요.
(C) 후한 제안이네요.

30 미국 ⇄ 미국

Will our travel company provide more all-day tours this summer?
(A) I really need to take a break from work.
(B) I'd love to go visit.
(C) Our customers prefer shorter ones.

올여름에는 여행사에서 종일 관광 제공을 늘릴까요?
(A) 전 정말 휴가가 간절해요.
(B) 너무 가고 싶어요.
(C) 우리 고객들은 짧은 관광을 선호해요.

31 미국 ⇄ 호주

Do you have Maxine's extension number?
(A) To some extent.
(B) Yes, they found some.
(C) She is on leave.

Maxine 내선 번호 아세요?
(A) 어느 정도는요.
(B) 네, 그들이 일부 찾아냈어요.
(C) 그녀는 휴가 중이에요.

PART 3

P. 35

미국 ⇄ 영국

Questions 32-34 refer to the following conversation.

M: Hello, you've reached the Johnson County Museum of History. This is Larry.

W: Hi, Larry. This is Anita from the *Blue Valley Sun Times*. I'm writing an article in our newspaper about an old trolley line, and I'd like to use one of the pictures from your exhibit.(32)/(33)

M: That should be fine. Could you tell me the exact title of the picture you want to use?(34) I'll get approval and then email you a digital copy.

32-34번은 다음 대화에 관한 문제입니다.

남: 안녕하세요, Johnson 카운티 역사박물관입니다. 저는 Larry라고 합니다.

여: 안녕하세요, Larry. 저는 <Blue Valley Sun Times>의 Anita입니다. 제가 저희 신문에 실을 옛 시가 전차 노선에 관한 기사를 쓰고 있는데, 이곳에 전시된 사진들 중 한 장을 사용하고 싶어요.(32)/(33)

남: 괜찮을 겁니다. 제게 사용하고 싶으신 사진의 정확한 제목을 알려 주시겠어요?(34) 제가 승인을 받고 나서 디지털 파일을 이메일로 보내 드리겠습니다.

32 여자는 어디서 일하는가?
(A) 공립대학교에서
(B) 여행사에서
(C) 미술관에서
(D) 신문사에서

33 여자는 왜 전화하는가?
(A) 장비 이용을 요청하기 위해
(B) 구매에 관한 불만을 제기하기 위해
(C) 사진 이용에 대한 관심을 표하기 위해
(D) 출간물 몇 부를 주문하기 위해

34 남자가 여자에게 무엇을 요청하는가?
(A) 물건 이름
(B) 이메일 주소
(C) 신분증명서
(D) 제품 코드

미국 ⇄ 미국

Questions 35-37 refer to the following conversation.

M: Florence, I just got a message from Quincy Concert Hall. Apparently, they'll be closed for some urgent repairs. We'll have to find another place for our orchestra rehearsals.(35)

W: Oh, no. Well, at least we didn't transport all our instruments there yet. You know, I've practiced at Deanville Cultural Center before.(36)

M: But that place is an hour drive from downtown.(36) I don't think our members would like that.

W: Ah, you're right. Hmm... My brother is in event planning. I'll ask him if he knows of a more suitable venue.(37)

35-37번은 다음 대화에 관한 문제입니다.

남: Florence, 제가 방금 Quincy 콘서트홀에서 메시지를 받았어요.

보아하니, 긴급 보수로 폐쇄될 건가 봐요. 저희 오케스트라 리허설 장소로 다른 곳을 찾아봐야 해요.(35)

여: 아, 어떡해요. 음, 적어도 우리가 아직 악기를 옮겨놓지는 않았네요. 저기, 제가 예전에 Deanville 문화 센터에서 연습했었어요.(36)

남: 근데 그곳은 시내에서 차로 한 시간 거리잖아요.(36) 단원들이 좋아할 것 같지 않은데요.

여: 아, 그렇네요. 흠... 제 동생이 행사 기획 쪽에 있어요. 더 적당한 장소를 아는지 물어볼게요.(37)

35 화자들은 무엇을 하려고 준비하고 있는가?
(A) 영상을 녹화하려고
(B) 음악 축제에 가려고
(C) 연극에서 공연하려고
(D) 리허설하려고

36 남자는 Deanville 문화 센터에 관하여 뭐라고 말하는가?
(A) 음향 상태가 안 좋다.
(B) 너무 좁다.
(C) 예산을 초과한다.
(D) 도시에서 멀다.

37 여자는 다음에 무엇을 하겠는가?
(A) 배송 주소를 변경할 것이다
(B) 행사 일정을 다시 잡을 것이다
(C) 가족에게 연락할 것이다
(D) 행사장을 방문할 것이다

호주 ⇄ 미국

Questions 38-40 refer to the following conversation.

M: Stephanie, regarding the conference here next month. We were going to send a few interns down.(38) However, it has been announced that Kolo Partners will be unveiling their new engine there. Tickets are selling out quickly now.(39)

W: I can see why. That would make a great piece. I suppose we should send some of our senior writers down instead of the interns.(38) Also, is Mr. Ashman available? He has the most knowledge on Kolo Partners.

M: Right. Mr. Ashman would have been perfect, but he's currently on leave. Let's send our most experienced people down to the conference instead.(40)

38-40번은 다음 대화에 관한 문제입니다.

남: Stephanie, 다음 달 여기서 있을 회의 말이에요. 저희가 인턴 몇 명을 보내려고 했었어요.(38) 그런데, Kolo Partners가 그 자리에서 자사 신규 엔진을 공개할 예정이라고 발표했어요. 지금 표가 빠르게 팔리고 있고요.(39)

여: 그렇겠네요. 멋진 기사가 나오겠어요. 우리도 인턴 대신 선임 기자를 보내야겠어요.(38) 그리고, Mr. Ashman이 시간 되나요? 그가 Kolo Partners에 대해서 가장 많이 알고 있어요.

남: 맞아요. Mr. Ashman이 가면 더할 나위 없겠지만, 현재 휴가 중이에요. 대신, 가장 경험 많은 사람들을 회의에 보냅시다.(40)

38 화자들은 어느 분야에 일하겠는가?
(A) 언론계
(B) 기술
(C) 의료
(D) 재무

39 왜 많은 사람들이 회의 참석에 관심을 보이는가?
(A) 저명한 잡지에 실릴 것이다.
(B) 업계 리더가 참석할 것이다.
(C) 인맥을 쌓을 기회가 있을 것이다.
(D) 제품 발표가 있을 것이다.

40 누가 회의에 참석하게 되겠는가?
(A) 경험이 가장 많은 직원들
(B) 현재 해외에 있지 않은 직원들
(C) 상품에 대해 가장 많이 아는 직원들
(D) 입장료를 지불할 의향이 있는 직원들

영국 ⇄ 미국 ⇄ 호주

Questions 41-43 refer to the following conversation with three speakers.

W: I hope your stay at our inn was pleasant. Did you enjoy your time here?**(41)**

M1: We did. This place made us really comfortable during our business trip. But the fitness room seemed a bit outdated. **Have you considered replacing the old exercise machines with new ones?(42)**

M2: Yeah, I imagine other guests have complained that the machines are too old.**(42)**

W: We've actually been meaning to renovate that facility, but I'm not sure when that will be. **My manager might be able to give you a better answer.(43)**

M2: Ah, yes. I'd like to know about that before we leave today.

W: OK, I'll give her a call and see if she can come down now to talk to you.**(43)**

M1: Thank you.

41-43번은 다음 세 화자의 대화에 관한 문제입니다.

여: 저희 호텔 투숙이 즐거우셨기를 바랍니다. 이곳에서 좋은 시간 보내셨나요?**(41)**

남1: 네. 이곳은 출장 기간 동안 저희를 정말 편안하게 해줬어요. 그런데 헬스장은 약간 구식인 것 같았어요. **오래된 운동기구들을 새 걸로 교체하는 걸 고려해보셨나요?(42)**

남2: 네. 다른 투숙객들도 장비가 너무 낡았다고 불평했을 것 같아요.**(42)**

여: 안 그래도 그 시설을 개조하려고 하는데, 그게 언제가 될지는 모르겠습니다. **저희 지배인이 더 나은 답변을 드릴 수 있을지도 모르겠네요.(43)**

남2: 아, 그렇군요. 오늘 떠나기 전에 알고 싶어요.

여: 알겠습니다, 지금 내려서 손님과 이야기 나눌 수 있는지 전화해보겠습니다.**(43)**

남1: 고맙습니다.

41 여자는 누구겠는가?
(A) 호텔 직원
(B) 비행기 승무원
(C) 여행사 직원
(D) 헬스 트레이너

42 남자들은 무엇에 관하여 문의하는가?
(A) 항공권 구매하는 것
(B) 수업 등록하는 것
(C) 장비 개선하는 것
(D) 시설 견학하는 것

43 여자는 무엇을 하겠다고 제안하는가?
(A) 가격을 할인해 주겠다고
(B) 송장을 인쇄하겠다고
(C) 상사에게 연락하겠다고
(D) 지도를 제공해 주겠다고

호주 ⇄ 미국

Questions 44-46 refer to the following conversation.

M: You know, **with the move here to our new company headquarters, this past week has been completely exhausting.(44)**

W: You can say that again. By the way, **did you see my day planner?(45)** It's dark blue, and I usually keep it on my desk. I'm pretty sure I packed it, but I can't find it in any of our boxes.

M: No, sorry, I haven't. But you know what? **I'm also missing some things.(45)**

W: Oh, wait. When I came into work today, **I saw a few boxes by the reception desk.(46)** Maybe our things are in those boxes.

M: Let's go find out.**(46)**

44-46번은 다음 대화에 관한 문제입니다.

남: 저기, **신규 본사로 이사하느라 지난주엔 완전히 진이 다 빠졌어요.(44)**

여: 동감이에요. 그나저나, **제 수첩 보셨어요?(45)** 남색이고, 제가 항상 책상 위에 두던 거요. 분명히 챙겨왔는데, 상자 아무 데도 안 보여요.

남: 아니요, 죄송해요, 못 봤어요. 근데 있잖아요. **저도 물건 몇 개가 안 보여요.(45)**

여: 아, 잠시만요. 제가 오늘 출근하면서 **접수처에서 상자 몇 개를 봤어요.(46)** 우리 물건들이 그 상자에 있을지도 몰라요.

남: 가서 알아봅시다.**(46)**

44 지난주 화자들의 회사는 무엇을 했는가?
(A) 주요 해외 고객을 확보했다.
(B) 부사장을 새로 임명했다.
(C) 본사를 이전했다.
(D) 조직 개편을 단행했다.

45 화자들은 어떤 문제점을 언급하는가?
(A) 출장이 연기되어야 한다.
(B) 사무실 개조 공사가 완료되지 않았다.
(C) 일부 직원을 내보내야 한다.
(D) 일부 개인 소지품이 분실됐다.

46 화자들은 다음으로 어디로 갈 것인가?
(A) 보관 공간으로
(B) 접수처로
(C) 건물 주차장으로
(D) 회의실로

미국 ⇄ 미국

Questions 47-49 refer to the following conversation.

W: What a relief! **I finally got around to changing the wallpaper in my living room last weekend.(47)** The entire space looks so different now. It really reflects my style.

M: Wow, I've been thinking of redoing my walls too. Do you have any advice?

W: Well, it's pretty straightforward. But I think the quality of wallpaper paste makes a big difference. **I have a lot of extra paste at home, so I can send it to you this afternoon.**(48)

M: That'd be great, thanks! It'll inspire me to get the job done. Now I just need to choose a new wallpaper.

W: Oh I recommend using this website. They have a lot of options, **and once you choose your wallpaper, they can deliver it the next day.**(49)

47-49번은 다음 대화에 관한 문제입니다.

여: 마음이 놓이네요! **드디어 지난 주말 거실 벽지까지 바꿨어요.**(47) 이제 전체 공간이 완전히 달라 보여요. 정말 제 스타일이에요.

남: 와, 저도 벽지를 다시 하려고 계속 생각 중이었어요. 알려줄 팁 같은 게 있어요?

여: 음, 꽤 간단해요. 근데 제 생각엔 벽지 반죽의 질에서 큰 차이가 생기는 것 같아요. **집에 반죽 여분이 많으니까, 제가 오늘 오후에 보내 줄게요.**(48)

남: 그럼 정말 좋죠, 고마워요! 일을 끝내는 데 자극이 될 거예요. 이제 새 벽지만 고르면 되네요.

여: 아, 이 웹사이트를 이용해 보세요. 옵션이 엄청 많고, **벽지를 고르면 다음 날 배송해줘요.**(49)

47 여자는 주말에 무엇을 했는가?
(A) 뒷마당에 창고를 설치했다.
(B) 새로운 조리법을 배웠다.
(C) 사진을 촬영했다.
(D) 새로운 벽지를 설치했다.

48 여자는 오늘 오후에 남자에게 무엇을 보낼 것인가?
(A) 제품
(B) 설명서
(C) 할인 코드
(D) 상점 주소

49 여자는 어떤 장점을 언급하는가?
(A) 주문 제작 디자인
(B) 방수 재료
(C) 빠른 배송
(D) 낮은 가격

영국 ⇄ 호주

Questions 50-52 refer to the following conversation.

W: Hey, Angelo. How are you coming along with the new sneakers?

M: Pretty well. **I've completed the sketch of the running shoes, and I'm really pleased with the unique patterns.** (50) They're going to look great.

W: Glad to hear that. What about the men's formal wear? **Did you make a new design for the boots?**(51)

M: Oh, **Tina told me not to make design changes to the boots.**(51)

W: Really? Didn't we decide to revise the design? We haven't been able to sell a lot of our men's boots lately. **I'll email our recent sales figures to Tina.** (52) She'll probably want to reconsider after looking them over.

50-52번은 다음 대화에 관한 문제입니다.

여: 저기, Angelo. 새 운동화는 어떻게 진행되고 있어요?

남: 꽤 순조로워요. 운동화 스케치를 완성했는데 독특한 무늬가 아주 마음에 들어요.(50) 아주 근사할 거예요.

여: 잘됐군요. 남성 정장은 어떤가요? **부츠 디자인을 새로 했나요?**(51)

남: 아, **Tina가 부츠는 디자인을 바꾸지 말라고 하더군요.**(51)

여: 그래요? 디자인을 수정하기로 하지 않았나요? 최근에 남성용 부츠를 많이 못 팔았잖아요. 제가 Tina에게 최근 매출 수치를 이메일로 보낼게요.(52) 그걸 살펴보고 나면 아마 재고해 볼지도 몰라요.

50 남자는 신발의 어떤 특징에 만족하는가?
(A) 편안한 밑창
(B) 친환경 소재
(C) 비용
(D) 무늬

51 남자는 왜 "Tina가 부츠는 디자인을 바꾸지 말라고 하더군요"라고 말하는가?
(A) 예산이 한정돼 있다는 점을 언급하기 위해
(B) Tina가 스케치를 수정할 것임을 알리기 위해
(C) 제품이 잘 팔리고 있다는 점을 지적하기 위해
(D) 어떤 업무를 하지 않는 이유를 대기 위해

52 여자는 Tina에게 무엇을 보낼 것인가?
(A) 매출 자료
(B) 새 디자인
(C) 초대 손님 명단
(D) 프로젝트 기획안

미국 ⇄ 영국

Questions 53-55 refer to the following conversation.

M: I'm Tommy, and I'll be helping you with your loan request. First, please tell me why you need a loan.

W: My company's earrings were recently featured in an international fashion magazine. Since then, **many customers overseas have wanted to purchase my products. I would like to open a new website to cater to them in time for the holiday season.**(53)

M: I'm sorry, but you'll have to wait a few months for our standard business loan. However, **there are other financing options that wouldn't take as long. Why don't you apply for these instead?**(54)

W: Sure. **What's the application process like?**(55) I'm not too familiar with this.

M: Don't worry. I'll be here to help you.

53-55번은 다음 대화에 관한 문제입니다.

남: 저는 Tommy라 하고요, 고객님의 대출 신청을 도와드리겠습니다. 우선, 대출이 필요한 이유를 말씀해 주세요.

여: 저희 회사의 귀걸이가 최근 국제 패션 잡지에 실렸습니다. 그 이후로, 많은 해외 고객분들이 저희 제품을 구매하길 원했어요. 휴가철에 맞춰 그들을 만족시키기 위해 새 웹사이트를 개설하고 싶습니다.(53)

남: 죄송합니다만, 저희의 일반 사업 대출을 받으시려면 몇 달 기다리셔야 합니다. 하지만, 그만큼 오래는 안 걸릴 다른 금융 옵션들도 있습니다. 대신 이런 상품들을 신청해보는 건 어떠세요?(54)

여: 그럼요. **지원 절차는 어떻게 되나요?**(55) 제가 이런 걸 잘 몰라서요.

남: 걱정하지 마세요. 제가 도와 드리겠습니다.

53 여자의 회사는 무엇을 제공할 계획인가?
(A) 더 빨라진 국제 배송
(B) 무료 설치
(C) 온라인 쇼핑
(D) 맞춤형 디자인 서비스

54 남자는 여자에게 무엇을 해보라고 제안하는가?
(A) 다른 금융 옵션을 선택해보라고
(B) 다른 지사를 방문해보라고
(C) 새 은행 계좌를 개설해보라고
(D) 세무 고문에게 문의해보라고

55 여자가 남자에게 무엇에 관하여 물어보는가?
(A) 납부 일정
(B) 회원 신청서
(C) 직원 안내서
(D) 신청 절차

Questions 56-58 refer to the following conversation with three speakers.

M1: The blueprint for Spier Hotel's ground floor renovations looks great.**(56)** I do have one suggestion, though. The entrance doors should be enlarged to accommodate more foot traffic.

M2: Hmm... That's a good point, Eddie. Let me make that adjustment.

W: Excuse me, you two. I'm sorry for the interruption. I wanted to let you know that Mr. Benson from Spier Hotel just contacted us. He wants to postpone the meeting to tomorrow morning instead.**(57)**

M2: Thank you for letting us know, Sheryl. Eddie, that gives us more time to go over our ideas. Why don't we grab something to eat now and make some changes to the plan afterwards?**(58)**

M1: Yeah, let's do that.**(58)**

56-58번은 다음 세 화자의 대화에 관한 문제입니다.
남1: Spier 호텔의 1층 개조용 설계도가 아주 훌륭해 보이네요.**(56)** 다만, 한 가지 제안이 있어요. 유동 인구를 더 많이 수용하려면 출입구가 더 커져야 해요.

남2: 흠... 좋은 지적이에요, Eddie. 그렇게 수정할게요.

여: 두 분, 실례합니다. 방해해서 죄송해요. Spier 호텔의 Mr. Benson께서 방금 연락하셨다고 알려드리고 싶었어요. 회의를 내일 오전으로 연기하고 싶어하세요.**(57)**

남2: 알려줘서 고마워요, Sheryl. Eddie, 그러면 우리가 아이디어를 검토할 시간이 좀 더 생기네요. 지금 뭐 좀 먹고 나서 도면을 수정할까요?**(58)**

남1: 네, 그렇게 해요.**(58)**

56 화자들은 어떤 업계에 일하겠는가?
(A) 금융
(B) 소매
(C) 서비스
(D) 건축

57 여자는 남자들을 왜 방해하는가?
(A) 회의 위치에 대해 물어보기 위해
(B) 변경된 일정에 대해 알려주기 위해

(C) 사무실 장비를 빌리기 위해
(D) 프로젝트를 지원해 주기 위해

58 남자들은 다음에 무엇을 할 것인가?
(A) 식사하러 갈 것이다
(B) 고객 사무실을 방문할 것이다
(C) 견적서를 살펴볼 것이다
(D) 동료에게 연락할 것이다

Questions 59-61 refer to the following conversation.

W: Welcome to Rosaline's Garden Care. We offer customers a variety of landscaping services.**(59)** We're currently providing complimentary consultations on how to prepare your lawn for the cold weather.

M: Oh, can you give me more details?

W: Sure. Once you set up a time and date, a specialist will come by your home to check out the lawn.**(60)**

M: Well, it's going to be winter soon.**(60)** But the thing is, I'm going to be working overtime this entire month, so I don't know if I can make the time.

W: That's OK. We have flexible hours to accommodate our customers.

M: Hmm... I'll get back to you on this.

W: All right. Here's a pamphlet with complete details about our business.**(61)**

59-61번은 다음 대화에 관한 문제입니다.
여: Rosaline 정원 관리에 오신 것을 환영합니다. 저희는 고객 여러분께 다양한 조경 서비스를 제공합니다.**(59)** 저희가 현재 추운 날씨에 여러분의 잔디를 어떻게 대비해야 하는지에 관한 무료 상담을 제공하고 있습니다.

남: 아, 더 자세히 말씀해 주시겠어요?

여: 그럼요. 일단 시간과 날짜를 정하시면, 전문가가 귀하의 댁에 방문해 잔디를 점검해드립니다.**(60)**

남: 음, 곧 겨울이 올 거예요.**(60)** 그런데 문제는 제가 이번 달 내내 야근을 할 거라서, 시간을 낼 수 있을지 모르겠다는 거예요.

여: 괜찮습니다. 저희는 고객님들의 시간에 맞춰 유연하게 운영합니다.

남: 음... 이 문제에 대해 다시 연락드릴게요.

여: 알겠습니다. 이건 저희 업체에 관한 전체 내용이 들어있는 팸플릿입니다.**(61)**

59 화자들은 어디에 있는가?
(A) 스키 리조트에
(B) 철물점에
(C) 제조 공장에
(D) 조경 회사에

60 남자는 왜 "곧 겨울이 올 거예요"라고 말하는가?
(A) 다가오는 마감 기한을 지적하기 위해
(B) 여행으로 들떠 있음을 나타내기 위해
(C) 서비스에 관심이 있음을 보이기 위해
(D) 새 제품을 주문하기 위해

61 여자는 남자에게 무엇을 주는가?
(A) 프로젝트 포트폴리오
(B) 작업 일정
(C) 샘플 계약서
(D) 정보 팸플릿

Questions 62-64 refer to the following conversation and schedule.

W: Mr. Evans, this is Ivy Dental Clinic. We have you scheduled for a 2 P.M. appointment with Dr. Baker.**(62)**

M: Yes. Is my appointment still on?

W: We would like to extend our deepest apologies. **Our clinic experienced a power cut, so many of our appointments got pushed back.(63)** Would you be free to come in at 4 P.M.?

M: Unfortunately, no. Would I be able to come in on Thursday?

W: Let me check our schedule. Thursday is free for us. Is there a particular time you would like to come in?

M: **I'll be in the area past 11, but I have a meeting at 1.(64)**

62-64번은 다음 대화와 일정표에 관한 문제입니다.

여: Mr. Evans, Ivy 치과입니다. Dr. Baker께 오후 2시로 예약하셨죠.**(62)**

남: 맞아요. 예약은 그대로인가요?

여: 깊은 사과의 말씀 드립니다. **저희 병원이 정전이 돼서, 예약이 많이 밀렸습니다.(63)** 오후 4시에 오실 수 있으신가요?

남: 불행히도, 아니요. 목요일에 갈 수 있을까요?

여: 일정을 확인해 보겠습니다. 목요일 가능합니다. 원하시는 특정한 시간이 있으신가요?

남: **11시 넘어서 그 지역에 있을 건데, 1시에 회의가 있습니다.(64)**

Ivy 치과 목요일 일정				
	Dr. Sharp	Dr. Baker	Dr. Olson	Dr. Ross
오전 10시	X	예약없음	X	예약없음
오전 11시	X	X	X	X
오후 12시	X	X	X	예약없음
오후 1시	예약없음	X	예약없음	X
오후 2시	X	X	예약없음	X

62 여자는 어디서 일하겠는가?
(A) 치과에서
(B) 정부 기관에서
(C) 극장에서
(D) 공장에서

63 왜 예약 일정을 변경해야 하는가?
(A) 진료가 예상보다 길어졌다.
(B) 결제 시스템이 고장 났다.
(C) 계획에 없던 정전이 있었다.
(D) 일부 직원이 지각했다.

64 시각 자료를 보시오. 남자는 누구를 보겠는가?
(A) Dr. Sharp
(B) Dr. Baker
(C) Dr. Olson
(D) Dr. Ross

Questions 65-67 refer to the following conversation and map.

M: Good morning. Welcome to Lange and Associates.

W: Hello. My name is Tin Yan Lee. I have an appointment with Lucas Doyle at 11. **I'm here for an interview with him for an accounting position.(65)**

M: Let me check the system for your appointment. Ah, here it is. Mr. Doyle's office is on the fifth floor, room 518. The elevators are on your right. But **don't use the elevator closest to the entrance.(66)** We've been having some problems with that one today.

W: Thanks for your help.

M: I'll give Mr. Doyle a call and let him know that you're heading upstairs. But before you do, **I need you to sign in as a visitor. Do you have a picture ID?(67)**

65-67번은 다음 대화와 지도에 관한 문제입니다.

남: 좋은 아침입니다. Lange and Associates에 오신 걸 환영합니다.

여: 안녕하세요. 저는 Tin Yan Lee입니다. 제가 11시에 Lucas Doyle과 약속이 있어요. **회계직 면접을 보러 왔습니다.(65)**

남: 시스템에 예약이 있는지 확인해 볼게요. 아, 여기 있네요. Mr. Doyle의 사무실은 5층, 518호예요. 엘리베이터는 오른편에 있어요. 그런데 **출입구에 가장 가까운 엘리베이터는 이용하지 마세요.(66)** 그 엘리베이터는 오늘 문제가 좀 있어요.

여: 도와주셔서 감사합니다.

남: 제가 Mr. Doyle께 전화해서 당신이 올라가고 있다고 알릴게요. 그런데 가시기 전에, **방문객으로 서명을 해주셔야 해요. 사진이 있는 신분증 있으세요?(67)**

65 여자는 왜 Lange and Associates에 방문하고 있는가?
(A) 고장 난 장비를 수리하기 위해
(B) 금융 서류를 검토하기 위해
(C) 면접에 참석하기 위해
(D) 세금 환급을 신청하기 위해

66 시각 자료를 보시오. 여자는 어떤 엘리베이터를 피해야 하는가?
(A) 엘리베이터 A
(B) 엘리베이터 B
(C) 엘리베이터 C
(D) 엘리베이터 D

67 여자는 다음에 무엇을 하겠는가?
(A) 자신의 신분증을 보여줄 것이다
(B) 신청서를 작성할 것이다
(C) 다시 바깥으로 나갈 것이다
(D) 동료에게 연락할 것이다

(C) 프레젠테이션이 지연되었다.

(D) 여자의 신용카드가 처리될 수 없다.

미국 ⇌ 미국

Questions 68-70 refer to the following conversation and sign.

W: Hello. I forgot to sign up in advance for today's convention. Is it still possible to participate?

M: That's fine. You can sign up right now.

W: Thanks. **I was worried that you wouldn't accept last-minute registrations.(68)** I'm here because I heard **Baymox, Inc. is giving a product demonstration on their newest tablet device.(69)** That's still happening, right?

M: Yes. **They will be doing that during the last morning session, following Professor Salinsky's presentation on the future of the Internet.(69)**

W: All right. Where is it being held?

M: You'll find a guide in this registration packet. Also, **it looks like we're all out of free convention pens. I'm sorry.(70)** We brought just enough pens for all the participants who registered ahead of time.

W: That's OK.

68-70번은 다음 대화와 표지판에 관한 문제입니다.

여: 안녕하세요. 제가 오늘 컨벤션에 사전 등록하는 것을 깜박했는데요.(68) 아직 참가하는 것이 가능한가요?

남: 괜찮습니다. 지금 바로 등록하실 수 있어요.

여: 고맙습니다. **막판 등록을 안 받아줄까 봐 걱정했어요.(68)** 저는 **Baymox사가 자사 최신 태블릿 기기의 시연을 한다고(69)** 들어서 여기 왔어요. 그대로 하는 거죠, 맞죠?

남: 맞아요. **Salinsky 교수의 인터넷의 미래에 관한 프레젠테이션에 뒤이어, 오전 마지막 세션에서 할 거예요.(69)**

여: 알겠습니다. 어디서 하나요?

남: 이 등록자료집에 안내서가 있습니다. 그리고, **저희 무료 컨벤션 펜이 다 떨어진 것 같네요. 죄송합니다.(70)** 저희가 미리 등록한 전체 참가자 수에 딱 맞게 펜을 가져왔거든요.

여: 괜찮아요.

Statesville 기술 컨벤션 [오전 세션]				
	Diamond 홀	Star 룸	Emerald 라운지	Crystal 강당
오전 7시 30분 - 오전 9시 30분	소셜 미디어 사용하기	인터넷의 미래(69)		
오전 9시 40분 - 오전 11시 40분		태블릿과 스마트폰(69)		온라인 결제 플랫폼

68 여자는 무엇에 관하여 우려했는가?
(A) 신분증을 가져오지 않은 것
(B) 중요한 자료집을 잃어버린 것
(C) 등록할 수 없는 것
(D) 잘못된 장소로 가는 것

69 시각 자료를 보시오. Baymox사는 어디서 제품 시연을 할 것인가?
(A) Diamond 홀에서
(B) Star 룸에서
(C) Emerald 라운지에서
(D) Crystal 강당에서

70 남자는 왜 사과하는가?
(A) 더 이상 무료 펜이 없다.
(B) 가이드에 있는 일부 정보가 잘못됐다.

PART 4

P. 39

영국

Questions 71-73 refer to the following advertisement.

W: **Need a quiet place to study or read? Come grab a beverage at Pearl Garden.(71)** We offer a range of specialist teas and coffees, brewed to perfection. **We have just opened another location in downtown Carville.(72)** The new location has private meeting rooms that can be booked using our online reservation system. Once you see our locations, you will be amazed. **Go on to our website and take a detailed look at the photos.(73)** We hope to serve you soon at Pearl Garden.

71-73번은 다음 광고에 관한 문제입니다.

여: 공부하거나 책을 읽을 조용한 장소가 필요하세요? Pearl Garden에 오셔서 음료를 드세요.(71) 저희는 전문가가 완벽하게 끓여낸 다양한 차와 커피를 제공합니다. 얼마 전 Carville 시내에 지점을 하나 더 개장했습니다.(72) 신규 지점에는 온라인 예약 시스템으로 예약할 수 있는 전용 회의실이 있습니다. 저희 지점을 보시면, 깜짝 놀랄 겁니다. 웹사이트에 방문하셔서 사진을 자세히 살펴보세요.(73) 조만간 Pearl Garden에서 모시게 되길 바랍니다.

71 무엇이 광고되고 있겠는가?
(A) 회의장
(B) 피트니스 센터
(C) 소매점
(D) 카페

72 화자에 따르면, 최근에 사업체에서 무엇을 했는가?
(A) 매니저를 추가로 채용했다.
(B) 새로운 지역으로 확장했다.
(C) 회사와 합병했다.
(D) 권위 있는 상을 받았다.

73 청자들은 왜 웹사이트를 방문하도록 권장받는가?
(A) 사진을 보기 위해
(B) 회원으로 등록하기 위해
(C) 경품을 타기 위해
(D) 서비스 목록을 보기 위해

미국

Questions 74-76 refer to the following telephone message.

W: Hi. This message is for the property manager of Begamot Plaza. I'm the owner of Leah's Gift Shop at the plaza, and **I'm calling regarding an issue I have with the store next door, CS Diner.(74)** As you know, there are garbage bins for each store at the back of the building. But the diner has been leaving their trash outside. Our customers have been complaining about the smell, and **I've already spoken to the restaurant owner,(75)** but the issue has not been resolved. **I'm going to take pictures of the trash left outside and send them to you today(76)** so that you can see for yourself. Please call me back when you get this message. Thank you.

74-76번은 다음 전화 메시지에 관한 문제입니다.

여: 안녕하세요. Begamot Plaza 건물 관리자님께 메시지 드립니다. 저는 플라자에 있는 Leah 선물 가게의 주인이며, **저희 옆 가게인 CS 식당과 문제가 있어 이에 관하여 전화 드립니다.(74)** 아시다시피, 건물 뒤에 각 상점의 쓰레기통이 있습니다. 하지만 그 식당은 쓰레기를 밖에 버리고 있어요. 저희 손님들이 냄새 때문에 불만을 제기해서, **제가 이미 식당 주인과도 이야기해봤지만,(75)** 이 문제가 해결되지 않았습니다. 직접 보실 수 있도록, **오늘 밖에 버려진 쓰레기 사진들을 찍어서 보내드리겠습니다.(76)** 이 메시지를 받으시면 제게 전화해주세요. 감사합니다.

74 화자는 왜 메시지를 남겼는가?
(A) 일정을 설명하기 위해
(B) 문제를 알리기 위해
(C) 회의를 잡기 위해
(D) 실수를 사과하기 위해

75 화자가 이미 무엇을 했는가?
(A) 사업주와 이야기했다
(B) 서비스 비용을 지불했다
(C) 테이블을 예약했다
(D) 장비를 확인했다

76 화자는 오늘 무엇을 하겠다고 하는가?
(A) 점검을 진행하겠다고
(B) 사진을 보내겠다고
(C) 상점을 개조하겠다고
(D) 사무실을 방문하겠다고

Questions 77-79 refer to the following announcement.

M: I've called this meeting to make an announcement. First, I'd like to thank you for your prompt feedback on the survey(77) we emailed to everyone last week. Based on your responses, the company has decided to renovate our offices to create more workspace for all employees. (78) However, as this will be a major remodeling project, employees will be asked to either relocate to the Middleborough branch or work from home for the next month.(79) Please let your manager know what you'd like to do as soon as possible. Also, direct any questions that you may have to the HR Department.

77-79번은 다음 공지에 관한 문제입니다.

남: 공지할 사항이 있어서 이번 회의를 소집했습니다. 우선 지난주에 모든 분께 이메일로 보내드린 **설문조사에 빠르게 답변해주셔서 감사합니다.(77)** 여러분의 응답에 근거하여 회사 측에서는 사무실을 개조하여 전 직원을 위한 업무공간을 더 만들기로 했습니다.(78) 그러나 이것은 대규모 리모델링 프로젝트가 될 것이기 때문에 **다음 달 동안은 직원 여러분께 Middleborough 지점으로 가시거나 재택 근무 하실 것을 부탁드립니다.(79)** 여러분 매니저에게 어떻게 하고 싶으신지 가능한 한 빨리 알려주시기 바랍니다. 또한, 혹시 질문이 있으면 인사부로 직접 문의해 주시기 바랍니다.

77 화자는 왜 청자들에게 고마워하는가?
(A) 초과근무를 해줘서
(B) 영업 목표를 달성해줘서
(C) 잡지를 구독해줘서
(D) 설문조사에 응답해줘서

78 회사는 무엇을 하기로 했는가?
(A) 소프트웨어를 업데이트하기로
(B) 행사를 연기하기로
(C) 회사 정책을 변경하기로
(D) 사무 공간을 확장하기로

79 화자에 따르면, 청자들은 다음 달에 무엇을 하겠는가?
(A) 고과평가에 참여할 것이다
(B) 다른 장소에서 근무할 것이다
(C) 신입직원들을 만날 것이다
(D) 무역박람회에 참가할 것이다

Questions 80-82 refer to the following talk.

M: My name is Min-ho, and during today's demonstration, I'll be introducing you all to the DX Portable Wireless Speaker.(80) Available at the end of this month, this speaker provides amazing sound quality in a lightweight and compact size. The feature that really makes this audio equipment unique, however, is that it is waterproof.(81) That means you can play your favorite music at the beach or the pool without any worries. The speaker will most likely sell out quickly, so I recommend that you reserve one in advance on the DX Electronics' website.(82) This will ensure that you receive it in a timely manner.

80-82번은 다음 담화에 관한 문제입니다.

남: 제 이름은 Min-ho이며, 저는 오늘 시연회에서 **DX 휴대용 무선 스피커를 여러분께 소개해 드리겠습니다.(80)** 이달 말부터 구입하실 수 있는 이 스피커는 가볍고 작은 크기로 놀라운 음질을 제공합니다. 그러나 이 오디오 장비를 정말 독특하게 만들어주는 특징은 **방수 제품이라는 점입니다.(81)** 여러분이 가장 좋아하는 음악을 아무 걱정 없이 해변이나 수영장에서 틀 수 있다는 걸 의미합니다. 이 스피커는 금세 매진될 가능성이 크므로 **DX 전자 웹사이트에서 사전 예약하실 것을 권장해드립니다.(82)** 이렇게 하면, 물건을 빠른 시일 내 받아보실 수 있을 거예요.

80 무엇이 논의되고 있는가?
(A) 최첨단 스포츠 시계
(B) 무선 오디오 장치
(C) 디지털카메라
(D) 휴대용 히터

81 화자에 따르면, 제품에 관하여 무엇이 특별한가?
(A) 에너지 효율성이 높다.
(B) 착용하기 편하다.
(C) 방수가 된다.
(D) 비싸지 않다.

82 화자는 무엇을 하라고 권장하는가?
(A) 온라인으로 제품 예약하라고
(B) 사용 안내 프로그램 시청하라고
(C) 연장된 품질보증 구입하라고
(D) 제품을 직접 찾아가라고

Questions 83-85 refer to the following excerpt from a meeting.

M: Now that you've been given an overview of our new electric car's functions, **we need to talk about how you're going to relay this information to car buyers.**(83) When describing electric automotive technology to customers, always keep this in mind: they probably have limited knowledge about it. Many people will especially want to learn more about the batteries that are in our vehicles.(84) Each of you will receive a diagram that will show how the battery works. Be sure to use it when explaining it to customers. Don't forget that your goal is to sell five electric vehicles a month. Try your best to achieve this quota.(85)

83-85번은 다음 회의 발췌록에 관한 문제입니다.

남: 우리의 신형 전기차 기능에 대한 개요를 들으셨으니, **여러분이 이 정보를 자동차 구매자에게 어떻게 전달할지에 대해 이야기를 나눠야 합니다.**(83) 전기 자동차 기술을 고객에게 설명할 때에, 항상 이 점을 명심하십시오: 그들이 이 분야에 대해 가진 지식은 한정적일 겁니다. 많은 사람들이 우리 차량에 탑재된 배터리에 대해 특히 더 알고 싶어 할 겁니다.(84) 여러분 모두 배터리 작동원리를 보여주는 도표를 받으실 겁니다. 고객에게 설명할 때 꼭 사용하도록 하세요. **매달 전기차 다섯 대를 판매하는 게 목표라는 걸 잊지 마세요. 이 할당량을 맞출 수 있게 최선을 다해 주세요.**(85)

83 담화는 누구를 대상으로 하겠는가?
(A) 자동차 정비공
(B) 공장 직원
(C) 영업사원
(D) 컴퓨터 기술자

84 화자가 "그들이 이 분야에 대해 가진 지식은 한정적일 겁니다"라고 말할 때 무엇을 내비치는가?
(A) 청자들이 주제를 명확하게 설명해야 한다.
(B) 청자들이 동영상을 보여주어야 한다.
(C) 청자들이 세미나에 참석해야 한다.
(D) 청자들이 전문가와 만나야 한다.

85 화자는 청자들에게 무엇을 상기시키는가?
(A) 직원들 채용하는 것
(B) 할당량 채우는 것
(C) 문서 출력하는 것
(D) 비용 절감하는 것

영국

Questions 86-88 refer to the following instructions.

W: Welcome to my channel, "Shapes and Angles." **In today's video, I want to show you how to create your very own chair.**(86) The first thing you will need is to get some **pieces of wood.**(87) Ideally, you want the softest wood you can get your hands on as they are easier to work with. I read some comments on my last video asking which wood I like to use for my own pieces. That's a really great question, so thank you for asking.(88) I'll show you a few options today, from oak to mahogany, and discuss the major differences between them.

86-88번은 다음 설명에 관한 문제입니다.

여: 제 채널 '형태와 각도'에 잘 오셨습니다. 오늘 영상에서는 여러분이 각자 자신만의 의자를 만드는 방법을 알려드릴게요.(86) 첫 번째로 할 일은 나무 조각을 구하는 겁니다.(87) 이상적인 건, 작업하기 쉽기 때문에 최대한 부드러운 나무를 구하는 겁니다. 지난 영상의 댓글에서 제가 작품에 어떤 목재를 쓰는 걸 좋아하는지 묻는 글을 읽었어요. 아주 좋은 질문이에요, 질문해주셔서 감사합니다.(88) 제가 오늘 오크에서 마호가니까지 선택지를 몇 가지 보여드리고, 주요 차이점에 대해 설명해 드릴게요.

86 화자의 직업은 무엇이겠는가?
(A) 프로젝트 매니저
(B) 플로리스트
(C) 목수
(D) 전기 기술자

87 화자는 가장 먼저 무엇을 하라고 제안하는가?
(A) 치수 재라고
(B) 몇몇 자재 구하라고
(C) 장비 청소하라고
(D) 쇼핑 목록 만들라고

88 화자는 시청자에게 무엇을 해줘서 고마워하는가?
(A) 질문하는 것
(B) 대의에 기부하는 것
(C) 채널 홍보하는 것
(D) 사진 전송하는 것

미국

Questions 89-91 refer to the following tour information.

W: Here at the Endicott Museum of History, you will learn about the history of cinema from the earliest motion picture to the latest visual effects technology seen in most films today.(89) This permanent exhibit at our museum is displayed throughout ten rooms. However, **as our collection is constantly growing, you might see some artifacts without labels.**(90) Don't worry, though. **We have a curator in every room.**(90) Please feel free to take as many pictures as you want. You are also welcome to post them on your social media accounts.(91) Make sure to tag our museum.

89-91번은 다음 투어 정보에 관한 문제입니다.

여: 이곳 Endicott 역사박물관에서 여러분은 최초의 영화에서부터 오늘날 대부분의 영화에서 볼 수 있는 최신 시각효과 기법에 이르기까지 영화의 역사에 관해 배우게 됩니다.(89) 우리 박물관의 이 상설 전시는 10곳의 공간에 걸쳐 진열되어 있습니다. 하지만 저희 소장품이 계속 증가하고 있어서, 라벨이 안 붙은 작품을 보게 되실 수도 있습니다.(90) 하지만 걱정 마세요. 모든 공간에 큐레이터가 상주합니다.(90) 원하시는 만큼 편하게 사진을 찍으셔도 됩니다. 또한 얼마든지 소셜 미디어 계정에 올리셔도 됩니다.(91) 저희 박물관을 태그해 주시는 것 잊지 마세요.

89 청자들은 박물관에서 무엇을 배우게 되는가?
(A) 영화의 역사
(B) 인쇄술의 역사
(C) 언어의 역사
(D) 예술의 역사

90 화자는 "모든 공간에 큐레이터가 상주합니다"라고 말할 때 무엇을 의미하는가?
(A) 박물관이 방문객으로 북적인다.
(B) 박물관에 재정지원이 더 필요하다.
(C) 전시품이 보호된다.
(D) 청자들이 질문을 할 수 있다.

91 화자는 청자들에게 무엇을 하라고 청하는가?
(A) 전시 카탈로그를 참고하라고
(B) 사진을 올리라고
(C) 박물관에 기부하라고
(D) 기념품을 구입하라고

호주

Questions 92-94 refer to the following telephone message.

M: Good morning. I represent Covington's Tools and Supplies. We will be setting up a kiosk at an upcoming expo this fall and would like an eye-catching banner for our stand. (92) I was browsing through some of your creations on your online catalog, and it's completely different from what I've seen in the past! I knew that we had to go with you.(93) Our designated area isn't that big, but I don't think it will be much of an issue. I'll email you the dimensions of our kiosk. Would it be possible to get a price quote by the end of the week?(94)

92-94번은 다음 전화 메시지에 관한 문제입니다.

남: 안녕하세요. 저는 Covington's Tools and Supplies를 대표하고 있습니다. 저희가 올가을에 있을 박람회에 키오스크를 설치할 예정이어서 저희 가판대를 위해 눈길을 끄는 현수막을 원합니다.(92) 당신의 온라인 카탈로그에 있는 제작물들 몇 개를 훑어봤는데, 제가 이전에 봤던 거랑은 완전히 다르더라고요! 저는 우리가 당신과 함께해야 한다는 것을 알았어요.(93) 우리의 지정 구역이 그렇게 크지는 않지만, 크게 문제가 되진 않을 거라고 봐요. 제가 저희 키오스크의 치수를 이메일로 보내 드릴게요. 가격 견적을 이번 주까지 받아 볼 수 있을까요?(94)

92 화자의 회사는 올가을에 무엇을 할 계획인가?
(A) 박람회에 참석할 것이다
(B) 세미나를 진행할 것이다
(C) 인턴을 고용할 것이다
(D) 웹사이트를 출시할 것이다

93 화자는 "제가 이전에 봤던 거랑은 완전히 다르더라고요"라고 말할 때 무엇을 의미하는가?
(A) 결과에 기분이 상했다.
(B) 디자인에 만족해한다.
(C) 공구와 물건들을 옮기는 데 도움이 필요하다.
(D) 제안을 따르는 것에 대해 확신이 없다.

94 화자는 무엇을 요청하는가?
(A) 비용 견적
(B) 전화번호
(C) 크기 측정
(D) 샘플 카탈로그

미국

Questions 95-97 refer to the following speech and costume designs.

W: Good afternoon. Thank you very much to the South Bank Film Association for inviting me to speak about my work on the Victorian-era history piece, which premiered last month. It was an honor being able to work on this project because the director is somebody I've looked up to for a long time.(95) And because of his reputation for his strong attention to detail, much of my work involved conducting extensive research. For instance, the gloves you saw in the opening scene used a specific kind of leather not often seen in fashion.(96) In fact, I brought some behind-the-scenes footage of the design process.(97) After we take a look, I'll take some questions.

95-97번은 다음 연설과 의상 디자인에 관한 문제입니다.

여: 안녕하세요. 지난달 개봉한 빅토리아 시대 역사극에서 제가 한 작업에 관해 말할 자리를 마련해 주신 South Bank 영화 협회 측에 깊은 감사의 말씀 드립니다. 제가 오래도록 존경하던 분이 감독님이었기에 이 프로젝트에서 작업할 수 있어 영광이었습니다.(95) 게다가 그분이 엄청난 꼼꼼함으로 명성이 자자하셔서 제 작업의 상당 부분을 방대한 조사에 할애했습니다. 이를테면, 오프닝 장면에서 보신 장갑에는 의류에서 흔히 볼 수 없는 특수 가죽을 사용했습니다.(96) 실은 제가 디자인 과정을 담은 비하인드 영상을 가져왔어요.(97) 함께 본 후, 질문을 받겠습니다.

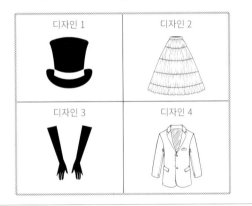

디자인 1	디자인 2
디자인 3	디자인 4

95 영화는 화자에게 왜 특별한가?
(A) 자신의 첫 번째 주요 작품이다.
(B) 친한 친구가 썼다.
(C) 언론에 의해 큰 기대를 받았다.
(D) 자신이 존경하는 사람이 감독했다.

96 시각 자료를 보시오. 화자는 어떤 디자인을 언급하는가?
(A) 디자인 1
(B) 디자인 2
(C) 디자인 3
(D) 디자인 4

97 다음에 무슨 일이 있겠는가?
(A) 영상이 공개될 것이다.
(B) 짧은 휴식 시간이 시작될 것이다.
(C) 몇몇 질문이 답변될 것이다.
(D) 몇몇 샘플을 돌려볼 것이다.

Questions 98-100 refer to the following announcement and list.

M: Hello, everyone. Part of my job as a manager at this restaurant is to notify you of any major changes.(98) We recently had a government official conduct a health and safety inspection.(99) We passed, but there were a few provisions that we should bear in mind. I've taken the liberty and created some new signs for us to put up as a reminder to all of us.(100) I do have to make one change to one of the areas. In addition to wearing protective gloves, staff will be required to dry their shoes before going inside.(100) The inspector will be following up on us next month, so let's make sure we follow the new rules.

98-100번은 다음 발표와 목록에 관한 문제입니다.

남: 모두 안녕하세요. 이 레스토랑의 매니저로서 제 역할 중 하나는 중요한 변경 사항을 여러분께 알려드리는 것인데요.(98) 최근 저희는 공무원에게 보건 및 안전 점검을 받았습니다.(99) 통과는 했지만, 저희가 유념해야 할 몇 가지 준비 사항이 있습니다. 모든 분이 보고 기억을 떠올릴 수 있도록 세워둘 새로운 표지판 몇 개를 제가 임의로 만들었습니다.(100) 구역 중 한 곳에는 변경 사항을 하나 적용해야 합니다. 보호 장갑 착용 외에, 직원들은 실내로 들어오기 전에 신발을 말려야 합니다.(100) 다음 달에 검사관이 후속 검사를 실시할 예정이니, 반드시 새로운 규칙을 잘 지키도록 합시다.

장소	필요한 안전 표지판
냉동고	개봉된 용기에 라벨 붙이기
레인지	핸드폰 사용 금지
식당 구역	젖은 곳 물기 닦기
저장고	보호 장갑 착용(100)

98 화자는 누구인가?
(A) 관광 가이드
(B) 식당 매니저
(C) 정부 공무원
(D) 변호사

99 화자에 따르면, 최근 무슨 일이 있었는가?
(A) 직원 오리엔테이션
(B) 팀워크 개발 워크숍
(C) 시설 보수 공사
(D) 보건 및 안전 점검

100 시각 자료를 보시오. 추가 표지판은 어디에 놓이겠는가?
(A) 냉동고 근처에
(B) 레인지 근처에
(C) 식당 구역에
(D) 저장고 바깥에

TEST 03

PART 1   P. 44

1 (D)   **2** (C)   (A)   **4** (C)   **5** (D)   **6** (D)

PART 2   P. 48

7 (A)   **8** (C)   **9** (A)   **10** (B)   **11** (B)   **12** (B)
13 (C)   **14** (C)   **15** (B)   **16** (B)   **17** (A)   **18** (C)
19 (B)   **20** (B)   **21** (C)   **22** (C)   **23** (A)   **24** (B)
25 (B)   **26** (A)   **27** (B)   **28** (C)   **29** (C)   **30** (A)
31 (A)

PART 3   P. 49

32 (C)   **33** (D)   **34** (A)   **35** (B)   **36** (D)   **37** (D)
38 (D)   **39** (B)   **40** (B)   **41** (C)   **42** (C)   **43** (B)
44 (D)   **45** (C)   **46** (C)   **47** (D)   **48** (C)   **49** (D)
50 (A)   **51** (B)   **52** (A)   **53** (C)   **54** (B)   **55** (D)
56 (B)   **57** (D)   **58** (A)   **59** (A)   **60** (C)   **61** (D)
62 (B)   **63** (D)   **64** (D)   **65** (A)   **66** (D)   **67** (B)
68 (C)   **69** (B)   **70** (A)

PART 4   P. 53

71 (B)   **72** (D)   **73** (B)   **74** (B)   **75** (D)   **76** (C)
77 (B)   **78** (D)   **79** (A)   **80** (D)   **81** (B)   **82** (C)
83 (D)   **84** (B)   **85** (A)   **86** (C)   **87** (B)   **88** (C)
89 (C)   **90** (D)   **91** (B)   **92** (D)   **93** (D)   **94** (B)
95 (A)   **96** (D)   **97** (D)   **98** (C)   **99** (A)   **100** (D)

PART 1   P. 44

1   미국
(A) A sculpture is being washed with water.
(B) There's a parking area near the building.
(C) He's putting on a jacket.
(D) He's standing in front of a fountain.

(A) 조각상이 물에 씻기고 있다.
(B) 건물 근처에 주차장이 있다.
(C) 남자가 재킷을 입는 중이다.
(D) 남자가 분수 앞에 서 있다.

2   호주
(A) A man is closing a meeting room door.
(B) A man is writing on a piece of paper.
(C) A woman is adding notes to a whiteboard.
(D) A woman is sitting at her desk.

(A) 남자가 회의실 문을 닫고 있다.
(B) 남자가 종이에 글을 쓰고 있다.
(C) 여자가 화이트보드에 메모하고 있다.
(D) 여자가 책상에 앉아 있다.

3   미국
(A) Some supplies have been left on a kitchen floor.
(B) Some rags are being washed in a sink.
(C) A man is adjusting the temperature of an oven.
(D) Some cupboard doors are being opened.

(A) 몇몇 물건들이 주방 바닥에 놓여 있다.
(B) 싱크대에서 행주가 빨리고 있다.
(C) 남자가 오븐의 온도를 조절하고 있다.
(D) 몇몇 찬장 문들이 열리고 있다.

4   미국
(A) One of the women is sipping from a mug.
(B) One of the women is using a writing instrument.
(C) One of the women is on the phone.
(D) One of the women is pointing at a computer monitor.

(A) 여자들 중 한 명이 머그잔에서 음료를 마시고 있다.
(B) 여자들 중 한 명이 필기도구를 사용하고 있다.
(C) 여자들 중 한 명이 전화 통화 중이다.
(D) 여자들 중 한 명이 컴퓨터 모니터를 가리키고 있다.

5   영국
(A) Computers are being assembled in the room.
(B) Documents are being cleared from a table.
(C) One of the men is handing out some papers.
(D) A woman is presenting at a meeting.

(A) 컴퓨터들이 방에서 조립되고 있다.
(B) 서류들이 테이블에서 치워지고 있다.
(C) 남자들 중 한 명이 서류를 나누어 주고 있다.
(D) 여자가 회의에서 발표하고 있다.

6   미국
(A) A living room chair is occupied.
(B) Some refreshments have been set on a table.
(C) Some drawers have been left open.
(D) Some decorations have been put on the shelves.

(A) 거실 의자가 사용 중이다.
(B) 몇몇 다과가 테이블 위에 놓여 있다.
(C) 몇몇 서랍들이 열려 있다.
(D) 선반 위에 몇몇 장식품이 놓여 있다.

PART 2   P. 48

7   영국 ⇄ 호주
You'll be at Ruth's birthday party, won't you?
(A) Yes, I'll be joining.
(B) A room for 20 people.
(C) She is the finance director.

Ruth의 생일파티에 계실 거죠, 그렇죠?
(A) 네, 참석할 거예요.
(B) 20명이 들어갈 방이요.
(C) 그녀는 재무 이사예요.

8 미국 ⇄ 미국

Where can I get some flowers?
(A) Yes, I enjoy gardening.
(B) A floral arrangement.
(C) There's a shop on Bloor Road.

어디서 꽃을 좀 살 수 있을까요?
(A) 네, 저는 정원 가꾸기를 즐겨요.
(B) 꽃꽂이요.
(C) Bloor로에 가게가 하나 있어요.

9 호주 ⇄ 영국

Are you signing up for the two-week or the three-week course?
(A) The two-week course.
(B) She'll be out of town for four weeks.
(C) Mr. Bryant took the test.

신청하실 과정이 2주 과정인가요, 아니면 3주 과정인가요?
(A) 2주 과정이요.
(B) 그녀는 4주 내내 출장 가 있을 거예요.
(C) Mr. Bryant가 그 시험을 봤어요.

10 미국 ⇄ 호주

How long do you plan to stay with our company?
(A) I'll contact the HR Department.
(B) I don't have any immediate plans to move.
(C) At a hotel downtown.

우리 회사에서 얼마 동안 근무할 계획이신가요?
(A) 제가 인사 부서에 연락할게요.
(B) 당장은 옮길 계획이 없습니다.
(C) 시내 호텔에서요.

11 미국 ⇄ 미국

Why isn't my credit card working?
(A) At the bank.
(B) It's expired.
(C) I pay my bills on the 10th of every month.

제 신용카드가 왜 안 되는 거죠?
(A) 은행에서요.
(B) 만료됐어요.
(C) 매달 10일에 요금을 납부해요.

12 영국 ⇄ 미국

We should get started so we won't run late.
(A) I start work on Monday.
(B) Nate will be here soon.
(C) We're running out of space.

우리가 늦지 않으려면 시작해야 해요.
(A) 저는 월요일에 근무를 시작해요.
(B) Nate가 금방 올 거예요.
(C) 자리가 점점 없어지고 있어요.

13 미국 ⇄ 호주

When did they decide to move our office?
(A) To make the commute more convenient.
(B) No, I don't think we should.
(C) Weren't you at yesterday's meeting?

그들이 우리 사무실을 언제 옮기기로 한 건가요?
(A) 통근을 더 편리하게 하기 위해서요.
(B) 아니요, 우리가 그래야 한다고 생각하지 않아요.
(C) 어제 회의에 안 계셨어요?

14 미국 ⇄ 영국

What is this tea made of?
(A) That T-shirt looks great on you.
(B) At a nearby café.
(C) Why don't you check the packaging?

이 차는 무엇으로 만들어졌나요?
(A) 그 티셔츠가 잘 어울리시네요.
(B) 근처 카페에서요.
(C) 포장을 확인해보는 건 어때요?

15 호주 ⇄ 미국

This magazine cover looks nice, doesn't it?
(A) Yes, it was a great article.
(B) I think you should try a different font.
(C) At the newspaper stand down the street.

잡지 표지가 좋아 보여요, 그렇지 않아요?
(A) 네, 좋은 기사였어요.
(B) 다른 폰트를 사용해 보셔야 할 것 같아요.
(C) 길 아래에 있는 신문 가판대에서요.

16 미국 ⇄ 미국

Who should I ask for when I get to the office?
(A) In the waiting room.
(B) Ask for Jason.
(C) Yes, the reception desk.

사무실에 도착하면 누구를 찾아야 할까요?
(A) 대기실에서요.
(B) Jason을 찾으세요.
(C) 네, 접수 데스크요.

17 영국 ⇄ 미국

Has anyone made copies of the meeting agenda?
(A) The meeting has been canceled.
(B) We'll be presenting the new product.
(C) Did you use the coffee maker?

누가 회의 안건을 복사했나요?
(A) 회의가 취소되었어요.
(B) 저희가 신제품을 발표할 거예요.
(C) 커피 메이커를 사용하셨나요?

18 호주 ⇄ 영국

Would you like to make an appointment for another time?
(A) I have another laptop.
(B) No, the clock's broken.
(C) Sure. What are the available times?

다른 시간으로 예약하시겠어요?
(A) 저는 또 다른 노트북이 있습니다.
(B) 아니요, 시계가 고장 났어요.
(C) 그러죠. 가능한 시간이 언제인가요?

19 미국 ⇄ 미국

Do you think our team members should vote on the party venue?
(A) The next presidential election.
(B) Yes, that's a great suggestion.
(C) No, he works on the second floor.

팀원들이 파티 장소에 투표해야 할까요?
(A) 다음 대통령 선거요.
(B) 네, 아주 좋은 제안이에요.
(C) 아니요, 그는 2층에서 근무해요.

20 미국 ⇄ 호주
Who is going to oversee the Berlin office when James moves?
(A) The IT team.
(B) They haven't made a decision yet.
(C) It has a great view.

James가 이동하면 누가 Berlin 지사를 관리하나요?
(A) IT팀이요.
(B) 그들이 아직 결정하지 않았어요.
(C) 그곳의 전망이 매우 좋아요.

21 영국 ⇄ 미국
You don't mind if I use your laptop while you're away from the office, do you?
(A) I enjoyed my holiday.
(B) From BSS Electronics.
(C) No, be my guest.

사무실에 안 계시는 동안 제가 노트북 좀 써도 괜찮으시죠, 그렇죠?
(A) 휴가 잘 보냈어요.
(B) BSS 전자사요.
(C) 네, 그렇게 하세요.

22 호주 ⇄ 미국
Why hasn't the company profile been updated on the website?
(A) A photograph of the employees.
(B) Amelia will set the date.
(C) We're having technical difficulties.

회사 프로필이 왜 웹사이트에 업데이트되지 않았죠?
(A) 직원들 사진이요.
(B) Amelia가 날짜를 정할 거예요.
(C) 기술적인 문제가 있어서요.

23 미국 ⇄ 미국
Have you chosen the color for the walls?
(A) Do you know what pattern the carpet will be?
(B) Mr. Chan is on his way to the lobby to meet the clients.
(C) I'm thinking about wearing a grey suit.

벽 색상은 고르셨어요?
(A) 카펫이 어떤 무늬일지 아세요?
(B) Mr. Chan은 고객을 만나러 로비로 가는 중이에요.
(C) 회색 정장을 입을까 생각 중이에요.

24 영국 ⇄ 미국
The university is organizing a leadership conference.
(A) I majored in business administration in college.
(B) When's the registration deadline?
(C) Over ten years of experience.

대학교에서 리더십 콘퍼런스를 준비하고 있어요.
(A) 저는 대학에서 경영학을 전공했어요.
(B) 등록 마감일이 언제예요?
(C) 경력이 10년 넘었어요.

25 미국 ⇄ 미국
What do you think of the blueprint we received this morning?
(A) The new printer should be a lot faster.
(B) Oh. I was stuck in meetings all day.
(C) Because the renovation has been rescheduled.

오늘 아침에 받은 설계도에 대해 어떻게 생각하세요?
(A) 새로운 프린터는 훨씬 더 빠를 거예요.
(B) 아. 전 하루 종일 회의에 갇혀 있었어요.
(C) 수리 일정이 변경됐거든요.

26 호주 ⇄ 영국
Should the holiday cards be printed or sent through e-mail?
(A) How do we usually do it?
(B) To all of our clients.
(C) Sure, I'll mail them for you.

연하장을 출력할까요, 아니면 이메일로 발송할까요?
(A) 보통 어떻게 하세요?
(B) 전체 고객에게요.
(C) 네, 제가 우편 발송할게요.

27 미국 ⇄ 미국
Wouldn't it be more convenient to take the plane?
(A) A three-hour layover in Boston.
(B) I wonder if there are any tickets left.
(C) Yes, I'm planning to attend the workshop.

비행기를 타는 게 더 편리하지 않겠어요?
(A) Boston에서 세 시간 경유요.
(B) 티켓이 남아 있을지 모르겠네요.
(C) 네, 워크숍에 참석할 계획이에요.

28 영국 ⇄ 미국
Do you have this jacket in medium?
(A) No, early this morning.
(B) Medium rare, please.
(C) Yes, I'll get it for you.

이 재킷이 미디엄 사이즈로 있나요?
(A) 아니요, 오늘 아침 일찍요.
(B) 미디엄 레어로 해주세요.
(C) 네, 가져다드릴게요.

29 미국 ⇄ 영국
Could I get your opinion on this design?
(A) Tom has an extra one.
(B) No, with the computer software.
(C) I was just about to leave.

이 디자인에 대한 당신의 의견 좀 얻을 수 있을까요?
(A) Tom이 여분을 하나 가지고 있어요.
(B) 아니요, 컴퓨터 소프트웨어로요.
(C) 저는 막 퇴근하려던 참이었어요.

30 미국 ⇄ 호주
When will the hotel's event hall be remodeled?
(A) Floor plans will be reviewed in June.
(B) Can I see the suit in a different color?
(C) This is the latest and most popular model.

호텔 이벤트 홀은 언제 리모델링되나요?
(A) 평면도가 6월에 검토될 거예요.
(B) 정장을 다른 색으로 볼 수 있을까요?
(C) 이게 가장 인기 있는 최신 모델이에요.

31 호주 ⇄ 미국
I don't think Ms. Graves is back from her vacation yet.
(A) I just saw her in the break room.
(B) Yes, you can register on the first floor.
(C) I thought the check-in was at 3 P.M.

Ms. Graves가 아직 휴가에서 돌아오지 않은 것 같아요.
(A) 제가 방금 휴게실에서 봤어요.
(B) 네, 1층에서 등록하시면 됩니다.
(C) 전 체크인이 오후 3시인 줄 알았어요.

PART 3

P. 49

미국 ⇄ 미국

Questions 32-34 refer to the following conversation.

M: Hi, Liz. It looks like you have created a very interesting new exercise machine.(32)

W: Thanks. This machine is quite unique. You can ride it like a typical stationary bicycle, but it also has special handles so you can exercise your arms and shoulders at the same time. I think our customers will like it.

M: That sounds promising. Do you know how much it will cost?(33)

W: Actually, we're still working on that. We have a general idea, but we can't seem to decide on an exact figure.(33)

M: Well, you should mention it at the monthly meeting tomorrow. It could help to get feedback from people in other departments.(34)

32-34번은 다음 대화에 관한 문제입니다.

남: 안녕하세요, Liz. 아주 흥미로운 운동 기구를 새로 제작하셨나 봐요.(32)

여: 감사합니다. 이 기구는 상당히 독특해요. 일반 고정형 자전거처럼 탈 수도 있지만, 특별한 손잡이도 있어서 동시에 팔과 어깨 운동을 할 수도 있어요. 우리 고객들이 좋아할 것 같아요.

남: 잘될 것 같은데요. 가격이 얼마일지 아세요?(33)

여: 실은, 아직 고민 중이에요. 대략적인 아이디어는 있지만, 정확한 금액을 결정하기 힘든 것 같아요.(33)

남: 음, 그걸 내일 월례 회의 때 얘기해보세요. 다른 부서에 계신 분들에게 피드백을 받는 게 도움이 될 거예요.(34)

32 화자들은 어떤 종류의 상품에 관해 이야기하고 있는가?
(A) 차량
(B) 휴대전화
(C) 운동기구
(D) 사무용 가구

33 무엇이 여전히 결정되어야 하는가?
(A) 이름
(B) 마케팅 캠페인
(C) 출시일
(D) 가격

34 남자는 무엇을 하라고 권장하는가?
(A) 동료들과 얘기하라고
(B) 회의 일정 잡으라고
(C) 기한 수정하라고
(D) 몇 가지 기능들 수정하라고

영국 ⇄ 미국

Questions 35-37 refer to the following conversation.

W: Nice to meet you, Mr. Gao. The first question I would like to ask today is this: why do you want to work here at Percell Publishing?(35)

M: Well, my sister, Sharon Gao, used to work here. She was in the graphic design team and told me that I would really enjoy the work.(36)

W: Ah, yes. I remember Sharon. Anyway, why do you want to leave your current company? It looks like you've been there for four years.

M: Well, all my work there involves creating logos and banners for various clients. But my real interest is Web design. I want to concentrate on that more.(37)

35-37번은 다음 대화에 관한 문제입니다.

여: 만나서 반갑습니다, Mr. Gao. 제가 오늘 첫 번째로 물어보고 싶은 질문은요: 왜 이곳 Percell 출판사에서 일하고 싶으신가요?(35)

남: 음, 제 여동생 Sharon Gao가 여기서 일했어요. 그래픽 디자인팀에 있었는데, 제가 일을 아주 즐기게 될 거라고 이야기해줬어요.(36)

여: 아, 네. Sharon 기억나네요. 그러면, 왜 현재 회사를 떠나고 싶으신가요? 그곳에 4년 동안 계셨던 것 같은데요.

남: 음, 거기서 모든 제 업무는 다양한 고객들을 위한 로고와 배너 제작과 관련되어 있습니다. 하지만 저의 진짜 관심사는 웹 디자인이에요. 거기에 더 집중하고 싶습니다.(37)

35 남자는 왜 여자와 만나고 있는가?
(A) 이용 가능한 사무실 공간을 확인하기 위해
(B) 취업 면접에 참여하기 위해
(C) 서비스에 관해 문의하기 위해
(D) 계약을 타결하기 위해

36 남자는 왜 자신의 여동생을 언급하는가?
(A) 잘 알려진 작가에 관해 논의하기 위해
(B) 자신이 기술을 배운 곳을 설명하기 위해
(C) 특별 금액을 요청하기 위해
(D) 회사에 관해 어떻게 알게 되었는지 설명하기 위해

37 남자는 어느 분야에 집중하고 싶어 하는가?
(A) 소프트웨어 프로그래밍
(B) 도서 편집
(C) 고객 관리
(D) 웹 디자인

미국 ⇄ 미국

Questions 38-40 refer to the following conversation.

W: Thank you for stopping by last minute. As you can see, one of the pipes is leaking onto the hardwood floors.(38) I'm worried about water damage.

M: I'm afraid this doesn't look good. That pipe is badly corroded. This is an old building, so there may be more corroded pipes that could leak and cause damage.

W: Well, good thing you're here. Do you think you could fix it? We're hosting a dinner party next Friday evening.(39) Will the repairs be done before then?

M: Lucky for you, I have some water pipes in the car. I'll just do a quick scan of the building and then get started on the repairs.(40)

38-40번은 다음 대화에 관한 문제입니다.

여: 급하게 요청했는데 들러주셔서 감사합니다. 보시다시피, 수도관 하나에서 원목 바닥으로 물이 새고 있어요.(38) 물로 인한 피해가 걱정돼요.

남: 보기에 안 좋겠네요. 그 수도관이 심하게 부식됐어요. 오래된 건물이라서, 누수로 피해를 줄 수 있는 부식된 수도관이 더 있을 거예요.

TEST 03

여: 음, 당신이 여기 계셔서 다행이에요. 고칠 수 있을 것 같으세요? **저희가 다음 주 금요일 저녁에 디너파티를 열어요.**(39) 그 전에 수리가 완료될까요?

남: 운이 좋으시네요, 차에 수도관이 몇 개 있거든요. **건물을 빠르게 살펴본 후 수리를 시작할게요.**(40)

38 남자의 직업은 무엇이겠는가?
(A) 예술가
(B) 행사 기획자
(C) 부동산 중개인
(D) 수리공

39 여자는 다음 주 금요일에 무슨 일이 있을거라고 말하는가?
(A) 업무 회의
(B) 디너파티
(C) 판촉 행사
(D) 중고품 판매

40 남자는 다음에 무엇을 할 것인가?
(A) 차량을 견인할 것이다
(B) 건물을 확인할 것이다
(C) 새로운 장비를 주문할 것이다
(D) 에어컨을 설치할 것이다

호주 ⇄ 영국 ⇄ 미국

Questions 41-43 refer to the following conversation with three speakers.

M: Hello, Kristie. Hello, Tiffany. **I heard you wanted to talk to me about our chocolate mixing machine.**(41) What's going on?

W1: **The mixing unit keeps shutting down every 30 minutes.**(42) Tiffany called a technician about the problem.

W2: Yes. The technician checked it out and found that the motor is overheating. He said that we will have to get a new one.

M: All right. **Why don't we place an order today for a new motor?**(43)

41-43번은 다음 세 화자의 대화에 관한 문제입니다.

남: 안녕하세요, Kristie. 안녕하세요, Tiffany. **초콜릿 혼합 기계에 대해 저와 이야기하고 싶으시다고 들었어요.**(41) 무슨 일이신가요?

여1: **혼합 장치가 30분마다 꺼지네요.**(42) Tiffany가 이 문제로 기술자에게 연락했어요.

여2: 네. 기술자가 확인했는데, 모터가 과열되었다고 해요. 새것을 사야 한다고 하더라고요.

남: 알았어요. **오늘 새 모터를 주문하는 건 어때요?**(43)

41 화자들은 어느 산업에 일하겠는가?
(A) 가전제품 판매
(B) 자동차 생산
(C) 식품 제조
(D) 컴퓨터 프로그래밍

42 어떤 문제가 논의되고 있는가?
(A) 장비가 계속 꺼진다.
(B) 매니저가 부재중이다.
(C) 몇몇 고객들이 불만을 표했다.
(D) 물품 재고 목록이 정확하지 않다.

43 남자는 무엇을 추천하는가?
(A) 새로운 판매처 선택하는 것
(B) 대체 부품 주문하는 것
(C) 쿠폰 제공하는 것
(D) 배송 지연하는 것

호주 ⇄ 미국 ⇄ 영국

Questions 44-46 refer to the following conversation with three speakers.

M1: Hey, Spencer. Congratulations! **We decided to promote you to assistant manager.**(44) It's been great having you on our team.

M2: Wow, thank you! I'm glad I made a good impression here.

M1: **We actually need someone to hire stylists for our new branch opening next month.**(45) Would you be able to do that?

M2: Of course! I have a few contacts that may be interested in the position.

M1: That's great.

M2: Okay, I'll get started on that right after I help this customer. Hi, are you here for an appointment?

W: No, **I'd like to schedule a haircut for later today. Are there any openings for five o'clock?**(46)

44-46번은 다음 세 화자의 대화에 관한 문제입니다.

남1: Spencer. 축하해요! **당신을 부매니저로 승진시키기로 했어요.**(44) 우리 팀에 함께 해서 정말 좋았어요.

남2: 와, 감사합니다! 제가 여기서 좋은 인상을 드렸다니 다행이에요.

남1: **실은 다음 달 개장하는 신규 지점에서 일할 스타일리스트를 채용할 사람이 필요해요.**(45) 그 일을 맡을 수 있겠어요?

남2: 그럼요! 그 자리에 관심있어 할만한 사람들이 몇 명 있어요.

남1: 잘됐네요.

남2: 네, 제가 이 고객분부터 도와드리고 나서 바로 시작할게요. 어서 오세요, 예약하셨어요?

여: 아니요, **이따 커트 예약을 하고 싶어서요. 5시에 자리가 있나요?**(46)

44 Spencer는 무엇에 관해 축하받는가?
(A) 상을 받은 것
(B) 기록을 깬 것
(C) 대학을 졸업한 것
(D) 승진한 것

45 다음 달에 무슨 일이 있을 것인가?
(A) 신규 승진이 있을 것이다.
(B) 교육 워크숍이 열릴 것이다.
(C) 다른 지점이 문을 열 것이다.
(D) 미용실이 문을 닫을 것이다.

46 여자는 무엇을 하려고 묻는가?
(A) 쿠폰을 쓰려고
(B) 일자리에 지원하려고
(C) 예약을 잡으려고
(D) 설문조사하려고

미국 ⇄ 미국

Questions 47-49 refer to the following conversation.

W: Sunil, I just got a call from the marketing director. **It turns out the representatives from Reed Pharmaceuticals would like us to change the subtitles on the TV advertisement clip we sent them yesterday.**(47)/(48)

M: What kind of changes?

W: They said the subtitles were a little hard to read. We'll have to enlarge the font and change the color.

M: I see. When do we have to finish this by?

W: **Today would be best.**(49)

M: Umm... You know, **the Vasquez account is due today.**(49)

47-49번은 다음 대화에 관한 문제입니다.

여: Sunil, 제가 방금 마케팅 감독님한테 전화를 받았어요. **Reed 제약회사 쪽에서 저희가 어제 발송한 TV 광고 영상 자막을 변경해달라고 하네요.**(47)/(48)

남: 어떤 변경이요?

여: 자막이 읽기 좀 힘들대요. 글자를 키우고 색상을 변경해야 해요.

남: 알았어요. 언제까지 끝내야 해요?

여: **오늘이 가장 좋을 거예요.**(49)

남: 음... 그게, **Vasquez건이 오늘 마감이에요.**(49)

47 화자들은 누구겠는가?
(A) 실험실 과학자들
(B) 그래픽 디자이너들
(C) TV 프로그램 작가들
(D) 영상 편집자들

48 고객은 화자들이 무엇을 하기를 원하는가?
(A) 계약서를 갱신해달라고
(B) 프로젝트 일정을 변경해달라고
(C) 광고를 변경해달라고
(D) 견적서를 새로 고쳐 달라고

49 남자는 왜 "Vasquez건이 오늘 마감이에요"라고 말하는가?
(A) 고객과의 소통 부족에 대해 불평하기 위해
(B) 자신의 동료에게 계정을 등록해달라고 요청하기 위해
(C) 재정 문제에 관한 우려를 표하기 위해
(D) 즉시 도와줄 수 없음을 설명하기 위해

호주 ⇄ 미국

Questions 50-52 refer to the following conversation.

M: Welcome to Conwell Corner.(50) What can I help you with?

W: I recently heard that Josh Wood released his autobiography. I was wondering if you had any in stock right now.(50)

M: I'm sorry. I don't think we have any left, but I think our downtown location does. Let me check.(51)

W: Great. I've been all around town looking for a copy.

M: OK, we do have a few left at our downtown location.(51) Would you like me to reserve you one?

W: Oh, yes, please. I'll head there right away.

M: Sure. While I have you, would you like to sign up for our alerts? It will notify you when a book you want is in stock.(52)

50-52번은 다음 대화에 관한 문제입니다.

남: Conwell Corner입니다.(50) 무엇을 도와드릴까요?

여: Josh Wood가 자서전을 출간했다는 소식을 최근 들었어요. 지금 재고가 있는지 궁금해서요.(50)

남: 죄송합니다. 남은 게 없을 거예요, 그런데 저희 시내 매장에는 있을 것 같아요. 확인해드릴게요.(51)

여: 잘됐네요. 책을 구하려 온 시내를 돌아다녔거든요.

남: 네, 시내 매장에 몇 부 남아 있습니다.(51) 한 부 예약해 드릴까요?

여: 아, 네, 그렇게 해주세요. 제가 바로 그쪽으로 갈게요.

남: 알겠습니다. 오신 김에, 저희 알림 서비스에 가입하시겠어요? 원하는 책의 재고가 있을 때 알려드릴 거예요.(52)

50 화자들은 어디에 있는가?
(A) 서점에
(B) 대학교에
(C) 슈퍼마켓에
(D) 은행에

51 남자는 무엇을 확인해 주는가?
(A) 매장의 위치
(B) 상품 구입가능 여부
(C) 주문품 배송일
(D) 제안의 실효성

52 남자는 여자에게 무엇을 하라고 제안하는가?
(A) 서비스에 가입하라고
(B) 시내에서 택시를 타라고
(C) 매니저와 이야기하라고
(D) 주문품을 예약하라고

영국 ⇄ 미국

Questions 53-55 refer to the following conversation.

W: Hey, Matt. I just spoke with the director of all Techno Tree Computer Education Centers in the Chicago area. **It looks like all the equipment in our branch will be replaced in the first week of August,**(53) so we'll be closed for seven days.

M: Oh. Our students need to know about that right away, so they can go to another center.

W: Right. **The director also mentioned that the students should receive 25 percent of their tuition back for this month to make up for any inconvenience.**(54)

M: That's good. **I'll start calling our students now to let them know.**(55)

53-55번은 다음 대화에 관한 문제입니다.

여: Matt. 제가 방금 Chicago 지역의 Techno Tree 컴퓨터 교육센터 총괄이사님과 얘기를 나눴는데요. **저희 지점에 있는 전체 장비가 8월 첫 번째 주에 교체될 것 같아서,**(53) 7일간 문을 닫을 거예요.

남: 아. 그럼 저희 학생들이 다른 센터로 갈 수 있게, 지금 바로 알려야겠네요.

여: 네. 그리고 이사님이 학생들이 겪을 불편함을 만회할 수 있게 이번 달 **수업료의 25퍼센트를 돌려받아야 한다고 말씀하셨어요.**(54)

남: 좋네요. **제가 지금부터 저희 학생들에게 전화해서 알려 줄게요.**(55)

53 8월 첫째 주에 무슨 일이 있을 것인가?

(A) 새 강사들이 채용될 것이다.

(B) 시상식이 열릴 것이다.

(C) 기계가 교체될 것이다.

(D) 이사가 Chicago 지역을 방문할 것이다.

54 학생들에게 무엇이 제공될 것인가?

(A) 무료 기기

(B) 환불

(C) 할인

(D) 온라인 상담

55 남자는 다음에 무엇을 하겠는가?

(A) 컴퓨터를 점검할 것이다

(B) 수업을 진행할 것이다

(C) 웹사이트를 디자인할 것이다

(D) 학생들과 이야기할 것이다

영국 ⇄ 호주

Questions 56-58 refer to the following conversation.

W: Hi, I just moved to this city. **Can I get a guide that lists local attractions and restaurants?(56)**

M: Of course. Take this one right here. By the way, **I highly suggest checking out the Pearl Art Gallery. It was remodeled last week.(57)**

W: Thank you for the recommendation! I'll read about it in the guide before I go.

M: Great. One more thing: **there will be live music performances on Sunday at Manitz Park.(58)** Admission is free, but you'll want to arrive early because parking spaces will fill up fast.

56-58번은 다음 대화에 관한 문제입니다.

여: 안녕하세요, 제가 최근에 이 도시로 이사 왔거든요. **지역 명소와 식당 목록이 있는 안내서를 받을 수 있을까요?(56)**

남: 물론이죠. 여기 이거 가져가세요. 그나저나, **저는 Pearl 미술관에 가보시는 걸 강력히 추천합니다. 지난주에 리모델링이 됐거든요.(57)**

여: 추천 고맙습니다! 가기 전에 안내서에서 그곳에 관해 읽어볼게요.

남: 좋아요. 한 가지 더요: **일요일에 Manitz 공원에서 라이브 음악공연이 있어요.(58)** 입장은 무료이지만, 주차장이 금세 다 차버리니까 일찍 가시는 게 좋을 거예요.

56 여자는 무엇을 요청하는가?

(A) 주차권

(B) 지역 안내서

(C) 버스 탑승권

(D) 제품 카탈로그

57 남자는 미술관에 관하여 뭐라고 말하는가?

(A) 주인이 바뀌었다.

(B) 입장이 무료이다.

(C) 명화를 전시한다.

(D) 최근 개조되었다.

58 일요일에 어떤 행사가 열릴 것인가?

(A) 콘서트

(B) 공원 개장

(C) 스포츠 경기

(D) 퍼레이드

미국 ⇄ 미국

Questions 59-61 refer to the following conversation.

M: Samantha, you've been here a long time, right? I'm having trouble putting up a vacation day request through our system.(59)

W: Did you install the computer update?(60)

M: Yes, **I downloaded it yesterday.(60)** I don't think that's the issue, though. Look at this... When I click the submit button, the page refreshes, and the form resets.

W: Hmm... That's strange. In that case, I don't know what the problem is. Sorry.

M: It's OK. **I'll just call the IT team.(61)** They'll probably know what's going on.

59-61번은 다음 대화에 관한 문제입니다.

남: Samantha, 여기서 오래 근무하셨죠, 맞죠? 제가 우리 시스템으로 휴가 신청서를 제출하려는 데 잘 안되네요.(59)

여: 컴퓨터 업데이트는 설치하셨어요?(60)

남: 네, **어제 다운로드했어요.(60)** 그런데 그게 문제는 아닌 것 같아요. 이것 좀 보세요... 제출 버튼을 클릭하면 페이지가 새로고침 되면서 양식이 지워져요.

여: 음... 이상하군요. 이런 경우에는 뭐가 문제인지 모르겠네요. 미안해요.

남: 괜찮아요. **IT팀에 전화해 보죠 뭐.(61)** 그분들은 뭐가 문제인지 아실 거예요.

59 남자는 왜 "Samantha, 여기서 오래 근무하셨죠, 맞죠"라고 말하는가?

(A) 도움을 요청하기 위해

(B) 동료를 칭찬하기 위해

(C) 추천을 받기 위해

(D) 승인을 요청하기 위해

60 남자는 어제 무엇을 했는가?

(A) 문서를 수정했다.

(B) 워크숍에 참석했다.

(C) 업데이트를 다운로드했다.

(D) 고객과 만났다.

61 남자는 다음에 무엇을 하겠는가?

(A) 교육 과정에 등록할 것이다

(B) 웹사이트를 확인할 것이다

(C) 회의실을 예약할 것이다

(D) IT 부서에 연락할 것이다

영국 ⇄ 호주

Questions 62-64 refer to the following conversation and bill.

W: Hi, **could I pay the bill, please?(62)**

M: Of course. **Did you find your room comfortable?(62)**

W: Yes, thank you. It was really nice. **Oh, it looks like I was charged for one of the premium rooms. I stayed in a double room.(63)**

M: Oh, you're right. Sorry about that. I'll update your bill.

W: Thank you. Also, I have to leave for the airport at 2 P.M. **Could I have the number of a taxi service?(64)**

62-64번은 다음 대화와 청구서에 관한 문제입니다.

여: 안녕하세요, 계산해 주시겠어요?(62)

남: 물론이죠. 방은 편안하셨나요?(62)

여: 네, 감사합니다. 아주 좋았어요. 아, 프리미엄룸으로 청구가 된 것 같네요. 저는 더블룸에 묵었어요.(63)

남: 아, 그러네요. 죄송합니다. 청구서를 수정해 드릴게요.

여: 감사합니다. 그리고, 제가 2시에 공항으로 출발해야 하는데요. 택시 서비스 번호를 알 수 있을까요?(64)

```
              Carlton 호텔
                청구서

  발렛주차            10달러
  룸서비스            30달러
  조식               7달러
  디럭스 룸          250달러(63)
```

62 남자는 누구겠는가?
    (A) 소매점 직원
    (B) 호텔 접수 직원
    (C) 식당 종업원
    (D) 전기 기술자

63 시각 자료를 보시오. 청구서에서 어떤 금액이 잘못됐는가?
    (A) 7달러
    (B) 10달러
    (C) 30달러
    (D) 250달러

64 여자는 2시에 무엇을 할 것인가?
    (A) 회의에 참석할 것이다
    (B) 예약할 것이다
    (C) 관광지를 방문할 것이다
    (D) 공항에 갈 것이다

미국 ⇌ 호주

Questions 65-67 refer to the following conversation and advertisement.

W: You've reached Macmore's Flooring. This is Katie speaking.

M: Hello, **I want to install new floor tiles in my living room. I haven't changed the current ones since I moved in here which was 40 years ago.**(65)

W: You called the right place. And just so you know, we're offering discounts on our products right now. The price varies depending on what kind of floor tiles you want.

M: Hmm… The ones I have right now are stone, so this time **I'd like to go with ceramic tiles.**(66)

W: Ceramic? You should be able to get an extra low price on your order then.

M: Perfect!

W: Also, **all of our floor tiles are very sturdy. They don't crack easily, so they look good for a long time.**(67)

65-67번은 다음 대화와 광고에 관한 문제입니다.

여: Macmore Flooring에 전화 주셨습니다. 저는 Katie입니다.

남: 안녕하세요, 저희 집 거실에 바닥 타일을 새로 깔고 싶은데요. 지금 있는 건 이곳으로 이사 오고 나서 바꾼 적이 없어요, 그게 40년 전이네요.(65)

여: 연락 잘 주셨습니다. 그리고 참고로 말씀드리면, 현재 저희 제품들에 대한 할인을 제공하고 있습니다. 가격은 어떤 종류의 바닥 타일을 원하시는지에 따라 다릅니다.

남: 음... 지금 있는 것은 석재라서요, 이번에는 **세라믹 타일로 하고 싶어요.**(66)

여: 세라믹이요? 그러시다면 더 낮은 가격으로 주문하실 수 있을 겁니다.

남: 너무 좋네요!

여: 게다가 저희 바닥 타일은 모두 매우 튼튼합니다. 쉽게 깨지지도 않아 외관도 오랫동안 좋게 유지됩니다.(67)

```
              Macmore's Flooring
               특별 할인 행사!
            (6월 30일까지 할인)

  세라믹 타일 설치: 40퍼센트 할인(66)
  도자기 타일 설치: 30퍼센트 할인
  석재 타일 설치: 20퍼센트 할인
  대리석 타일 설치: 10퍼센트 할인
```

65 남자는 왜 새 바닥 타일을 설치하고 싶어 하는가?
    (A) 오래된 바닥재를 교체하기 위해
    (B) 거실 벽지와 어울리게 하기 위해
    (C) 더 많은 바닥 면적을 제공하기 위해
    (D) 집을 팔기 위해

66 시각 자료를 보시오. 남자의 주문 금액에서 얼마나 할인되겠는가?
    (A) 10퍼센트
    (B) 20퍼센트
    (C) 30퍼센트
    (D) 40퍼센트

67 여자는 바닥 타일에 관하여 무엇을 강조하는가?
    (A) 가볍다.
    (B) 내구성이 있다.
    (C) 환경친화적이다.
    (D) 저렴하다.

영국 ⇌ 미국

Questions 68-70 refer to the following conversation and seating chart.

W: Hello. According to your website, **the performing arts center was remodeled last week**(68) and offers wider seats now.

M: Yes. But that's not all. The seats are also cushioned for comfort. Just remember to try to purchase tickets in advance to ensure a good view.

W: All right. Actually, I want to purchase four seats for the Wingding Orchestra concert next Friday. Can I do that right now?

M: Of course. OK, **it looks like the gold section is the only area with four seats together.**(69) If you're fine with that, I'll go ahead and reserve them now.

W: **Yes.**(69) And one more thing. **I have a 20-percent-off voucher I want to use.**(70)

M: Sure. Just read me the 12-digit number on the voucher.

68-70번은 다음 대화와 좌석 배치도에 관한 문제입니다.

여: 안녕하세요. 귀사의 웹사이트를 보니, **공연 예술 센터가 지난주에 개조되어**(68) 이제 더 넓은 좌석을 제공한다고 나오네요.

남: 네. 그런데 그게 다가 아닙니다. 안락할 수 있게 좌석들에 쿠션도 덧대어 있습니다. 좋은 시야를 확보할 수 있게 미리 티켓을 구매하시는 것만 기억하세요.

여: 알겠습니다. 실은 제가 다음 주 금요일 Wingding 오케스트라 콘서트에 네 좌석을 구매하고 싶은데요. 지금 할 수 있을까요?

남: 물론이죠. 자, **골드 섹션이 좌석 4개가 붙어있는 유일한 구역인 것 같네요.**(69) 괜찮으시면, 제가 지금 예약해드리겠습니다.

여: **네.**(69) 그리고 한 가지 더 있는데요. **사용하고 싶은 20퍼센트 할인 쿠폰이 있어요.**(70)

남: 그럼요. 쿠폰에 있는 12자리 숫자를 저에게 알려주세요.

```
┌─────────────────────────┐
│        중앙 무대          │
└─────────────────────────┘
        (골드 섹션)
```

A열 ■ ■ ■ ■ ■ ■ ■ A열
(69)B열 □ □ □ □ ■ ■ ■ B열
C열 ■ ■ ■ ■ ■ ■ □ C열
D열 ■ ■ ■ ■ □ □ □ ■ D열

공석 □

68 최근에 공연 예술 센터에서 무슨 일이 있었는가?
(A) 새로운 매니저가 채용되었다.
(B) 공연의 날짜가 변경되었다.
(C) 시설의 개조가 마무리되었다.
(D) 주차장이 건설되었다.

69 시각 자료를 보시오. 여자는 어느 열의 티켓을 사겠는가?
(A) A열
(B) B열
(C) C열
(D) D열

70 여자는 무엇을 하고 싶다고 말하는가?
(A) 쿠폰을 사용하고 싶다고
(B) 회원으로 가입하고 싶다고
(C) 전자 티켓을 받고 싶다고
(D) 좌석을 업그레이드하고 싶다고

PART 4

P. 53

미국

Questions 71-73 refer to the following excerpt from a meeting.

W: I want to thank the district managers for attending today's meeting to talk about a new approach our restaurant will be taking.(71) In the coming weeks, our entire menu will be available for delivery.(72) The purpose is to be more accessible for our customers. Some people may want to eat our food for lunch but can't because of their short lunch hours. By offering delivery, these customers can place their order beforehand, so their food can arrive in time for lunch. José Alvarez, the Director of Operations, is in charge of this task. **José, what will the restaurants need to plan in order to properly execute this arrangement?**(73)

71-73번은 다음 회의 발췌록에 관한 문제입니다.

여: 우리 식당이 도입할 새로운 접근법에 관해 논의하려고 마련한 오늘 회의에 참석해 주신 지역 매니저들께 감사의 말씀을 드립니다.(71) 다음 몇 주 동안, 전체 메뉴의 배달이 가능해질 것입니다.(72) 목적은 우리 고객들이 더 쉽게 이용할 수 있게 하는 것입니다. 어떤 분들은 점심으로 우리의 음식을 먹고 싶어 할 수 있는데, 점심시간이 짧아 그럴 수가 없습니다. 배달을 제공함으로써, 이러한 고객들이 미리 주문을 할 수 있게 되어서 음식이 점심시간에 맞춰 도착할 수 있습니다. 운영 책임자인 José Alvarez이 이 업무를 담당하고 있습니다. **José, 이 일을 제대로 실행하려면, 식당에서는 무슨 계획을 세워야 할까요?**(73)

71 회사는 어떤 종류의 사업체를 소유하는가?
(A) 문구점
(B) 음식 서비스
(C) 도매 시장
(D) 자동차 대여

72 사업체들은 무엇을 하기 시작할 것인가?
(A) 자동 결제 준비
(B) 시간대별 할인 제공
(C) 영업시간 연장
(D) 물품 배송 제공

73 화자는 José Alvarez에게 무엇을 하라고 요청하는가?
(A) 이메일을 발송하라고
(B) 실행 계획을 설명하라고
(C) 일정표를 나눠주라고
(D) 음식 공급 업체에 전화하라고

호주

Questions 74-76 refer to the following recorded message.

M: You have reached Hello Telecommunications' support line.(74) We understand that many of our customers are experiencing difficulties connecting to the Internet right now due to last night's heavy rainfall.(75) We hope to restore all connections by 3 P.M. Saturday afternoon. If you continue to have problems after this time, please speak to one of our representatives directly by dialing this number again and then pressing "0."(76)

74-76번은 다음 녹음 메시지에 관한 문제입니다.

남: Hello 텔레콤 지원팀입니다.(74) 어젯밤 폭우로 인하여 현재 많은 고객이 인터넷 연결에 어려움을 겪고 계신 걸 알고 있습니다.(75) 저희는 토요일 오후 3시까지 모든 연결 문제들을 복구하기를 바라고 있습니다. 이 시간 이후에도 계속 문제를 겪으신다면, 이 번호로 다시 전화하신 다음 0번을 누르셔서 저희 직원에게 직접 말씀해 주세요.(76)

74 화자는 어디에서 일하겠는가?
(A) 컴퓨터 제조업체에서
(B) 인터넷 서비스 공급업체에서
(C) 집수리 회사에서
(D) 방송국에서

75 문제의 원인은 무엇인가?
(A) 기술적인 오류가 있었다.
(B) 작업 일부가 마무리되지 않았다.
(C) 일부 기계들이 파손되었다.
(D) 날씨가 안 좋았다.

76 청자들은 문제가 계속될 경우에 무엇을 해야 하는가?
(A) 서류를 제출해야한다
(B) 장비를 교체해야한다
(C) 나중에 다시 전화해야한다
(D) 업체에 방문해야한다

Questions 77-79 refer to the following announcement.

W: Thank you everyone for attending the grand opening of the latest addition to our theater, the memorabilia showroom.(77) I'm thrilled to share this moment with the movie fans in our city. The showroom will display props from some of the most popular films ever made. Before you enter, we'd like you to fill out this survey letting us know your movie preferences.(78) Also, to show our appreciation for your support, everyone here will be getting a $10 voucher to our concession stand.(79)

77-79번은 다음 안내에 관한 문제입니다.

여: 최근 저희 극장의 수집품 전시실 증축의 개장 행사에 참석해 주신 모든 분들께 감사드립니다.(77) 우리 시의 영화 팬분들과 이 시간을 함께하게 되어 무척이나 기쁩니다. 전시실에는 지금껏 만들어진 가장 인기 있는 일부 영화들의 소품들을 전시할 것입니다. 입장하시기 전에, 여러분이 선호하는 영화들을 저희가 알 수 있도록 이 설문을 작성해 주시기 바랍니다.(78) 또한, 여러분의 지원에 대한 감사의 표시로, 여기 계신 모든 분들은 저희 구매매장에서 사용하실 수 있는 10달러 할인권을 받게 됩니다.(79)

77 극장은 무엇을 기념하고 있는가?
(A) 영화 개봉
(B) 전시실 개장
(C) 건물 개조
(D) 기념일

78 청자들은 처음에 무엇을 할 것인가?
(A) 영상을 시청할 것이다
(B) 투어를 할 것이다
(C) 사진을 찍을 것이다
(D) 질문에 답할 것이다

79 청자들은 무엇을 받을 것인가?
(A) 구매매장 할인권
(B) 영화전시 소품
(C) 무료입장 티켓
(D) 상영시간 일정표

Questions 80-82 refer to the following telephone message.

W: Hello. My manager, Vince, was praising your company after returning from his holiday.(81) I need your company's help preparing for my own travel this spring. (80)/(81) I was researching the Grand Mediterranean Cruises website and saw a 5-city package for $670 during the month of May. I understand that this is one of the busier months, which explains why it's so expensive. But, I'm told that the Mediterranean is breathtaking during that season. That's why I wanted to get in touch with you before I finalize my plans.(82) You can contact me at 555-9328.

80-82번은 다음 전화 메시지에 관한 문제입니다.

여: 안녕하세요. 제 매니저이신 Vince가 휴가를 다녀오신 후에 귀사에 대해 칭찬해 주셨는데요.(81) 제가 올봄에 저 혼자 가는 여행을 준비하는 데 귀사의 도움이 필요해서요.(80)/(81) 제가 그랜드 지중해 크루즈 웹사이트를 조사했는데 5월 한 달 동안에 670달러에 5개 도시 패키지를 보았어요. 이게 비싼 극성수기 중 한 때라는 건 알고 있습니다. 하지만 지중해는 그 시기에 숨 막힐 듯 아름답다고 들었습니다. 그래서 제가 계획을 확정하기 전에 연락드리고 싶었습니다.(82) 555-9328번으로 저에게 연락해주세요.

80 화자는 무엇을 준비하고 있는가?
(A) 연구 조사 발표
(B) 고객 방문
(C) 기념일 파티
(D) 휴가

81 청자는 누구겠는가?
(A) 선장
(B) 여행사 직원
(C) 리조트 매니저
(D) 전시회 코디네이터

82 화자는 "지중해는 그 시기에 숨 막힐 듯 아름답다고 들었어요"라고 말할 때 무엇을 의미하는가?
(A) 서비스에 만족하지 않는다.
(B) 추천에 동의한다.
(C) 그 가격에 구매할 가치가 있다고 생각한다.
(D) 청자가 그녀와 동행하기를 원한다.

Questions 83-85 refer to the following talk.

M: I understand that Sunrise Avenue has partnered with some local universities to let some students gain some work experience while studying.(83) However, some of people from my IT company pointed out that there may be potential security risks that come with internship programs. To put it simply, the risk of confidential documents being leaked to the public increases with such programs. Our program specializes in keeping confidential documents secure.(84) We believe our program can confer enormous benefits for your company. **Before we talk about fees, let's talk about what this program can do.(85)**

83-85번은 다음 담화에 관한 문제입니다.

남: Sunrise Avenue에서 지역 대학들과 협력해 학생들에게 재학하는 동안 근무 경험을 쌓을 수 있게 한 것으로 알고 있습니다.(83) 하지만 저희 IT 기업의 일부 직원들은 인턴십 프로그램으로 인해 생겨나는 보안상 위험 요인이 있을지도 모른다고 지적합니다. 간단히 말하면, 그런 프로그램으로 기밀문서가 대중에 유출될 위험이 증가합니다. 저희 프로그램은 기밀문서를 안전하게 보관하는 것을 전문으로 합니다.(84) 저희 프로그램이 귀사에 엄청난 이득을 가져다 줄 거라고 믿습니다. 요금 얘기를 하기 전에, 이 프로그램으로 무엇을 할 수 있는지 이야기 나눠 봅시다.(85)

83 Sunrise Avenue에서 어떤 결정을 내렸는가?
(A) 직원 재택근무를 허용하기로
(B) 해외 일자리를 광고하기로
(C) 세부 계획을 대중에 공개하기로
(D) 인턴십 프로그램을 시작하기로

84 화자에 따르면, 그의 회사에서는 청자들이 무엇을 관리하도록 도와줄 수 있는가?
(A) 사무 공간을 확보하는 것
(B) 안보 위험을 최소화하는 것
(C) 광고를 강화하는 것
(D) 대기 시간을 줄이는 것

85 다음에 무엇이 논의될 것인가?
(A) 기능
(B) 일정
(C) 요금
(D) 명성

호주

Questions 86-88 refer to the following excerpt from a meeting.

M: Thank you all for attending this morning's HR meeting. **Today, we'll be preparing a new evaluation form that we'll send out to all department managers.(86)** The executives decided that we will now be holding quarterly employee reviews rather than biannual ones. Remember, **our major objective this year is to increase staff productivity,(87)** and we believe keeping track of employees' performance more often will help with that. Now, for the next 20 minutes, I'd like you all to come up with some ideas for the format of the evaluation form. **So please get into groups of three and start brainstorming some ideas.(88)** Thanks.

86-88번은 다음 회의 발췌록에 관한 문제입니다.

남: 오늘 오전 인사부 회의에 참석해 주신 여러분께 감사 드립니다. 오늘 우리는 모든 부서장에게 발송할 새 평가 양식을 준비할 예정입니다.(86) 경영진에서 이제부터 직원 평가를 연 2회가 아니라 분기별로 진행하기로 했습니다. 기억하세요, 올해 주요 목표는 직원 생산성을 향상하는 것이며,(87) 직원들의 성과를 더 자주 파악해두는 것이 이에 도움이 될 것이라고 믿습니다. 자, 이제 20분 동안 평가 양식의 형식에 대해 아이디어를 구상해 주셨으면 합니다. 3명씩 그룹 지어서 떠오르는 아이디어를 나눠 보세요.(88) 감사합니다.

86 회의의 목적은 무엇인가?
(A) 입사 지원자를 평가하기 위해
(B) 행사를 준비하기 위해
(C) 평가 양식을 개발하기 위해
(D) 직원들을 소개하기 위해

87 화자에 따르면, 올해 목표는 무엇인가?
(A) 사업을 확장하는 것
(B) 생산성을 향상하는 것
(C) 부서를 합치는 것
(D) 운영비를 절감하는 것

88 화자는 청자들에게 무엇을 하라고 지시하는가?
(A) 다른 방으로 이동하라고
(B) 노트북 컴퓨터를 켜라고
(C) 그룹 토론을 하라고
(D) 몇 가지 서류에 서명하라고

영국

Questions 89-91 refer to the following speech.

W: Good evening. Thank you for coming to this career fair. Those of you who are currently studying or have studied statistics may find my speech quite interesting. **Much of my work has been in modeling and quantifying risk, primarily in the finance industry.(89)** I would look at new companies, for instance, and calculate how risky of an investment they would be. It is by no means easy, but no two days will be the same. In that sense, it's a job where you will never get stuck in a routine.(90) The most surprising part about my job is how many different people I get to meet.(91) With new companies coming in every day, there's always someone new to get to know.

89-91번은 다음 연설에 관한 문제입니다.

여: 안녕하세요. 이번 취업 박람회에 와주셔서 감사합니다. 현재 통계를 공부하거나 공부하신 분들은 제 강연이 아주 흥미롭다고 느끼실 겁니다. 이제까지 제가 담당한 일은 상당 부분 주로 금융업에서 리스크를 설계하고 수량화하는 것입니다.(89) 예를 들면, 신생 회사들을 살펴보고 투자 위험이 얼마나 클지 산출합니다. 결코 쉽지 않지만, 같은 날은 단 하루도 없습니다. 그런 면에서는 매일 절대 똑같은 일을 하지 않게 될 직업입니다.(90) 제 직업에서 가장 놀라운 부분은 매일 다양한 사람들을 많이 만나게 된다는 것입니다.(91) 매일 새로운 회사가 들어오기에, 항상 새로운 사람을 알게 됩니다.

89 화자의 직업은 무엇인가?
(A) 사업가
(B) 우주선 엔지니어
(C) 리스크 분석가
(D) 제품 디자이너

90 화자는 왜 "같은 날은 단 하루도 없습니다"라고 말하는가?
(A) 공통된 위험을 강조하기 위해
(B) 자신의 과거 고용주를 추천하기 위해
(C) 교육의 중요성을 강조하기 위해
(D) 잠재 혜택에 대해 언급하기 위해

91 화자의 직업에서 어떤 면이 그녀를 놀라게 했는가?
(A) 승진 기회
(B) 교류 기회
(C) 높은 기본 보수
(D) 출장 정도

미국

Questions 92-94 refer to the following excerpt from a meeting.

M: Thank you all PRM Legal staff for coming to today's meeting.(92) Today is officially the first day for Laurence Kim, our new chief operating officer. Mr. Kim has over 20 years of leadership experience in this industry, and he is excited to lead PRM Legal as we scale up our operations. Mr. Kim is very keen on meeting everyone here and understanding how we have been operating. Therefore, he has gratefully opened up his entire afternoon to get to know everyone on a personal level.(93) As your schedule allows, feel free to pop into his office for a short chat. A reminder that it is rare for executives to dedicate entire days to meetings.(94)

- -

92-94번은 다음 회의 발췌록에 관한 문제입니다.

남: 오늘 회의에 와주신 모든 PRM Legal 직원 여러분께 감사드립니다.(92) 오늘은 저희 신임 최고 운영 책임자이신 Laurence Kim의 공식 부임 첫날입니다. Mr. Kim이 이 업계에서 20년이 넘는 관리 경험을 갖고 계시고, 저희가 사업 규모를 확장함에 따라 PRM Legal을 이끄는 일에 의욕이 높으십니다. Mr. Kim은 여기 계신 모든 분과 만나고 저희가 지금까지 어떻게 운영해왔는지 파악하는 데 대단히 관심이 많으십니다. 이에, 모든 분과 개별적으로 친분을 쌓으시겠다고 기꺼이 오후 시간을 모두 비워 두셨습니다.(93) 일정이 되는대로 자유롭게 그분의 사무실에 방문하셔서 짧게 이야기 나누는 시간을 가져주세요. 임원이 하루를 통째로 만남에 할애하는 경우는 드물다는 것을 다시 한번 알려드립니다.(94)

92 청자들은 어디서 일하겠는가?
(A) 쇼핑몰에서
(B) 출판사에서
(C) 시장조사기관에서
(D) 법률 사무소에서

93 Laurence Kim은 점심시간 이후 무엇을 할 것인가?
(A) 다른 지점을 방문할 것이다
(B) 개별 지도에 참석할 것이다
(C) 계약을 협상할 것이다
(D) 직원들과 만날 것이다

94 화자는 "임원이 하루를 통째로 만남에 할애하는 경우는 드물다"라고 말할 때 무엇을 의미하는가?
(A) 관리자들은 겹치는 일정을 알고 있어야 한다.
(B) 청자들은 기회를 활용해야 한다.
(C) 오늘 사무실은 방문객에게 적합하지 않을 수 있다.
(D) 청자들은 프레젠테이션을 준비해야 한다.

미국

Questions 95-97 refer to the following excerpt from a meeting and graph.

W: Welcome to Johnson County Community College. My name is Teresa Hernandez, and I am the admissions director.(95) I'd like to talk about our Workplace Learning Program. In the past, instructors would be sent out to various companies in the area, and about 1,000 students completed a class every month. But when the college's Extension Services started offering the courses online, the number of people who registered for the classes dropped to just

500.(96) In hopes of figuring out why we had such a large drop, we conducted questionnaires with several hundred participants. I'm going to share that data with you now, and then, we will discuss what to do next.(97)

- -

95-97번은 다음 회의 발췌록과 그래프에 관한 문제입니다.

여: Johnson 카운티 전문대학에 오신 것을 환영합니다. 제 이름은 Teresa Hernandez이고 입학처장입니다.(95) 저는 저희 직장 교육 프로그램에 관하여 말씀드리려고 합니다. 과거에는 지역 내의 다양한 기업들에 강사들이 파견되었고 매달 약 1,000명의 학생이 수업을 수료했습니다. 그러나 대학의 순회 교육 부서에서 온라인으로 수업을 제공하기 시작하자 수업 등록자 수가 500명으로 떨어졌습니다.(96) 저희는 왜 이렇게 큰 폭의 감소가 있었는지 알아내기 위해 수백 명의 참가자들을 대상으로 설문조사를 실시했습니다. 제가 지금 여러분께 그 자료를 공유해 드리고 나서, 저희가 앞으로 무엇을 해야 할지 의논해 보겠습니다.(97)

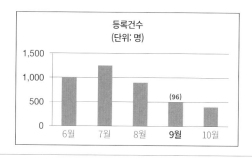

95 화자는 어디에서 일하겠는가?
(A) 교육기관에서
(B) 백화점에서
(C) 택배사에서
(D) 콘퍼런스 센터에서

96 시각 자료를 보시오. 온라인 프로그램은 어느 달에 시작되었는가?
(A) 6월
(B) 7월
(C) 8월
(D) 9월

97 이후에 어떤 일이 있겠는가?
(A) 청자들이 웹사이트에 접속할 것이다.
(B) 청자들을 여러 그룹으로 나눌 것이다.
(C) 인터뷰가 실시될 것이다.
(D) 설문조사 데이터가 발표될 것이다.

호주

Questions 98-100 refer to the following announcement and map.

M: We hope you are having a good weekend, shoppers. This is to let you know that we will be shutting down one hour earlier today due to the upcoming holiday.(98) Accordingly, the complimentary shuttles which can take you to the central bus station will also depart one hour earlier. Its departure location has not changed. It will still depart from the parking area parallel to Highway 24 and just north of CamCom.(99) Also, be sure to mark your calendars for next Saturday. We will be joined by the actors from the movie *Night Watch*, and they will be signing autographs. (100)

98-100번은 다음 안내방송과 지도에 관한 문제입니다.

남: 쇼핑객 여러분, 즐거운 주말 보내고 계시길 바랍니다. 다가오는 연휴로 인해 저희는 금일 한 시간 일찍 폐장할 예정임을 알려드립니다.(98) 이에, 중앙 버스 정류장까지 운행하는 무료 셔틀버스 또한 한 시간 일찍 출발합니다. 출발 장소는 변함없습니다. 그대로 24번 고속도로와 나란히 있으며 CamCom 북쪽에 위치한 주차 구역에서 출발합니다.(99) 그리고, 다음 주 토요일을 달력에 표시해 주시기를 바랍니다. 영화 <Night Watch>의 출연 배우들이 방문하며, 사인회를 할 예정입니다.(100)

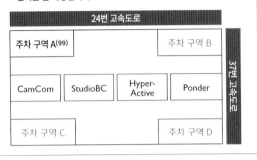

98 어떤 변화가 공지되고 있는가?
(A) 주차 요금 인상
(B) 곧 있을 수리
(C) 이른 폐장 시간
(D) 업데이트된 판매 행사

99 시각 자료를 보시오. 셔틀버스는 어디서 출발하는가?
(A) 주차 구역 A
(B) 주차 구역 B
(C) 주차 구역 C
(D) 주차 구역 D

100 다음 주 토요일에 어떤 행사가 열리는가?
(A) 경품 증정 행사
(B) 연휴 기념행사
(C) 음식 박람회
(D) 연예인 만남

TEST 04

PART 1
P. 58

1 (A) **2** (A) **3** (C) **4** (B) **5** (A) **6** (A)

PART 2
P. 62

7 (B) **8** (B) **9** (B) **10** (C) **11** (C) **12** (B)
13 (C) **14** (A) **15** (A) **16** (A) **17** (B) **18** (B)
19 (A) **20** (B) **21** (A) **22** (B) **23** (B) **24** (C)
25 (A) **26** (B) **27** (A) **28** (B) **29** (C) **30** (A)
31 (A)

PART 3
P. 63

32 (A) **33** (B) **34** (B) **35** (B) **36** (A) **37** (C)
38 (D) **39** (B) **40** (D) **41** (C) **42** (D) **43** (C)
44 (C) **45** (B) **46** (A) **47** (C) **48** (C) **49** (D)
50 (C) **51** (B) **52** (D) **53** (C) **54** (B) **55** (A)
56 (A) **57** (D) **58** (A) **59** (B) **60** (C) **61** (B)
62 (B) **63** (A) **64** (B) **65** (D) **66** (C) **67** (B)
68 (D) **69** (C) **70** (D)

PART 4
P. 67

71 (A) **72** (D) **73** (C) **74** (A) **75** (B) **76** (D)
77 (A) **78** (A) **79** (D) **80** (A) **81** (B) **82** (C)
83 (B) **84** (B) **85** (C) **86** (A) **87** (B) **88** (B)
89 (C) **90** (A) **91** (C) **92** (B) **93** (B) **94** (A)
95 (C) **96** (C) **97** (D) **98** (A) **99** (A) **100** (A)

PART 1
P. 58

1 미국
(A) A woman is examining some products.
(B) A woman is wiping off her sunglasses.
(C) A woman is filling a shopping cart.
(D) A woman is placing a basket on a counter.

(A) 여자가 몇몇 제품들을 살펴보고 있다.
(B) 여자가 선글라스를 닦고 있다.
(C) 여자가 쇼핑 카트를 채우고 있다.
(D) 여자가 계산대에 바구니를 놓고 있다.

2 미국
(A) He's resting his hands on a laptop computer.
(B) He's extending his arm to reach for a chair.
(C) He's walking through an aisle of bookshelves.
(D) He's checking out some books at a library.

(A) 남자가 노트북에 손을 얹고 있다.
(B) 남자가 의자를 잡으려고 팔을 뻗고 있다.
(C) 남자가 책꽂이 통로를 걷고 있다.
(D) 남자가 도서관에서 책을 대출하고 있다.

3 영국
(A) The man is typing on a keyboard.
(B) The man is seated under a window.
(C) Some pieces of paper have been stuck on a notice board.
(D) A plate has been left on the coffee table.

(A) 남자가 키보드로 입력하고 있다.
(B) 남자가 창문 아래에 앉아 있다.
(C) 종이 여러 장이 게시판에 붙어 있다.
(D) 접시가 커피 테이블 위에 놓여 있다.

4 호주
(A) A woman is reaching into her bag.
(B) A woman is holding onto a railing.
(C) The walkway is closed for maintenance.
(D) The staircase is being constructed.

(A) 여자가 가방 안에 손을 넣고 있다.
(B) 여자가 난간을 꼭 잡고 있다.
(C) 보도가 보수공사로 폐쇄되어 있다.
(D) 계단이 지어지고 있다.

5 미국
(A) Some people are seated in front of a window.
(B) Some people are gathered around a table.
(C) One of the men is looking down at a clipboard.
(D) One of the women is adjusting a chair.

(A) 몇몇 사람들이 창문 앞에 앉아 있다.
(B) 몇몇 사람들이 테이블 주위에 모여 있다.
(C) 남자들 중 한 명이 클립보드를 내려다보고 있다.
(D) 여자들 중 한 명이 의자를 조절하고 있다.

6 미국
(A) Cushions have been propped up on a sofa.
(B) A coffee table has been positioned between two armchairs.
(C) A painting has been mounted to the wall.
(D) A lamp has been placed on a corner of a table.

(A) 쿠션들이 소파에 받쳐져 있다.
(B) 두 개의 안락의자 사이에 커피 테이블이 놓여 있다.
(C) 그림이 벽에 걸려 있다.
(D) 램프가 탁자 모서리에 놓여 있다.

PART 2
P. 62

7 호주 ⇄ 미국
Why did you upload the job posting?
(A) Sure, I can do that right away.
(B) Because Barbara is retiring.
(C) No, not since last week.

왜 구인 공고를 올리셨나요?
(A) 그럼요, 바로 할 수 있어요.
(B) Barbara가 은퇴하거든요.
(C) 아니요, 지난주 이후로 아니에요.

8 미국 ⇄ 영국

Where is the nearest stationery shop?
(A) A few notepads.
(B) There's a city map.
(C) No, it closes at 8 o'clock.

가장 가까운 문구점이 어디인가요?
(A) 메모장 몇 개요.
(B) 시내 지도가 있어요.
(C) 아니요, 8시에 문을 닫아요.

9 호주 ⇄ 영국

How much do you estimate we'll use for car rental?
(A) For three days.
(B) About 500 dollars.
(C) I usually drive.

자동차 대여 비용은 얼마를 예상하고 있어요?
(A) 3일 동안이요.
(B) 500달러 정도요.
(C) 저는 보통 운전해서 가요.

10 미국 ⇄ 미국

Which beverage would you prefer?
(A) Sure. With extra ice, please.
(B) At the diner.
(C) I'll have some tea. Thanks.

어떤 음료를 드시겠어요?
(A) 네. 얼음을 추가해 주세요.
(B) 작은 식당에서요.
(C) 저는 차 마실게요. 감사해요.

11 미국 ⇄ 영국

Should we install the carpet on Wednesday or Thursday?
(A) Please read over the installation manual.
(B) I vacuumed the floor.
(C) Thursday would be more convenient.

카펫을 수요일에 설치할까요, 아니면 목요일에 할까요?
(A) 설치 매뉴얼을 꼼꼼히 읽어주세요.
(B) 진공청소기로 바닥을 청소했어요.
(C) 목요일이 더 편할 거예요.

12 미국 ⇄ 호주

Aren't you going to attend the client dinner with us?
(A) Can I have some water, please?
(B) I'm afraid I have a prior engagement.
(C) The deadline was extended.

고객 저녁 식사 자리에 저희와 함께 안 가세요?
(A) 물 좀 주시겠어요?
(B) 죄송하지만 선약이 있어요.
(C) 마감일이 연장됐어요.

13 미국 ⇄ 영국

How can I reach Mr. Chase?
(A) No, he isn't here.
(B) OK, he can meet you there.
(C) Let me transfer your call.

제가 Mr. Chase와 어떻게 연락할 수 있을까요?
(A) 아니요, 지금 안 계세요.
(B) 네, 거기서 당신을 만날 수 있으세요.
(C) 통화 연결해 드릴게요.

14 미국 ⇄ 미국

Where do you usually have lunch?
(A) At Hopewell Shopping Center.
(B) Around 12.
(C) I'll have the daily special.

보통 점심을 어디서 드세요?
(A) Hopewell 쇼핑센터에서요.
(B) 12시쯤에요.
(C) 저는 일일 특선으로 할게요.

15 영국 ⇄ 호주

The advertisement campaign was very successful, wasn't it?
(A) Yes, our sales have increased.
(B) She's the marketing manager.
(C) The end of the quarter.

광고 캠페인이 매우 성공적이었어요, 그렇죠?
(A) 네, 매출이 증가했어요.
(B) 그녀는 마케팅부장이에요.
(C) 분기 말이요.

16 미국 ⇄ 미국

Can you get some milk from the supermarket?
(A) It's not open on Sundays.
(B) With cereal for breakfast.
(C) Excellent market conditions.

슈퍼마켓에서 우유 좀 사다 줄래요?
(A) 일요일엔 문을 안 열어요.
(B) 아침 식사로 시리얼에 곁들여요.
(C) 시장 상황이 최고예요.

17 호주 ⇄ 미국

Does the subway go to your office?
(A) Did you check the schedule?
(B) Actually, I'll be taking a cab.
(C) The records are on my desk.

지하철이 당신 사무실 쪽으로 가나요?
(A) 일정표를 확인하셨나요?
(B) 실은, 저는 택시를 탈 거예요.
(C) 그 기록들은 제 책상에 있어요.

18 미국 ⇄ 미국

You've attended the annual marketing convention, haven't you?
(A) Yes, a new marketing strategy.
(B) There were some great sessions.
(C) Is that why we haven't?

연례 마케팅 총회에 참석하셨죠, 그렇지 않나요?
(A) 네, 새로운 마케팅 전략이요.
(B) 훌륭한 세션들이 좀 있었어요.
(C) 그래서 우리가 안 한 건가요?

19 영국 ⇄ 미국

Should I go to the art museum or the history museum?
(A) There's a new exhibition at the history museum.
(B) It was repainted last month.
(C) Can we go in a few minutes?

미술관으로 갈까요, 역사박물관으로 갈까요?
(A) 역사박물관에서 신규 전시가 있어요.
(B) 지난달에 새로 도색했어요.
(C) 몇 분 후에 출발할까요?

20 미국 ⇄ 호주

When will the autumn performance series start?
(A) This is the 8th episode of the documentary series.
(B) You should ask Ji-hoon.
(C) In room 406.

가을 공연 시리즈는 언제 시작하나요?
(A) 이번이 다큐 시리즈의 여덟 번째 에피소드예요.
(B) Ji-hoon한테 물어보세요.
(C) 406호에서요.

21 미국 ⇄ 영국

Do you want me to make the dinner reservation?
(A) No, I'll take care of it.
(B) I made a mistake.
(C) For the client dinner.

제가 저녁 식사 예약을 할까요?
(A) 아니에요, 제가 할게요.
(B) 제가 실수했어요.
(C) 고객 저녁 식사를 위해서요.

22 미국 ⇄ 미국

How do you know that this new flavor will be more popular?
(A) That was a delicious meal.
(B) We conducted many surveys.
(C) This design seems quite popular.

이 새로운 맛이 더 인기 있을지 어떻게 아세요?
(A) 맛있는 식사였어요.
(B) 저희가 설문조사를 많이 했어요.
(C) 이 디자인이 꽤 인기 있는 것 같아요.

23 호주 ⇄ 미국

Are you going to the annual conference next month?
(A) Some product demonstrations.
(B) I won't be attending this year.
(C) She's a guest speaker.

다음 달 연례 총회에 가실 거예요?
(A) 몇 번의 제품 시연이요.
(B) 올해는 참석하지 않을 거예요.
(C) 그녀는 초청 연사입니다.

24 영국 ⇄ 호주

When will you need my help with the furniture we ordered?
(A) We need many parts for the assembly.
(B) Each one costs around 500 dollars.
(C) The delivery truck just got here.

주문한 가구에 언제 도움이 필요하세요?
(A) 조립에 부품이 많이 필요해요.
(B) 한 개에 비용이 500달러 정도 해요.
(C) 방금 배송 트럭이 도착했어요.

25 미국 ⇄ 미국

We should buy some decorations for Melissa's birthday party, shouldn't we?
(A) Yes, I'll do that right away.
(B) By Saturday morning at 11.
(C) It's not a good location.

우리가 Melissa의 생일 파티용 장식용품을 좀 사야 해요, 그렇죠?
(A) 네, 제가 지금 바로 할게요.
(B) 토요일 오전 11시까지요.
(C) 좋은 장소는 아니네요.

26 미국 ⇄ 영국

There's a bit of coffee left in the coffeemaker if you would like some.
(A) Should I turn left or right?
(B) Thanks. I could really use some.
(C) Not as much as I used to.

원하시면, 커피메이커에 커피가 좀 남았어요.
(A) 좌회전할까요, 우회전할까요?
(B) 고마워요. 정말 필요했어요.
(C) 예전만큼은 아니에요.

27 미국 ⇄ 호주

Who's demonstrating our latest software at the trade expo?
(A) An e-mail was just sent out.
(B) During the presentation.
(C) Automatically check for updates.

누가 무역 박람회에서 최신 소프트웨어를 시연할 예정인가요?
(A) 방금 이메일이 발송됐어요.
(B) 프레젠테이션 중에요.
(C) 자동으로 업데이트를 확인해요.

28 영국 ⇄ 미국

Doesn't the coffee machine on the fourth floor need to be fixed?
(A) We produce machine parts.
(B) Thanks for the reminder.
(C) I need to make 50 copies.

4층에 있는 커피 머신 수리해야 하지 않아요?
(A) 저희는 기계 부품을 생산합니다.
(B) 상기시켜줘서 고마워요.
(C) 50부 만들어야 해요.

29 영국 ⇄ 호주

Where is Elijah's desk?
(A) In the latest city election.
(B) Could you pass me some office supplies?
(C) The finance team moved upstairs.

Elijah 자리가 어디죠?
(A) 최근 시 선거에서요.
(B) 사무용품 좀 주실래요?
(C) 재무팀은 위층으로 옮겼어요.

30 미국 ⇄ 미국

The deadline for submitting the report to the CEO is next Wednesday.
(A) Our team completed it last night.
(B) I watched that news report.
(C) No, just one signature is necessary.

CEO 보고서 제출 마감일은 다음 주 수요일이에요.
(A) 저희 팀은 어젯밤에 완료했어요.
(B) 그 뉴스 봤어요.
(C) 아니요, 서명 하나만 있으면 돼요.

31 호주 ⇄ 미국

Why is the trade show being held in Hong Kong?
(A) That's where the organization is located.
(B) We don't provide refunds on registration fees.
(C) I won't be giving a presentation until the last day.

무역 박람회가 왜 Hong Kong에서 열리나요?
(A) 조직이 그곳에 있거든요.

(B) 등록비는 환불해 드리지 않습니다.

(C) 저는 마지막 날에 발표할 예정이에요.

PART 3

P. 63

미국 ⇄ 미국

Questions 32-34 refer to the following conversation.

W: Jordan, ever since we began expanding our clothing store, I've noticed we haven't been getting many customers.(32) Let's discuss some ways we can increase our sales.

M: You know, construction workers are always going in and out of the building. So it might look like our store is closed. **We should put a big sign out front**(33) to show that we're open.

W: That's a great idea. We should make sure the text on the sign stands out so that it catches the customers' attention right away.

M: All right. **Let's get Kay to make it. She's skilled in graphic design.**(34) She's the one who created the store's logo.

32-34번은 다음 대화에 관한 문제입니다.

여: Jordan, 제가 보니까 우리가 옷 가게를 확장한 이후로 손님이 많지 않네요.(32) 판매량을 늘릴 수 있는 방법을 의논해 봅시다.

남: 아시다시피, 공사 인부들이 항상 건물을 드나들고 있잖아요. 그래서 우리 가게가 문을 닫은 것처럼 보일 수 있어요. 우리가 영업 중이라는 걸 보여줄 수 있게 **입구 쪽에 큰 표지판을 내걸어야겠어요.**(33)

여: 정말 좋은 생각이에요. 고객들의 시선을 바로 사로잡을 수 있게 표지판의 문구는 반드시 눈에 잘 띄게 해야 해요.

남: 알겠어요. Kay가 만들게 하죠. 그래픽 디자인을 잘하거든요.(34) 그 친구가 바로 매장 로고를 만든 사람이에요.

---

32 화자들은 어떤 종류의 사업체에서 일하는가?

(A) 의류 소매업체

(B) 광고 대행사

(C) 건설회사

(D) 식료품점

33 남자는 무엇을 권장하는가?

(A) 할인을 제공하는 것

(B) 표지판을 거는 것

(C) 회사를 고용하는 것

(D) 예산을 조정하는 것

34 남자는 Kay가 무엇에 능숙하다고 말하는가?

(A) 상품을 판매하는 것

(B) 그래픽을 디자인하는 것

(C) 웹사이트를 제작하는 것

(D) 신규 입사자를 교육하는 것

미국 ⇄ 호주

Questions 35-37 refer to the following conversation.

W: Hey, Glenn. I finished reviewing feedback from our recent questionnaire. According to the responses, a lot of customers are dissatisfied with our online store's new payment application.(35)

M: Really? There were some security issues with our previous version, but our development team already worked hard to fix that.

W: Well, the main issue now is that the process is a lot more complex.(36) Customers are complaining that they have to install unnecessary programs just to make a purchase.

M: Hmm... I think we should post a note on our website to explain that these programs are required for security purposes.(37)

W: I can do that today.

35-37번은 다음 대화에 관한 문제입니다.

여: 안녕하세요, Glenn. 최근 설문에서 얻은 의견 검토를 마무리했어요. 응답에 따르면, 많은 고객이 우리 온라인 매장의 새로운 결제 애플리케이션을 불만스러워해요.(35)

남: 정말요? 이전 버전에 보안 문제가 있었지만, 우리 개발팀에서 그걸 해결하려고 이미 아주 열심히 작업했는데요.

여: 음, 현재 가장 큰 문제는 절차가 훨씬 더 복잡해졌다는 거예요.(36) 고객들이 결제하려면 불필요한 프로그램을 설치해야 한다고 불평하네요.

남: 흠... 이들 프로그램이 보안을 위해 필요하다는 내용을 우리 웹사이트에 게시하는 게 좋겠어요.(37)

여: 제가 오늘 할 수 있어요.

---

35 대화의 주제는 무엇인가?

(A) 사업 확장

(B) 설문 응답

(C) 연간 예산

(D) 채용 가능성이 있는 입사 지원자

36 여자는 무엇이 가장 큰 문제라고 말하는가?

(A) 애플리케이션 사용이 어렵다.

(B) 팀에 인력이 부족하다.

(C) 몇몇 비용이 너무 많이 든다.

(D) 몇몇 직원들이 의욕이 없다.

37 남자는 무엇을 하는 것을 권장하는가?

(A) 하드웨어를 업그레이드하는 것

(B) 보안 직원과 이야기하는 것

(C) 설명을 게시하는 것

(D) 웹사이트를 다시 디자인하는 것

미국 ⇄ 영국

Questions 38-40 refer to the following conversation.

M: Daisy, our new delivery option has been very popular at all of our dining locations.(38) That's been great for business. But have you looked at the customer reviews from our social media page? I'm a bit worried.

W: I have. There were some comments about the styrofoam containers we use for takeout orders. The styrofoam isn't recyclable, so customers are worried about the environmental impact.(39) I think it's a valid concern.

M: Well, why don't we start using recyclable cardboard containers from now on?

W: Yes, that's a great idea. Customers will appreciate our eco-friendly packaging.(40)

38-40번은 다음 대화에 관한 문제입니다.

남: Daisy, 새로운 배송 옵션이 저희 식당 전 지점에서 아주 인기가 많아요.(38) 사업에는 아주 좋았어요. 그런데 소셜 미디어 페이지에 있는 고객 후기 보셨나요? 좀 걱정돼요.

여: 봤어요. 테이크아웃 주문에 사용하는 스티로폼 용기에 관한 언급이 있었죠. 스티로폼이 재활용이 안 돼서, 고객들이 환경에 미치는 영향을 걱정하고 있어요.(39) 타당한 우려인 것 같아요.

남: 그럼, 이제부터 재활용되는 종이 용기를 사용해볼까요?

여: 네, 아주 좋은 생각이에요. 고객은 저희 친환경 포장재를 환영할 거예요.(40)

38 화자들은 어떤 종류의 사업체에서 일하겠는가?
(A) 세탁 서비스
(B) 법률 사무소
(C) 소매업체
(D) 식당

39 여자는 어떤 우려를 언급하는가?
(A) 비닐봉지가 잘 찢어진다.
(B) 용기를 재활용할 수 없다.
(C) 음식이 빨리 식는다.
(D) 배송비가 너무 비싸다.

40 여자는 왜 남자의 제안이 마음에 든다고 말하는가?
(A) 이익을 증대시킬 것이다.
(B) 배송 시간이 단축될 것이다.
(C) 투자자를 끌어들일 것이다.
(D) 고객을 만족시킬 것이다.

미국 ⇄ 미국

Questions 41-43 refer to the following conversation.

W: Metro System. How can I help you?

M: Hello. I'm trying to head over to Prince Edward station. I've been waiting for the subway train for more than 20 minutes, but the train still hasn't arrived.(41) I have a job interview in 30 minutes, and I can't be late!

W: I apologize for the inconvenience. I'll take a look into this matter right away. Which station are you at?(42)

M: Quarry Bay, on the blue line.

W: Let me check the circuit board. Ah, there has been a delay due to a mechanical failure.(43) Your train should arrive in less than five minutes, though.

41-43번은 다음 대화에 관한 문제입니다.

여: Metro System입니다. 무엇을 도와드릴까요?

남: 안녕하세요. 제가 Prince Edward역을 가려고 하는데요. 20분 넘게 지하철을 기다리는 중인데, 아직도 안 왔어요.(41) 제가 30분 후에 면접이 있어서 늦으면 안 돼요!

여: 불편을 끼쳐드려 죄송합니다. 바로 확인할게요. 어느 역에 계세요?(42)

남: 블루라인 Quarry Bay요.

여: 노선도를 확인해 볼게요. 아, 기계 결함으로 지연이 있었네요.(43) 하지만 열차가 5분 안으로는 도착할 거예요.

41 남자는 왜 전화하는가?
(A) 좌석을 업그레이드하기 위해
(B) 추천을 해주기 위해
(C) 불만을 접수하기 위해
(D) 길을 물어보기 위해

42 여자는 어떤 정보를 요청하는가?
(A) 전화번호
(B) 신분증
(C) 이동 시간
(D) 역명

43 여자는 무엇이 지연을 초래하고 있다고 말하는가?
(A) 교통사고
(B) 험한 날씨
(C) 시설 고장
(D) 도로 보수

영국 ⇄ 호주

Questions 44-46 refer to the following conversation.

W: Rodney, the company's 20th anniversary is coming up soon, and I'm responsible for ordering the cake for the party.(44) You live nearby, right?

M: Yes, right down the street. Why do you ask?

W: I found some bakeries near the office. Cake Walk seems to have good reviews. Have you been there before?(45)

M: Well, I've ordered from The Baking Room for special occasions. They made my mother's birthday cake this year.(45)

W: I see. I'll give them a call today or go down to the store so I can see some of their cake designs.(46)

M: You know what? I might still have the catalog they sent me from when I was ordering the cake for my mom. Oh, here it is!(46)

44-46번은 다음 대화에 관한 문제입니다.

여: Rodney, 곧 회사 20주년 창립 기념일인데, 제가 행사용 케이크 주문 담당이에요.(44) 이 근처 사시죠, 맞죠?

남: 맞아요, 바로 아래쪽이에요. 왜 물어보세요?

여: 제가 사무실 근처 베이커리를 발견했어요. Cake Walk의 후기가 좋은 것 같아요. 거기 가본 적 있으세요?(45)

남: 음, 저는 특별 행사용으로 The Baking Room에서 주문해봤어요. 거기서 올해 어머니 생신용 케이크를 만들었어요.(45)

여: 그렇군요. 제가 오늘 케이크 디자인을 살펴볼 겸 매장에 전화해보거나 방문해 봐야겠어요.(46)

남: 있잖아요. 제가 어머니께 드릴 케이크 주문할 때 받은 카탈로그를 아직 가지고 있을지도 몰라요. 오, 여기 있네요!(46)

44 어떤 종류의 행사가 준비되고 있는가?
(A) 생일 축하 행사
(B) 미술 전시회
(C) 회사 창립기념일
(D) 시즌 홍보 행사

45 남자는 왜 "저는 특별 행사용으로 The Baking Room에서 주문해봤어요"라고 말하는가?
(A) 의견에 동의하기 위해
(B) 다른 옵션을 제안하기 위해
(C) 제안에 거절하기 위해
(D) 불만을 제기하기 위해

46 화자들은 다음에 무엇을 하겠는가?

(A) 제품들을 살펴볼 것이다

(B) 행사장을 예약할 것이다

(C) 고객에게 전화할 것이다

(D) 청구서를 요청할 것이다

호주 ⇄ 영국 ⇄ 미국

Questions 47-49 refer to the following conversation with three speakers.

M1: Welcome to Genie Sports Emporium.**(47)** Do you require any assistance?

W: Yes, I'm looking for a baseball bat.**(47)** I want to buy it for my nephew. Can you suggest a good brand?

M1: Actually, my coworker would probably know better. James, this customer would like a recommendation for a good baseball bat.

M2: Hmm... I'd go for a Baton Co. bat. I'm sure you know the company. They've been operating in this city for nearly 100 years.**(48)**

W: Oh yeah. I've heard of them.

M2: Also, this bat includes a 10-percent-off voucher for any other Baton Co. product. But you can only use it online. **(49)**

47-49번은 다음 세 화자의 대화에 관한 문제입니다.

남1: Genie 스포츠 백화점에 오신 것을 환영합니다.**(47)** 도움이 필요하신가요?

여: 네, 야구 배트를 찾고 있어요.**(47)** 조카에게 사 주려고요. 괜찮은 브랜드를 추천해 주시겠어요?

남1: 실은 제 동료가 더 잘 알 겁니다. James, 이 손님께서 괜찮은 야구 배트를 추천받고 싶어 하세요.

남2: 음... 저라면 Baton사의 야구 배트로 고를 겁니다. 그 회사는 잘 아실 거예요. 이곳에서 영업한 지 거의 100년이 다 돼 가죠.**(48)**

여: 아, 네. 들어 봤어요.

남2: 그리고, 이 배트에는 Baton사에서 나온 다른 모든 제품에 쓸 수 있는 10퍼센트 할인쿠폰이 포함돼 있어요. 인터넷에서만 사용하실 수 있긴 하지만요.**(49)**

47 대화는 어디에서 일어나겠는가?

(A) 의류 액세서리 매장에서

(B) 골동품 매장에서

(C) 스포츠용품점에서

(D) 축구 경기장에서

48 Baton사는 무엇으로 알려져 있는가?

(A) 저렴한 제품을 판매하는 것

(B) 자격을 갖춘 직원을 채용하는 것

(C) 오랫동안 영업한 것

(D) 상을 받은 것

49 제품에 어떤 추가 혜택이 있는가?

(A) 청소 도구가 포함돼 있다.

(B) 큰 운반용 가방이 딸려 있다.

(C) 10년 품질보증이 포함돼 있다.

(D) 온라인 할인 쿠폰이 딸려 있다.

호주 ⇄ 영국

Questions 50-52 refer to the following conversation.

M: Welcome to Beachside Resort.

W: Hi, I was wondering if you have any rooms available tonight?

M: Let me check.

W: My connecting flight was canceled so I need to find a place to stay last minute.**(50)** It's just been a disastrous day.

M: Oh, what an inconvenience. Lucky for you, we have one room available. Room 710. It comes with fast internet connection in case you need to send any e-mails.**(51)**

W: That's great, thanks. That reminds me. Do you have a shuttle bus that goes to the airport by any chance?

M: Unfortunately, we don't. The shuttles only run downtown. However, we offer our guests a reduced fare if you use our chauffeur service.**(52)** All rides are air-conditioned and provide refreshments.

50-52번은 다음 대화에 관한 문제입니다.

남: Beachside 리조트에 오신 것을 환영합니다.

여: 안녕하세요, 오늘 밤 묵을 수 있는 방이 있을까요?

남: 확인해 볼게요.

여: 제 연결 항공편이 취소돼서 급하게 묵을 곳을 마련해야 합니다.**(50)** 끔찍한 하루네요.

남: 아, 불편하시겠네요. 다행히도, 객실이 하나 있습니다. 710호입니다. 혹시 이메일을 보내야 하실 경우에 대비해서 초고속 인터넷 연결이 제공됩니다.**(51)**

여: 정말 좋네요, 감사합니다. 그러고 보니 생각나서 그런데요. 혹시 공항으로 가는 셔틀버스가 있나요?

남: 아쉽게도, 없습니다. 시내로 가는 셔틀만 운행합니다. 그런데 저희 기사서비스를 이용하실 경우 숙박객께는 할인된 가격을 제공해 드립니다.**(52)** 모든 차량에는 에어컨이 설치되어 있고 다과가 제공됩니다.

50 여자는 자신의 항공편에 관하여 무엇을 언급하는가?

(A) 짐이 분실됐다.

(B) 항공기가 시끄러웠다.

(C) 항공편이 취소되었다.

(D) 좌석이 불편했다.

51 남자는 710호에 관하여 뭐라고 말하는가?

(A) 바다 전망이다.

(B) 초고속 인터넷이 된다.

(C) 침대가 하나 더 있다.

(D) 발코니가 있다.

52 남자는 여자에게 어떤 추가 서비스를 제안하는가?

(A) 세탁 서비스

(B) 무료 조식

(C) 객실 할인

(D) 운전기사

미국 ⇄ 미국

Questions 53-55 refer to the following conversation.

M: Hi, there. I need to hire a catering service for the opening of my gallery.**(53)**

W: You've certainly come to the right place. When will the opening be?

M: Friday. I know it's short notice, but the other catering company pulled out last minute. **Would you be able to cater for us this Friday at 7 P.M?**(54)

W: We normally require more notice than that, but we do happen to have an opening. We offer a couple of dining options for events. We can serve appetizers and drinks or dinner.

M: I think appetizers and drinks sound appropriate.

W: Great, **I'll send you some menu options that you can choose from.**(55)

53-55번은 다음 대화에 관한 문제입니다.

남: 안녕하세요. 제가 화랑을 개관해서 출장연회 서비스를 이용해야 합니다.(53)

여: 제대로 찾아오셨습니다. 개관일이 언제세요?

남: 금요일이에요. 촉박한 건 아는데요, 다른 업체에서 막판에 취소해서요. **이번 주 금요일 저녁 7시에 저희에게 음식 공급을 해주실 수 있으신가요?**(54)

여: 보통은 그보다 먼저 알려주셔야 하는데요, 때마침 빈 자리가 하나 있네요. 저희는 행사에 두 가지 식사 옵션을 제공합니다. 저희는 애피타이저와 음료 또는 저녁 식사를 준비해 드릴 수 있습니다.

남: 애피타이저와 음료가 적당할 것 같아요.

여: 좋습니다, **선택하실 수 있는 메뉴 옵션을 보내드릴게요.**(55)

53 남자는 어디서 일하는가?
(A) 연예기획사에서
(B) 사립학교에서
(C) 화랑에서
(D) 병원에서

54 남자는 무엇에 관하여 묻는가?
(A) 장소의 위치
(B) 서비스의 이용 가능성
(C) 행사 날짜
(D) 계약 조건

55 여자는 무엇을 하겠다고 말하는가?
(A) 메뉴를 보내겠다고
(B) 제품을 배송하겠다고
(C) 비용을 결정하겠다고
(D) 오락거리를 고용하겠다고

미국 ⇄ 호주

Questions 56-58 refer to the following conversation.

W: Darren, before your team gets started, **I'd like to discuss what renovation work you'll be doing on the backyard this afternoon.**(56) Please follow me.

M: Oh, **check out these fountains. They've got to be at least 50 years old!**(57) I don't think they'll suit the new backyard design.

W: The patio isn't great, either. Everything there needs to be removed and replaced. So the first thing you'll do today is install floor tiles and put in new furniture in that area.

M: Hmm... **This patio area is larger than I thought. Do we also have to finish planting all the flowers today?**(58)

W: No. When I saw how big the patio was, I decided to put that work off until tomorrow.

56-58번은 다음 대화에 관한 문제입니다.

여: Darren, 당신 팀이 일을 시작하기 전에 오늘 오후에 뒤뜰에서 어떤 개조 작업을 하실 건지 의논했으면 좋겠어요.(56) 저를 따라오세요.

남: 오, 이 분수대 좀 보세요. 최소 50년은 되었을 거예요!(57) 새 뒤뜰 디자인에 어울릴 것 같지는 않군요.

여: 테라스도 그리 좋지는 않아요. 거기 있는 걸 전부 다 제거하고 교체해야 해요. 그래서 오늘 할 첫 작업은 그 구역에 바닥 타일을 깔고 새 가구를 넣는 거예요.

남: 음... 이 테라스는 제가 생각했던 것보다 넓네요. 꽃 심는 것도 전부 오늘 다 끝내야 하나요?(58)

여: 아니요. 테라스가 얼마나 큰지 봤을 때 그 작업은 내일로 미루기로 했어요.

56 대화의 주제는 무엇인가?
(A) 조경 프로젝트
(B) 가격 견적
(C) 비어 있는 부동산
(D) 원예 도구

57 남자는 분수대에 관하여 뭐라고 말하는가?
(A) 제대로 작동하지 않는다.
(B) 내일 설치될 것이다.
(C) 너무 무겁다.
(D) 구식으로 보인다.

58 남자가 "이 테라스는 제가 생각했던 것보다 넓네요"라고 말할 때 무엇을 내비치는가?
(A) 업무를 끝내는 데 시간이 좀 걸릴 것이다.
(B) 매니저의 승인이 필요하다.
(C) 추가 용품을 주문해야 한다.
(D) 인부들을 더 요청하고자 한다.

미국 ⇄ 영국 ⇄ 호주

Questions 59-61 refer to the following conversation with three speakers.

M1: Hi, Isabel. **Good to see you again this year at the leadership conference.**(59)

W: Glad to see you, too, Edwin. **Let me introduce you to my colleague, Lester. He recently started working at our company as the director of finance,**(60) so I asked him to join me at the convention.

M1: Nice to meet you, Lester. The keynote speaker for this year is actually from a top financial services company. Did you sign up for that?

M2: Yes, I've signed up for several sessions in advance, but I still haven't checked in yet.(61)

M1: I have to do that as well. **Why don't we head over to the registration desk together?**(61)

59-61번은 다음 세 화자의 대화에 관한 문제입니다.

남1: 안녕하세요, Isabel. 올해 리더십 학회에서 다시 뵙게 되어 반갑습니다.(59)

여: 저도 뵙게 되어 기쁩니다, Edwin. 제 동료 Lester를 소개할게요. 그는 최근 우리 회사에서 재무 담당 이사로 근무하기 시작해서,(60) 제가 그에게 대화에 참석해 달라고 부탁했습니다.

남1: 만나서 반가워요, Lester. 올해의 기조연설자는 실제로 일류 금융 서비스 회사 출신입니다. 신청하셨어요?

남2: 네, 세션 몇 개를 미리 신청하긴 했는데, 아직 체크인하지는 않았습니다.(61)

남1: 저도 그걸 해야 합니다. 우리 같이 접수처로 가는 게 어때요?(61)

59 화자들은 어디에 있는가?
(A) 기자회견에
(B) 전문가 대회에
(C) 제품 시연회에
(D) 직원 세미나에

60 여자는 Lester에 관하여 뭐라고 말하는가?
(A) 수습 기간 중이다.
(B) 다른 부서로 옮겼다.
(C) 최근에 직장을 옮겼다.
(D) 최근에 승진했다.

61 화자들은 다음에 무엇을 할 것인가?
(A) 몇몇 세션에 등록할 것이다
(B) 행사에 체크인할 것이다
(C) 서류를 찾아올 것이다
(D) 등록 양식을 작성할 것이다

미국 ⇄ 미국

Questions 62-64 refer to the following conversation and sign.

M: Hello. I just put gas in my car at pump 8, but the receipt wouldn't print. Can I get it here?(62)

W: Sure. Give me a second.

M: Of course. By the way, I'm surprised at how cheap your gas prices are. **It was only $1.10 per gallon. I've paid a lot more at other gas stations.(63)**

W: Yeah, a lot of customers say that. Anyway, here you go. **Also, today, we're offering complimentary bottled water with every fuel purchase.(64)**

62-64번은 다음 대화와 안내판에 관한 문제입니다.

남: 안녕하세요. 제가 방금 8번 펌프에서 차에 기름을 넣었는데, 영수증이 출력되지 않네요. 여기서 받을 수 있나요?(62)

여: 물론이죠. 잠깐만 기다려 주세요.

남: 네. 그런데 기름값이 너무 싸서 놀랐어요. 갤런당 1.10달러밖에 안 하네요. 다른 주유소에서는 훨씬 더 많이 냈거든요.(63)

여: 네, 많은 고객이 그렇게 말씀하시죠. 자, 여기 있습니다. 그리고 오늘은 주유하시는 모든 분께 무료 생수를 제공해 드립니다.(64)

휘발유 종류	갤런당 가격
무연	1.10달러(63)
고급	1.20달러
최고급	1.35달러
디젤	1.55달러

62 남자는 무엇을 요청하는가?
(A) 비밀번호
(B) 영수증
(C) 안내서
(D) 환불

63 시각 자료를 보시오. 남자는 어떤 종류의 휘발유를 선택했는가?
(A) 무연
(B) 고급
(C) 최고급
(D) 디젤

64 남자는 연료 구입으로 무엇을 받을 것인가?
(A) 영화표
(B) 음료
(C) 상품권
(D) 자동차 액세서리

호주 ⇄ 미국

Questions 65-67 refer to the following conversation and computer screen.

M: You've reached Invoice Design's IT Department. How may I be of assistance?

W: Hello, I run an auto shop. **I purchased your program to create invoices for the repair and maintenance work I do on customers' vehicles. But I'm having some trouble making one.(65)** I've entered all the items, but **I don't know how to display the discount for replacing the vehicle's battery.(65)/(66)**

M: First, click on the DISCOUNT tab at the bottom of your screen. Your list will then have a box appear next to each item. Just check the ones you want to have the discount.

W: OK, **I was able to apply 15 percent to battery replacement. (66)** This should reflect the discount, right?

M: Yes. By the way, **next time, you might want to use our Web messenger service(67)** to get help more quickly.

65-67번은 다음 대화와 컴퓨터 화면에 관한 문제입니다.

남: Invoice Design IT 부서입니다. 어떻게 도와드릴까요?

여: 안녕하세요, 제가 자동차 정비소를 운영하는데요. 제가 고객 차량에 해드리는 수리 및 정비 작업용 청구서를 만들려고 귀사의 프로그램을 구입했는데요. 그런데 송장을 생성하는 데 문제가 좀 있어서요.(65) 모든 항목을 입력했지만, 차량 배터리 교체에 대한 할인을 나타내는 방법을 모르겠네요.(65)/(66)

남: 우선, 화면 아래에 DISCOUNT 탭을 클릭하세요. 그러면 목록에서 각 항목 옆에 박스가 나타날 겁니다. 할인을 적용하고 싶으신 것들에 체크하시면 됩니다.

여: 알았어요, 배터리 교체에 15퍼센트를 적용할 수 있었는데요.(66) 이게 할인을 반영해야 하는 거 맞죠?

남: 네. 그런데, 다음번에는 더 빠르게 도움을 받아보시려면 저희 웹 메신저 서비스를 이용해 보세요.(67)

송장	
작업 내용	가격
오일 교환	30달러
전면 유리 수리	70달러
배터리 교체	120달러(66)
타이어 설치	600달러

65 여자는 왜 전화하고 있는가?
(A) 보수점검 일정을 잡기 위해
(B) 특별 할인에 관해 문의하기 위해
(C) 비품을 구매하기 위해
(D) 프로그램에 대한 도움을 받기 위해

66 시각 자료를 보시오. 어느 가격이 변경될 것인가?
(A) 30달러
(B) 70달러
(C) 120달러
(D) 600달러

67 남자는 여자에게 다음번에 무엇을 하라고 권장하는가?
(A) 신용카드로 지불하라고
(B) 온라인 커뮤니케이션 서비스를 이용하라고
(C) 동영상 설명을 보라고
(D) 고객 후기를 확인하라고

호주 ⇄ 영국

Questions 68-70 refer to the following conversation and design options.

M: Hello, Jenny. **Here's the revised schedule for the world environment congress.**(68) The event is several months away, but we should make the final adjustments to the handbook.

W: I'm free to take care of that right now. While I work on the handbook, would you mind looking at some of the design options I made for the cover?

M: I like the one with the hands holding a globe since we're trying to save the earth.(69)

W: I like that one as well. By the way, **I'm putting together the video for the opening ceremony, but these clips are too pixelated. I'll need files with higher resolution. If you could send them...**(70)

M: Of course. I'll take care of that.

68-70번은 다음 대화와 디자인 옵션에 관한 문제입니다.

남: 안녕하세요, Jenny. **여기 수정된 세계 환경 회의 일정이에요.**(68) 행사까지 몇 달 남았지만, 핸드북에 최종 수정 작업을 해야 해요.

여: 지금 바로 처리할 시간 있어요. 제가 핸드북을 작업하는 동안 제가 커버용으로 만든 도안 옵션 좀 봐줄래요?

남: 우리가 지구를 구하려고 노력하는 거니까 손으로 지구를 잡고 있는 게 전 마음에 들어요.(69)

여: 저도 그게 좋아요. 그런데, 제가 개회식용 영상을 합치고 있는데, 이 영상들은 화질이 너무 안 좋네요. 해상도가 더 높은 파일이 필요해요. 혹시 보내주실 수 있으면...(70)

남: 그럼요. 제가 처리할게요.

68 화자들은 무엇을 계획하고 있는가?
(A) 비즈니스 컨벤션
(B) 도시 축제
(C) 기금 마련 캠페인
(D) 국제회의

69 시각 자료를 보시오. 남자는 어떤 디자인을 좋아하는가?
(A) 도안 A
(B) 도안 B
(C) 도안 C
(D) 도안 D

70 여자는 남자에게 무엇을 보내달라고 요청하는가?
(A) 편집실 주소
(B) 팀원 이름
(C) 일부 촬영 장비
(D) 일부 동영상 파일

PART 4
P. 67

미국

Questions 71-73 refer to the following excerpt from a meeting.

W: I've called this emergency meeting to discuss one of our T-shirt orders.(71) Initially, we were asked by BTA Marketing Co. to prepare 300 custom T-shirts for their sports festival on April 25. However, I just received a call from them saying that they'll now be having the event on April 15.(72) I know that leaves us with less time, but I think we can still get it done. I'll be requesting that everyone put in some extra hours over the next two weeks.(73) Of course, you'll be compensated for your time.

71-73번은 다음 회의 발췌록에 관한 문제입니다.

여: 저희 티셔츠 주문 건에 대해 논의 드리려고 이 긴급회의를 소집했습니다.(71) 처음에 BTA 마케팅사로부터 4월 25일에 있을 체육대회용 주문제작 티셔츠 300장을 준비해달라고 의뢰 받았습니다. 그런데 방금 행사를 4월 15일에 할 거라는 전화를 받았습니다.(72) 우리에게 시간이 얼마 없다는 건 알지만, 그래도 해낼 수 있다고 생각합니다. 여러분께 앞으로 2주간 몇 시간 정도 추가 근무를 해주기를 요청 드립니다.(73) 물론 근무 시간에 대한 보상은 받으실 겁니다.

71 화자는 어디에서 일하겠는가?
(A) 의류 제조업체에서
(B) 스포츠 경기장에서
(C) 마케팅 회사에서
(D) 회계 법인에서

72 화자는 주로 무엇을 논하고 있는가?
(A) 서비스 요금
(B) 새로운 회사 방침
(C) 행사 장소
(D) 일정 변동

73 화자는 청자들이 무엇을 하길 요청하는가?
(A) 배송을 준비하라고
(B) 보고서를 제출하라고
(C) 추가 근무를 하라고
(D) 고객에게 연락하라고

Questions 74-76 refer to the following talk.

M: Hello everyone. I hope everyone has had a chance to meet everyone in the room. **We have a very diverse crowd today, and I'm hearing a lot of chatter about the latest trends in building designs. I'm sure many of you have incorporated these trends into your work recently. (74)** Over the next few days in this program, we'll be highlighting some new important safety rules that the government will be implementing. (75) Earthquake protection is probably the one you would have heard the most about. **On the final day, we'll be hearing from a consulting team located in New Zealand. (76)** They'll be explaining to us some of their experiences regarding earthquakes.

74-76번은 다음 담화에 관한 문제입니다.

남: 여러분, 안녕하세요. 이 방에 계신 분들 모두 서로 만나볼 기회를 가지셨기를 바랍니다. 오늘은 아주 다양한 분들이 한자리에 모여 있기에, 건축 디자인의 최신 트렌드에 대한 많은 이야기가 들립니다. 많은 분들이 최근에 이러한 트렌드를 작업에 포함시키셨다고 확신합니다. (74) 이 프로그램에서는 앞으로 몇 일에 걸쳐, 정부에서 시행할 예정인 중요한 안전 규칙 몇 가지를 집중적으로 살펴볼 예정입니다. (75) 아마도 여러분이 가장 많이 들어본 건 지진 보호일 겁니다. 마지막 날에는 뉴질랜드에 있는 컨설팅 팀의 이야기를 들을 예정입니다. (76) 그들은 지진에 관한 경험을 설명해 줄 거예요.

74 청자들은 누구겠는가?
(A) 전문 건축가들
(B) 인터넷 광고주들
(C) 사업 컨설턴트들
(D) 기업 회계사들

75 프로그램의 주요 목적은 무엇인가?
(A) 회사 인지도를 확장하기 위해
(B) 새로운 지침을 설명하기 위해
(C) 장래 직원을 채용하기 위해
(D) 연말 행사를 계획하기 위해

76 화자는 청자들에게 마지막 날에 무엇을 할 거라고 말하는가?
(A) 회사를 방문할 거라고
(B) 시연회를 시청할 거라고
(C) 프로그램을 평가할 거라고
(D) 강연을 들을 거라고

Questions 77-79 refer to the following telephone message.

W: Good morning. My name is Yuka Matsumoto. **I was shopping at your store last night, checking out some sofas, (77)** and... **I believe I left my scarf there. (78)** It's made of silk with a green and red pattern on it. I remember having it when I was sitting on one of the brown leather couches. **I'm planning to come by after work tonight to have a look. (79)** But if you find it before then, please give me a call. My number is 555-4598. Thank you.

77-79번은 다음 전화 메시지에 관한 문제입니다.

여: 안녕하세요. 제 이름은 Yuka Matsumoto입니다. 제가 어제 저녁에 그쪽 매장에서 소파들을 좀 보면서 쇼핑을 했어요, (77) 그리고...

스카프를 두고 온 것 같아요. (78) 실크재질이고, 녹색과 빨간색 무늬가 있습니다. 제가 갈색 가죽 소파 중 하나에 앉아 있었을 때 가지고 있었다는 걸 기억합니다. 오늘 저녁 퇴근 후에 들러서 살펴보려고 합니다. (79) 하지만 그 전에 찾게 되신다면 전화 좀 부탁드립니다. 제 번호는 555-4598입니다. 고맙습니다.

77 여자는 어떤 종류의 사업체에 전화했겠는가?
(A) 가구 매장
(B) 카페
(C) 페인트 시공업체
(D) 도서관

78 여자는 왜 전화했는가?
(A) 분실된 물건에 관하여 문의하기 위해
(B) 영업시간을 알아보기 위해
(C) 할인을 요청하기 위해
(D) 예약을 다시 잡기 위해

79 여자는 오늘 저녁에 무엇을 할 것이라고 말하는가?
(A) 고객을 데리러 갈 거라고
(B) 다른 지점에 전화할 거라고
(C) 초과근무를 할 거라고
(D) 사업장을 살펴볼 거라고

Questions 80-82 refer to the following speech.

M: I would like to welcome all of you to the opening ceremony of the new city hall building. **The building now has a vertical garden that I'm particularly excited about. The garden wall extends from the first floor all the way up to the tenth floor. (80)** It's a great honor for me, your mayor, to be the first person to step through these doors after a 16-month-long construction work. **Many citizens have expressed concern with the length of time it took to finish. But, as you will be able to see, this is a unique space. (81)** Now, I invite you to join me as we tour the brand-new city hall building. (82)

80-82번은 다음 연설에 관한 문제입니다.

남: 새로운 시청사 개관식에 오신 모든 분을 환영합니다. 이제 건물에 제가 특히 좋아하는 수직 정원이 생겼습니다. 정원 벽은 1층부터 10층까지 이어져 있습니다. (80) 16개월에 걸친 긴 공사 끝에 제가 시장으로서 첫 번째로 이 문을 통과하게 되어 대단히 영광입니다. 많은 시민 여러분께서 완공되기까지 걸린 기간에 우려를 표하셨습니다. 하지만 보시게 되겠지만, 이곳은 독특한 공간입니다. (81) 이제, 저와 함께 새롭게 문을 연 시청 건물을 둘러보시기 바랍니다. (82)

80 화자는 무엇에 열정적인가?
(A) 정원 벽
(B) 에스컬레이터 시스템
(C) 설치 예술
(D) 창문 디자인

81 화자는 왜 "이곳은 독특한 공간입니다"라고 말하는가?
(A) 잠재 투자자를 설득하기 위해
(B) 프로젝트 기간을 정당화하기 위해
(C) 직원들에게 감사를 표하기 위해
(D) 더 높은 예산을 요구하기 위해

82 화자는 다음에 무엇을 하겠는가?
(A) 구조물의 사진을 찍을 것이다
(B) 식사를 할 것이다
(C) 견학을 할 것이다
(D) 프레젠테이션을 주도할 것이다

미국

Questions 83-85 refer to the following tour information.

M: Thank you for coming to today's hike. My name is Bruce, and I'll be guiding you today. **This sign marks the beginning of the Flower Road Trail. This will take us through Cauthon Forest and put us on the other side of Lethon.(83)** This trail can be fairly challenging, so please let me know if you need to take a break. **During breaks, I can pass around some snacks while we take in the views.(84)** We have plenty of time today, and I have a few activities planned throughout the trail. **When we get to an activity spot, I'll stop the group and explain what we are doing.(85)**

83-85번은 다음 투어 정보에 관한 문제입니다.

남: 오늘 하이킹에 와주셔서 감사합니다. 제 이름은 Bruce이고, 제가 오늘 여러분을 안내해 드릴 예정입니다. **이 표지판은 Flower Road 산책로의 시작을 나타냅니다. 이 길로 가면 Cauthon 숲을 통해 Lethon의 반대편으로 가게 됩니다.(83)** 이 산책로는 꽤 힘들 수 있으니, 휴식이 필요하시면 저에게 알려주세요. **휴식을 취하는 동안, 경치를 감상하면서 드시도록 제가 간식을 나눠드립니다.(84)** 오늘은 시간이 여유 있어, 제가 산책로를 걷는 동안 할만한 몇 가지 활동을 마련했습니다. **활동 장소에 도달하면, 제가 그룹을 멈춰 세우고 무엇을 하게 될지 설명해 드릴게요.(85)**

83 화자는 산책로에 관하여 무엇을 설명하는가?
(A) 언제 발견되었는지
(B) 어디로 그룹을 데려가는지
(C) 왜 이따금 통제되는지
(D) 어떤 야생동물이 발견되는지

84 화자는 청자들에게 기다리는 동안 무엇을 하라고 제안하는가?
(A) 운동을 하라고
(B) 경치를 즐기라고
(C) 선물을 구입하라고
(D) 안내서를 읽으라고

85 화자는 왜 멈출 예정이라고 말하는가?
(A) 기상 상황을 주기적으로 보기 위해
(B) 단체 사진을 찍기 위해
(C) 몇몇 활동을 하기 위해
(D) 안전 수칙을 설명하기 위해

영국

Questions 86-88 refer to the following telephone message.

W: Good afternoon, Mr. Herzog. When we spoke on the phone yesterday, I asked you to come by our office to give us your bank account details to ensure that your wages get deposited correctly.(86)/(87) But I just realized that we already have your information from the last job you did for us.(87) Your payment will be sent to that account on the tenth of next month. Additionally, I suggest that you contact Human Resources and arrange to collect the

official papers you'll need when filing your taxes. I'd do that sooner rather than later.(88)

86-88번은 다음 전화 메시지에 관한 문제입니다.

여: 안녕하세요, Mr. Herzog. 어제 통화할 때, 임금이 제대로 입금되는지 확인할 수 있게 저희 사무실에 들러서 은행 계좌 정보를 알려달라고 요청했습니다.(86)/(87) 그런데 지난번에 해주신 작업 때문에 정보를 이미 가지고 있다는 걸 방금 알았어요.(87) 다음 달 10일에 그 계좌로 입금될 거예요. 그리고 세금을 신고하실 때 필요한 공식 서류를 받아 가실 수 있도록 인사팀에 연락하시기를 권해드립니다. 빨리하시는 게 나을 거예요.(88)

86 화자는 어느 부서에서 근무하겠는가?
(A) 급여 관리
(B) 정보 기술
(C) 영업
(D) 연구 개발

87 화자는 "지난번에 해주신 작업 때문에 정보를 이미 가지고 있다"라고 말할 때 무엇을 의미하는가?
(A) 청자가 파일을 복구할 수 있었다.
(B) 청자가 방문할 필요가 없다.
(C) 화자에게 다른 업무가 있다.
(D) 화자에게 전화번호가 없다.

88 화자는 청자에게 무엇을 얼른 하라고 권장하는가?
(A) 신규 계좌를 개설하라고
(B) 문서를 찾아가라고
(C) 다른 일자리에 대해 문의하라고
(D) 이력서를 이메일로 보내라고

미국

Questions 89-91 refer to the following speech.

W: I'm excited to be speaking at this press conference today to announce our new graduate recruitment program, the Garden Path Program. **Our program is designed to offer film school graduates the opportunity to work on some of our productions.(89)** This will let them gain valuable experience while also providing pathways into becoming full-time employees. **Ms. Beck, who has been in charge of our recruiting needs for years, came up with the idea after realizing that most talent goes undiscovered in today's world.(90)** To celebrate our new program, we will be paying for a full scholarship to any college in the country. **All students are welcome to enter the contest, and we will announce the winner next week.(91)**

89-91번은 다음 연설에 관한 문제입니다.

여: 오늘 기자 회견에서 저희의 새로운 졸업생 채용 프로그램인 Garden Path Program을 발표하는 자리를 갖게 되어 기쁩니다. **저희 프로그램은 영화 학교 졸업생에게 저희 영화 제작에 참여할 기회를 제공하기 위해 마련되었습니다.(89)** 이는 정규직 직원이 되는 길을 제공하면서 동시에 그들이 귀중한 경험을 쌓게 합니다. **수년간 저희 채용을 담당해온 Ms. Beck이 요즘 세상에서 대부분의 인재가 발굴되지 못하는 것을 깨닫고 아이디어를 떠올렸습니다.(90)** 새로운 프로그램을 기념하기 위해 저희는 전국 대학에 전액 장학금을 지급할 예정입니다. **모든 학생은 얼마든지 대회에 참가할 수 있으며, 다음 주에 우승자를 발표합니다.(91)**

89 화자는 어떤 업계에 일하겠는가?
(A) 기술
(B) 비디오 게임
(C) 영화
(D) 교육

90 화자에 따르면, 누가 Garden Path Program을 개발했는가?
(A) 채용 컨설턴트
(B) 디자이너
(C) 교수
(D) 행정 보조

91 화자는 다음 주에 무슨 일이 있을 거라고 말하는가?
(A) 신임 관리자가 임명될 것이다.
(B) 제휴가 발표될 것이다.
(C) 학생이 선발될 것이다.
(D) 프로젝트가 마무리될 것이다.

호주

Questions 92-94 refer to the following excerpt from a meeting.
M: The usability on this was the issue. **All kitchen appliances should be very simple to use, but the buttons on this were not intuitive enough.(92)** I've taken some time to redesign the buttons as well as the menus on the blender.**(92)/(93)** I've put the newly designed icons on the wall. As you can see, it should make for a smoother experience for everyone. While I think they look great, I don't think we should make the final decision. We made the product, after all. Let's put a focus group together. **(94)**

92-94번은 다음 회의 발췌록에 관한 문제입니다.
남: 이것의 사용 편의성이 문제였어요. 모든 주방 제품은 사용이 아주 간단해야 하는데, 여기서는 버튼이 충분히 직관적이지 않았어요.**(92)** 제가 시간을 들여 믹서기의 메뉴뿐만 아니라 버튼을 다시 디자인했습니다.**(92)/(93)** 제가 새로 디자인된 아이콘을 벽에 붙여 놓았습니다. 보시다시피, 누구에게나 보다 매끄러운 경험을 선사해야 합니다. 제 생각에는 아주 괜찮아 보이지만, 최종 결정을 내려야 한다고는 생각하지 않습니다. 어쨌든, 저희가 만든 건 상품이니까요. 포커스 그룹을 구성합시다.**(94)**

92 화자는 누구겠는가?
(A) 마케팅 보조
(B) 상품 디자이너
(C) 영화 프로듀서
(D) 소매상인

93 어떤 종류의 제품이 논의되고 있는가?
(A) 음료
(B) 믹서기
(C) 노트북
(D) 사무용 의자

94 화자는 왜 "어쨌든, 저희가 만든 건 상품이니까요"라고 말하는가?
(A) 의견을 요청하기 위해
(B) 업데이트를 제공하기 위해
(C) 제안을 거절하기 위해
(D) 획기적인 사건을 축하하기 위해

미국

Questions 95-97 refer to the following instructions and map.
M: It's great to see all of you here at our city's yearly half-marathon race.**(95)** I'd like to wish each of you a safe and successful event. To get started, participants should make their way to the welcome desk by 10 A.M. **There, you'll complete your registration and pick up a complimentary towel to use during the event.(96)** Keep in mind that you need to stay on the running course as it is marked. **Once you get to the finish line, please cross Dover Avenue to participate in a group photo.(97)** It shouldn't take too long.

95-97번은 다음 지문과 지도에 관한 문제입니다.
남: 시 연례 하프 마라톤 경기에서 여러분 모두를 보게 되어 기쁩니다.**(95)** 여러분 모두에게 안전하고 성공적인 행사가 되시길 바랍니다. 우선, 참가자들은 오전 10시까지 환영 데스크로 가셔야 합니다. 그곳에서 신청서를 작성하시고 행사에서 사용할 무료 타월을 받으세요.**(96)** 표시되어 있는대로 경주 코스를 지켜야 한다는 점을 명심하세요. 결승전에 도착하시면, Dover가를 건너서 단체 사진 촬영에 참여해 주세요.**(97)** 아주 오래 걸리진 않을 거예요.

코스 지도

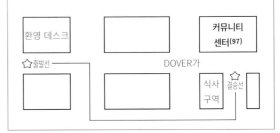

95 청자들은 어느 행사에 참석하고 있겠는가?
(A) 가이드 투어
(B) 청소 계획
(C) 육상 대회
(D) 거리 행진

96 화자에 따르면, 청자들은 무엇을 받아야 하는가?
(A) 허가증
(B) 음료
(C) 타월
(D) 모자

97 시각 자료를 보시오. 청자들은 단체 사진을 어디에서 찍을 것인가?
(A) 환영 데스크에서
(B) 출발선에서
(C) 식사 구역에서
(D) 커뮤니티 센터에서

Questions 98-100 refer to the following excerpt from a meeting and form.

W: Thank you all for attending the Langston Community Center staff meeting.(98) If you don't know me, I'm Paula Wong, the director here. As you know, **our annual membership registration initiative is this weekend, and I wanted to give my appreciation to all of our employees who volunteered to help.(99)** Our center relies heavily on the financial support of its members. Therefore, we'll be going around our neighborhood asking people to register for a membership. For those that do agree to join, we have this application form. There are four types of membership. **If you are familiar with our pricing, you'll notice that the fee for children has decreased this year.(100)**

98-100번은 다음 회의 발췌록과 서식에 관한 문제입니다.

여: Langston 시민문화회관 직원회의에 참석해주신 분들께 모두 감사드립니다.(98) 저를 모르신다면, 저는 Paula Wong이고 이곳의 책임자입니다. 아시다시피, **이번 주말에 저희 연간 회원등록이 시작되어, 자원해주신 모든 직원분들께 감사의 말씀을 전하고 싶었습니다.(99)** 우리 회관은 회원분들의 금전적인 지원에 많이 의존하고 있습니다. 그래서 저희는 동네를 돌며 회원 가입을 요청할 겁니다. 가입에 동의하시는 분들을 위해 이 신청서를 준비했습니다. 회원권에는 4가지 종류가 있습니다. **금액을 잘 아시는 분들은 올해 아이들 가입비가 낮아졌다는 걸 보실 수 있을 겁니다.(100)**

회원 신청서

이름: _____   날짜: _____
주소: _____

성인 50달러 ___   (100)청년 25달러 ___
고령자 30달러 ___   가족 90달러 ___

---

98 회의는 어디에서 하고 있겠는가?
(A) 시민문화회관에서
(B) 놀이공원에서
(C) 백화점에서
(D) 헬스클럽에서

99 화자는 왜 청자들에게 고마워하는가?
(A) 업무에 도움을 주어서
(B) 잡지를 구독해서
(C) 오리엔테이션에 참석해서
(D) 회원권을 구입해서

100 시각 자료를 보시오. 어떤 금액이 변경되었는가?
(A) 25달러
(B) 30달러
(C) 50달러
(D) 90달러

TEST 05

PART 1
P. 72

1 (D)   **2** (D)   **3** (C)   **4** (C)   **5** (A)   **6** (D)

PART 2
P. 76

7 (C)   **8** (C)   **9** (C)   **10** (C)   **11** (A)   **12** (C)

13 (C)   **14** (A)   **15** (A)   **16** (C)   **17** (B)   **18** (A)

19 (A)   **20** (A)   **21** (B)   **22** (A)   **23** (A)   **24** (C)

25 (C)   **26** (C)   **27** (C)   **28** (C)   **29** (C)   **30** (B)

31 (A)

PART 3
P. 77

32 (A)   **33** (D)   **34** (D)   **35** (A)   **36** (D)   **37** (C)

38 (C)   **39** (D)   **40** (B)   **41** (B)   **42** (D)   **43** (C)

44 (D)   **45** (B)   **46** (B)   **47** (D)   **48** (B)   **49** (B)

50 (C)   **51** (D)   **52** (A)   **53** (C)   **54** (C)   **55** (B)

56 (B)   **57** (B)   **58** (C)   **59** (C)   **60** (D)   **61** (C)

62 (C)   **63** (A)   **64** (A)   **65** (C)   **66** (A)   **67** (A)

68 (C)   **69** (B)   **70** (B)

PART 4
P. 81

71 (B)   **72** (A)   **73** (D)   **74** (D)   **75** (C)   **76** (D)

77 (C)   **78** (D)   **79** (A)   **80** (B)   **81** (B)   **82** (D)

83 (B)   **84** (C)   **85** (C)   **86** (D)   **87** (B)   **88** (A)

89 (D)   **90** (A)   **91** (A)   **92** (D)   **93** (A)   **94** (A)

95 (D)   **96** (D)   **97** (B)   **98** (A)   **99** (A)   **100** (B)

PART 1
P. 72

1 영국

(A) A woman is writing with a pen.
(B) A woman is arranging books on a shelf.
(C) A woman is setting her glasses on a desk.
(D) A woman is typing on a computer.

(A) 여자가 펜으로 글을 쓰고 있다.
(B) 여자가 책꽂이 위의 책들을 정리하고 있다.
(C) 여자가 책상 위에 안경을 놓고 있다.
(D) 여자가 컴퓨터로 타이핑하고 있다.

2 호주

(A) Some people are standing near some bushes.
(B) Some people are dining in a garden.
(C) Some people are getting ready for a meal.
(D) Some people are gathered around a table.

(A) 몇몇 사람들이 덤불 근처에 서 있다.
(B) 몇몇 사람들이 정원에서 식사를 하고 있다.
(C) 몇몇 사람들이 식사를 준비하고 있다.
(D) 몇몇 사람들이 테이블 주위에 모여 있다.

3 미국

(A) The man is waiting to board a train.
(B) The man is pulling his suitcase down the hallway.
(C) The woman is coming down some stairs.
(D) The woman is holding onto a railing.

(A) 남자가 열차에 타려고 기다리고 있다.
(B) 남자가 복도를 따라 여행 가방을 끌고 있다.
(C) 여자가 계단을 내려오고 있다.
(D) 여자가 난간을 잡고 있다.

4 영국

(A) A pot has been put in an oven.
(B) Utensils have been hung from hooks.
(C) Some food has been prepared.
(D) Some plates are beside a sink.

(A) 오븐에 냄비가 놓여있다.
(B) 주방 기구들이 고리에 걸려있다.
(C) 음식이 준비되어 있다.
(D) 접시들이 싱크대 옆에 있다.

5 미국

(A) The ground is being paved with tiles.
(B) A bucket is hanging from a hook.
(C) A man is pushing a wheelbarrow.
(D) A man is kneeling on the floor.

(A) 땅이 타일로 포장되고 있다.
(B) 양동이가 고리에 매달려 있다.
(C) 남자가 손수레를 밀고 있다.
(D) 남자가 바닥에 무릎을 꿇고 있다.

6 미국

(A) A woman is taking a seat at a café.
(B) A man is serving a beverage in a bottle.
(C) A patron is carrying a tray to a table.
(D) A man has put on a pair of glasses.

(A) 여자가 카페에서 자리에 앉고 있다.
(B) 남자가 병에 담긴 음료를 서빙하고 있다.
(C) 고객이 쟁반을 테이블로 가져가고 있다.
(D) 남자가 안경을 착용했다.

PART 2
P. 76

7 미국 ⇄ 미국

When did you start taking exercise classes?
(A) I usually listen to classical music.
(B) It starts early.
(C) Sometime last spring.

운동 수업 듣는 건 언제 시작했어요?
(A) 저는 보통 클래식 음악을 들어요.
(B) 일찍 시작해요.
(C) 지난 봄에요.

8 영국 ⇄ 호주

Who are you baking the cake for?
(A) By tomorrow morning.
(B) OK, I can pick it up.
(C) A customer from Southport.

누구를 위해 케이크를 굽고 계신 거예요?
(A) 내일 오전까지요.
(B) 알겠어요, 제가 갖다 드릴게요.
(C) Southport의 고객이요.

9 미국 ⇄ 영국

Where should I go when I finish filling out these forms?
(A) By Friday morning.
(B) Thank you. I'm feeling much better.
(C) To the registration office.

이 서류를 작성하면 어디로 가야 하나요?
(A) 금요일 아침까지요.
(B) 감사합니다. 훨씬 나아졌어요.
(C) 등록 사무소요.

10 호주 ⇄ 미국

Why didn't the managers report the budget update to the CEO?
(A) Yes, the financial advisors were here.
(B) No, that was last Wednesday.
(C) Because they are still working on it.

매니저들이 왜 CEO에게 개정 예산안을 보고하지 않았나요?
(A) 네, 재정 고문들이 계셨습니다.
(B) 아니요, 그건 지난주 수요일이었습니다.
(C) 아직 작업하는 중이니까요.

11 미국 ⇄ 호주

How are we advertising our new laptop to young consumers?
(A) Claudia's responsible for that project.
(B) The warranty has expired.
(C) I'd like to get my computer repaired.

젊은 소비자들에게 우리 신상 노트북을 어떻게 광고하나요?
(A) Claudia가 그 프로젝트를 담당하고 있어요.
(B) 보증서가 만료되었어요.
(C) 제 컴퓨터를 수리받고 싶어요.

12 미국 ⇄ 미국

Which laptop do you prefer, the silver one or the white one?
(A) I contacted the IT Department.
(B) It comes with a wireless mouse.
(C) The silver one looks better.

어떤 노트북 컴퓨터를 선호하세요, 은색인가요 아니면 흰색인가요?
(A) 제가 IT 부서에 연락했어요.
(B) 무선 마우스도 딸려 있어요.
(C) 은색이 더 좋아 보여요.

13 미국 ⇄ 영국

Please notify your team members about the anniversary dinner on Friday.
(A) For 35 years.
(B) The department head.
(C) I've already let them know.

팀원들에게 금요일에 있을 기념일 만찬에 대해 알려주세요.
(A) 35년 동안이요.
(B) 부서장이요.
(C) 제가 이미 알려줬어요.

14 영국 ⇄ 호주

Have you received the revised company directory?
(A) Yes, I got the e-mail a few minutes ago.
(B) The revision will not be necessary.
(C) For the board of directors.

회사 안내 책자 개정본 받았어요?
(A) 네, 몇 분 전에 이메일 받았어요.
(B) 수정 안 해도 될 거예요.
(C) 이사회용이요.

15 미국 ⇄ 미국

How will you get to the awards ceremony?
(A) Angela is giving me a ride.
(B) For highest number of sales this year.
(C) At the Marbella Hotel banquet room.

시상식에 어떻게 가실 건가요?
(A) Angela가 절 태워다 줄 거예요.
(B) 올해 최고 판매량에 대해서요.
(C) Marbella 호텔 연회장에서요.

16 미국 ⇄ 미국

What time does the pottery class begin?
(A) Some bowls and cups.
(B) In Room 402.
(C) I didn't sign up for it.

도예 수업은 몇 시에 시작해요?
(A) 그릇이랑 컵 몇 개요.
(B) 402호에서요.
(C) 전 등록 안 했어요.

17 영국 ⇄ 미국

I'm having a hard time printing out the evaluation form.
(A) My supervisor evaluated me.
(B) Let me give you a hand with that.
(C) A form of identification.

제가 평가 서식을 인쇄하는 데 고생하고 있어요.
(A) 제 관리자가 저를 평가했어요.
(B) 제가 도와드릴게요.
(C) 신분증이요.

18 미국 ⇄ 호주

Do you have a receipt for this purchase?
(A) Yes, it's right here.
(B) I received the order.
(C) At the shopping mall.

이 구매품의 영수증 가지고 있으세요?
(A) 네, 여기 있어요.
(B) 주문품을 받았어요.
(C) 쇼핑몰에서요.

19 미국 ⇄ 미국

When will the speaker arrive?
(A) I'm not sure. He's in a traffic jam.
(B) The keynote speech was inspiring.
(C) The conference center is right across the street.

연사는 언제 도착할까요?
(A) 모르겠어요. 교통 체증에 갇혀 있어요.
(B) 기조연설이 감명 깊었어요.
(C) 회의장은 길 바로 건너편이에요.

20 영국 ⇄ 미국

Who sent in the work request?
(A) I have to check my e-mail first.
(B) By Friday morning.
(C) To fix the faulty wiring.

누가 업무 요청서를 보냈어요?
(A) 제 메일함 먼저 확인해봐야 해요.
(B) 금요일 오전까지요.
(C) 잘못된 배선을 손보려고요.

21 미국 ⇄ 미국

Should I make the dinner reservation by phone or online?
(A) That is an interesting idea.
(B) Calling would be much faster.
(C) That restaurant serves great food.

저녁 예약은 전화로 할까요, 아니면 온라인으로 할까요?
(A) 흥미로운 아이디어네요.
(B) 전화하는 게 훨씬 빠를 거예요.
(C) 그 식당은 음식이 정말 훌륭해요.

22 영국 ⇄ 호주

Could you send someone to repair my air-conditioner, please?
(A) Maintenance requests should be made online.
(B) The temperature in the server room is higher than usual.
(C) Not enough to run all the machinery without overheating.

제 에어컨을 수리해 줄 사람을 보내주시겠어요?
(A) 보수 신청은 온라인으로 하셔야 해요.
(B) 서버실 온도가 평소보다 높아요.
(C) 과열 없이 모든 기계를 작동시킬 정도는 아니에요.

23 미국 ⇄ 미국

The van came into the auto shop this morning, right?
(A) Yes, we'll be done soon.
(B) All four wheels.
(C) The shop is having a sale.

오늘 아침에 정비소에 밴이 입고됐죠, 맞죠?
(A) 네, 곧 끝낼 거예요.
(B) 바퀴 네 개 다요.
(C) 가게에서 할인판매 중이에요.

24 미국 ⇄ 영국

Would you like to have dinner with us after work?
(A) Let me take you to your table.
(B) The supermarket should have them in stock.
(C) I have to go to the airport early tomorrow morning.

퇴근하고 저희랑 저녁 식사 같이하시겠어요?
(A) 앉으실 테이블로 안내해 드릴게요.
(B) 그 슈퍼마켓에 재고가 있을 거예요.
(C) 제가 내일 아침 일찍 공항에 가야 해요.

25 미국 ⇄ 호주

Are you planning to join that gym?
(A) The monthly cable plan.
(B) An invoice for some new equipment.
(C) I'd like to check out other options first.

그 체육관에 등록할 계획이에요?
(A) 케이블 월간 요금제요.
(B) 최신 장비 송장이요.
(C) 다른 옵션부터 먼저 살펴보고 싶어요.

26 영국 ⇄ 미국

How does the magazine cover look?
(A) The publication is long overdue.
(B) The consultation with our graphic designer.
(C) I could show you if you want.

잡지 표지는 어때 보여요?
(A) 출판물 기한이 많이 지났어요.
(B) 저희 그래픽 디자이너와의 협의요.
(C) 원하시면 보여드릴게요.

27 호주 ⇄ 영국

You should replace your car battery.
(A) I can drive you to the airport.
(B) The power is out.
(C) I'm going to see the mechanic.

차량 배터리를 교체하셔야 해요.
(A) 제가 공항까지 태워다 줄 수 있어요.
(B) 전기가 나갔어요.
(C) 정비소에 가보려고요.

28 호주 ⇄ 미국

We haven't sent out the attendance list yet, have we?
(A) For the awards ceremony.
(B) A list of corporate sponsors.
(C) Yes, we did.

우리가 아직 참석자 명단을 발송하지 않았죠, 그렇죠?
(A) 시상식용이요.
(B) 후원 업체 명단이요.
(C) 네, 이미 했어요.

29 미국 ⇄ 호주

Don't you want to rehearse your presentation before the orientation?
(A) Thanks for the thoughtful present.
(B) At the performance center down the block.
(C) Paul is training the new recruits.

오리엔테이션 전에 프레젠테이션을 연습하고 싶지 않으세요?
(A) 정성스런 선물 감사해요.
(B) 한 블록 아래에 있는 공연장에서요.
(C) Paul이 신입직원 교육을 하고 있어요.

30 미국 ⇄ 영국

Aren't you coming to the awards ceremony with us?
(A) Award for the Employee of the Year.
(B) This will only take five more minutes.
(C) On the other side of the venue.

저희랑 같이 시상식에 안 가세요?
(A) 올해의 직원상요.
(B) 5분만 더 있으면 될 거예요.
(C) 행사장 건너편에서요.

31 호주 ⇄ 미국

Apparently, this has been our company's most profitable quarter so far.
(A) We've all been working overtime.
(B) I sent out half of the shipment.
(C) I sold it at a profit.

보아하니, 지금까지 중 이번 분기에 우리 회사 수익이 가장 좋은 것 같아요.
(A) 저희 모두 초과 근무를 해왔어요.
(B) 제가 수송품 절반을 발송했어요.
(C) 이익을 남기고 팔았어요.

PART 3

영국 ⇄ 호주

Questions 32-34 refer to the following conversation.

W: Drew, **could I get an update on the new cooling fan you've been working on?**(32) Any stumbling blocks you've encountered?

M: It's going great. I managed to drastically reduce the amount of noise it makes without sacrificing any performance. This is a feature our customers have been requesting for a long time.

W: These are really nice. **I really like how small it is. That should make it easier for people to store them.**(33)

M: Thanks. I've worked quite hard on this.

W: I can tell. **Let's go ahead and show this to the other team members. We need to get some more opinions.**(34)

32-34번은 다음 대화에 관한 문제입니다.

여: Drew, 작업하고 계신 신규 냉각 팬에 대해 업데이트를 받아볼 수 있을까요?(32) 장애 요인이 있었나요?

남: 잘 진행되고 있어요. 성능을 저하시키지 않고 소음 발생량을 대폭 낮출 수 있었습니다. 우리 고객들이 오랫동안 요청해왔던 기능이에요.

여: 정말 좋네요. 작아서 정말 맘에 들어요. 사람들이 보관하기가 더 수월해질 거예요.(33)

남: 감사합니다. 여기에 아주 공을 많이 들였어요.

여: 그래 보여요. 그럼 이걸 다른 팀원에게 보여줍시다. 여러 다른 의견을 받아봐야 해요.(34)

32 화자들은 어떤 종류의 상품에 관해 이야기하고 있는가?
(A) 냉각 팬
(B) 컴퓨터 모니터
(C) 휴대용 라디오
(D) 밥솥

33 여자는 제품에 관하여 무엇이 마음에 든다고 말하는가?
(A) 튼튼하게 지어졌다.
(B) 에너지 효율이 높다.
(C) 사용하기 쉽다.
(D) 보관이 더 수월하다.

34 여자는 무엇을 하자고 제안하는가?
(A) 몇몇 시제품을 설계하자고
(B) 견적서를 만들자고
(C) 투자자를 발굴하자고
(D) 피드백을 얻자고

미국 ⇄ 영국

Questions 35-37 refer to the following conversation.

M: Ms. Fieldman, **the representatives from CTM, Inc. just called to cancel. I rescheduled them for tomorrow afternoon.**(35)

W: OK. That'll actually give me more time to prepare for that meeting. Anyway, since no more clients are coming in, **I'll let the staff leave an hour early today.**(36)

M: Oh, I'm sure everyone will be happy to hear that! By the way, **some workers are coming by this evening to begin renovations on the dining lounge.**(37) They'll be here every day until Friday.

35-37번은 다음 대화에 관한 문제입니다.

남: Ms. Fieldman, CTM사 직원들이 방금 전화해서 취소했어요. 내일 오후로 일정을 다시 잡았습니다.(35)

여: 알겠어요. 사실 그게 회의를 준비할 시간을 더 벌어주겠네요. 그러면, 더 올 고객이 없으니, 오늘은 직원들을 한 시간 일찍 퇴근시켜야겠어요.(36)

남: 오, 그 얘길 들으면 모두 기뻐할 거예요! 그런데, 인부들 몇 명이 오늘 저녁에 식당 구역에 개조 작업을 시작하러 잠깐 들를 거예요.(37) 금요일까지 매일 올 거예요.

35 남자는 자신이 무엇을 했다고 말하는가?
(A) 회의 시간을 옮겼다고
(B) 고객 사무실을 방문했다고
(C) 배송을 처리했다고
(D) 프레젠테이션을 수정했다고

36 여자는 무엇을 하기로 하는가?
(A) 출장을 가기로
(B) 휴게실 비품을 더 주문하기로
(C) 출장연회 메뉴를 변경하기로
(D) 직원들을 일찍 퇴근하게 하기로

37 남자에 따르면, 저녁에 무슨 일이 있을 것인가?
(A) 주차장이 폐쇄될 것이다.
(B) 기계가 수리될 것이다.
(C) 어떤 구역이 개조될 것이다.
(D) 시스템이 다시 시작될 것이다.

미국 ⇄ 미국

Questions 38-40 refer to the following conversation.

M: Hi, my name is Shawn Lamar, and **I made a reservation for a deluxe suite. I'm here to check in.**(38)

W: Of course. Welcome to Granier Hotel. You'll need to complete this short form before I can give you your room key.

M: All right. Ahm... **It says here that I have to provide my confirmation code, but unfortunately, I don't have it with me.**(39)

W: That's OK. **I can just search for it in our system.**(40) Can you give me your phone number?

38-40번은 다음 대화에 관한 문제입니다.

남: 안녕하세요, 제 이름은 Shawn Lamar이고, 디럭스 스위트룸을 예약했어요. 체크인하려고요.(38)

여: 네. Granier 호텔에 오신 것을 환영합니다. 제가 방 열쇠를 드리기 전에 이 간단한 서식을 작성해주셔야 해요.

남: 알겠습니다. 음... 여기 보니 확인 코드를 적으라고 되어 있는데, 유감스럽게도 제가 지금 몰라요.(39)

여: 괜찮습니다. 제가 시스템에서 검색할 수 있어요.(40) 전화번호를 알려주시겠어요?

38 남자는 무엇을 하려고 하는가?
(A) 테이블 예약하려고
(B) 기차표를 예매하려고
(C) 방에 체크인하려고
(D) 자기소개서를 제출하려고

TEST 05

39 남자는 무엇을 빠트렸는가?
(A) 사진이 부착된 신분증
(B) 할인권
(C) 휴대전화
(D) 확인 코드

40 여자는 무엇을 하겠다고 제안하는가?
(A) 동료에게 전화하겠다고
(B) 시스템을 검색하겠다고
(C) 작업요청서를 전송하겠다고
(D) 청구서를 검토하겠다고

영국 ⇄ 호주 ⇄ 미국

Questions 41-43 refer to the following conversation with three speakers.

W1: Thank you for meeting with us today, Shane. I'm sure you've been very busy rehearsing for your national tour.**(41)**

M: I've been practicing my vocals all morning with my band,**(41)** and I could definitely use this break. I'm pleased you have selected me to represent your brand.**(42)**

W2: Your involvement with our brand would be great for our company.

W1: We believe you'll be the ideal spokesperson for our products.

M: I agree. I've been taking your vitamins and supplements regularly for a few years now, and my body feels healthier than ever.**(43)**

W2: That's exactly the message we would like to spread to our target demographic.

41-43번은 다음 세 화자의 대화에 관한 문제입니다.
여1: 오늘 저희와 만나 주셔서 감사합니다, Shane. 전국 투어 준비하느라 아주 바쁘시죠.**(41)**
남: 오전 내내 밴드랑 보컬 연습했더니,**(41)** 이런 휴식 시간이 간절했어요. 귀사 브랜드를 대표하는 데 저를 선택해 주셔서 기쁩니다.**(42)**
여2: 저희 브랜드와 함께해 주시면 저희 회사에 아주 힘이 될 거예요.
여1: 저희 제품에 이상적인 대변인이 되실 거라고 생각해요.
남: 맞아요. 제가 지금 몇 년째 귀사 비타민과 건강 보조 식품을 먹고 있는데, 몸이 전보다 건강해진 것 같아요.**(43)**
여2: 그게 바로 저희가 목표 인구층에 전하고 싶은 메시지예요.

41 남자는 누구겠는가?
(A) 영화감독
(B) 가수
(C) 배우
(D) TV쇼 진행자

42 회의의 목적은 무엇인가?
(A) 공연을 준비하기 위해
(B) 촬영 스케줄을 확인하기 위해
(C) 사진을 검토하기 위해
(D) 광고 캠페인을 논의하기 위해

43 남자는 제품에 관하여 뭐라고 말하는가?
(A) 가격이 저렴하다.
(B) 수요가 아주 많다.
(C) 본인에게 효과가 있었다.
(D) 제조법이 바뀌었다.

호주 ⇄ 미국

Questions 44-46 refer to the following conversation.

M: Hey, Shannon. It looks like some new county tax regulations will be implemented next month.**(44)** We'll have to keep these laws in mind when our accounting team handles the company's financial transactions.

W: Yes, and a few of them might be confusing. Why don't we conduct a training workshop for our team members?**(45)**

M: Good idea. Are you available this Friday to hold the session?

W: I am, but I'm not sure that day will work because some of the accountants will be attending the Finance Expo on Friday.**(46)**

44-46번은 다음 대화에 관한 문제입니다.
남: 저기, Shannon. 다음 달에 새로운 카운티 조세 규정이 시행될 것 같아요.**(44)** 우리 회계팀에서 회사 금융거래를 처리할 때 이 법규들을 명심해야 해요.
여: 맞아요, 그리고 그중 일부는 헷갈릴 수 있어요. 우리 팀원들을 위한 교육 워크숍을 실시하는 게 어떨까요?**(45)**
남: 좋은 생각이에요. 이번 주 금요일에 교육할 시간 있으세요?
여: 네, 그런데 일부 회계사들이 금요일에 금융박람회에 참석할 거라서 **(46)** 그날이 괜찮을지 모르겠어요.

44 화자들은 주로 무엇을 논하고 있는가?
(A) 카운티 행사
(B) 최근 거래
(C) 월급
(D) 새로운 법규

45 여자는 무엇을 제안하는가?
(A) 공무원에게 연락하는 것
(B) 교육을 제공하는 것
(C) 초과근무를 하는 것
(D) 양식을 검토하는 것

46 여자는 일부 회계사들이 금요일에 무엇을 할 거라고 말하는가?
(A) 은행을 방문할 거라고
(B) 박람회에 참가할 거라고
(C) 다른 지점에 갈 거라고
(D) 고객과 만날 거라고

미국 ⇄ 미국

Questions 47-49 refer to the following conversation.

W: Hello. I'm looking for Celia Ho. I'm here to make a delivery.

M: Celia isn't here at the pharmacy today,**(47)** but she did tell me I should expect to receive a delivery today. Umm, wait a minute. Shouldn't there be three boxes? Do you have the other one for her?**(48)**

W: My delivery tracker app says two.**(48)**

M: I see... Thank you.

W: No problem. Could I ask you a question? The road I usually take was closed for repairs, and I had to take a long detour. Is there another way downtown?

M: Oh, yes. If you take a left down the street, you will be able to take the expressway straight back into the city.**(49)**

47-49번은 다음 대화에 관한 문제입니다.

여: 안녕하세요. Celia Ho를 찾고 있는데요. 배송 왔어요.

남: Celia는 오늘 약국에 안 계세요.(47) 그런데 오늘 배송 올 게 있다고 저한테 말씀하셨어요. 음, 잠시만요, 상자가 3개 있어야 하지 않아요? 한 개 더 가지고 계세요?(48)

여: 제 배송 추적 앱에는 2개라고 나와 있어요.(48)

남: 그렇군요... 감사합니다.

여: 아닙니다. 뭐 하나 여쭤봐도 될까요? 제가 주로 다니는 길이 보수작업으로 폐쇄돼서 우회로로 돌아와야 했어요. 시내로 가는 다른 길이 있나요?

남: 아, 있어요. 길 끝에서 좌회전하시면, 시내로 바로 가는 고속도로를 탈 수 있으세요.(49)

47 대화는 어디서 이루어지는가?
(A) 창고에서
(B) 식료품점에서
(C) 우체국에서
(D) 약국에서

48 여자가 "제 배송 추적 앱에는 2개라고 나와 있어요"라고 말할 때 무엇을 내비치는가?
(A) 남자를 도와줄 수 있을 것이다.
(B) 남자가 잘못 알고 있다고 여긴다.
(C) 추가 작업 할당이 필요하다.
(D) 업무를 거의 마쳤다.

49 남자는 여자에게 무엇을 하라고 권장하는가?
(A) 동료에게 연락하라고
(B) 다른 길을 이용하라고
(C) 재고를 확인하라고
(D) 문서를 검토하라고

미국 ⇄ 영국

Questions 50-52 refer to the following conversation.

M: Please feel free to browse around. Right now, I'm cleaning this antique bookshelf, but I'll be right there if you need help with anything.(50)

W: Thanks. I'm looking to purchase some jewelry—specifically some earrings from late 19th century.

M: You can find them right over there in the display case. Are you looking to use it as decoration or...

W: No, I'm responsible for designing costumes for a musical.(51) The setting is in the 1890s, so I was hoping to purchase an authentic piece of jewelry for the female lead.

M: I understand. Let me show you what we have in stock, but **please remember that they are very delicate.**(52) You should be very careful when handling them.

50-52번은 다음 대화에 관한 문제입니다.

남: 편하게 둘러보세요. 제가 지금 골동품 책장을 청소 중인데, 도움이 필요하시면 바로 갈게요.(50)

여: 고마워요. 제가 보석을 구입하려고 하는데요, 구체적으로 말하자면 19세기 후반 귀걸이요.

남: 바로 저기 진열장에서 찾으실 수 있어요. 장식용으로 사용하시나요, 아니면...

여: 아니요, 전 뮤지컬 의상 디자인을 담당하고 있어요.(51) 배경이 1890년대라, 여자 주인공이 착용할 진짜 보석을 구입하고 싶어서요.

남: 그러시군요. 저희가 재고로 가지고 있는 물건을 보여드릴게요, 그런데 망가지기 쉽다는 점을 기억해 주세요.(52) 다룰 때 아주 주의하셔야 해요.

50 남자는 어디서 일하겠는가?
(A) 패션 부티크에서
(B) 극장에서
(C) 골동품점에서
(D) 서점에서

51 여자는 무엇을 담당하는가?
(A) 대본 편집
(B) 뮤지컬 악보
(C) 무대 조명
(D) 의상 디자인

52 남자는 여자에게 무엇에 관해 상기시켜주는가?
(A) 몇몇 물품은 망가지기 쉽다.
(B) 몇몇 물품은 비싸다.
(C) 몇몇 물품은 희귀하다.
(D) 몇몇 물품은 너무 크다.

호주 ⇄ 미국

Questions 53-55 refer to the following conversation.

M: Hi, Julia. I'd like to talk to you about our company's anniversary banquet. It's just six weeks away, so we need to decide who should be given the prize as Writer of the Year.(53)/(54)

W: Let's see. How about Irina? Her magazine articles are always highly rated in our reader surveys.(53)/(54)

M: She won it last year.(54) And there are others who have helped increase our subscription recently.

W: You're right. Well, what if we took a vote among the employees and see who they think deserves it the most?(55)

M: I like that idea. I've always thought we should let everybody who works here vote on it.(55)

53-55번은 다음 대화에 관한 문제입니다.

남: 안녕하세요, Julia. 우리 회사 기념일 연회에 관해 얘기하고 싶어요. 6주밖에 안 남아서, 누가 <올해의 작가> 상을 받아야 할지 결정해야 해요.(53)/(54)

여: 어디 봅시다. Irina는 어때요? 그녀가 쓴 잡지 기사는 저희 독자 설문에서 항상 높은 평가를 받거든요.(53)/(54)

남: 그분은 작년에 받았어요.(54) 그리고 최근에 구독을 늘리는 데 도움을 주신 다른 분들이 있어요.

여: 그렇네요. 직원들끼리 투표를 해서 그들이 생각하기에 가장 받을만한 사람이 누구라고 생각하는지 알아보면 어떨까요?(55)

남: 그 아이디어 좋은데요. 여기서 일하는 사람들 모두가 투표를 해야 한다고 항상 생각했거든요.(55)

53 화자들은 어디서 일하겠는가?
(A) 호텔에서
(B) 조경 회사에서
(C) 잡지 출판사에서
(D) 건설 회사에서

54 남자는 왜 "그분은 작년에 받았어요"라고 말하는가?

(A) 존경을 표하기 위해

(B) 세부 사항을 확인하기 위해

(C) 추천을 거절하기 위해

(D) 해결책을 제안하기 위해

55 화자들은 무엇을 하기로 결정하는가?

(A) 회의를 취소하기로

(B) 직원들의 의견을 구하기로

(C) 근무 시간을 연장하기로

(D) 교육을 받기로

영국 ⇄ 미국

Questions 56-58 refer to the following conversation.

W: George, thank you for providing a detailed résumé with your work experiences. Having looked at the document, though, **I'd like to know why you decided to leave your previous work in the hospitality industry.**[56]

M: Working as a hotel receptionist was an excellent starting point for my career, but after a few years, I couldn't help but think I learned everything there is to know about the job. **That's why I got a master's degree to move up to a managerial position.**[57]

W: Yes, it seems like you'd be a great fit as an operations manager based on your qualifications.

M: According to the job description posted online, this position will require working closely with the hotel headquarters in New York. Could you explain how that would work?[58]

56-58번은 다음 대화에 관한 문제입니다.

여: George, 경력에 관한 상세한 이력서를 제공해 주셔서 감사합니다. 그런데 서류를 살펴보니, **왜 이전 서비스 분야 업무를 그만두셨는지 궁금하네요.**[56]

남: 호텔 접수 직원으로 근무한 것은 제 경력의 출발점으로 아주 좋았지만, 몇 년이 지나니 이 직업에 관한 모든 것을 배웠다는 생각이 머릿속에서 떠나지 않았습니다. **그래서 관리직으로 올라가기 위해 석사 학위를 땄습니다.**[57]

여: 그렇군요, 자격 사항을 놓고 보면 운영 관리자직에 아주 잘 맞으실 것 같아요.

남: 온라인에 게시된 직무 설명에 따르면, 이 직무는 New York에 있는 호텔 본사와 긴밀히 협력해야 하는데요. 어떤 식으로 이루어지는지 설명해 주실 수 있으세요?[58]

56 화자들은 어떤 분야에 일하는가?

(A) 제조

(B) 서비스

(C) 교육

(D) 소매업

57 남자는 왜 이전 일을 관뒀는가?

(A) 다른 도시로 이사했다.

(B) 고위직을 원했다.

(C) 자유 시간이 더 많이 필요했다.

(D) 다른 분야를 경험해보고 싶었다.

58 여자는 다음에 무엇에 관해 이야기하겠는가?

(A) 추가 서류를 제출하는 것

(B) 계약 조건을 협상하는 것

(C) 본사와 협력하는 것

(D) 업무 시작일을 조정하는 것

미국 ⇄ 미국 ⇄ 영국

Questions 59-61 refer to the following conversation with three speakers.

M: Hi, Fatima and Karen. **Do you have any updates on the progress of our new wireless device? We're expecting to showcase the earphones at our next press conference.** [59] We can't miss this opportunity.

W1: We tested the device while performing a variety of activities. The quality was always top-notch. We did notice that the earphones tended to fall out while the user was exercising.

W2: **We need to make sure the earphones will stay put for regular use.**[60] As soon as we make a few adjustments to the prototype, we'll send it back for testing before the launch.

M: All right. **Fatima, can you update the development timeline to reflect recent changes?**[61]

W1: Yes, I'll update it today.

59-61번은 다음 세 화자의 대화에 관한 문제입니다.

남: Fatima, Karen, 안녕하세요. **저희 새로운 무선 기기의 진척 상황이 있나요? 다음 기자회견 때 이어폰을 선보일 예정이에요.**[59] 이 기회를 놓치면 안 돼요.

여1: 다양한 활동을 하면서 제품을 테스트했습니다. 품질은 언제나 최고였어요. 다만 사용자가 운동하는 동안 이어폰이 잘 빠져나온다는 것을 알게 됐습니다.

여2: **평상시 사용할 때 이어폰이 잘 고정되어 있어야 해요.**[60] 시제품에서 몇 가지 부분을 수정하면 바로, 출시 전에 테스트로 다시 보낼 거예요.

남: 알았어요. **Fatima, 최신 변경 사항을 반영해서 개발 진행 일정을 업데이트해 주겠어요?**[61]

여1: 네, 오늘 업데이트할게요.

59 화자들은 어떤 제품에 관해 이야기하고 있는가?

(A) 노트북

(B) 충전 기기

(C) 무선 이어폰

(D) 전화기

60 시제품이 왜 변경되고 있는가?

(A) 가격을 낮추기 위해

(B) 배터리 수명을 늘리기 위해

(C) 노이즈 캔슬링 기능을 추가하기 위해

(D) 착용감을 개선하기 위해

61 남자는 Fatima에게 무엇을 해달라고 요청하는가?

(A) 기간 연장을 요청하라고

(B) 보고서를 보내라고

(C) 일정을 변경하라고

(D) 컨설턴트를 채용하라고

Questions 62-64 refer to the following conversation and map.

W: Hello. I signed up to hand out water to the participants in today's 16-mile mini-marathon race.(62) An event staff member said that I should talk to you about what I need to do.

M: Ah, OK. Thank you for volunteering. Take this map of the mini-marathon route. **You'll be stationed at the 4-mile mark to give water to the runners.(63)**

W: Sounds good. I'll go over there right now and get ready for the event.

M: All right. Also, **once the race ends, please help clean up any trash around your station.(64)**

62-64번은 다음 대화와 지도에 관한 문제입니다.

여: 안녕하세요. 저는 오늘 16마일 미니 마라톤 경주에서 참가자들에게 물을 나누어 주는 일에 신청했는데요.(62) 행사 직원이 제가 해야 할 일에 관해서 당신과 이야기하라고 알려줬어요.

남: 아, 그러시군요. 자원해주셔서 고맙습니다. 이 미니 마라톤 경로 지도를 받으세요. **4마일 지점에서 선수들에게 물을 주시면 됩니다.(63)**

여: 네. 바로 거기로 가서 행사를 준비할게요.

남: 좋습니다. 그리고 **경주가 끝나면, 자리 주변의 쓰레기 치우는 일을 좀 도와주세요.(64)**

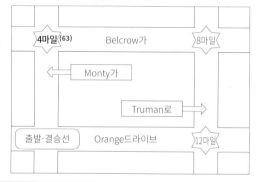

16마일 미니 마라톤 지도

62 여자는 마라톤 대회에서 무엇을 할 것인가?
(A) 사진을 촬영할 것이다
(B) 교통정리를 할 것이다
(C) 음료를 제공할 것이다
(D) 참가자들을 인터뷰할 것이다

63 시각 자료를 보시오. 여자는 어느 교차로로 갈 것인가?
(A) Monty가와 Belcrow가
(B) Belcrow가와 Truman로
(C) Truman로와 Orange드라이브
(D) Orange드라이브와 Monty가

64 여자는 마라톤이 끝난 후 무엇을 하라고 지시받는가?
(A) 구역을 청소하라고
(B) 상을 나누어 주라고
(C) 설문지를 작성하라고
(D) 사진을 공유하라고

Questions 65-67 refer to the following conversation and graph.

W: Can you take a look at this monthly sales report for our X5 Slim Laptop?(65) I'd like to get your thoughts.

M: Let's see... I figured that sales for this product would be high for February. But, I didn't expect that they'd drop so much in the following month.(66)

W: Yeah, but we did have that month-long special deal in February. And there haven't been any promotions since that month.

M: I think we should set up a meeting with Catherine Burke, the new head of marketing.(67) She has overseen some successful ad campaigns.

65-67번은 다음 대화와 그래프에 관한 문제입니다.

여: 저희 X5 슬림 노트북의 이번 월간 매출 보고서를 봐주시겠어요?(65) 당신의 생각을 듣고 싶어요.

남: 봅시다... 이 제품의 매출이 2월에는 높았던 걸로 보이네요. 그런데, 그다음 달에 그렇게 많이 떨어질 거라고는 예상하지 못했어요.(66)

여: 네, 그런데 저희가 2월 내내 특별 할인을 했거든요. 그리고 그달 이후로는 아무런 프로모션도 하지 않았고요.

남: 새 마케팅 책임자인 Catherine Burke와 회의를 잡아야 할 것 같은데요.(67) 그분이 여러 광고 캠페인을 성공적으로 감독한 경험이 있거든요.

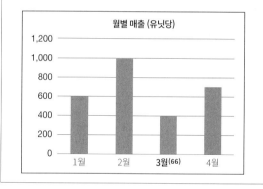

월별 매출 (유닛당)

65 화자들은 어떤 종류의 사업체에서 일하겠는가?
(A) 사무용품점
(B) 자동차 영업소
(C) 전자제품 제조사
(D) 스포츠용품 소매점

66 시각 자료를 보시오. 남자는 어떤 매출액에 놀랐는가?
(A) 400
(B) 600
(C) 700
(D) 1,000

67 Catherine Burke는 누구인가?
(A) 마케팅 전문가
(B) 금융 컨설턴트
(C) IT 관리자
(D) 인사 채용 담당자

Questions 68-70 refer to the following conversation and pricing list.

M: I simply love the location of these apartments! It has everything within walking distance.(68) I don't think I would even need a car if I lived here.

W: That is one of our biggest selling points. It's perfect for working professionals.

M: I can see why.

W: As requested, here are the available apartments as well as their rates.

M: Let's see here. I really liked the view from 348, but for $100 cheaper, I think I can go without that. 213 for me, please.(69)

W: Excellent choice. I'll start drawing up the contract. As part of our leasing requirements, we do require that you submit paystubs from the last two months.(70)

68-70번은 다음 대화와 가격표에 관한 문제입니다.

남: 여기 아파트들 위치가 정말 맘에 들어요! 도보 거리에 모든 게 다 있어요.(68) 여기 살면 차도 필요 없겠어요.

여: 그게 최대 장점 중 하나예요. 전문직 종사자들에겐 최적이에요.

남: 그렇겠네요.

여: 여기 요청하신 이용 가능한 아파트하고 요금이에요.

남: 어디 봅시다. 348호 전망이 정말 맘에 들었는데, 100달러 더 싼 값이면, 그거 없어도 될 것 같아요. 213호로 할게요.(69)

여: 탁월한 선택이세요. 제가 계약서 작성을 시작할게요. 저희는 임대 요건으로 최근 두 달 치 급여 명세서 제출을 요청 드립니다.(70)

이용 가능 호실	
아파트	요금
213	1,296달러(69)
275	1,341달러
348	1,396달러
425	1,195달러

68 남자는 아파트의 어떤 점이 마음에 든다고 하는가?
(A) 건물 안에서 애완동물을 키울 수 있다.
(B) 최근에 보수되었다.
(C) 위치가 편리하다.
(D) 다른 곳보다 가격이 싸다.

69 시각 자료를 보시오. 남자는 월세를 얼마 지불할 것인가?
(A) 1,195달러
(B) 1,296달러
(C) 1,341달러
(D) 1,396달러

70 여자는 무엇이 필요하다고 말하는가?
(A) 추천서
(B) 소득 증빙
(C) 서명한 임대 계약서
(D) 보험 증서

PART 4

Questions 71-73 refer to the following talk.

W: Today is the final part of your training at Samadi Boutique.(71) I'm going to take the morning to show you how to allow our customers to pay for some of the more expensive clothing items in monthly installments. After that, you'll have been taught everything you need to know to begin working.(72) I've organized a shadowing session for this afternoon with one of our experienced employees. She will walk you through an average day here. I'll also issue you your uniforms now.(73) I'll give everyone a few minutes now to put them on.

71-73번은 다음 담화에 관한 문제입니다.

여: 오늘은 Samadi Boutique에서의 교육 마지막 날입니다.(71) 오전에는 제가 고객에게 고가 의류 제품을 월 할부로 결제 처리하는 방법을 알려드릴 거예요. 그다음에는, 근무를 시작하려면 알아야 할 모든 것을 배우게 됩니다.(72) 오늘 오후에는 경력 직원과 함께 지내는 시간을 마련했습니다. 그분이 이곳에서의 평범한 하루 일상에 대해 차근차근 알려줄 거예요. 제가 지금 여러분의 유니폼도 지급할 거예요.(73) 모두 그것을 입도록 시간을 몇 분 드리겠습니다.

71 담화는 어디서 일어나겠는가?
(A) 창고에서
(B) 의류점에서
(C) 식당에서
(D) 기차역에서

72 청자들은 오늘 아침에 무엇을 할 것인가?
(A) 교육 프로그램을 마칠 것이다
(B) 안전 점검을 할 것이다
(C) 계약서에 서명할 것이다
(D) 몇몇 선반의 재고를 채울 것이다

73 화자는 청자들에게 무엇을 입으라고 요청하는가?
(A) 헤드폰
(B) 작업용 장갑
(C) 명찰
(D) 유니폼

Questions 74-76 refer to the following excerpt from a meeting.

W: We can see that our sales numbers for blenders and juicers have fallen a lot recently.(74) This is concerning because other stores have said that these products are their best sellers this season. Rick, our subject matter expert, has suggested that we don't do enough to promote our products. What he's saying is that we have to advertise more aggressively, particularly in the Internet space.(75) I've invited Shawna Black to come speak to us. She's an expert when it comes to increasing social media presence. I think this is where our biggest opportunity is. Here she is now.(76)

74-76번은 다음 회의 발췌록에 관한 문제입니다.

여: 최근 우리 블렌더와 착즙기 매출이 급감한 것을 볼 수 있습니다.(74) 다른 매장에서는 이 제품이 이번 시즌 베스트셀러라고 했다는 점에서 우려스러운 상황입니다. 주제 전문가 Rick은 우리가 제품 홍보를 충분히 하지 않는다고 했습니다. 그분 말에 따르면, 우리는 특히 인터넷 공간에서 좀 더 공격적으로 광고해야 합니다.(75) 제가 이 이야기를 들려주실 분으로 Shawna Black을 모셨습니다. 그녀는 소셜 미디어상에서 인지도를 높이는 방법에 있어서 전문가입니다. 우리에게 아주 큰 기회가 될 것 같습니다. 지금 여기로 모실게요.(76)

74 화자의 회사에서는 무엇을 판매하는가?
(A) 중고 책
(B) 자동차 부품
(C) 운동 장비
(D) 주방용품

75 Rick은 무엇을 추천하는가?
(A) 가격 낮추기
(B) 전문가 고용하기
(C) 광고 늘리기
(D) 비용 최적화하기

76 청자들은 다음에 무엇을 하겠는가?
(A) 매장을 조사할 것이다
(B) 수신함을 확인할 것이다
(C) 회의 일정을 잡을 것이다
(D) 연사의 말을 경청할 것이다

미국

Questions 77-79 refer to the following telephone message.

M: Hi, Judith. This is Oliver returning your call. I am free on Saturday, so it would be great to meet up then. However, it will have to be after 11 o'clock as I will have to stop by my gym locker to pick up my shoes.(77) I have a soccer match on Sunday. Also, I ran into our college roommate at the art center the other day. He started working there about a month ago.(78) Anyway let's meet at Jungle Juice. I have to see why everyone waits in lines.(79) Let me know if 1 P.M. works for you. If not, we can meet later.

77-79번은 다음 전화 메시지에 관한 문제입니다.

남: 안녕하세요, Judith. Oliver인데, 회신 전화드립니다. 제가 토요일에 시간이 돼서 그때 만나면 좋겠어요. 그런데 제가 신발을 가지러 체육관 보관함에 들러야 해서 11시 이후로 해야 해요.(77) 일요일에는 축구 시합이 있어요. 그리고 제가 얼마 전에 아트센터에서 대학 룸메이트를 우연히 만났어요. 한 달쯤 전부터 거기서 근무하기 시작했더라고요.(78) 어쨌든 Jungle Juice에서 만납시다. 왜 다들 줄을 서는지 알아봐야겠어요.(79) 오후 1시가 괜찮은지 알려주세요. 안 되면, 다음에 만나요.

77 화자는 왜 토요일 11시 전에는 시간을 낼 수 없는가?
(A) 동료를 만날 것이다.
(B) 다른 지역에서 돌아올 예정이다.
(C) 장비를 찾아와야 한다.
(D) 수업에 참석해야 한다.

78 화자는 서로 아는 친구에 관하여 뭐라고 말하는가?
(A) 해외로 이주할 예정이다.
(B) 텔레비전에 출연했다.
(C) 승진했다.
(D) 새로운 일을 시작했다.

79 화자는 왜 "왜 다들 줄을 서는지 알아봐야겠어요"라고 말하는가?
(A) 제안을 정당화하기 위해
(B) 동향에 논평하기 위해
(C) 제안을 거절하기 위해
(D) 요점을 입증하기 위해

호주

Questions 80-82 refer to the following introduction.

M: Thank you all for joining us for the 15th Annual World Convention on Wildlife and Ecology.(80) I am excited to introduce our keynote speaker for today, Benedict Freeman from the Endangered Animals Association. Mr. Freeman is recognized as one of the leading activists involved in protecting endangered species.(81) For the past decade, he has gone on countless tours across the world advocating the preservation of wildlife habitats. But before we bring Mr. Freeman to the stage, I'd like to urge each of you to consider donating to the association.(82) Anything you can give will be a big help.

80-82번은 다음 소개에 관한 문제입니다.

남: 제15회 연례 세계 야생 동물 및 생태계 박람회에 와주신 모든 분께 감사의 말씀 드립니다.(80) 오늘의 기조연설자이신 멸종 위기 동물협회의 Benedict Freeman을 소개해드리게 되어 정말 기쁩니다. Mr. Freeman은 멸종 위기종 보호에 관여하는 주요 활동가 중 한 분으로 인정받고 있습니다.(81) 그는 지난 10년 동안 전 세계를 수없이 다니시며 야생 동물 서식지의 보존을 주장해오셨습니다. 하지만 Mr. Freeman을 무대로 모시기 전에, 협회에 대한 기부를 고려해주실 것을 여러분 모두에게 강력히 권장 드립니다.(82) 얼마를 기부하시든 큰 도움이 될 것입니다.

80 소개는 어디에서 이루어지고 있는가?
(A) 시상식에서
(B) 국제 박람회에서
(C) 기념일 파티에서
(D) 직원 오찬에서

81 화자는 Benedict Freeman이 무엇으로 유명하다고 말하는가?
(A) 여행 서적
(B) 멸종 위기종을 위한 일
(C) 문제 해결 능력
(D) 삽화를 넣은 식물도감

82 청자들은 무엇을 하도록 권장받는가?
(A) 초청 연사를 환영해달라고
(B) 설문지를 작성하라고
(C) 여행을 가라고
(D) 기부를 하라고

Questions 83-85 refer to the following telephone message.

W: Hi, Dr. Craig. This is Dr. Robbins from Davidson Unlimited. We're holding a conference for entrepreneurs in the Davidson area, and I would like to extend an invite to you to be one of our speakers.[83] I'm familiar with your work from my time in Luton, where I was assigned for a work project.[84] We would love your expertise and insights to help our community. It may also benefit you as many prestigious firms will be in attendance. Personally, I'm excited to expand my network of contacts.[85] If you'd like to find out more, please give me a call.

83-85번은 다음 전화 메시지에 관한 문제입니다.

여: 안녕하세요, Dr. Craig. 저는 Davidson Unlimited의 Dr. Robbins입니다. 저희가 Davidson 지역 내 기업가를 위한 컨퍼런스를 개최하는데, 귀하를 저희 연사 중 한 분으로 모시고 싶습니다.[83] 저는 Luton에서 있던 시절을 통해 귀하의 업적에 대해 잘 알고 있는데요, 그곳에서 업무 프로젝트를 맡은 적이 있습니다.[84] 귀하의 전문성과 통찰로 저희 지역사회에 도움을 주시면 너무 좋을 것 같습니다. 명망 있는 회사가 많이 참석하는 만큼 귀하에게도 도움이 될 것입니다. 개인적으로 저는 인맥을 넓힐 생각에 기대됩니다.[85] 더 많은 내용을 알고 싶으시면, 저에게 전화해 주십시오.

83 화자는 왜 전화하고 있는가?
(A) 최신 일정표를 요청하기 위해
(B) 청자를 행사에 초대하기 위해
(C) 청자에게 추천서를 부탁하기 위해
(D) 새로운 역할에 대한 관심을 표하기 위해

84 화자는 Luton에서 무엇을 했는가?
(A) 부모님을 방문했다.
(B) 창업했다.
(C) 프로젝트 작업을 했다.
(D) 대학에 다녔다.

85 화자는 무엇에 관해 기대된다고 말하는가?
(A) 연설을 하는 것
(B) 텔레비전에 출연하는 것
(C) 기업인과 만나는 것
(D) 상을 받는 것

Questions 86-88 refer to the following excerpt from a meeting.

W: Good morning, everyone. This quarter has been unexpectedly hot for us. It seems like multiple car companies are demanding our parts, which has been great for our sales.[86] To top it off, we have received some excellent feedback from our clients. Our parts are clearly a cut above the competition. However, there is some bad news. We have received complaints that our delivery times are simply too long. Compared to our competitors, we take nearly a month longer. I mean, we are manufacturing overseas.[87] I'm going to talk to our manufacturers and see what we can do. We have our company's anniversary event next month.[88] I'd like for us to decide on some changes by then.

86-88번은 다음 회의 발췌록에 관한 문제입니다.

여: 여러분, 안녕하세요. 이번 분기는 예상외로 아주 치열했습니다. 보아하니 여러 자동차 회사에서 저희 부품을 요구하고 있어서, 우리 매출에 큰 도움이 되었어요.[86] 게다가 고객들에게 우수한 피드백도 받았습니다. 저희 부품이 단연 경쟁사보다 뛰어납니다. 하지만 안 좋은 소식이 있어요. 우리 배송 시간이 그야말로 너무 길다는 불만을 받았습니다. 경쟁사 대비, 우리 회사가 거의 한 달이나 더 걸립니다. 제 말은, 우리는 해외에서 제조하고 있어요.[87] 제가 우리 제조업체들과 이야기를 나누며 조치 방안에 대해 알아볼게요. 다음 달에는 우리 회사 창립기념 행사가 있습니다.[88] 그때까지는 우리가 몇 가지 변경 사항을 결정했으면 합니다.

86 화자의 회사에서는 무엇을 판매하는가?
(A) 건설 장비
(B) 컴퓨터 소프트웨어
(C) 옥외 광고
(D) 자동차 부품

87 화자는 "우리는 해외에서 제조하고 있어요"라고 말할 때 무엇을 의미하는가?
(A) 의견을 듣고 싶어 한다.
(B) 유력한 이유를 알고 있다.
(C) 청자들이 요점에 귀 기울이지 않았다.
(D) 경쟁사들이 유용한 정보를 제공하지 않았다.

88 다음 달에 무슨 행사가 열릴 것인가?
(A) 회사 창립기념일
(B) 연휴
(C) 내부 감사
(D) 업계 무역 박람회

Questions 89-91 refer to the following recorded message.

M: You have reached the Quigley Recreation Center. For the next two months of spring, our building will be inaccessible due to some reconstruction. In the meantime, we have rented a space on the other side of town at 748 Yosemite Road.[89] For directions on how to get there, please check our website.[90] Because this rental property isn't as big as our facility, it does not have a fitness center. You will, however, be able to check out various sports equipment. In order to do so, please hand over your recreation center ID card at the front desk.[91]

89-91번은 다음 녹음 메시지에 관한 문제입니다.

남: Quigley 레크리에이션 센터입니다. 봄 시즌인 다음 두 달 동안, 복원 공사로 인해 저희 건물을 이용하실 수 없습니다. 그동안, 저희가 시 맞은 편, Yosemite로 748번지에 있는 장소를 하나 임차했습니다.[89] 찾아오시는 법은 저희 웹사이트를 확인해 주세요.[90] 이 임차 건물이 저희 시설만큼 크지 않아서, 피트니스 센터는 없습니다. 하지만, 다양한 운동 기구를 대여하실 수 있습니다. 그렇게 하시려면, 안내 데스크에서 고객님의 레크리에이션 센터 ID 카드를 건네주세요.[91]

89 메시지는 주로 무엇에 관한 것인가?
(A) 봄철 프로그램
(B) 도로변 공사
(C) 스포츠 경기
(D) 장소 변경

90 화자에 따르면, 웹사이트에서 무엇을 이용할 수 있는가?
(A) 길 안내
(B) 사진
(C) 신청서
(D) 행사 일정표

91 청자들은 스포츠용품을 어떻게 빌릴 수 있는가?
(A) ID 카드를 제출함으로써
(B) 신청서를 작성함으로써
(C) 요금을 지불함으로써
(D) 온라인으로 예약함으로써

Questions 92-94 refer to the following news report.

W: Good evening, Daniela McAdams here with KMG 3 News. Tonight's Your Money segment features Landing Financial Services' new banking app for mobile devices.**(92)** One key aspect of the app is that users can link multiple accounts, making it easier to transfer money from their savings to checking account. Many experts have questioned the adoption of mixing banking and technology. Nevertheless, after only being released a few days ago, it has over 25,000 downloads.**(93)** In an effort to gain more users, everyone who signs up and completes at least two transactions within the first 72 hours of downloading the app will automatically become eligible for their electric bike sweepstakes.**(94)**

92-94번은 다음 뉴스 보도에 관한 문제입니다.

여: 안녕하세요, KMG 3 뉴스의 Daniela McAdams입니다. 오늘 밤 <Your Money> 코너에서는 Landing Financial Services의 모바일 기기용 신규 은행 앱을 특집으로 다룹니다.**(92)** 이 앱의 한 가지 중요한 특징은 사용자가 여러 계좌에 접속할 수 있다는 점인데, 이는 보통 예금에서 당좌 예금으로 돈을 더 쉽게 이체할 수 있게 해 줍니다. 많은 전문가들은 금융 거래와 기술을 혼합한 방식을 도입하는 것에 의문을 제기했습니다. 그럼에도 불구하고, 며칠 전에 출시되었을 뿐인데, 25,000건 이상 다운로드 되었습니다.**(93)** 더 많은 사용자들을 확보하기 위한 노력의 일환으로, 앱을 다운로드한 후 첫 72시간 이내에 최소 두 건의 거래를 이행한 분들은 모두 자동으로 전기 자전거 경품 행사에 응모됩니다.**(94)**

92 모바일 애플리케이션은 사용자들에게 무엇을 가능하게 해줄 것인가?
(A) 업체 검색하기
(B) 게임 하기
(C) 사진 올리기
(D) 온라인 뱅킹하기

93 화자는 "25,000건 이상 다운로드 되었습니다"라고 말할 때 무엇을 의미하는가?
(A) 프로그램이 인기가 있다.
(B) 마케팅 캠페인이 필요하다.
(C) 서버가 업그레이드되어야 한다.
(D) 사이트가 제대로 작동하지 않는다.

94 일부 사용자들은 무엇에 참가할 수 있는가?
(A) 추첨 대회
(B) 시범 사용기간
(C) 연구 조사
(D) 육상 경기

Questions 95-97 refer to the following instructions and table arrangements.

M: Attention, everyone. Today is the night Boodle Estates is hosting a retirement party for one of their employees. **(95)** They requested a specific arrangement for the tables, so here's what we need to do. They would like to sit within their teams, so let's get multiple small tables. Let's use the smallest ones so that we can accommodate more people.**(96)** We'll also need to install some speakers high up on the walls. That way, everyone in the restaurant will be able to hear. There's a ladder in the closet you can use to do that.**(97)** Can someone volunteer to do that?

95-97번은 다음 설명과 테이블 배치에 관한 문제입니다.

남: 모두, 주목해 주세요. 오늘은 Boodle Estates에서 직원 한 분을 위한 퇴임식을 개최하는 밤입니다.**(95)** 그쪽에서 특정 테이블 배치를 요청해서, 저희가 해야 할 일은 다음과 같습니다. 그쪽에서는 팀 단위로 앉고 싶어하니, 작은 테이블을 여러 개 마련합시다. 더 많은 사람을 수용할 수 있도록 가장 작은 것을 사용하죠.**(96)** 벽 위쪽에 스피커도 몇 개 설치해야 합니다. 그렇게 하면 식당 내 모든 사람이 들을 수 있어요. 벽장에 사다리가 있으니 사용해서 하셔도 됩니다.**(97)** 누가 자원해서 작업을 해 주실래요?

테이블 배치

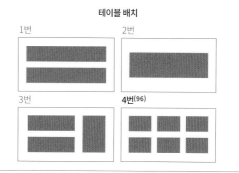

1번   2번   3번   4번**(96)**

95 청자들은 어떤 행사를 준비하는 중인가?
(A) 세미나 후 만찬
(B) 창립기념일 행사
(C) 친목 도모 행사
(D) 직원 퇴임식

96 시각 자료를 보시오. 어떤 테이블 배치가 사용될 것인가?
(A) 배치 1번
(B) 배치 2번
(C) 배치 3번
(D) 배치 4번

97 화자에 따르면, 사다리가 왜 필요한가?
(A) 조명을 교체하기 위해
(B) 스피커를 놓기 위해
(C) 천장을 청소하기 위해
(D) 배너를 걸기 위해

Questions 98-100 refer to the following announcement and catalog.

M: If we could have your attention for a moment, we have a few announcements to make before our overnight flight to Honolulu takes off. **(98)** First of all, complimentary bottled water is available at all times during this flight. If you are thirsty, simply tell me or one of the other cabin crew members, and we will be glad to bring you a bottle. **(99)** And don't forget, we have all kinds of gifts available for purchase to delight your friends and family. Shop from the catalog now! **Just one thing—I'm afraid that Product #82 has sold out. (100)** But there are plenty of other great choices!

98-100번은 다음 안내와 카탈로그에 관한 문제입니다.

남: 잠시 주목해 주시면, Honolulu로 가는 야간 비행 편이 이륙하기 전, 몇 가지 안내 말씀드리겠습니다. **(98)** 먼저, 비행하시는 동안 생수를 언제든 무료로 이용하실 수 있습니다. 목이 마르시면, 저나 다른 승무원에게 말씀만 해주시면 고객님께 가져다드리겠습니다. **(99)** 그리고 기억해 주세요, 승객 여러분의 친지분들을 기쁘게 해드릴 모든 종류의 선물을 구매하실 수 있습니다. 지금 카탈로그를 보시면서 쇼핑하세요! 하나만 더 말씀드리면, 아쉽게도 82번 제품은 매진되었습니다. **(100)** 하지만 그 밖에도 선택하실 좋은 물건들이 많이 있습니다.

75번 제품 초콜릿 상자 (25달러)	**82번 제품(100)** **지갑** (55달러)
79번 제품 선글라스 (70달러)	95번 제품 무선 충전기 (40달러)

98 청자들은 누구겠는가?

    (A) 항공기 승객들
    (B) 콘서트 참석자들
    (C) 리조트 고객들
    (D) 쇼핑몰 방문객들

99 화자는 무엇을 해주겠다고 제안하는가?

    (A) 음료를 제공해 주겠다고
    (B) 불을 꺼 주겠다고
    (C) 소지품을 보관해 주겠다고
    (D) 돈을 환불해 주겠다고

100 시각 자료를 보시오. 어떤 물건을 더 이상 구할 수 없는가?

    (A) 초콜릿 상자
    (B) 지갑
    (C) 선글라스
    (D) 무선 충전기

TEST 06

PART 1
P. 86

1 (A) **2** (D) **3** (D) **4** (D) **5** (C) **6** (A)

PART 2
P. 90

7 (A) **8** (B) **9** (A) **10** (B) **11** (A) **12** (B)
13 (C) **14** (A) **15** (B) **16** (C) **17** (B) **18** (B)
19 (C) **20** (C) **21** (C) **22** (C) **23** (A) **24** (C)
25 (A) **26** (C) **27** (C) **28** (C) **29** (A) **30** (B)
31 (B)

PART 3
P. 91

32 (D) **33** (C) **34** (B) **35** (D) **36** (B) **37** (D)
38 (D) **39** (B) **40** (A) **41** (A) **42** (C) **43** (D)
44 (A) **45** (C) **46** (B) **47** (A) **48** (A) **49** (D)
50 (A) **51** (C) **52** (D) **53** (C) **54** (D) **55** (A)
56 (A) **57** (B) **58** (A) **59** (B) **60** (C) **61** (B)
62 (B) **63** (A) **64** (C) **65** (D) **66** (A) **67** (B)
68 (A) **69** (D) **70** (C)

PART 4
P. 95

71 (A) **72** (A) **73** (A) **74** (B) **75** (A) **76** (B)
77 (A) **78** (B) **79** (D) **80** (A) **81** (B) **82** (D)
83 (A) **84** (B) **85** (B) **86** (A) **87** (A) **88** (C)
89 (A) **90** (B) **91** (B) **92** (A) **93** (B) **94** (C)
95 (A) **96** (D) **97** (D) **98** (A) **99** (B) **100** (C)

PART 1
P. 86

1 호주
(A) A woman is facing a monitor.
(B) A woman is typing on a keyboard.
(C) A woman is looking at a calendar.
(D) A woman is arranging some files.

(A) 여자가 모니터를 바라보고 있다.
(B) 여자가 키보드를 치고 있다.
(C) 여자가 달력을 보고 있다.
(D) 여자가 몇몇 파일을 정리하고 있다.

2 영국
(A) One of the men is nailing some boards together.
(B) One of the men is tightening his utility belt.
(C) The men are removing some protective gear.
(D) The men are carrying some wooden planks.

(A) 남자들 중 한 명이 합판들을 못으로 박고 있다.
(B) 남자들 중 한 명이 그가 맨 다용도 벨트를 조이고 있다.
(C) 남자들이 보호 장구를 벗고 있다.
(D) 남자들이 나무판자들을 나르고 있다.

3 미국
(A) A man is raking the lawn.
(B) A man is repairing a fence.
(C) A man is trimming some bushes.
(D) A man is working on some equipment.

(A) 남자가 잔디에 갈퀴질을 하고 있다.
(B) 남자가 울타리를 고치고 있다.
(C) 남자가 관목을 다듬고 있다.
(D) 남자가 장비를 살피고 있다.

4 미국
(A) A woman is attaching a label on a package.
(B) A woman is erasing a whiteboard.
(C) A woman is putting together a cardboard box.
(D) A woman is grabbing a box on a shelf.

(A) 여자가 소포에 라벨을 붙이고 있다.
(B) 여자가 화이트보드를 지우고 있다.
(C) 여자가 판지 상자를 조립하고 있다.
(D) 여자가 선반 위 상자를 잡고 있다.

5 영국
(A) A metal railing is being repaired.
(B) A pedestrian is crossing a street.
(C) Some bicycles are parked next to a road.
(D) Some passengers are boarding a bus.

(A) 금속 난간이 수리되고 있다.
(B) 보행자가 길을 건너고 있다.
(C) 몇몇 자전거들이 도로 옆에 주차되어 있다.
(D) 몇몇 승객들이 버스에 탑승하고 있다.

6 미국
(A) Some containers have been stocked with a variety of foods.
(B) Some jars have been stacked on top of one another.
(C) A cash register is in the corner of a store.
(D) A store employee is arranging some cartons.

(A) 몇몇 용기들이 다양한 음식으로 채워져 있다.
(B) 몇몇 병들이 차곡차곡 쌓여 있다.
(C) 계산대가 상점 구석에 있다.
(D) 상점 직원이 몇몇 상자들을 정리하고 있다.

PART 2
P. 90

7 영국 ⇄ 미국
Our manager printed the agenda for us, right?
(A) No, he had Ms. Long do it.
(B) Thanks, I just printed one.
(C) We'll be discussing the new project.

저희 매니저가 안건을 출력했죠, 그렇죠?
(A) 아니요, Ms. Long에게 시켰어요.
(B) 고마워요, 제가 방금 하나 출력했어요.
(C) 새 프로젝트를 논의하게 될 거예요.

8 호주 ⇄ 영국

When are we going to have our salary negotiations?
(A) Almost 50 thousand dollars a year.
(B) The president is away on business this month.
(C) Yes, they offer excellent employee benefits.

임금협상은 언제 하나요?
(A) 매년 거의 5만달러요.
(B) 이번 달에는 사장님께서 출장 중이시라 안 계세요.
(C) 네, 그들은 훌륭한 복리후생을 제공해요.

9 미국 ⇄ 미국

How long is the TV commercial you're editing?
(A) Less than 30 seconds.
(B) It's 10 kilometers from here.
(C) Yes, I'm the chief editor.

편집하고 있는 TV 광고는 얼마나 길어요?
(A) 30초 미만이요.
(B) 여기서부터 10킬로미터예요.
(C) 네, 제가 편집장이에요.

10 영국 ⇄ 호주

Who could I speak with about my ID badge?
(A) May 2nd.
(B) Ms. Song in Maintenance.
(C) The registration forms are online.

제 사원증에 대해서는 누구에게 얘기하면 되나요?
(A) 5월 2일이요.
(B) 시설관리부의 Ms. Song이요.
(C) 신청서는 인터넷에 있어요.

11 미국 ⇄ 미국

Where is the international symposium taking place?
(A) I think it's in Hong Kong this year.
(B) Since I won't be going, you can take my place.
(C) That's where Cathy usually sits.

국제 심포지엄은 어디서 열리나요?
(A) 올해는 Hong Kong인 것 같아요.
(B) 전 안 갈 거니까, 제 자리에 앉으세요.
(C) 거긴 Cathy가 주로 앉는 자리예요.

12 미국 ⇄ 영국

How do you like your new apartment?
(A) Last Saturday.
(B) It has a nice view.
(C) The department office is downstairs.

새 아파트는 어떠세요?
(A) 지난 토요일이요.
(B) 전망이 좋아요.
(C) 부서 사무실은 아래층에 있어요.

13 호주 ⇄ 미국

Why is this file cabinet here?
(A) From the furniture catalog.
(B) The official documents.
(C) I'll move it to the storage room.

이 파일 캐비닛이 왜 여기에 있죠?
(A) 가구 카탈로그에서요.
(B) 공식 서류요.
(C) 제가 그걸 창고로 옮겨 놓을게요.

14 영국 ⇄ 미국

Don't you want to watch the movie with us today?
(A) When does it start?
(B) Emma bought it last night.
(C) A documentary on birds.

오늘 저희와 영화 보지 않으시겠어요?
(A) 언제 시작하는데요?
(B) Emma가 어젯밤에 샀어요.
(C) 조류에 관한 다큐멘터리요.

15 미국 ⇄ 영국

Where can I get the tourist visa application form?
(A) For Shanghai and Beijing.
(B) At the information desk.
(C) A travel schedule.

관광비자 신청서는 어디서 받을 수 있나요?
(A) Shanghai와 Beijing행이요.
(B) 안내 데스크에서요.
(C) 여행일정표요.

16 미국 ⇄ 호주

Consumers seem to be pleased with our new car model, right?
(A) They'll travel by public transportation.
(B) A new company vehicle policy.
(C) I haven't read the reviews yet.

소비자들이 우리 신형 자동차 모델에 만족하는 것 같아요, 그렇죠?
(A) 그들은 대중교통으로 이동할 거예요.
(B) 새로운 회사 차량 정책이요.
(C) 아직 평을 읽어 보지 못했어요.

17 미국 ⇄ 미국

Should I contact the shipping company or the retailer?
(A) Ship it to my home address.
(B) Try the store first.
(C) Do you have an express option?

제가 택배사에 연락해야 할까요, 아니면 소매점에 연락해야 할까요?
(A) 그것을 저희 집 주소로 보내주세요.
(B) 먼저 매장에 연락해봐요.
(C) 속달 옵션이 있나요?

18 영국 ⇄ 미국

You should take woodworking classes after work.
(A) Sorry, our classes are full.
(B) Yes, I'd love to pick up a new hobby.
(C) Well, I enjoy walking to the office.

퇴근 후에 목공 수업을 들어보세요.
(A) 죄송해요, 저희 수업이 마감됐네요.
(B) 네, 정말 새 취미를 만들고 싶어요.
(C) 음, 저는 사무실까지 걸어가는 걸 좋아해요.

19 호주 ⇄ 영국

Is Mr. Reed's team on the 6th floor or the 7th floor?
(A) I have several certificates.
(B) By the end of the month.
(C) They're on the 6th.

Mr. Reed의 부서가 6층인가요, 7층인가요?
(A) 저는 자격증이 여러 개 있어요.
(B) 이달 말까지요.
(C) 6층이에요.

20 미국 ⇄ 호주

Why was Greg late to the meeting?
(A) It was nice to finally meet him in person.
(B) From 9:30 A.M. to 10 A.M.
(C) Route 4 was closed for maintenance.

Greg는 회의에 왜 늦었죠?
(A) 드디어 직접 만나 봬서 좋았습니다.
(B) 오전 9시 30분부터 10시까지요.
(C) 4번 국도가 보수작업으로 폐쇄됐어요.

21 영국 ⇄ 미국

Would you mind coming in to the store this weekend?
(A) The warehouse is full.
(B) Yes, I had an enjoyable weekend.
(C) Do you need me on both days?

이번 주말에 매장에 와주시겠어요?
(A) 창고가 가득 찼어요.
(B) 네, 즐거운 주말이었어요.
(C) 이틀 모두 제가 필요하신가요?

22 미국 ⇄ 미국

Do you need the website link for the Department of Health?
(A) Let's go for a run.
(B) I went to see a doctor last week.
(C) That's OK. I got it.

보건부 웹사이트 링크 필요하세요?
(A) 달리기하러 가요.
(B) 지난주에 병원에 다녀왔어요.
(C) 괜찮아요. 있어요.

23 미국 ⇄ 미국

When will the new interns finish their training?
(A) I'm not in charge of them.
(B) We should have enough office supplies.
(C) The train schedule is posted online.

신규 인턴 교육은 언제 끝나나요?
(A) 제 담당이 아니에요.
(B) 사무용품이 충분히 있어야 해요.
(C) 열차 시간표는 온라인에 게시되어 있어요.

24 영국 ⇄ 호주

I need to meet with Chase before I leave work for the day.
(A) The Wi-Fi router is over there.
(B) Yes, the convention is a week long.
(C) He'll be with a client until 5.

퇴근하기 전에 Chase와 만나야 해요.
(A) 와이파이 라우터는 저기 있어요.
(B) 네, 컨벤션은 일주일간 해요.
(C) 5시까지 고객과 함께 계실 거예요.

25 호주 ⇄ 미국

Which of these online marketing strategies is the best?
(A) I work in finance.
(B) At an offline market.
(C) A 30-percent increase.

이 중에서 어떤 온라인 마케팅 전략이 가장 좋으세요?
(A) 전 금융업에 종사해요.
(B) 오프라인 시장에서요.
(C) 30퍼센트 인상이요.

26 미국 ⇄ 미국

Should we start a hiking club for our employees?
(A) No, I've never been there before.
(B) Sure, let me make a hotel reservation for you.
(C) Ming Hao mentioned that the other day.

직원 산악회를 시작해야 할까요?
(A) 아니요, 한 번도 안 가봤어요.
(B) 네, 호텔을 예약해 드릴게요.
(C) Ming Hao가 지난번에 그 얘기 했어요.

27 미국 ⇄ 영국

Hasn't the refrigerator been repaired yet?
(A) In the kitchen.
(B) No, I made the dish with pears.
(C) The technician canceled.

냉장고가 아직 수리되지 않았나요?
(A) 주방에요.
(B) 아니요, 제가 배로 요리를 만들었어요.
(C) 기사가 취소했어요.

28 호주 ⇄ 미국

How did you make this delicious pastry?
(A) I'm fine, thank you.
(B) No, you should copy and paste it.
(C) It's our special recipe.

이렇게 맛있는 페이스트리는 어떻게 만든 거예요?
(A) 전 괜찮아요, 감사합니다.
(B) 아니요, 복사해서 붙여 넣어야 해요.
(C) 저희 특별 조리법이에요.

29 영국 ⇄ 호주

Can you start working from the week of the 16th?
(A) I have a trip planned for that week.
(B) Well, I think we're all quite satisfied.
(C) I'd just need 18 copies instead.

16일 주부터 근무 시작할 수 있으세요?
(A) 그 주에 여행 계획이 잡혀 있어요.
(B) 음, 우리 모두 상당히 만족한 것 같아요.
(C) 대신에 18부만 있으면 돼요.

30 미국 ⇄ 미국

The building elevators are running well, aren't they?
(A) A parking garage is being built.
(B) They're the most recent model.
(C) I try to go running every morning.

건물 엘리베이터가 잘 작동하고 있죠, 그렇죠?
(A) 주차장이 건설되고 있어요.
(B) 최신 모델이에요.
(C) 전 아침마다 뛰려고 노력해요.

31 호주 ⇄ 미국

The filing cabinets in the reference room are all full.
(A) Yes, the file has been deleted.
(B) We'll have to order more then.
(C) It's on the bottom shelf.

자료실에 있는 서류 정리함이 다 꽉 찼어요.
(A) 네, 파일이 삭제되었어요.
(B) 더 주문해야겠네요.
(C) 맨 아래 칸에 있어요.

PART 3

P. 91

호주 ⇄ 영국

Questions 32-34 refer to the following conversation.

M: Excuse me, could you explain something? According to your store's website, **you're offering a 15-percent discount on the Cross Adventure hiking boots. But I don't see them in the footwear aisle.**(32)

W: Unfortunately, we are all out of those at the moment. **A new shipment did come in this morning, but it was damaged.**(33) We'll receive a new one tomorrow.

M: Ah, OK. Well, the website said the promotion was valid through today. Will you still offer the same deal tomorrow?

W: Yes. **Just visit our help desk,**(34) and an employee will give you a voucher to use when purchasing the boots.

32-34번은 다음 대화에 관한 문제입니다.

남: 저기요, 뭐 설명 좀 해주시겠어요? 상점 웹사이트를 보면, Cross Adventure 등산화가 15퍼센트 할인하고 있다고 나오는데요. 그런데 등산화가 신발 섹션에서 안 보여요.(32)

여: 유감스럽게도, 현재 재고가 없어요. 새 배송품이 오늘 오전에 들어왔는데, 파손이 되었어요.(33) 내일 새 제품이 들어옵니다.

남: 아, 그렇군요. 음, 웹사이트에서는 그 프로모션이 오늘까지 유효하다고 되어 있는데요. 내일도 동일하게 할인해 주시나요?

여: 네. **저희 안내 데스크에 방문하시면,**(34) 직원이 등산화를 구매하실 때 이용하실 쿠폰을 드릴 겁니다.

32 남자는 무엇에 도움이 필요한가?
(A) 제품을 교환하는 것
(B) 차에서 소포들을 내리는 것
(C) 상점 회원권을 갱신하는 것
(D) 상품을 찾는 것

33 문제의 원인은 무엇인가?
(A) 창고가 일찍 문을 닫았다.
(B) 관리자가 시간이 없다.
(C) 배송품이 파손되었다.
(D) 가격표가 잘못되었다.

34 여자는 남자에게 어디로 가라고 알려주는가?
(A) 계산대로
(B) 안내 데스크로
(C) 다른 통로로
(D) 창고로

호주 ⇄ 미국 ⇄ 영국

Questions 35-37 refer to the following conversation with three speakers.

M: Hello, Katie and Myra. I'm Harold from Human Resources. I'll be spending the morning helping the two of you understand your roles on your new team.(35)

W1: I see. Would you mind if we send off a few e-mails to our clients? I'd like to tell them who they should refer to now.(36)

W2: That's a great idea.(36)

M: Absolutely. The plan is to go over your new responsibilities in the morning and set up your desks. **Then after lunch, I'll formally introduce you to your new team.**(37)

35-37번은 다음 세 화자의 대화에 관한 문제입니다.

남: Katie, Myra, 안녕하세요. 저는 인사팀의 Harold입니다. 저는 오전 시간 동안 두 분이 새로운 부서에서 맡게 될 역할에 대해 알려 드릴 예정입니다.(35)

여1: 그러시군요. 저희가 고객들에게 이메일을 몇 통 발송해도 괜찮을까요? 이제 누구에게 문의를 해야 하는지 안내해 드리고 싶어서요.(36)

여2: 아주 좋은 생각이에요.(36)

남: 그럼요. 오전에는 여러분의 새로운 업무에 대해 살펴보고, 책상을 마련할 계획이에요. 그리고 점심시간 이후에는 여러분을 새로운 부서에 정식으로 소개해 드릴게요.(37)

35 어떤 활동이 오전에 예정되어 있는가?
(A) 중재 절차
(B) 퇴임식
(C) 제품 시연
(D) 오리엔테이션 시간

36 여자들은 무엇을 하고 싶다고 말하는가?
(A) 계획을 취소하고 싶다고
(B) 이메일을 보내고 싶다고
(C) 주문하고 싶다고
(D) 메모하고 싶다고

37 남자는 점심 이후 무슨 일이 있을 거라고 말하는가?
(A) 서류가 서명될 것이다.
(B) 자리가 배정될 것이다.
(C) 시험이 치러질 것이다.
(D) 회의가 열릴 것이다.

호주 ⇄ 미국

Questions 38-40 refer to the following conversation.

M: You've reached Lastow Home Improvement. This is Martin speaking.

W: Hello, **I just received the four cans of blue paint I purchased from your online store three days ago.**(38) However, **I noticed that one of the cans was opened, and some of the paint spilled. It wasn't sealed properly.**(39)

M: I'm so sorry about that.

W: I can get this exchanged for another one, right?

M: Definitely. We'll send you a new one at no cost. **Please give me your name and phone number, so I can look up your order.**(40)

38-40번은 다음 대화에 관한 문제입니다.

남: Lastow 주거용품점입니다. 저는 Martin입니다.

여: 안녕하세요, 제가 3일 전에 그곳 온라인 상점에서 구입한 파란색 페인트 4통을 방금 받았는데요.(38) 그런데, 보니까 통 하나가 개봉된 상태고 페인트도 좀 쏟아졌네요. 밀봉이 제대로 안 돼 있더라고요.(39)

남: 정말 죄송합니다.

여: 이거 다른 걸로 교환 받을 수 있죠, 맞죠?

남: 물론입니다. 새 제품을 무료로 보내드리겠습니다. 주문 정보를 찾을 수 있도록 성함과 전화번호를 알려주세요.(40)

38 여자는 최근에 무엇을 했는가?
(A) 소포를 배달했다.
(B) 상사와 만났다.
(C) 새집으로 이사했다.
(D) 비품을 샀다.

39 여자가 전화를 건 이유는 무엇인가?
- (A) 대금을 납입하기 위해
- (B) 불만을 제기하기 위해
- (C) 추가 물품을 구매하기 위해
- (D) 상담 일정을 잡기 위해

40 남자는 무엇을 요청하는가?
- (A) 개인정보
- (B) 쿠폰 번호
- (C) 매장 안내도
- (D) 제품 견본

미국 ⇄ 미국

Questions 41-43 refer to the following conversation.

M: Hi, Irina. I just found out that our CEO rescheduled his travel plans. He'll be here this Thursday, rather than the next.(41)

W: Then we should finish our sales report quickly.(42) It's not even half done!

M: I don't think it will be too difficult, but you're right. We need to get it done. Let me just finish looking over these customer feedback surveys.

W: Isn't the assistant manager coming in at 1 o'clock? **Why don't you have her review them?**(43) That way, we can get started right away.

M: That's a great idea.

41-43번은 다음 대화에 관한 문제입니다.

남: 안녕하세요, Irina. 저희 CEO가 출장 계획을 변경했다는 사실을 방금 알게 됐어요. 그분이 다음 주 목요일이 아니고 이번 주 목요일에 이곳에 오실 거예요.(41)

여: 그러면 영업 보고서를 빨리 끝내야겠네요.(42) 아직 반도 못 끝냈거든요!

남: 그렇게 어려운 것은 아니지만, 당신 말이 맞아요. 그걸 마무리해야 해요. 제가 일단 이 고객 피드백 설문 검토부터 끝낼게요.

여: 1시에 부매니저가 오지 않아요? 그녀에게 검토를 맡기는 건 어때요?(43) 그렇게 하면, 우리가 바로 시작할 수 있잖아요.

남: 좋은 생각이에요.

---

41 남자는 최근에 무엇을 알게 됐는가?
- (A) CEO의 방문 날짜가 변경됐다.
- (B) 직원이 승진했다.
- (C) 미팅 장소가 옮겨졌다.
- (D) 잡지사가 그 회사에 대해 보도할 것이다.

42 화자들은 무엇을 해야 하는가?
- (A) 소프트웨어를 업데이트해야 한다
- (B) 후보자들을 만나야 한다
- (C) 보고서를 끝내야 한다
- (D) 고객에게 답장해야 한다

43 여자는 남자에게 무엇을 제안하는가?
- (A) 영업 보고서를 수정할 것
- (B) 점심시간을 가질 것
- (C) 전화 회의에 참가할 것
- (D) 동료에게 업무를 처리하게 할 것

영국 ⇄ 미국

Questions 44-46 refer to the following conversation

W: Hi, Nobuhiko. How do you like this year's food technology convention?

M: I'm really impressed. **There's a lot of new technology I could use in my restaurants' kitchens.**(44) And this location is so much nicer than the last year's. **The auditorium is just a short drive from the airport!**(45)

W: I agree. I flew in this morning, and it was so easy to get here.(45) By the way, at the convention last year, you were planning to install a new computer network for your service staff. How has that been going?

M: Very well. It helps the service staff stay organized, and they love it. It's a lot easier to get customer orders right during busy times.(46)

44-46번은 다음 대화에 관한 문제입니다.

여: 안녕하세요, Nobuhiko. 올해 음식 기술 대회는 어때요?

남: 정말 인상 깊었어요. 제 식당 주방에서 사용할 만한 신기술이 많더라고요.(44) 그리고 이번 장소가 작년보다 훨씬 더 좋아요. 강당이 공항에서 조금만 운전하면 있어요!(45)

여: 맞아요. 제가 오늘 아침에 비행기를 타고 왔는데, 이곳에 아주 쉽게 왔어요.(45) 그런데, 작년 대회 때, 당신의 서비스 직원들을 위해 컴퓨터 네트워크를 새로 설치하려고 했었잖아요. 그건 어떻게 돼 가고 있어요?

남: 아주 잘 되고 있어요. 서비스 직원들이 계속 체계적으로 일할 수 있게 도와줘서 그들이 아주 좋아해요. 바쁜 시간대에 고객 주문을 제대로 받기가 훨씬 더 수월해졌어요.(46)

---

44 남자는 어떤 종류의 사업체를 소유하는가?
- (A) 식당
- (B) 무역 회사
- (C) IT 회사
- (D) 택시업

45 화자들은 강당의 어떤 점을 좋아하는가?
- (A) 음식을 살 곳이 있다.
- (B) 공간이 넓다.
- (C) 여행객들에게 편리하다.
- (D) 경치 좋은 곳에 있다.

46 남자의 사업체에서 컴퓨터 네트워크는 어떻게 사용되는가?
- (A) 비용을 계산하기 위해
- (B) 주문을 처리하기 위해
- (C) 일정을 생성하기
- (D) 상품을 점검하기 위해

미국 ⇄ 미국

Questions 47-49 refer to the following conversation.

W: Sorry for calling you over here on such short notice, David. **There is an issue with the air conditioning unit your technician installed in our conference room this morning. No cold air is coming out.**(47)

M: We're the ones who need to apologize! You've been a loyal client for many years, and we'd like to keep it that way. All right, let me turn the unit on.

W: As you can see, the air isn't cool. **I tried setting the unit to the lowest temperature, but nothing happened. We use this room frequently for meetings.**(48)

M: I'm so sorry about that. We'll take care of it right away. **I'll call the shop right now**(49) and have someone deliver a new unit within the hour.

47-49번은 다음 대화에 관한 문제입니다.

여: 이렇게 갑자기 오시라고 연락드려서 죄송해요, David. 오늘 아침에 기사분께서 저희 회의실에 설치해주신 에어컨에 문제가 있어서요. 찬 바람이 나오지 않아요.(47)

남: 사과는 저희가 드려야죠! 여러 해 동안 단골 고객이셨고, 계속 이렇게 유지되었으면 좋겠습니다. 그럼, 제가 장치를 켜볼게요.

여: 보시다시피 바람이 차갑지 않아요. **장치를 최저 온도로 설정해 보기도 했는데, 아무 변화도 없었어요. 저희가 회의할 때 이 방을 자주 사용하거든요.**(48)

남: 정말 죄송합니다. 즉시 처리해드리겠습니다. **지금 바로 매장에 전화해서**(49) 한 시간 내에 새 기계를 배송해 드리겠습니다.

47 화자들은 주로 무엇을 논하고 있는가?
- (A) 오작동하는 기계
- (B) 다가오는 회의
- (C) 방 예약
- (D) 배송요금

48 여자는 왜 "저희가 회의할 때 이 방을 자주 사용하거든요"라고 말하는가?
- (A) 요청이 중요한 이유를 설명하기 위해
- (B) 회의 장소를 변경하기 위해
- (C) 추가 가구 구매를 권장하기 위해
- (D) 장소가 너무 좁다는 것을 나타내기 위해

49 남자는 다음에 무엇을 할 것인가?
- (A) 절차를 설명할 것이다
- (B) 환불을 해줄 것이다
- (C) 보고서를 수정할 것이다
- (D) 매장에 연락할 것이다

[미국] ⇄ [호주] ⇄ [미국]

Questions 50-52 refer to the following conversation with three speakers.

M1: I'd like to welcome everyone to this afternoon's training seminar. Please turn on the laptop in front of you. This afternoon, **you'll be learning how to input customer information into our new system.**(50) But before we start, does anyone have questions or comments about yesterday's session?

M2: I do. I was out sick yesterday. What do I...

W: Actually, Michael, **I can give you the notes I took yesterday.**(51)

M1: Thank you, Krista. OK. Now, **I'd like all of you to open the document labeled "System Instructions."**(52) It contains basic guidelines on how to use the program.

50-52번은 다음 세 화자의 대화에 관한 문제입니다.

남1: 오늘 오후 교육 세미나에 오신 모든 분들을 환영합니다. 여러분 앞에 있는 노트북을 켜주세요. 오늘 오후에는, **새로운 시스템에 고객 정보를 입력하는 방법을 배울 것입니다.**(50) 그런데 시작하기 전에, 어제 수업에 관해 질문이나 의견 있는 분 계신가요?

남2: 저요. 제가 어제 아파서 결석했거든요. 제가 무엇을 하면...

여: 어, Michael, 제가 어제 필기한 것을 줄 수 있어요.(51)

남1: 고마워요, Krista. 좋습니다. 이제, 여러분 모두 "시스템 설명"이라고 되어 있는 문서를 열어 주세요.(52) 거기에 프로그램 사용법에 관한 기본 가이드라인이 들어 있습니다.

50 청자들은 무엇에 관하여 배울 것인가?
- (A) 고객 데이터를 입력하는 것
- (B) 비용 보고서를 올리는 것
- (C) 프로그램을 설치하는 것
- (D) 기기를 수리하는 것

51 여자는 무엇을 하겠다고 제안하는가?
- (A) 다른 자리를 찾겠다고
- (B) 새 장비를 가져오겠다고
- (C) 자신의 필기를 제공하겠다고
- (D) 발표하겠다고

52 청자들은 다음에 무엇을 하겠는가?
- (A) 설문지를 작성할 것이다
- (B) 제품을 테스트할 것이다
- (C) 업데이트를 다운로드할 것이다
- (D) 파일을 검토할 것이다

[호주] ⇄ [영국]

Questions 53-55 refer to the following conversation.

M: **Kioko, our automobile company will be audited this quarter.**(53) The two of us have been chosen to search for an ideal auditing agency for our needs.

W: I see. I believe this is the first time for our company, right?

M: Correct. With our recent initial public offering, we have acquired new shareholders. This means that an annual audit is necessary. It's to examine that our financial reports are accurate and up to date.

W: OK. Well, **it would make sense for us to look for an agency that has previously worked with clients similar to us.**(54)

M: That's a good idea. **That's very important.**(54) By the way, **I forgot to mention the CEO wants us to present the search results by next Tuesday.**(55)

53-55번은 다음 대화에 관한 문제입니다.

남: **Kioko, 우리 자동차 회사에서 이번 분기에 회계 감사를 받아요.**(53) 저희 둘이 우리의 필요에 맞는 이상적인 회계 감사 기관을 물색하는 거로 선정됐어요.

여: 그렇군요. 우리 회사는 이번이 처음인 거죠, 맞죠?

남: 맞아요. 최근에 기업 공개를 하면서 새로운 주주들을 확보했어요. 즉, 연례 감사가 필요하다는 말이죠. 우리 재무 보고서가 정확하고 최신 정보를 반영하고 있는지 검토하는 거예요.

여: 알았어요. 음, 이전에 우리와 비슷한 고객과 일해본 기관을 물색하는 게 맞겠네요.(54)

남: 좋은 생각이에요. **아주 중요해요.**(54) 그런데, **CEO께서 다음 주 화요일까지 검색 결과를 보고하길 원하신다고 말한다는 걸 깜박했네요.**(55)

53 화자들은 주로 무엇을 논하고 있는가?
- (A) 마케팅 캠페인
- (B) 투자자 미팅
- (C) 기업 회계 감사
- (D) 예산안

54 기관의 어떤 부분이 화자들에게 가장 중요한가?
(A) 서비스가 시기적절하다.
(B) 비용이 저렴하다.
(C) 세계적으로 인정받는다.
(D) 관련 경험이 있다.

55 남자는 무엇을 언급하는 걸 깜박했다고 말하는가?
(A) 마감일
(B) 재정적 제약
(C) 위치
(D) 출장

미국 ⇄ 미국

Questions 56-58 refer to the following conversation.

W: Hello, Mr. Marone. **I wanted to give you an update on the office spaces you were interested in.**(56) Unfortunately, those downtown locations are a bit above your budget. (57) There is, however, a nice building in the East District, if you're interested.

M: Hmm… **That's not good news. I really want to open an office in the downtown area.**(57)

W: I understand, but this place is quite affordable, and it's also right across from a park.

M: Oh! The park would be a nice spot for my employees to take a break. **Can I check out the property at 2 P.M. this Thursday?**(58)

W: Of course. I'll add you to my schedule.(58)

56-58번은 다음 대화에 관한 문제입니다.

여: 안녕하세요, Mr. Marone. 관심 보이셨던 사무실 부지와 관련해 최신 소식을 전해 드리려고 합니다.(56) 안타깝게도 시내 소재의 해당 부지들은 귀하의 예산을 약간 초과합니다.(57) 그런데 혹시 관심 있으시다면 동부 지구에 괜찮은 건물이 하나 있긴 합니다.

남: 음… 희소식은 아니네요. 시내에 사무실을 열고 싶은 마음이 크거든요.(57)

여: 이해합니다, 그런데 이곳은 꽤 저렴한데다 공원 바로 맞은 편이에요.

남: 아! 공원이 있으면 저희 직원들이 휴식을 취하기에 좋겠네요. **이번 주 목요일 오후 2시에 건물을 볼 수 있을까요?**(58)

여: **물론이죠. 제 일정에 추가해 놓겠습니다.**(58)

56 여자는 누구겠는가?
(A) 부동산업자
(B) 엔지니어
(C) 사무실 관리자
(D) 시설관리 직원

57 남자는 왜 실망하는가?
(A) 일정을 조율할 수 없다.
(B) 몇몇 장소가 너무 비싸다.
(C) 일부 설치물들이 고장 났다.
(D) 직원이 시간이 되지 않는다.

58 화자들은 목요일에 무엇을 할 것인가?
(A) 건물을 둘러볼 것이다
(B) 마감 기한을 정할 것이다
(C) 예산을 검토할 것이다
(D) 회의에 참석할 것이다

영국 ⇄ 호주

Questions 59-61 refer to the following conversation.

W: Leighton Landscaping. How can we help you today?

M: Hello. **My colleague Carey recommended your services.** (59) I saw that you planted some beautiful flowers in his garden. I have a gardening project in mind for my property as well.

W: Sure thing. What kind of work do you need?

M: I'm hoping to find someone with extensive experience in water features. **I want to install a fountain in my backyard.**(60)

W: We've handled five projects like that this year.(60)

M: Wonderful!

W: If you would like to see some of our previous works, I could forward you some pictures.(61)

M: Yes, I'd appreciate that.

59-61번은 다음 대화에 관한 문제입니다.

여: Leighton 조경입니다. 무엇을 도와드릴까요?

남: 안녕하세요. 제 동료 Carey가 귀사 서비스를 추천해 줬어요.(59) 그분 정원에 아름다운 꽃을 심어놓은 걸 봤어요. 저희 집에도 정원을 가꾸는 작업을 하려고 계획 중이에요.

여: 네. 어떤 작업이 필요하신가요?

남: 인공 폭포에 경험이 풍부한 분을 구하려고 해요. **뒷마당에 분수를 설치하고 싶어요.**(60)

여: **저희가 올해 그런 프로젝트를 다섯 건 처리했어요.**(60)

남: 잘됐네요!

여: **저희 이전 작업을 보고 싶으시면, 사진을 보내드릴게요.**(61)

남: 네, 그렇게 해주시면 감사하겠습니다.

59 남자는 회사에 대해 어떻게 들었는가?
(A) 이웃에게서
(B) 동료에게서
(C) 가족에게서
(D) 온라인 광고에서

60 여자는 "저희가 올해 그런 프로젝트를 다섯 건 처리했어요"라고 말할 때 무엇을 의미하는가?
(A) 일부 작업은 시간이 많이 걸릴지도 모른다.
(B) 특정 프로젝트가 인기가 많다.
(C) 사업체가 전문 기술을 가지고 있다.
(D) 올해에는 일정이 꽉 차 있다.

61 여자는 무엇을 보내준다고 제안하는가?
(A) 웹사이트 링크
(B) 사진
(C) 견적
(D) 참고 자료

미국 ⇄ 영국

Questions 62-64 refer to the following conversation and table of contents.

M: Irina, I just read your proposal, and I think you have some really good ideas. **This is a very unique plan for your new fitness center.**(62) I was especially impressed with the amount of research you did for where you wanted to set up your facility.

W: Thanks, **that's something that my previous business undertaking has taught me. I opened my store in the same area as all my competitors, which I realize now was a bad choice. This time, I made sure to identify a place where we'd be in demand.(63)**

M: Great. Now, you're looking for investors, so **you'll want to provide more details about your expected profits.(64)** The time it will take before the business starts making money needs to be especially clear. It normally takes about three years for fitness centers in this region to break even.

62-64번은 다음 대화와 목차에 관한 문제입니다.

남: Irina, 지금 막 당신의 제안서를 읽었는데, 정말 좋은 아이디어가 많으신 것 같아요. **당신의 새 피트니스 센터에 맞는 매우 특별한 계획이네요.(62)** 시설을 세우실 장소에 관해 진행하셨던 연구량이 특히 인상 깊었어요.

여: 감사합니다. 이전 사업을 하면서 배운 것이에요. 경쟁업체들과 같은 지역에 제 상점을 열었는데, 이제야 나쁜 결정이었다는 걸 알게 되었어요. 이번에는 우리를 필요로 하는 곳을 확실히 알아봤어요.(63)

남: 좋습니다. 이제 투자자를 구하고 계시니, **예상 수익에 대한 세부 내용을 더 제공하셔야 해요.(64)** 특히 사업이 수익을 내기까지 걸리는 시간이 정확해야 해요. 이 지역의 피트니스 센터는 보통 손익 분기까지 대략 3년이 걸려요.

사업 제안서

1절	사업 설명
2절	장소 및 시설
3절	산업 동향
4절	**수익 예측(64)**
5절	마케팅

62 여자는 어떤 종류의 사업을 시작하고자 하는가?
(A) 여행사
(B) 피트니스 센터
(C) 시장 조사 회사
(D) 재무 설계 회사

63 여자에 따르면, 그녀는 지난 사업을 통해 무엇을 배웠는가?
(A) 이상적인 장소를 찾는 법
(B) 효과적인 광고를 디자인하는 법
(C) 단골 고객층을 만드는 법
(D) 사업자등록증을 받는 법

64 시각 자료를 보시오. 남자에 따르면, 사업기획서에 어느 절이 수정되어야 하는가?
(A) 2절
(B) 3절
(C) 4절
(D) 5절

Questions 65-67 refer to the following conversation and store layout.

M: Hi, Jeanette. **I have here the scented candles we ordered last month.(65)** I heard these are selling extremely well in other locations. I'm hoping they will take off here as well.

W: They smell great. I'm sure they'll be a hit. Where should we put them?

M: I don't want the scents to be a nuisance to our checkout staff. Let's put them in the furthest corner from the counter.(66)

W: Done. Anything else I can do for you?

M: Yes. **I know summer holidays are coming up, and many of our employees have plans to travel. Let's meet regarding when everyone has made plans.(67)** That way, we can avoid any conflicting dates.

65-67번은 다음 대화와 매장 배치도에 관한 문제입니다.

남: Jeanette, 안녕하세요. 저희가 지난달에 주문한 향초가 저한테 있어요.(65) 다른 매장에서 엄청 잘 팔린다고 들었어요. 여기서도 인기가 많아지면 좋겠어요.

여: 향이 아주 좋네요. 히트작이 될 거예요. 어디에 놓을까요?

남: 향기가 계산대 직원에게 방해가 되지 않으면 좋겠어요. 계산대에서 가장 멀리 있는 코너에 놓읍시다.(66)

여: 네. 더 말씀하실 거 있으세요?

남: 네. 여름 휴가철이 오고 있고, 많은 직원들이 여행 계획을 세운 걸로 알고 있어요. 모두 언제로 계획을 세웠는지 만나서 이야기합시다.(67) 그렇게 하면 날짜가 겹치는 걸 피할 수 있어요.

65 화자들은 어떤 종류의 제품에 관해 이야기하고 있는가?
(A) 수건
(B) 신발
(C) 책
(D) 초

66 시각 자료를 보시오. 상품은 어디에 놓일 것인가?
(A) 1번 진열대
(B) 2번 진열대
(C) 3번 진열대
(D) 4번 진열대

67 남자는 왜 직원회의가 열릴거라고 말하는가?
(A) 계약서를 수정하기 위해
(B) 날짜를 확인하기 위해
(C) 지불을 요청하기 위해
(D) 양식을 작성하기 위해

Questions 68-70 refer to the following conversation and company survey.

W: Hey Tyler, did you look over the memo this morning? **Apparently the company is considering changing the work schedule.(68)** That would mean we might not work from 9 to 5 anymore.

M: Really? I'm not sure I want it to change. **My morning commute is really relaxing. I'm worried the bus will be more crowded at a different time, and I won't get a seat.** (69)

W: The good news is that the hours would be based on your preference. And depending on your department head, members of your team could all start at different times. They sent us the link to a survey to get feedback.

M: Oh, I see. **There's a section where I can choose to keep my schedule the same.** (70)

68-70번은 다음 대화와 회사 설문조사에 관한 문제입니다.

여: Tyler, 안녕하세요, 오늘 아침에 온 회람 봤어요? **회사에서 근무 일정 변경을 고려 중인가 봐요.** (68) 그럼 이제 더 이상 9시부터 5시까지 일하지 않을 수도 있어요.

남: 정말요? 전 바뀌는 걸 원하지 않아요. **아침 출근길이 정말 여유롭거든요. 다른 시간대에는 버스가 너무 혼잡해서 자리에 못 앉을까 봐 걱정돼요.** (69)

여: 다행인 건, 업무시간이 선호도를 바탕으로 할 거라는 점이에요. 그리고 부서장에 따라, 팀원 모두 서로 다른 시간에 출근할 수 있어요. 의견 달라고 설문조사 링크를 보내왔어요.

남: 아, 그렇군요. **제 일정을 동일하게 유지하는 걸로 선택할 수 있는 부분이 있네요.** (70)

```
┌─────────────────────────────────────┐
│            회사 설문조사              │
│                                       │
│  1. 고용 상태                         │
│     ☐ 정규직        ☐ 시간제          │
│                                       │
│  2. 부서: _____              │
│                                       │
│  3. 변경 제안사항 중 선호 항목: (70)   │
│     ☐ 동일 근무 시간  ☐ 이른 시작  ☐ 늦은 시작 │
│                                       │
│  4. 의견: _____              │
└─────────────────────────────────────┘
```

68 회사는 어떤 변화를 고려하고 있는가?
(A) 근무 시간을 변경하는 것
(B) 소프트웨어를 업데이트하는 것
(C) 새로운 사무실로 이사하는 것
(D) 신규 지점을 개장하는 것

69 남자는 무엇에 관하여 염려하는가?
(A) 분실된 서류
(B) 새로운 관리자
(C) 비생산적인 회의
(D) 혼잡한 통근

70 시각 자료를 보시오. 남자는 어떤 조사 항목을 언급하는가?
(A) 1번 항목
(B) 2번 항목
(C) 3번 항목
(D) 4번 항목

영국

Questions 71-73 refer to the following tour information.

W: Hello. I'd like to thank you all for joining us today at Twin Peaks Arts & Crafts Studio. Today, I'll be showing you **around our workshop,** (71) where you'll get to see how our beautiful hand-made jewelry is created by our experienced staff of designers. **As we proceed through the tour, please refrain from asking questions to the designers while they are working.** (72) If you have any questions, I'll be glad to answer them for you. **After the tour ends, we kindly ask you to complete a short survey about your experience today.** (73) It'll only take a few minutes.

71-73번은 다음 여행 정보에 관한 문제입니다.

여: 안녕하세요. Twin Peaks 공예 스튜디오에서 오늘 저희와 함께해 주신 여러분 모두에게 감사드립니다. 오늘 여러분에게 **저희 작업장을 구경시켜드릴 텐데,** (71) 저희 경험 많은 디자이너 직원들에 의해 아름다운 수공예 장신구가 어떻게 만들어지는지 보시게 될 것입니다. **투어가 진행되는 동안 작업 중인 디자이너들에게 질문하는 일은 삼가시기를 바랍니다.** (72) 질문이 있으면 제가 기꺼이 대답해 드리겠습니다. **투어가 끝난 후에는 오늘 여러분의 경험에 관한 짧은 설문조사를 작성해 주실 것을 부탁드립니다.** (73) 몇 분밖에 걸리지 않을 겁니다.

71 투어는 어디에서 이루어질 것인가?
(A) 공예 작업장에서
(B) 연구소에서
(C) 미술관에서
(D) 사진 스튜디오에서

72 청자들은 무엇을 삼가야 하는가?
(A) 디자이너들에게 말 걸기
(B) 휴대전화 사용하기
(C) 음식 가져오기
(D) 그룹에서 이탈하기

73 화자는 청자들에게 무엇을 해달라고 요청하는가?
(A) 피드백을 제공하라고
(B) 기념품점을 둘러보라고
(C) 회원으로 등록하라고
(D) 대회에 참가하라고

미국

Questions 74-76 refer to the following talk.

W: I'd like to inform all of you about the tablet PCs that will arrive soon. They will be used by all supervisors to keep track of the inventory in our manufacturing plant. (74) This means the data you enter into the tablets will be updated in real time, and we will be able to keep a better record of our inventory. **These tablets will be kept in this locked safe. You can open it by simply using your employee numbers.** (75) That is all for the time being. **The tablets are expected to arrive next week.** (76)

TEST 06

여: 곧 도착할 태블릿 PC와 관련하여 모든 분께 알려드립니다. 제조 공장 내 재고를 파악하는 용도로 모든 관리자가 사용하게 됩니다.**(74)** 이는 태블릿에 입력하는 데이터는 실시간으로 업데이트되며, 재고 기록 관리를 더 잘 할 수 있게 된다는 의미입니다. 태블릿은 여기 잠금장치가 있는 금고에 보관됩니다. 사번을 이용해서 쉽게 열 수 있습니다.**(75)** 현재로선 여기까지입니다. 태블릿은 다음 주에 도착할 예정입니다.**(76)**

74 청자들은 누구겠는가?
(A) 해외 고객들
(B) 공장 관리자들
(C) 조경 근로자들
(D) 가구 디자이너들

75 화자에 따르면, 청자들은 사번으로 무엇을 할 수 있게 되는가?
(A) 금고를 열 수 있다
(B) 세미나에 등록할 수 있다
(C) 사무실에 들어갈 수 있다
(D) 웹사이트를 업데이트할 수 있다

76 다음 주에 무슨 일이 있을 것인가?
(A) 몇몇 고객들이 시설을 방문할 것이다.
(B) 몇몇 기기들이 배송될 것이다.
(C) 회사가 이전할 것이다.
(D) 직원 설문지가 제출될 것이다.

호주

Questions 77-79 refer to the following talk.

M: Apologies for starting off this meeting with this, but I would like to mention our issue with tools at this site. **(77)** I'm sure many of you have experienced instances where you have not been able to find the tools you need. Everyone needs to make an effort to put the tools back in the case at the end of the day. **(78)** I understand that it can be difficult after a long day, but it really only takes a few minutes. To assist with this, I'm going to put a sign-out sheet here. Whenever you take something, write your name and the date. **(79)** That way, we can keep track of who has what.

77-79번은 다음 담화에 관한 문제입니다.

남: 오늘 회의를 이렇게 시작해서 죄송하지만, 이곳 현장에서의 연장 문제에 대해 언급하려고 합니다.**(77)** 많은 분들이 필요한 연장을 찾지 못하는 경우를 겪어 보셨을 겁니다. 모든 분은 퇴근할 때 연장을 통에 다시 넣어 놓으려고 노력해야 합니다.**(78)** 긴 하루를 보내고 나면 힘들 수 있다는 건 알고 있지만, 몇 분이면 할 수 있는 일입니다. 도움을 드리고자, 제가 여기에 서명 용지를 놓을 예정입니다. 가져가실 때마다 이름과 날짜를 작성해 주세요.**(79)** 그렇게 하면, 누가 무엇을 가지고 있는지 파악할 수 있습니다.

77 담화는 어디서 일어나겠는가?
(A) 공사장에서
(B) 사무실에서
(C) 식품점에서
(D) 실험실에서

78 화자는 어떤 불만을 언급하는가?
(A) 일부 주문이 이행되지 않고 있다.
(B) 일부 연장이 다시 통에 놓이지 않고 있다.
(C) 일부 안전 규정이 제대로 지켜지지 않고 있다.
(D) 일부 사람들이 제시간에 나타나지 않고 있다.

79 이제 청자들은 무엇을 해야 할 것인가?
(A) 교육 과정을 이수해야 한다
(B) 공식 승인을 받아야 한다
(C) 벌금을 내야 한다
(D) 세부 사항을 기록해야 한다

미국

Questions 80-82 refer to the following broadcast.

W: In local news, Everson High School's history teacher, Mr. Matthew Barnes,**(80)** will be starting up his annual summer project again. Mr. Barnes will be recruiting local students to intern at the Gelson Museum during the summer. **(81)** This will give them a chance to work in an academic environment. Participating students will be given $3,000 in cash at the end of August.**(82)** More details can be found on the Gelson Museum website.

80-82번은 다음 방송에 관한 문제입니다.

여: 지역 소식입니다, Everson 고등학교의 역사 교사인 Mr. Matthew Barnes**(80)**가 또 한 번 연례 프로젝트를 시작합니다. Mr. Barnes는 여름 방학 동안 Gelson 박물관에서 인턴으로 근무할 지역 학생들을 모집할 예정입니다.**(81)** 이는 학생들에게 학구적 환경에서 일하는 기회를 줄 것입니다. 참가 학생들에게는 8월 말에 3,000달러가 현금으로 지급됩니다.**(82)** 더 자세한 사항은 Gelson 박물관 웹사이트에서 보실 수 있습니다.

80 Mr. Barnes는 누구인가?
(A) 교사
(B) 언론인
(C) 공무원
(D) 미술가

81 여름에 무슨 일이 있을 것인가?
(A) 박물관이 개조된다.
(B) 인턴십 프로그램이 열린다.
(C) 지역 공무원이 선출된다.
(D) 수상자가 발표된다.

82 화자에 따르면, 8월에 무엇이 주어질 것인가?
(A) 설문조사 양식
(B) 주차권
(C) 콘서트 티켓
(D) 현금

미국

Questions 83-85 refer to the following excerpt from a meeting.

M: An aspect of the business we traditionally spent a lot of time on is recruiting more checkout staff.**(83)** It's always been a huge challenge to retain our current staff, and this is quite common among grocers. Therefore, we added additional incentives and benefits to this position. We then prominently featured these incentives and bonuses into our Internet advertisements.(84) We weren't sure what to expect.(85) But over the past year, we haven't had to sit through many interviews at all.(85)

83-85번은 다음 회의 발췌록에 관한 문제입니다.

남: 우리가 전통적으로 많은 시간을 소비한 사업의 한 측면은 계산대 직원을 더 많이 채용한 것입니다.(83) 현 직원을 유지하는 일은 언제나 큰 도전이었고, 식품점에서는 아주 흔한 일입니다. 따라서 우리는 이 직무에 추가 인센티브와 복지를 더했습니다. 그리고 나서는 이러한 인센티브와 보너스를 인터넷 광고에 대문짝만하게 실었습니다.(84) 무슨 일이 일어날지 알 수 없었죠.(85) 하지만 지난 1년 동안, 우리는 면접을 많이 볼 필요가 전혀 없었습니다.(85)

83 화자는 어디서 일하겠는가?
(A) 슈퍼마켓에서
(B) 약국에서
(C) 건축회사에서
(D) 은행에서

84 광고는 어디에 실렸는가?
(A) 신문에
(B) 인터넷에
(C) 광고판에
(D) 텔레비전에

85 화자가 "우리는 면접을 많이 볼 필요가 전혀 없었습니다"라고 말할 때 무엇을 내비치는가?
(A) 시에 인구가 부족하다.
(B) 변화는 유익했다.
(C) 몇몇 직원들은 초과근무를 해야 한다.
(D) 더 많은 제안이 필요하다.

미국

Questions 86-88 refer to the following telephone message.

W: I'm Eunice Park from Uplifting Office Solutions. The draft of your review of our premium standing desks has been well received. Thank you for sharing the article with us,(86) and we are happy that our product will be featured in such a respected magazine. We are also happy to see that you rated the desk ten out of ten for its customizability.(87) But one issue caught us off guard. You said that you wished the desk height could be adjusted automatically with a touch of a button.(88) Well, that is a feature of the premium model.(88) You will be able to find this information on page six of the assembly manual. Please return this call at your earliest convenience. Thank you.

86-88번은 다음 전화 메시지에 관한 문제입니다.

여: 저는 Uplifting Office Solutions의 Eunice Park입니다. 저희 프리미엄 스탠딩 책상에 관해 작성해 주신 후기 초고는 잘 받아보았습니다. 기사를 공유해 주셔서 감사드리며,(86) 저희 제품이 그런 명망 있는 잡지에 실리게 되어 영광입니다. 더불어 고객 맞춤화 부분에서 저희 제품에 10점 만점에 10점을 주셔서 기쁩니다.(87) 다만 한 가지 문제를 보고 당황했습니다. 버튼 터치로 책상 높이가 자동 조절될 수 있으면 좋겠다고 하셨는데요.(88) 음, 그게 프리미엄 모델의 특징입니다.(88) 조립 설명서의 6쪽에서 관련 정보를 찾아보실 수 있으세요. 가급적 빨리 회신 부탁드립니다. 감사합니다.

86 화자는 청자에게 무엇을 받았다고 말하는가?
(A) 기사 초안
(B) 구매 주문
(C) 신용 카드 번호
(D) 입사 지원서

87 청자는 제품에서 무엇에 감명받았는가?
(A) 주문 제작 가능하다.
(B) 보증 기간을 연장해 준다.
(C) 조립이 용이하다.
(D) 가격이 저렴하다.

88 화자는 왜 "그게 프리미엄 모델의 특징입니다"라고 말하는가?
(A) 제안을 거절하기 위해
(B) 청자를 칭찬하기 위해
(C) 실수를 정정하기 위해
(D) 추천을 해주기 위해

미국

Questions 89-91 refer to the following speech.

M: I'm very excited to be speaking at the Centennial Center. I've been covering major events around Fizdale for ten years, but this is by far the biggest.(89) Today marks the opening of the Centennial Center, Fizdale's first ever mall.(90) The construction was wrapped up last month, and tenants have been eager to open for business. The project was initially started to promote Fizdale as a tourism spot,(91) but based on the large interest from locals, it has sparked a wave of interest in shopping. In a few moments, we will be interviewing some locals who have been waiting outside since 6 A.M.

89-91번은 다음 연설에 관한 문제입니다.

남: Centennial 센터에서 말하게 되어 무척 기쁩니다. 저는 10년간 Fizdale에서 하는 주요 행사를 보도해 왔지만, 이번이 단연 최대 규모입니다.(89) 오늘은 Fizdale의 최초 쇼핑몰인 Centennial 센터의 개장을 축하하는 날입니다.(90) 지난달 공사가 마무리되어, 입주민은 영업을 시작하기를 간절히 바라고 있습니다. 처음에 프로젝트는 Fizdale을 관광지로 증진하려고 시작되었지만,(91) 현지인의 큰 관심을 바탕으로, 쇼핑에 대한 관심을 촉발시켰습니다. 잠시 후에는 오전 6시부터 밖에서 기다리고 있는 현지인 몇 분을 인터뷰할 예정입니다.

89 화자는 어디서 일하는가?
(A) 통신사
(B) 건설사
(C) 관공서
(D) 컨설팅 회사

90 화자는 무엇에 관해 이야기하고 있는가?
(A) 아파트 단지 확장
(B) 쇼핑센터 개장
(C) 인근 도시와의 제휴
(D) 신규 시장 취임

91 프로젝트의 목적은 무엇인가?
(A) 추가 일자리를 만들기 위해
(B) 재활용을 촉진하기 위해
(C) 시의 자금을 절약하기 위해
(D) 관광을 증진하기 위해

Questions 92-94 refer to the following announcement.

W: As you may have heard, Greg Velasquez, who has always handled our website, will be retiring next month. **Here at Diamante Dairy, we fully understand the importance of the website for our Sales Department, which processes online orders from supermarkets and eateries all over the state for our farm's products.**(92) We've interviewed a few candidates but finally chose to work with an outside firm, Web Maestros, instead of hiring somebody to do Greg's job in-house. **This is a well-respected company that Greg himself thought would do a great job.**(93) Now, I know it's been great having Greg right here to help us, but keep in mind, Web Maestros will designate a qualified technician to us.(94)

92-94번은 다음 공지에 관한 문제입니다.

여: 아마 들으셨겠지만, 항상 우리 웹사이트를 관리해주셨던 Greg Velasquez께서 다음 달에 은퇴하십니다. Diamante Dairy는 우리 영업부에게 주 전역의 슈퍼마켓과 식당에서 들어오는 우리 농장 제품의 온라인 주문을 처리하는 웹사이트가 얼마나 중요한지 잘 알고 있습니다.(92) 몇 명의 지원자들을 인터뷰했지만, 사내에서 Greg의 업무를 맡을 직원을 채용하는 대신, 외부 업체 Web Maestros와 함께하기로 최종 선택했습니다. 이 회사는 높이 평가되며, Greg 본인이 생각하기에도 업무 수행을 잘 거예요.(93) 자, Greg가 여기 계시면서 저희에게 도움을 주셔서 정말 좋았지만, Web Maestros도 우리에게 능력 있는 전문가를 지정해줄 거라는 걸 기억해 주세요.(94)

92 청자들은 어디에서 근무하는가?
(A) 낙농장에서
(B) 식료품점에서
(C) 제과점에서
(D) 식당에서

93 회사는 Web Maestros에 관하여 어떻게 알게 되었는가?
(A) TV 광고를 통해
(B) 현 직원을 통해
(C) 전 고객을 통해
(D) 신문 광고를 통해

94 화자는 왜 "Web Maestros도 우리에게 능력 있는 전문가를 지정해줄 것입니다"라고 말하는가?
(A) 프로젝트가 지연될 것이다.
(B) 계약이 검토되어야 한다.
(C) 청자들은 걱정할 필요가 없다.
(D) 청자들이 입사 지원자 면접을 진행해야 한다.

Questions 95-97 refer to the following telephone message and floor plan.

M: It's Jordan Coppard, the head organizer for the food and beverage convention.(95) I emailed you a revised floor plan of your booth area. In addition to providing you with display shelves, **we'll set up one special display case so that your newest line of pasta sauces can be displayed in the front.**(96) Also, we acted on your suggestion that we add a section towards the back for customers to taste some samples. It'll be separated by a partition.(97) Please let me know if you have any other requests. Thank you.

95-97번은 다음 전화 메시지와 평면도에 관한 문제입니다.

남: 저는 식음료 컨벤션 책임기획자 Jordan Coppard입니다.(95) 수정된 부스 구역 평면도를 이메일로 보내드렸습니다. 진열대를 제공해 드릴 뿐 아니라, **최신 파스타 소스 제품군을 앞에 전시하실 수 있도록 특별 진열장 하나를 설치하도록 하겠습니다.**(96) 또한, 뒤쪽에 고객 시식 구역을 추가해달라고 제안하셨던 대로 해드렸습니다. 그곳은 칸막이로 분리될 것입니다.(97) 다른 요청사항이 있으시다면 알려주세요. 감사합니다.

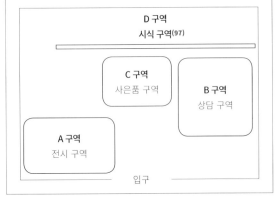

95 화자의 직업은 무엇이겠는가?
(A) 이벤트 기획자
(B) 수석 주방장
(C) 인테리어 디자이너
(D) 컴퓨터 기술자

96 화자는 파스타 소스에 관하여 뭐라고 말하는가?
(A) 서늘한 곳에 보관해야 한다.
(B) 할인가에 판매될 수 있다.
(C) 사은품으로 배포될 것이다.
(D) 앞쪽에 위치할 것이다.

97 시각 자료를 보시오. 어느 구역이 추가되었는가?
(A) A 구역
(B) B 구역
(C) C 구역
(D) D 구역

Questions 98-100 refer to the following speech and schedule.

M: It seems like every year, the education industry doesn't change at all. This wasn't true this year, and we have seen some tremendous innovations.(98) Today's focus will be on the intersection between education and fashion. Many of you will have no doubt seen devices such as tablets become more and more commonplace. This is one of the topics we will cover in today's conference. Before we get started, I have a few announcements. **If you have not already, please check in with your details so that we can send you your electronic tickets for the dinner event.** (99) Also, I've been informed that there is a last-minute scratch on the schedule. The session following the competition will unfortunately be canceled.(100) Now, let me welcome our first speaker Johnny Larson to the stage.

98-100번은 다음 연설과 일정표에 관한 문제입니다.

남: 매년 교육산업에는 전혀 변화가 없어 보입니다. 올해에는 그렇지 않았고, 우리는 어마어마한 혁신을 보았습니다.(98) 오늘은 교육과 패션의 교착 지점을 중점적으로 살펴볼 텐데요. 여러분 중 다수는 태블릿 같은 기기가 점점 더 흔해지는 걸 보게 될 거라는 데는 의심의 여지가 없습니다. 이게 바로 오늘 콘퍼런스에서 다룰 주제 중 하나입니다. 시작하기 전에, 몇 가지 안내 말씀드립니다. 아직 하지 않으셨다면, 저녁 행사용 전자 입장권을 보내드릴 수 있도록 여러분의 정보를 입력해 주세요.(99) 그리고, 막판에 일정에 지장이 생겼다는 소식을 받았습니다. 아쉽게도 경연 대회 다음 세션은 취소될 예정입니다.(100) 이제, 첫 번째 연사이신 Johnny Larson을 무대로 모시겠습니다.

행사 일정표	
오전 10시	기술의 현 위치
오전 11시	분석 및 회계
오후 12시	점심
오후 2시	모범 사례 경연 대회
오후 3시	**정확한 평가(100)**
오후 4시	온라인으로

98 화자에 따르면, 최근 어떤 분야에 많은 혁신이 있었는가?
  (A) 교육
  (B) 패션
  (C) 기술
  (D) 금융

99 화자는 청자들에게 무엇을 하라고 상기하는가?
  (A) 설문조사에 답하라고
  (B) 세부 정보를 등록하라고
  (C) 명함을 나눠주라고
  (D) 스터디에 등록하라고

100 시각 자료를 보시오. 어떤 세션이 취소되었는가?
  (A) 분석 및 회계
  (B) 모범 사례 경연 대회
  (C) 정확한 평가
  (D) 온라인으로

TEST 07

PART 1   P. 100

1 (C)	2 (C)	3 (B)	4 (C)	5 (B)	6 (D)

PART 2   P. 104

7 (C)	8 (C)	9 (B)	10 (A)	11 (A)	12 (C)
13 (C)	14 (B)	15 (B)	16 (C)	17 (B)	18 (B)
19 (B)	20 (C)	21 (A)	22 (B)	23 (A)	24 (B)
25 (B)	26 (A)	27 (A)	28 (A)	29 (C)	30 (A)
31 (A)					

PART 3   P. 105

32 (D)	33 (A)	34 (C)	35 (A)	36 (C)	37 (C)
38 (D)	39 (C)	40 (C)	41 (B)	42 (C)	43 (B)
44 (D)	45 (B)	46 (A)	47 (B)	48 (A)	49 (D)
50 (D)	51 (C)	52 (C)	53 (B)	54 (B)	55 (D)
56 (B)	57 (C)	58 (B)	59 (A)	60 (B)	61 (C)
62 (A)	63 (C)	64 (D)	65 (D)	66 (D)	67 (A)
68 (B)	69 (A)	70 (D)			

PART 4   P. 109

71 (D)	72 (A)	73 (C)	74 (C)	75 (B)	76 (C)
77 (B)	78 (D)	79 (B)	80 (C)	81 (A)	82 (D)
83 (D)	84 (A)	85 (D)	86 (C)	87 (A)	88 (A)
89 (B)	90 (C)	91 (B)	92 (C)	93 (A)	94 (B)
95 (C)	96 (C)	97 (A)	98 (A)	99 (A)	100 (B)

PART 1   P. 100

1   미국
(A) The woman is placing an order.
(B) The woman is taking a lid off a jar.
(C) The man is getting a beverage.
(D) The man is wiping off some spilled drink.

(A) 여자가 주문을 하고 있다.
(B) 여자가 병에서 뚜껑을 열고 있다.
(C) 남자가 음료를 받고 있다.
(D) 남자가 쏟아진 음료를 닦고 있다.

2   호주
(A) Some people are packing a suitcase.
(B) Some people are looking out a window.
(C) One of the people is pulling a piece of luggage.
(D) One of the people is opening a briefcase.

(A) 몇몇 사람들이 여행 가방을 싸고 있다.
(B) 몇몇 사람들이 창밖을 내다보고 있다.
(C) 사람들 중 한 명이 짐을 끌고 있다.
(D) 사람들 중 한 명이 서류 가방을 열고 있다.

3   미국
(A) A man is bending over to tie his shoe.
(B) Benches line a walkway outdoors.
(C) A lamppost is being repaired by workers.
(D) Leaves are being swept off a path.

(A) 남자가 신발 끈을 묶기 위해 몸을 굽히고 있다.
(B) 벤치들이 야외에 있는 보도를 따라 늘어서 있다.
(C) 가로등 기둥이 작업자들에 의해 수리되고 있다.
(D) 낙엽들이 길 위에서 쓸어지고 있다.

4   미국
(A) A man is plugging in a laptop computer.
(B) A man is closing window blinds.
(C) A man is working near some windows.
(D) A man is turning on a lamp.

(A) 남자가 노트북의 전원을 연결하고 있다.
(B) 남자가 창문의 블라인드를 닫고 있다.
(C) 남자가 창가에서 일하고 있다.
(D) 남자가 램프를 켜고 있다.

5   영국
(A) Some vehicles are being inspected in the garage.
(B) Some boxes are stacked in the warehouse.
(C) A man is packing a crate with merchandise.
(D) A man is loading a delivery truck.

(A) 몇몇 차량들이 차고에서 점검받고 있다.
(B) 몇몇 상자들이 창고에 쌓여있다.
(C) 남자가 상품이 들어있는 상자를 포장하고 있다.
(D) 남자가 배달 트럭에 짐을 싣고 있다.

6   호주
(A) A carpet has been rolled up against the window.
(B) A painting is positioned on a wall.
(C) Some light fixtures are hanging from the ceiling.
(D) Some cushions have been set on a sofa.

(A) 카펫이 창문에 기대어 말려 있다.
(B) 그림 한 점이 벽에 배치되어 있다.
(C) 몇몇 조명기구들이 천장에 매달려 있다.
(D) 몇몇 쿠션들이 소파 위에 놓여 있다.

PART 2   P. 104

7   미국 ↔ 영국
Which topic will be discussed at today's meeting?
(A) Let's meet in Room 526.
(B) Today's weather is great.
(C) Talent management.

오늘 회의에서 어떤 주제가 논의될까요?
(A) 526호에서 만나요.
(B) 오늘 날씨가 정말 좋아요.
(C) 인재 관리요.

8 영국 ⇄ 미국

Could you send me a copy of the proposal?
(A) Monday afternoon.
(B) I went to the copy center.
(C) OK, I'll do that for you.

저에게 제안서 사본 한 부를 보내주시겠어요?
(A) 월요일 오후요.
(B) 제가 복사실에 갔어요.
(C) 네, 그렇게 해 드릴게요.

9 미국 ⇄ 미국

When is the due date for the registration fee?
(A) From the Operations Department.
(B) You should call Eugene.
(C) Yes, on your desk.

등록비 납기일은 언제인가요?
(A) 운영 부서에서요.
(B) Eugene에게 전화해보세요.
(C) 네, 당신 책상 위에요.

10 호주 ⇄ 영국

How do I update my personal information?
(A) Didn't you check the online guide?
(B) No, it's up to date.
(C) Here is my business card.

제 개인정보를 어떻게 업데이트하나요?
(A) 온라인 가이드 안보셨나요?
(B) 아니요, 그것은 최신이에요.
(C) 여기 제 명함이요.

11 미국 ⇄ 미국

Who can help set up some chairs for the seminar?
(A) Daniel said he would.
(B) We'll both be attending.
(C) She was just promoted.

세미나용 의자 배치를 누가 도와줄 수 있나요?
(A) Daniel이 하겠다고 했어요.
(B) 저희 둘 다 참석할 거예요.
(C) 그녀는 막 승진되었어요.

12 미국 ⇄ 영국

Why was the meeting postponed to later in the week?
(A) In conference room B.
(B) Good idea. Let's do that.
(C) Helen is out of the office.

회의가 왜 주 후반으로 연기되었나요?
(A) B 회의실에서요.
(B) 좋은 생각이에요. 그렇게 하죠.
(C) Helen이 출장 중이거든요.

13 영국 ⇄ 호주

Where can I buy a good camera?
(A) By a renowned photographer.
(B) Just as good as I had hoped.
(C) There's a place across the street.

어디서 좋은 카메라를 살 수 있을까요?
(A) 유명한 사진작가가요.
(B) 제가 바랐던 대로 좋네요.
(C) 길 건너편에 상점이 있어요.

14 호주 ⇄ 미국

How many languages can you speak?
(A) Joey Zhang's trip to France.
(B) I'm fluent in three.
(C) They haven't spoken with me.

몇 개 언어를 구사할 수 있으세요?
(A) Joey Zhang의 프랑스 여행이요.
(B) 전 3개 국어에 유창해요.
(C) 그쪽에서 저랑 이야기 나눠보지 않았어요.

15 영국 ⇄ 호주

Let's stay longer to finish this budget report.
(A) Yes, a financial report.
(B) But I've already made plans.
(C) No, Sue no longer works here.

예산 보고서를 마무리하게 조금만 더 있읍시다.
(A) 네, 재무 보고서요.
(B) 근데 저는 선약이 있어요.
(C) 아니요, Sue는 이제 더 이상 여기서 근무하지 않아요.

16 미국 ⇄ 미국

Which brands of automobiles do you sell at this shop?
(A) I just got a new car.
(B) At the auto body shop.
(C) We only do repairs here.

이 상점에서는 어느 자동차 브랜드를 판매하시나요?
(A) 새 차 산 지 얼마 안 됐어요.
(B) 자동차 정비소에서요.
(C) 여기서는 수리만 해요.

17 호주 ⇄ 미국

Don't you provide a special discount for gym members?
(A) I left it in my locker.
(B) That offer ended last month.
(C) Yes, a membership fee.

체육관 회원에게 특별 할인을 제공하시지 않나요?
(A) 제 사물함에 두었어요.
(B) 그 할인은 지난달에 종료됐어요.
(C) 네, 회원가입비요.

18 미국 ⇄ 영국

Does your coffee shop deliver?
(A) Thank you. We roast our own beans.
(B) Only for orders within a 1-kilometer radius.
(C) Here are your drinks.

여기 커피숍에서 배달해 주나요?
(A) 감사합니다. 저희가 커피콩을 직접 볶아요.
(B) 1킬로미터 반경 내 주문만요.
(C) 음료 나왔습니다.

19 미국 ⇄ 호주

Weren't the department heads supposed to give us feedback on our proposal?
(A) It was supposed to be open.
(B) They're still at the CEO briefing.
(C) She's working at the cash register.

부서장분들이 우리 제안서에 대한 피드백을 주시기로 하지 않았나요?
(A) 그건 개봉되었어야 했어요.
(B) 그분들이 아직 CEO 브리핑 중이세요.
(C) 그녀는 계산대에서 일하고 있어요.

20 미국 ⇄ 미국

Did you see the advertisement for the new movie at Jameson Theater?
(A) I already met with him.
(B) Many moviegoers.
(C) Yes, and it looks like it'll be a lot of fun.

Jameson 극장에서 하는 새 영화 광고를 보셨나요?
(A) 이미 그를 만났어요.
(B) 많은 영화 애호가들이요.
(C) 네, 정말 재미있을 것 같아요.

21 미국 ⇄ 미국

Where's the nearest grocery store?
(A) The closest one is on Walnut Street.
(B) In aisle 8.
(C) For some fresh fruits and vegetables.

가장 가까운 식료품점이 어디죠?
(A) 가장 가까운 건 Walnut가에 있어요.
(B) 8번 통로예요.
(C) 신선한 과일이랑 야채 사려고요.

22 호주 ⇄ 영국

When are you going on your holidays?
(A) We'll be taking a direct flight.
(B) I haven't received approval from my manager yet.
(C) There's a travel agency at the airport.

언제 휴가 가세요?
(A) 저희는 직항편을 탈 거예요.
(B) 아직 관리자 승인을 받지 못했어요.
(C) 공항 근처에 여행사가 있어요.

23 미국 ⇄ 미국

Do you want to hold the banquet at Gold Coast Hotel?
(A) Do they have any openings?
(B) My supervisor and his colleagues.
(C) No, on November 21.

Gold Coast 호텔에서 연회를 열고 싶으세요?
(A) 그곳에 빈자리가 있나요?
(B) 제 상사와 그분 동료들이요.
(C) 아니요, 11월 21일에요.

24 미국 ⇄ 미국

The waiting list has been updated, right?
(A) They're all sold out.
(B) Yes, the names are finalized.
(C) Can you wait for me upstairs?

대기자 명단이 업데이트됐죠, 맞죠?
(A) 다 팔렸어요.
(B) 네, 이름이 확정됐어요.
(C) 위층에서 기다려 주실래요?

25 호주 ⇄ 미국

The ovens we ordered won't arrive by the weekend.
(A) Yes, I just saw her leave.
(B) We'll postpone the bakery's grand opening.
(C) Saturdays and Sundays work for me.

저희가 주문한 오븐이 주말까지 오지 않을 거예요.
(A) 네, 그녀가 방금 나가는 걸 봤어요.
(B) 빵집 개점을 연기할 거예요.
(C) 저는 토요일과 일요일이 좋아요.

26 미국 ⇄ 미국

Did you write up the proposal response, or will you need more time?
(A) It'll be ready by noon.
(B) Yes, the goal is clear.
(C) Are you sure you're right?

제안서 답변을 작성했나요, 아니면 시간이 더 필요하세요?
(A) 정오까지 준비됩니다.
(B) 네, 목표가 명확해요.
(C) 확실하세요?

27 미국 ⇄ 영국

Do you think we should go to the job fair?
(A) My boss reminded me several times.
(B) That's all there is to it.
(C) A few names on the list of attendees.

우리가 채용 박람회에 가야 할까요?
(A) 제 상사가 몇 번이나 얘기했어요.
(B) 그게 다예요.
(C) 참석자 명단에 있는 몇몇 이름이요.

28 미국 ⇄ 호주

You're leaving early for your doctor's appointment, aren't you?
(A) I'll be in meetings all day.
(B) It's actually on the right.
(C) The reception desk.

진료 예약 때문에 오늘 일찍 가시죠, 그렇죠?
(A) 하루 종일 회의가 있어요.
(B) 실은 오른쪽에 있어요.
(C) 접수처요.

29 영국 ⇄ 미국

I'd rather use the conference room on the fifth floor.
(A) No, this isn't the right amount.
(B) That software program is more helpful.
(C) The AC there is broken.

제가 5층 회의실을 사용할게요.
(A) 아니요, 이건 적정량이 아니에요.
(B) 그 소프트웨어 프로그램이 더 유익해요.
(C) 거기 에어컨이 고장 났어요.

30 미국 ⇄ 호주

Would you like to start renting the apartment this month or next month?
(A) I'll let you know by the end of the day.
(B) A lot of people like Swanson Avenue.
(C) The apartment is fully furnished.

아파트 임대는 이번 달에 시작하고 싶으세요, 아니면 다음 달에 시작하고 싶으세요?
(A) 오늘 중으로 알려드릴게요.
(B) 많은 분들이 Swanson가를 좋아해요.
(C) 아파트에는 가구가 완비되어 있어요.

31 영국 ⇄ 미국

The Finance Department recruited more staff this month.
(A) They won't have to work overtime now.
(B) Didn't Jason get a certificate in finance?
(C) She's a corporate banker.

회계부가 이번 달에 직원을 더 채용했어요.
(A) 그들은 이제 야근하지 않아도 되겠어요.
(B) Jason이 재무 자격증을 따지 않았나요?
(C) 그녀는 법인 담당 은행원이에요.

PART 3
P. 105

미국 ⇄ 미국

Questions 32-34 refer to the following conversation.

W: Hello, Dillon. **Roy's room is locked, and I'm supposed to give him some receipts**(32) from my recent business trip before noon. Would you mind taking them?

M: Not at all. I'll give them to him when he gets back. **He's been with the vice president all morning going over the next quarter's budget.**(33)

W: I really appreciate it! OK, **I need to go show some investors around our office now.**(34)

32-34번은 다음 대화에 관한 문제입니다.

여: 안녕하세요, Dillon. **Roy의 사무실이 잠겨있는데, 제가 정오 전에 최근 다녀온 출장 영수증을 드려야 하거든요.**(32) 받아주실 수 있나요?

남: 네, 그럼요. 그가 돌아오면 제가 전달하도록 할게요. **그는 오전 내내 부사장님과 다음 분기 예산을 검토하고 있어요.**(33)

여: 정말 감사드려요! 좋아요, 저는 이제 **투자자분께 우리 사무실을 구경시켜드리러 가야 해요.**(34)

32 여자는 왜 Roy의 사무실을 방문했는가?
(A) 물건을 반납하기 위해
(B) 장비를 고치기 위해
(C) 예산제안서를 논의하기 위해
(D) 서류를 제출하기 위해

33 Roy는 왜 부재중인가?
(A) 임원과 회의 중이다.
(B) 곧 공항으로 갈 것이다.
(C) 고객 설문조사를 진행 중이다.
(D) 컨벤션에 참석 중이다.

34 여자는 다음에 무엇을 할 것인가?
(A) 매니저에게 연락할 것이다
(B) 사용 설명서를 읽을 것이다
(C) 사무실을 구경시켜줄 것이다
(D) 프로그램을 다운로드할 것이다

영국 ⇄ 미국 ⇄ 미국

Questions 35-37 refer to the following conversation with three speakers.

W1: **Welcome to Central City Library.**(35) How can I help you today?

M: Hello. Is the periodical room on the fourth floor closed? The elevator won't stop there.

W1: Yes, unfortunately, it will be closed until July. **The whole floor is being renovated, so visitors cannot access the area.**(36)

M: Oh, no. I need to check some old journals for a research project due next week.

W1: I see. My coworker may be able to help you. Joanne, this man needs to view some old periodicals.(35)/(37)

W2: Sir, if you can write down the name of the journals and the issue, I can bring them to you.(37)

35-37번은 다음 세 화자의 대화에 관한 문제입니다.

여1: **Central City 도서관입니다.**(35) 무엇을 도와드릴까요?

남: 안녕하세요. 4층에 있는 정기 간행실이 문을 닫았나요? 엘리베이터가 그곳에 서지 않네요.

여1: 네, 아쉽게도 7월까지 문을 닫습니다. **전 층이 수리 중이어서, 방문객은 그 구역에 출입할 수 없어요.**(36)

남: 아, 안 돼요. 저는 다음 주까지인 연구 프로젝트에 필요한 예전 저널을 봐야 해요.

여1: 그러시군요. 제 동료가 도움을 드릴 수 있을지도 몰라요. Joanne, 이분이 예전 간행물을 보셔야 해요.(35)/(37)

여2: 선생님, 저널명과 호수를 적어주시면, 제가 가져다드릴게요.(37)

35 여자들은 누구겠는가?
(A) 사서
(B) 큐레이터
(C) 잡지 편집자
(D) 공사장 인부

36 남자는 왜 구역에 들어갈 수 없는가?
(A) 이전 중이다.
(B) 엘리베이터가 수리 중이다.
(C) 수리가 진행 중이다.
(D) 직원 점심시간이다.

37 Joanne은 남자를 어떻게 도울 수 있는가?
(A) 온라인 데이터베이스에 로그인함으로써
(B) 예약함으로써
(C) 일부 저널을 찾음으로써
(D) 출판사에 연락함으로써

미국 ⇄ 영국

Questions 38-40 refer to the following conversation.

M: Hello, Ms. Sanchez. It's Daniel Palmer. **I spoke with you about hiring your interior design firm to remodel our office, but you haven't sent me an estimate yet.**(38)

W: Ah, I apologize for that, Mr. Palmer. **I had to go on an urgent business trip a few days ago, and I just returned late last night.**(39)

M: I see. I just wanted to make sure that you could still begin the work in March.

W: Yes. I'll send the estimate to you by the end of the day. **We do have an important workshop in the first week of March,**(40) so we would probably start the work in the second week.

38-40번은 다음 대화에 관한 문제입니다.

남: 안녕하세요, Ms. Sanchez. 저는 Daniel Palmer예요. **귀하의 인테리어 디자인 회사에 저희 사무실 개조를 의뢰하는 문제로 이야기 나눴는데요, 아직 저에게 견적서를 보내지 않으셨네요.**(38)

여: 아, 죄송합니다, Mr. Palmer. 제가 며칠 전 급히 출장을 갔다가 어젯밤 늦게 막 돌아왔습니다.**(39)**

남: 그렇군요. 그대로 3월에 작업을 시작하실 수 있는지 확인하고 싶었어요.

여: 네. 오늘 중으로 견적서를 보내드리겠습니다. **저희가 3월 첫 주에 중요한 워크숍이 있어서,(40)** 아마 둘째 주에 작업을 시작하게 될 거예요.

38 남자는 왜 전화하는가?
(A) 추가 비용을 논의하기 위해
(B) 물품을 구매하기 위해
(C) 비즈니스 학회에 등록하기 위해
(D) 개조 프로젝트에 대한 후속 조치를 취하기 위해

39 여자는 최근에 무엇을 했는가?
(A) 자신의 회사를 매각했다.
(B) 책을 출판했다.
(C) 여행에서 돌아왔다.
(D) 새 제품을 디자인했다.

40 3월 첫째 주에 무슨 일이 있을 것인가?
(A) 일부 가격이 확정될 것이다.
(B) 일부 면접이 진행될 것이다.
(C) 워크숍이 열릴 것이다.
(D) 한 고객이 방문할 것이다.

미국 ⇄ 호주

Questions 41-43 refer to the following conversation.

W: I have great news, Ho-seok. SVH Incorporated wants to see me again for a second interview next week.

M: That sounds promising! You must have done well in your first interview.

W: I think I did OK. **They tested my knowledge about computer coding languages.(41)** During the second interview, they'll be seeing if I'd be a good fit for their position.

M: Ah, interesting.

W: Yeah, but **I'm concerned that I may not have enough managerial experience.(42)** The job post asked for at least five years of experience as a team manager.

M: Don't worry. You'll do a great job. **Would you still be able to work from home if you take on the job?(43)**

41-43번은 다음 대화에 관한 문제입니다.

여: 좋은 소식이 있어요, Ho-seok. SVH Incorporated에서 다음 주에 2차 면접을 보재요.

남: 느낌이 좋은데요! 1차 면접을 잘 봤나 봐요.

여: 괜찮게 봤다고 생각했어요. **컴퓨터 코딩 언어에 관한 지식을 테스트했어요.(41)** 2차 면접에서는 제가 그 직무에 잘 맞는지 볼 예정이에요.

남: 아, 흥미롭네요.

여: 네, 그런데 **제 관리직 경력이 부족할까봐 걱정이에요.(42)** 채용 공고에는 최소 5년의 팀장 경력을 요했거든요.

남: 걱정 말아요. 잘할 거예요. **일을 하게 돼도 계속 재택근무를 할 수 있겠어요?(43)**

41 여자의 직업은 무엇이겠는가?
(A) 인사 담당자
(B) 컴퓨터 프로그래머
(C) 수학자
(D) 번역가

42 여자는 왜 걱정하는가?
(A) 연봉 삭감을 받아들여야 할 것이다.
(B) 추천서가 필요하다.
(C) 경력이 부족하다.
(D) 1차 면접 때 지각했다.

43 남자는 여자에게 무엇에 관하여 물어보는가?
(A) 회사에서 연락을 받았는지
(B) 재택근무를 할 것인지
(C) 선별 검사를 치를 것인지
(D) 퇴직서를 제출했는지

영국 ⇄ 호주

Questions 44-46 refer to the following conversation.

W: Hi, Aaron. Did you enjoy the staff appreciation dinner yesterday?

M: I did. **I received a reward for acquiring the most client accounts(44)** this quarter.

W: That's great news. Congratulations! You are always very good at securing new clients. What's the reward?

M: Two front-row seats to next Friday's performance of the world-famous Newmore Orchestra.

W: Oh, that's nice!

M: Yeah, but unfortunately, **I'll be out of town all next week visiting my parents,(45)** so I can't go.

W: Ah, I see. **What will you do with the tickets then?(46)**

M: **I'll probably offer them to someone in my department. (46)**

44-46번은 다음 대화에 관한 문제입니다.

여: 안녕하세요, Aaron. 어제 직원 감사 만찬이 즐거우셨나요?

남: 네, 그랬어요. **저는 이번 분기 최다 고객 유치로 상품을 받았어요.(44)**

여: 정말 좋은 소식이네요. 축하드려요! 신규고객 유치를 항상 잘하시니깐요. 상품이 뭔가요?

남: 다음 주 금요일 세계적인 Newmore 오케스트라의 공연에 앞자리 좌석 티켓 두 장이요.

여: 오, 좋네요!

남: 네, 그런데 안타깝게도, **다음 주 내내 부모님 댁에 가 있을 거라,(45)** 못가요.

여: 아, 그렇군요. **그럼 티켓을 어떻게 하실 거예요?(46)**

남: **우리 부서에 있는 분에게 드릴까 해요.(46)**

44 남자는 무엇에 대한 상품을 받는가?
(A) 성공적인 제품을 디자인한 것
(B) 운영비를 절감한 것
(C) 해외 프로젝트를 감독한 것
(D) 많은 고객을 유치한 것

45 남자는 다음 주에 무엇을 할 계획인가?
(A) 스포츠 대회에 참가한다
(B) 가족을 만난다
(C) 공연에 참석한다
(D) 회사 연회를 주최한다

46 남자는 상품을 어떻게 하겠다고 하는가?
(A) 동료에게 주겠다고
(B) 온라인에서 판매하겠다고
(C) 나중에 사용하겠다고
(D) 액자에 넣겠다고

미국 ⇄ 영국

Questions 47-49 refer to the following conversation.

M: Hi, could you show me where the children's clothing section is? I've looked all over this department store.(47)

W: I can help you with that. We just renovated, and the facilities are a lot nicer now.(48) But everything is in different places. Children's clothing has been relocated to the third floor. Is there anything else you're looking for?

M: Just one thing. Do you still have El Gato Footwear?(49)

W: I'll check. I know we adjusted some of the brands that we carry.(49)

47-49번은 다음 대화에 관한 문제입니다.

남: 안녕하세요, 아동복 코너가 어디에 있는지 알려주시겠어요? 제가 이 백화점을 다 살펴봤거든요.(47)

여: 제가 도와드리겠습니다. 저희가 수리한 지 얼마 안 돼서, 이제 시설이 훨씬 더 좋아졌어요.(48) 그런데 장소가 모두 바뀌었어요. 아동복은 3층으로 옮겨졌어요. 찾으시는 게 또 있으신가요?

남: 하나만 더요. 아직 El Gato Footwear가 있나요?(49)

여: 확인하겠습니다. 저희가 취급하는 브랜드 중 일부가 조정된 걸로 알고 있어요.(49)

47 화자들은 어디에 있는가?
(A) 의류 소매점에
(B) 백화점에
(C) 건설 회사에
(D) 초등학교에

48 여자는 무슨 일이 있었다고 말하는가?
(A) 건물이 리모델링되었다.
(B) 마케팅 캠페인이 시작되었다.
(C) 새로운 근로자들이 고용되었다.
(D) 새로운 정책들이 채택되었다.

49 여자가 "저희가 취급하는 브랜드 중 일부가 조정된 걸로 알고 있어요"라고 말할 때 무엇을 내비치는가?
(A) 남자가 어떤 상품을 좋아할 것이다.
(B) 남자가 부서장과 얘기해야 한다.
(C) 남자가 다른 건물로 걸어가야 한다.
(D) 남자가 찾고 있는 것을 못 찾을 수도 있다.

미국 ⇄ 미국

Questions 50-52 refer to the following conversation.

W: You've reached Maxicar Fitness Club. How can I be of assistance?

M: Hello. I'm a member of your club, and I wanted to extend for another year.(50) I heard that you're taking 40 percent off the one-year membership rate.

W: Ah, unfortunately, that discount is only valid for new members. I'm so sorry.(51) We do, however, offer a free sports bag if you decide to renew for a year.

M: Oh, if that's the case, I'll just extend for six more months. I'm on a tight budget.

W: I understand. I'll still give you a complimentary T-shirt(52) to show our appreciation for your continued business.

50-52번은 다음 대화에 관한 문제입니다.

여: Maxicar 헬스클럽입니다. 무엇을 도와드릴까요?

남: 안녕하세요. 저는 클럽 회원인데요, 1년 더 연장하고 싶어서요.(50) 1년 회원가에서 40퍼센트를 할인해준다고 들었어요.

여: 아, 유감스럽게도 그 할인가는 신규 회원에게만 유효합니다. 정말 죄송해요.(51) 하지만 1년을 연장하시면 스포츠백을 무료로 드립니다.

남: 오, 그러면 6개월만 더 연장할게요. 예산이 빠듯하거든요.

여: 알겠습니다. 그래도 계속 이용해 주시는 것에 대한 감사의 표시로 무료 티셔츠를 드릴게요.(52)

50 남자가 전화한 목적은 무엇인가?
(A) 일자리에 지원하기 위해
(B) 환불을 요청하기 위해
(C) 문제점을 보고하기 위해
(D) 회원권을 연장하기 위해

51 여자가 왜 사과하는가?
(A) 남자는 잘못된 설명을 받았다
(B) 청구서에 추가 요금이 포함되었다.
(C) 남자는 할인 대상이 아니다.
(D) 신용카드가 처리되지 않는다.

52 여자가 무엇을 하겠다고 제안하는가?
(A) 연락처를 업데이트하겠다고
(B) 주문을 수정하겠다고
(C) 무료 상품을 제공하겠다고
(D) 다른 지점에 전화하겠다고

호주 ⇄ 미국 ⇄ 영국

Questions 53-55 refer to the following conversation with three speakers.

M: There's going to be an executive board meeting next Monday to decide on this year's Best Staff Member at our publishing firm.(53)/(54) We have some excellent nominees this time.(54) Did you read over the list?

W1: Jeremy Westfield in the Sales Department performed really well this year. He was responsible for increasing the company's sales by 15 percent last quarter.

M: And what about that editor?

W2: Ah, yes. Sally Muntz. She was in charge of the English language textbook series that received such high praise from the local high schools. I think I may vote for her.

M: Hmm... There are many factors to consider. It's a good thing that I have some time to make my choice.(55)

53-55번은 다음 세 화자의 대화에 관한 문제입니다.

남: 다음 주 월요일에 우리 출판사 올해의 최우수 직원을 결정하는 이사 회의가 있을 거예요.(53)/(54) 이번에는 아주 훌륭한 후보들이 몇 명 있어요.(54) 명단을 살펴보셨나요?

여1: 올해는 영업부의 Jeremy Westfield가 실적이 아주 좋더라고요. 지난 분기에 회사 매출을 15퍼센트나 증가시킨 주인공이죠.

남: 그 편집자는 어때요?

여2: 아, 네. Sally Muntz요. 이 지역 고등학교에서 극찬을 한 영어 교과서 시리즈를 담당했죠. 전 그녀에게 표를 줄까 해요.

남: 음... 고려할 요인들이 많네요. **결정할 시간이 아직 좀 있어서 다행이에요.(55)**

53 화자들은 어디에서 일하겠는가?
(A) 법률사무소에서
(B) 출판사에서
(C) 고등학교에서
(D) 방송국에서

54 대화의 주제는 무엇인가?
(A) 수정된 계약서
(B) 수상 후보들
(C) 은퇴 직원
(D) 일부 예산 수치

55 남자는 왜 안도하는가?
(A) 프로젝트가 추가 자금 지원을 받을 것이다.
(B) 고객이 작업에 만족한다.
(C) 업무에 더 많은 도움을 받을 것이다.
(D) 선택을 할 시간이 충분하다.

Questions 56-58 refer to the following conversation.

M: Vanessa, I'm sorry, but **analyzing the numbers for the annual sales report is taking much longer than I had anticipated.(56)**

W: Umm, OK. **When will the results be ready then? They need to be included in the presentation for our board of directors. And the presentation is this Friday.(57)**

M: I understand, but could we postpone it? I didn't think the figures would be this complex.

W: OK, **I'll speak with the directors then.(58)** Hopefully they could give us an extra week to finish up.

M: Yes, that would be much appreciated. I'm sorry for the inconvenience.

56-58번은 다음 대화에 관한 문제입니다.

남: Vanessa, 죄송하지만, **연간 매출 보고서용 수치 분석이 예상보다 훨씬 더 오래 걸리네요.(56)**

여: 음, 알았어요. 그러면 결과가 언제 준비될까요? 이사회 발표에 포함되어야 해요. 그리고 발표는 이번 주 금요일이에요.(57)

남: 그렇긴 한데, 연기할 수 있을까요? 수치가 이렇게까지 복잡할 줄은 몰랐어요.

여: 알았어요, 그러면 제가 이사진에게 말씀드려 볼게요.(58) 마무리할 수 있도록 일주일 더 주시길 바라요죠.

남: 네, 그렇게 해주시면 정말 감사드려요. 불편 끼쳐 드려 죄송합니다.

56 남자는 무엇을 작업하고 있는가?
(A) 출장 계획 세우기
(B) 매출액 분석하기
(C) 직원 안내 책자 업데이트하기
(D) 고객 만족도 설문조사 만들기

57 여자는 왜 "발표는 이번 주 금요일이에요"라고 말하는가?
(A) 감사를 표하기 위해
(B) 수정을 하기 위해
(C) 우려를 표하기 위해
(D) 문맥을 제공하기 위해

58 여자는 무엇을 할 거라고 말하는가?
(A) 교육을 실시할 것이다
(B) 이사진과 대화를 나눌 것이다
(C) 직원을 추가로 채용할 것이다
(D) 여행사에 연락할 것이다

Questions 59-61 refer to the following conversation.

M: Lana, I'm working on the packaging design for our new energy bar.(59) I have it open on my monitor right now. Could you take a look at it?

W: Sure. Well... I think it needs to be a little more appealing. **How about using more colors?(60)** A wider palette of colors would be more eye-catching.

M: That's a good idea. I'll try a couple of things out.

W: OK. And by the way, are you using that new computer program?

M: Yes, I am. I tried out other programs, too, but **this software was compatible with more file types.(61)** I've had a great experience so far.

59-61번은 다음 대화에 관한 문제입니다.

남: Lana, 제가 저희 신상 에너지 바용 포장 디자인 작업을 하는 중인데요.(59) 지금 모니터에 띄어 놨어요. 한번 봐줄 수 있으세요?

여: 그럼요. 음... 조금 더 끌려야 할 것 같아요. **색상을 더 사용하는 건 어때요?(60)** 좀 더 다채로운 색상을 사용하면 눈길을 더 끌 거예요.

남: 좋은 생각이에요. 몇 가지 시도해 볼게요.

여: 네. 그런데 그 신규 컴퓨터 프로그램 사용하세요?

남: 네, 맞아요. 다른 프로그램도 사용해 봤는데, **이 소프트웨어가 더 다양한 파일 종류와 호환이 됐어요.(61)** 지금까지는 훌륭해요.

59 화자들은 어떤 종류의 제품을 판매하는가?
(A) 음식
(B) 조리기구
(C) 의복
(D) 가전제품

60 여자는 포장을 어떻게 바꾸라고 제안하는가?
(A) 문구를 바꿈으로써
(B) 색을 더 사용함으로써
(C) 글자체를 변경함으로써
(D) 로고 크기를 조절함으로써

61 남자는 왜 그 컴퓨터 프로그램을 선택했는가?
(A) 여러 기기에서 사용될 수 있다.
(B) 무료 온라인 자원을 제공한다.
(C) 더 많은 파일 유형을 지원한다.
(D) 가장 흔하게 사용된다.

Questions 62-64 refer to the following conversation and schedule.

M: Good morning, Kotono. Are you available this week to go over the design plan? The client made some additional requests.

W: Hi, Leon. I'm free to meet this week. The thing is, **I'll be going out of town on vacation this Thursday.**(62) So we'll have to meet before then.

M: All right. Does Wednesday work for you, then? I have client meetings all afternoon, but I can make some time in the morning.

W: OK, **let's set something up for the morning.**(63)

M: I need to participate in a videoconference, so why don't we meet right after that?(63)

W: Sounds good.

M: OK. **I'll book the small conference room for that time right now.**(64)

62-64번은 다음 대화와 일정표에 관한 문제입니다.

남: 안녕하세요, Kotono. 이번 주에 디자인 계획을 검토할 시간이 있으세요? 고객이 몇 가지를 추가로 요청했어요.

여: 안녕하세요, Leon. 저는 이번 주에 시간 돼요. 그런데 문제는 **제가 이번 주 목요일에 휴가를 가거든요.**(62) 그래서 그 전에 만나야 해요.

남: 알았어요. 그럼 수요일 괜찮으세요? 제가 오후 내내 고객 회의가 있지만, 오전에는 시간을 좀 낼 수 있거든요.

여: 알겠어요, **오전으로 시간을 잡읍시다.**(63)

남: 제가 화상회의에 참석해야 하는데, 그 직후에 만나는 건 어때요?(63)

여: 좋아요.

남: 좋습니다. 제가 지금 소회의실을 그 시간으로 예약할게요.(64)

Leon의 수요일 일정	
오전 8시	부서 회의
오전 9시	
오전 10시	**화상회의 시간**(63)
오전 11시	
오후 12시	부서 오찬
오후 1시	
오후 2시 - 5시	고객 회의

62 여자에 따르면, 목요일에 무슨 일이 있을 것인가?
   (A) 그녀가 휴가를 떠날 것이다.
   (B) 고객들이 사무실을 방문할 것이다.
   (C) 그녀가 동영상을 촬영할 것이다.
   (D) 소프트웨어가 설치될 것이다.

63 시각 자료를 보시오. 화자들은 몇 시에 만나겠는가?
   (A) 오전 8시
   (B) 오전 10시
   (C) 오전 11시
   (D) 오후 1시

64 남자는 다음에 무엇을 하겠다고 말하는가?
   (A) 시스템을 업데이트하겠다고
   (B) 문서를 편집하겠다고
   (C) 동료에게 이메일을 보내겠다고
   (D) 방을 예약하겠다고

Questions 65-67 refer to the following conversation and bus seating chart.

M: Okay, **we're almost done getting ready for the company retreat next week.**(65) I booked a hotel and made lunch and dinner reservations for the trip. There's just a few more things I need to do.

W: Do you need any help?

M: Actually, yes. **Could you write up a schedule of the activities we have planned?**(66)

W: I can do that. I'll also email it to everyone so we're on the same page.

M: Thanks. Oh, and since most people are driving, we'll have to book our own bus tickets. I have the page open here... **I like having a window seat.**(67)

W: Okay, I don't mind the aisle as long as we're near the front. How about these seats right next to each other?(67)

65-67번은 다음 대화와 버스 좌석 배치도에 관한 문제입니다.

남: 이제, **다음 주에 있을 회사 야유회 준비는 거의 끝났어요.**(65) 제가 호텔이랑 여행 때 점심 및 저녁 식사를 예약해 놨어요. 몇 가지 할 일만 더 남았네요.

여: 도움이 필요하신가요?

남: 실은, 있어요. **저희가 계획한 활동 일정표를 작성해 주시겠어요?**(66)

여: 제가 할게요. 그리고 모두 다 알고 있도록 전원에게 이메일을 보낼게요.

남: 고마워요. 아, 그리고 사람들이 대부분 운전해서 올 거라서요, 버스표는 우리 것만 예약해야 할 거예요. 여기 화면 열어 놨어요... **저는 창가 좌석이 좋아요.**(67)

여: 네, 저는 앞쪽에만 앉는다면 통로 좌석도 상관없어요. 여기 나란히 붙어 있는 좌석 어떠세요?(67)

버스 앞 부분

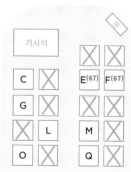

65 화자들은 어떤 행사를 준비하고 있는가?
   (A) 친목 도모 행사
   (B) 전시회
   (C) 무역 박람회
   (D) 회사 야유회

66 남자는 여자에게 무엇을 도와달라고 요청하는가?
   (A) 팸플릿을 인쇄하기
   (B) 비상 연락망을 업데이트하기
   (C) 여행 가방을 싸기
   (D) 일정표를 만들기

67 시각 자료를 보시오. 화자들은 어떤 좌석을 선택할 것인가?
(A) 좌석 E와 F
(B) 좌석 C와 G
(C) 좌석 L과 M
(D) 좌석 O와 Q

미국 ⇄ 미국

Questions 68-70 refer to the following conversation and sketch.

W: Thank you for calling Golden Horn Carpeting. This is Denise.

M: Hi, Denise. I spoke to you in the store yesterday about some carpeting for my coffee shop.(68)

W: Ah, yes. Mr. Jenkins, right? How did your business partner like the design?

M: She loved it.

W: So would you like us to make your carpeting based on yesterday's drawing?

M: Well, yes, but please make it wider(69) so that it will cover the entire interior of the shop. We'd like it to be 4.3 meters wide, if possible.(69)

W: Let's see. I think we can do that. But let me just email the new measurements to our factory to confirm.(70)

68-70번은 다음 대화와 스케치에 관한 문제입니다.

여: Golden Horn Carpeting에 전화 주셔서 감사합니다. 저는 Denise라고 합니다.

남: 안녕하세요, Denise. 제가 어제 매장에서 제 커피숍 카펫 작업에 관해서 당신과 이야기 나눴었는데요.(68)

여: 아, 네. Mr. Jenkins 맞으시죠? 동업자분은 디자인을 좋아하셨나요?

남: 아주 좋아했어요.

여: 그럼 어제 그린 것을 기준으로 해서 카펫을 제작해 드릴까요?

남: 음, 네, 그런데 폭을 더 넓게 만들어주세요.(69) 가게 실내 전체를 커버할 수 있게요. 가능하다면, 폭이 4.3미터가 되면 좋겠어요.(69)

여: 어디 봅시다. 가능할 것 같아요. 하지만 새 치수를 저희 공장에 이메일로 보내서 확실히 하겠습니다.(70)

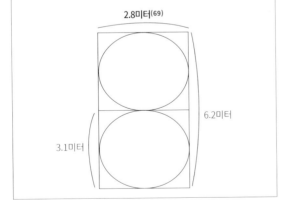

68 남자는 어떤 종류의 사업체를 소유하는가?
(A) 저장 시설
(B) 커피숍
(C) 직업소개소
(D) 미술관

69 시각 자료를 보시오. 남자는 어느 치수를 변경하고 싶어 하는가?
(A) 2.8미터
(B) 3.1미터
(C) 4.3미터
(D) 6.2미터

70 여자는 다음에 무엇을 하겠는가?
(A) 가격을 계산할 것이다
(B) 재료를 측정할 것이다
(C) 샘플을 제공할 것이다
(D) 제조업체에 연락할 것이다

PART 4   P. 109

영국

Questions 71-73 refer to the following excerpt from a meeting.

W: As part of our focus on improving the health of our employees, we partnered with a health club nearby, the Combustion Club. They have agreed to provide our employees with a special deal. It'd be great for our team, as we think we spend far too much time behind our monitors working on codes.(71) By signing up, not only will you have access to their facilities, but you will also receive nutrition plans from a licensed dietician.(72) I think it's best to first hear about the benefits of healthier living. I have a video we'll go over now that covers how we can lead healthier lives.(73)

71-73번은 다음 회의 발췌록에 관한 문제입니다.

여: 직원 건강 증진에 집중하려는 일환으로, 인근 헬스클럽인 Combustion 클럽과 제휴를 맺었습니다. 그곳에서 우리 직원에게 특별 할인가를 제공하기로 했습니다. 우리 팀에는 아주 잘된 일이에요, 코드 작업을 하느라 모니터 앞에서 너무 많은 시간을 보낸다고 생각하고 있으니까요.(71) 등록하면, 시설 이용뿐만 아니라, 공인 영양사에게 식단을 받아볼 수 있습니다.(72) 제 생각엔, 더 건강한 생활의 이점에 대한 이야기를 먼저 듣는 게 가장 좋을 것 같습니다. 이제 더 건강한 삶을 영위하는 방법에 대한 영상을 보여 드릴게요.(73)

71 청자들은 누구겠는가?
(A) 프로 운동선수들
(B) 건설 근로자들
(C) 시장 조사원들
(D) 컴퓨터 프로그래머들

72 회원이 되면 청자들은 무엇을 할 수 있을 것인가?
(A) 식단을 받을 것이다
(B) 시설을 빌릴 것이다
(C) 운동 기구를 빌릴 것이다
(D) 주차장을 이용할 것이다

73 청자들은 다음에 무엇을 할 것인가?
(A) 시설을 견학할 것이다
(B) 과정에 등록할 것이다
(C) 영상을 시청할 것이다
(D) 담당자와 이야기할 것이다

Questions 74-76 refer to the following recorded message.

M: You have reached Patel and Associates Medical Clinic. (74) Our hours of operation are 9 A.M. to 7 P.M., Monday to Friday, and 10 A.M. to 6 P.M., Saturday. **This coming weekend, we will be moving to a new office at 350 Markham Road, next to Silverthorn Insurance.**(75) We will reopen on Monday, March 4. If you have an inquiry or would like to make an appointment, **please call back during our regular hours.**(76) Thank you.

74-76번은 다음 녹음 메시지에 관한 문제입니다.

남: Patel and Associates 병원입니다.(74) 저희 영업시간은 월요일부터 금요일까지 오전 9시부터 오후 7시까지이며, 토요일은 오전 10시부터 오후 6시까지입니다. **저희는 이번 돌아오는 주말에 Silverthorn 보험사 옆 Markham로 350번지에 있는 새로운 장소로 이전합니다.**(75) 3월 4일 월요일에 다시 개원합니다. 문의 사항이 있으시거나 예약을 하시려면 **정상 영업시간에 다시 전화해 주시기를 바랍니다.**(76) 감사합니다.

74 어떤 사업체에서 메시지를 만들었겠는가?
(A) 직업소개소
(B) 보험회사
(C) 병원
(D) 법률사무소

75 사업체에 대해 무엇이 언급되는가?
(A) 개조되고 있다.
(B) 이전할 것이다.
(C) 영업시간이 변경될 것이다.
(D) 연휴로 인해 문을 닫았다.

76 화자는 청자들에게 무엇을 하라고 지시하는가?
(A) 웹사이트를 방문하라고
(B) 메시지를 남기라고
(C) 다른 시간에 전화하라고
(D) 서류를 제출하라고

Questions 77-79 refer to the following broadcast.

M: Good evening and thanks for tuning in to KS Radio's business report. **In a press statement today, WIE Motors, one of the top manufacturers of auto parts in the country, announced its long-awaited merger with JD Incorporated,**(77) who will start selling WIE Motors' car parts on their popular online shopping site. Also, during the press statement, **Terry Logan, the CEO of WIE Motors, said that the company plans to construct a new plant next year to make its renowned products.**(78)/(79) Mr. Logan added that the plant will create hundreds of new jobs in the community.

77-79번은 다음 방송에 관한 문제입니다.

남: 안녕하십니까, KS 라디오의 비즈니스 리포트를 청취해주셔서 감사합니다. **국내 최고 자동차 부품 제조업체 중 하나인 WIE 자동차가 오늘 언론 발표를 통해 오래 기다려온 JD 주식회사와의 합병을 발표했는데요,**(77) JD 주식회사는 인기 있는 자사 온라인 쇼핑 사이트에서 WIE 자동차의 차량 부품 판매를 시작할 것입니다. 또

한, 언론발표에서, **WIE 자동차 CEO인 Terry Logan이 자사 유명 제품을 만들기 위해 내년에 새로운 공장을 설립할 계획이라고 밝혔습니다.**(78)/(79) Mr. Logan은 공장이 지역 사회에 수백 개의 새로운 일자리를 창출할 것이라고 덧붙였습니다.

77 방송의 주제는 무엇인가?
(A) 자동차 콘퍼런스
(B) 법인 합병
(C) 최신 쇼핑 동향
(D) 개정된 채용 과정

78 화자에 따르면, Terry Logan은 누구인가?
(A) 웹 디자이너
(B) 뉴스 기자
(C) 공사 감독관
(D) 임원

79 화자에 따르면, WIE 자동차는 내년에 무엇을 할 것인가?
(A) 본사를 이전할 것이다
(B) 제조 시설을 지을 것이다
(C) 신제품을 출시할 것이다
(D) 재정 기부할 것이다

Questions 80-82 refer to the following talk.

W: Thank you for taking the time to meet with me today. I understand that your schedule as department heads is very hectic. **This makes me all the more grateful for this chance to share with you about Jarvis Cloud System.**(80) Jarvis Cloud System provides cloud computing services for businesses like yours. **According to research, cloud-based computing boosts employee productivity by up to 30 percent.**(81) I believe your company will benefit greatly from our service. **On the screen is a cost breakdown of our subscription plans. As you can see, our prices are very competitive.**(82)

80-82번은 다음 담화에 관한 문제입니다.

여: 오늘 시간 내주셔서 감사합니다. 부서장으로서 정신 없이 바쁘실 텐데요. **이렇게 Jarvis Cloud 시스템에 대해 여러분께 공유해 드릴 기회를 얻게 되어 더욱더 감사할 따름입니다.**(80) Jarvis Cloud 시스템에서는 귀사와 같은 사업체에 클라우드 컴퓨팅 서비스를 제공합니다. **연구에 따르면, 클라우드를 기반으로 한 컴퓨팅은 직원 생산성을 최대 30퍼센트까지 향상시킵니다.**(81) 저희 서비스가 귀사에 크게 도움이 될 것이라 생각합니다. **화면에는 구독 요금제를 비용별로 나눈 세부 내역이 나와 있습니다. 보시다시피, 저희 가격은 아주 경쟁력 있습니다.**(82)

80 화자는 청자들과 왜 만나고 있는가?
(A) 직원 교육을 제안하기 위해
(B) 투자 기회를 보여주기 위해
(C) 서비스를 광고하기 위해
(D) 연구 결과를 알려주기 위해

81 화자에 따르면, 연구로 어떤 이득이 제시되는가?
(A) 생산성 증대
(B) 배송 시간 단축
(C) 연간 수익 향상
(D) 인력 유지 개선

82 화자는 청자들에게 무엇을 보여주는가?
(A) 행사 일정표
(B) 마케팅 보고서
(C) 사용 설명서
(D) 가격표

호주

Questions 83-85 refer to the following advertisement.

M: Do you feel that too few people know about your company? If that's the case, you should attend the Welmont Global Marketing Conference, where you will learn how to build brand awareness.(83) Small conferences usually feature the same group of speakers from the local area. However, we invite experts from across the world.(84) And as an added incentive for your participation, we're giving businesses who register a month in advance a 15-percent discount.(85) Head over to our website to register now!

83-85번은 다음 광고에 관한 문제입니다.

남: 귀사를 아는 사람이 너무 적다고 생각하세요? 그러시다면, 브랜드 인지도 구축 방법을 배울 수 있는 Welmont 세계 마케팅 콘퍼런스에 참석하세요.(83) 보통 소규모 콘퍼런스에서는 해당 지역 출신의 동일한 강사들이 나와 강연합니다. 하지만 저희는 전 세계에서 전문가를 초청합니다.(84) 그리고 참가자 우대 추가 특전으로, 한 달 전에 등록하는 사업체에 15퍼센트 할인을 제공합니다.(85) 저희 웹사이트에서 지금 바로 등록하세요!

83 학회의 주제는 무엇인가?
(A) 자격을 갖춘 직원 채용하기
(B) 더 좋은 제품의 개발하기
(C) 운영 비용 삭감하기
(D) 브랜드 인지도 구축하기

84 화자가 "저희는 전 세계에서 전문가를 초청합니다"라고 말할 때 무엇을 내비치는가?
(A) 청자들이 다양한 연사들에게 배우게 된다.
(B) 청자들이 올해 더 많은 요금을 내야 한다.
(C) 컨벤션 입장권이 빠르게 매진될 것이라고 생각한다.
(D) 행사에 더 많은 통역사가 필요하다고 생각한다.

85 청자들은 어떻게 할인받을 수 있는가?
(A) 발표자를 추천함으로써
(B) 단체 패키지 상품을 준비함으로써
(C) 주최자에게 연락함으로써
(D) 일찍 등록함으로써

미국

Questions 86-88 refer to the following announcement.

W: Good morning. I have a quick announcement regarding the color copier our office just received today.(86) I understand that you all wanted new laptops instead, but it just wasn't in the company's budget this year. Anyway, the new photocopier is very simple to use.(87) If you need to make a copy, just place the document in the tray and follow the instructions on the display screen. If an error message shows up, you can contact the Maintenance Department. But keep in mind that they're pretty busy

this time of year. It may take a few hours for them to respond to your request.(88)

86-88번은 다음 공지에 관한 문제입니다.

여: 좋은 아침입니다. 오늘 사무실에 도착한 컬러복사기에 관련해 간단히 알려드립니다.(86) 여러분 모두가 대신에 새 노트북 컴퓨터를 원하셨던 걸 알지만, 올해 회사 예산에 포함되지 않았습니다. 아무튼, 새 복사기는 사용이 아주 간단합니다.(87) 복사하시려면, 트레이에 문서를 올려놓고 표시 화면에 적힌 설명만 따라 하시면 됩니다. 오류 메시지가 뜨면, 유지보수부서에 연락하시면 됩니다. 하지만, 매년 이맘때에 그 부서가 아주 바쁘다는 걸 명심하세요. 그쪽에서 요청에 응답하는 데 몇 시간이 걸릴 수도 있습니다.(88)

86 화자에 따르면, 오늘 무엇이 도착했는가?
(A) 에어컨
(B) 노트북 컴퓨터
(C) 복사기
(D) 라벨기

87 화자는 제품에 관하여 무엇을 강조하는가?
(A) 사용하기 쉽다.
(B) 가장 잘 팔리는 모델이다.
(C) 오래 지속된다.
(D) 환경친화적이다.

88 화자는 왜 "하지만, 매년 이맘때에 그 부서가 아주 바쁘다는 걸 명심하세요"라고 하는가?
(A) 청자들에게 인내심을 가져달라고 요청하기 위해
(B) 직원을 더 채용해달라고 요청하기 위해
(C) 무리한 프로젝트 일정을 지적하기 위해
(D) 제조사에 연락하는 걸 추천하기 위해

미국

Questions 89-91 refer to the following excerpt from a meeting.

M: Good afternoon everyone. I'm Kyle Patel from Safety Tech Services. I'm here at Brighton Realtors to show you how to use our new alarm system.(89) I'll briefly explain how the security system works.(90) First, every lock comes with a security pin that can be changed. This pin can also be used to log into the surveillance system on any internet enabled device. That means you can check on a location even when you're at the office. Now, I'll show you a tutorial on how to install the system. Then, after lunch, you can install the security devices at your properties.(91) Any questions?

89-91번은 다음 회의 발췌록에 관한 문제입니다.

남: 여러분, 안녕하세요. 저는 안전 기술 서비스 소속 Kyle Patel이라고 합니다. 저는 저희 신규 경보 시스템 사용법을 알려드리려고 이곳 Brighton 부동산에 왔습니다.(89) 제가 보안 시스템 작동원리를 간략하게 설명해 드리겠습니다.(90) 우선, 모든 잠금장치에는 변경 가능한 보안 번호가 제공됩니다. 이 식별 번호는 인터넷 접속 가능한 기기에서 감시 시스템에 로그인할 때도 사용됩니다. 즉, 사무실에 계실 때도 장소를 확인하실 수 있습니다. 이제, 시스템 설치 방법에 대해 알려 드리겠습니다. 그다음, 점심 식사를 하신 후 여러분의 물건에 보안 장치를 설치하실 수 있습니다.(91) 질문 있으신가요?

89 청자들은 누구겠는가?
(A) 경비원들
(B) 부동산 중개인들
(C) 보험사 직원들
(D) 전기 기술자들

90 화자는 어떤 종류의 제품에 관해 이야기하고 있는가?
(A) 전화기 부속품
(B) 블루투스 스피커
(C) 보안 시스템
(D) 무선 프린터

91 청자들은 점심 후에 무엇을 할 것인가?
(A) 사무실을 방문할 것이다
(B) 장치를 설치할 것이다
(C) 지불할 것이다
(D) 소프트웨어 프로그램을 업데이트할 것이다

호주

Questions 92-94 refer to the following talk.

M: Hello, everyone. **I am the project manager for the community center construction project.(92)** Mr. Scott asked me to provide an update on the project. I am proud to report that we are on track to finish within the deadline, and we are just about ready to wrap everything up. **We also went ahead and added something new. We foresaw the need for a storage shed, so we have added that in the back.(93)** This will help with storing equipment such as sporting gear and outdoor tools. Also, I've had some questions regarding how we are doing in terms of the budget. Melissa Richardson is your best bet. Other than that, I am happy to take any questions.(94)

92-94번은 다음 담화에 관한 문제입니다.

남: 모두 안녕하세요. **저는 커뮤니티 센터 건설 프로젝트를 맡은 프로젝트 매니저입니다.(92)** Mr. Scott께서 저에게 프로젝트에 관한 최신 정보를 제공해달라고 요청하셨습니다. 저희는 마감 기한 내 끝낼 수 있도록 진행 중이며, 모든 것을 마무리할 준비를 이제 곧 갖추게 된다고 알려드리게 되어 자랑스럽게 생각합니다. **또한 저희는 새로운 것을 추가했습니다. 저희는 창고의 필요성을 예견해서 뒤편에 추가했습니다.(93)** 이는 스포츠용품이나 야외 도구 같은 장비를 보관하는 데 유용할 겁니다. **또한, 예산 측면에서 저희가 어떻게 하고 있는지에 관한 질문이 있었습니다. Melissa Richardson이 최고의 선택입니다. 그 외에는 어떤 질문이든 받겠습니다.(94)**

92 화자는 어떤 종류의 건설 프로젝트에 관해 이야기하고 있는가?
(A) 시청
(B) 학교 체육관
(C) 커뮤니티 센터
(D) 스포츠 경기장

93 화자는 어떤 특성을 설명하는가?
(A) 창고
(B) 주차구역
(C) 보안 시스템
(D) 추가 화장실

94 화자는 왜 "Melissa Richardson이 최고의 선택입니다"라고 말하는가?
(A) 자신의 동료를 인정해 주기 위해
(B) 청자들을 맞는 사람에게 연결해 주기 위해
(C) 전문가에게 설명을 요청하기 위해
(D) 일부 문서상 일치하지 않는 부분을 설명하기 위해

미국

Questions 95-97 refer to the following announcement and sign.

W: Welcome to AA Driver Licenses. Due to the recent financial cutbacks, we've been short on staff, so we apologize for the longer wait times.(95) This is why we have introduced a new line system. **If you have filled out an online application, you may proceed immediately to the indicated counter.(96)** To help move things along, please have your ticket number and licenses ready. If you did not use our online application system, please find the appropriate counter using this chart. **Finally, we have recently launched an app that allows you to reserve appointments.(97)** Reserving bypasses this line system as there will be a dedicated server at your chosen time. If you don't like waiting, we highly recommend using it.

95-97번은 다음 안내와 표지판에 관한 문제입니다.

여: AA 운전면허에 오신 것을 환영합니다. 최근의 재정 감축으로 인원이 부족해, 더 길어진 대기 시간에 대해 사과의 말씀 드립니다.(95) 이런 이유로 저희는 새로운 라인 시스템을 도입했습니다. **온라인 신청서를 작성하신 경우, 표시된 카운터로 바로 이동하실 수 있습니다.(96)** 원활한 진행을 위해 티켓 번호와 면허증을 준비해 주시기 바랍니다. 저희 온라인 신청 시스템을 이용하지 않으셨다면, 이 도표를 이용해 해당 카운터를 찾으시기 바랍니다. **마지막으로, 최근 저희가 예약할 수 있는 앱을 출시했습니다.(97)** 선택한 시간에 전용 근무자가 있으므로, 예약하게 되면 이 라인 시스템을 건너뛰게 됩니다. 기다리는 것을 싫어하신다면, 이용하시길 강력 추천 드립니다.

AA 운전면허	
운전면허 시험 예약	카운터 1
운전면허 갱신	카운터 2
온라인 신청(96)	카운터 3
차량 등록	카운터 4

95 화자는 최근에 무슨 일이 있었다고 말하는가?
(A) 경영진이 바뀌었다.
(B) 일부 서비스를 이용할 수 없다.
(C) 예산 삭감이 있었다.
(D) 건물이 용도 변경되었다.

96 시각 자료를 보시오. 일부 청자들은 어떤 카운터로 곧장 가도 되는가?
(A) 카운터 1
(B) 카운터 2
(C) 카운터 3
(D) 카운터 4

97 화자에 따르면, 청자들은 무엇을 하는 것을 고려해야 하는가?
(A) 신규 앱을 이용하는 것
(B) 신용 카드를 사용해 지불하는 것
(C) 전문가와 상담하는 것
(D) 더 일찍 오는 것

Questions 98-100 refer to the following excerpt from a meeting and map.

W: Thank you for coming, everyone, and welcome to the monthly meeting of Glenwood Grocer's shop managers. First and foremost, **I want to congratulate Maddie Apodaca. According to our customer surveys, the store she runs received the highest score for customer service.** (98) This achievement is all the more impressive in that she manages the store in Greenview township.(99) That store only opened last year. Great job, Maddie. **The first item on our agenda today is to expand our stores to include coffee shops. I want to talk about this significant development with all of you.**(100)

98-100번은 다음 회의 발췌록과 지도에 관한 문제입니다.

여: 와 주신 모든 분께 감사드리며, Glenwood Grocer의 매장 관리자 월례 회의에 오신 것을 환영합니다. 무엇보다도, **Maddie Apodaca께 축하의 말씀을 드리고 싶습니다. 고객 설문조사에서 그녀가 운영하는 매장이 고객 서비스 최우수 점수를 받았습니다.**(98) 그녀가 Greenview 구역에 있는 매장을 관리한다는 점에서 이러한 성과는 더욱 인상적입니다.(99) 그 매장은 겨우 작년에 문을 열었습니다. 수고 많으셨어요, Maddie. **오늘 첫 번째 안건은 커피숍까지 매장을 확장하는 것입니다. 이러한 중요한 성장에 대해 모든 분과 이야기 나누고 싶습니다.**(100)

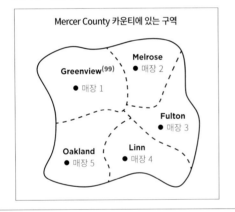

98 화자는 왜 Maddie Apodaca를 축하하는가?
(A) 그녀의 매장이 고객 서비스가 뛰어나다.
(B) 그녀의 매장이 작년에 최고 매출을 올렸다.
(C) 그녀가 매장 관리자로 승진했다.
(D) 그녀가 잡지 기사에 소개될 것이다.

99 시각 자료를 보시오. Maddie Apodaca는 어떤 매장을 관리하는가?
(A) 매장 1
(B) 매장 2
(C) 매장 3
(D) 매장 4

100 다음으로 무엇이 논의될 것인가?
(A) 업그레이드
(B) 확장
(C) 이전
(D) 워크숍

TEST 08

PART 1
P. 114

1 (D) **2** (D) **3** (B) **4** (D) **5** (D) **6** (C)

PART 2
P. 118

7 (B) **8** (A) **9** (B) **10** (C) **11** (A) **12** (C)
13 (B) **14** (A) **15** (A) **16** (C) **17** (A) **18** (A)
19 (C) **20** (C) **21** (C) **22** (B) **23** (A) **24** (C)
25 (B) **26** (B) **27** (B) **28** (C) **29** (B) **30** (C)
31 (B)

PART 3
P. 119

32 (A) **33** (C) **34** (A) **35** (B) **36** (D) **37** (C)
38 (B) **39** (C) **40** (D) **41** (B) **42** (A) **43** (B)
44 (A) **45** (C) **46** (B) **47** (A) **48** (C) **49** (A)
50 (B) **51** (C) **52** (A) **53** (B) **54** (A) **55** (C)
56 (C) **57** (A) **58** (A) **59** (D) **60** (A) **61** (B)
62 (A) **63** (D) **64** (B) **65** (C) **66** (C) **67** (C)
68 (A) **69** (B) **70** (D)

PART 4
P. 123

71 (B) **72** (D) **73** (B) **74** (B) **75** (C) **76** (D)
77 (C) **78** (D) **79** (A) **80** (C) **81** (A) **82** (B)
83 (C) **84** (A) **85** (B) **86** (C) **87** (A) **88** (B)
89 (A) **90** (B) **91** (B) **92** (B) **93** (A) **94** (D)
95 (C) **96** (B) **97** (A) **98** (B) **99** (B) **100** (B)

PART 1
P. 114

1 미국
(A) He's stirring a pot of soup.
(B) He's chopping some vegetables.
(C) He's heating a dish in a microwave.
(D) He's wearing an apron.

(A) 남자가 국이 든 냄비를 젓고 있다.
(B) 남자가 야채를 썰고 있다.
(C) 남자가 전자레인지에 음식을 데우고 있다.
(D) 남자가 앞치마를 두르고 있다.

2 영국
(A) A woman is repairing a wheel.
(B) A man is unzipping his backpack.
(C) They are locking up their bicycles.
(D) They are cycling on a path.

(A) 여자가 바퀴를 수리하고 있다.
(B) 남자가 배낭의 지퍼를 열고 있다.
(C) 사람들이 자전거에 자물쇠를 채우고 있다.
(D) 사람들이 길에서 자전거를 타고 있다.

3 미국
(A) He's putting some papers into a photocopier.
(B) He's holding down a book.
(C) He's plugging in a power cord.
(D) He's turning off some equipment.

(A) 남자가 복사기에 종이를 넣고 있다.
(B) 남자가 책을 누르고 있다.
(C) 남자가 전원 코드에 플러그를 꽂고 있다.
(D) 남자가 몇몇 장비를 끄고 있다.

4 호주
(A) A wooden structure is being erected.
(B) A camera has been placed on a tripod.
(C) Some people are sailing along the river.
(D) One of the men is seated near the water.

(A) 목조 건축물이 세워지고 있다.
(B) 카메라가 삼각대 위에 놓여 있다.
(C) 몇몇 사람들이 강을 따라 항해하고 있다.
(D) 남자들 중 한 명이 물가에 앉아 있다.

5 미국
(A) Some bushes have been planted by a door.
(B) Some gardening tools have been left on the lawn.
(C) A pathway leads to a courtyard.
(D) A ladder is propped on a wall.

(A) 몇몇 관목이 문 옆에 심어져 있다.
(B) 몇몇 원예 도구가 잔디 위에 놓여 있다.
(C) 오솔길이 안뜰로 이어진다.
(D) 사다리가 벽에 붙어 있다.

6 미국
(A) A woman is buttoning up a safety vest.
(B) A woman is stacking some packages by a wall.
(C) A woman is taping a box in a warehouse.
(D) A woman is moving some cartons with a forklift.

(A) 여자가 안전 조끼의 단추를 잠그고 있다.
(B) 여자가 벽 옆에 상자들을 쌓고 있다.
(C) 여자가 창고에서 상자에 테이프를 붙이고 있다.
(D) 여자가 지게차로 상자들을 옮기고 있다.

PART 2
P. 118

7 미국 ⇌ 영국
We should hire a caterer for Ken's retirement party, shouldn't we?
(A) On a higher floor.
(B) Yes, that sounds great.
(C) Next Thursday evening.

Ken의 은퇴 파티를 위해 출장 연회업체를 써야겠죠, 그렇죠?
(A) 더 높은 층에요.
(B) 네, 그게 좋겠네요.
(C) 다음 주 목요일 저녁에요.

8 호주 ⇄ 미국

Who will be leading the marketing seminar?
(A) It hasn't been decided yet.
(B) In conference room B.
(C) Yes, I'll be reading it.

누가 마케팅 세미나를 진행하나요?
(A) 아직 결정되지 않았어요.
(B) B 회의실에서요.
(C) 네, 제가 읽을 거예요.

9 영국 ⇄ 미국

Has anyone reserved the conference room for today's team meeting?
(A) The main course will be served now.
(B) We're meeting tomorrow.
(C) Did you see the patient in the waiting room?

오늘 팀 회의를 위해 누가 회의실을 예약했나요?
(A) 주요리가 지금 나올 거예요.
(B) 저희 회의는 내일이에요.
(C) 대기실에 있는 환자분 보셨어요?

10 호주 ⇄ 미국

The paper tray is empty.
(A) Yes, in the newspaper article.
(B) Please make some more copies.
(C) OK. I'll refill it.

용지 함이 비었어요.
(A) 네, 신문 기사에서요.
(B) 몇 장 더 복사해 주세요.
(C) 알았어요. 제가 다시 채울게요.

11 미국 ⇄ 호주

What brand of snacks should I get?
(A) You should get Hunter's Cookies.
(B) I don't remember getting it.
(C) No, that won't be necessary.

어느 브랜드의 스낵을 살까요?
(A) Hunter's Cookies를 한번 사 보세요.
(B) 그걸 산 기억이 없는데요.
(C) 아니요, 그러실 필요 없어요.

12 영국 ⇄ 미국

Would you prefer having the meeting at our office or at our client's?
(A) Let's get five more chairs.
(B) New clients from last month.
(C) I'd rather stay here.

회의를 우리 사무실에서 하는 걸 선호하시나요, 아니면 고객 사무실에서 하는 걸 선호하시나요?
(A) 의자를 다섯 개 더 가져오도록 하죠.
(B) 지난달에 새로 온 고객들이요.
(C) 여기 있는 게 낫겠어요.

13 호주 ⇄ 미국

Where's the subway station?
(A) I stopped taking the bus.
(B) Down the block from the museum.
(C) I like that radio station.

지하철역이 어디에 있나요?
(A) 저는 버스를 안 타요.
(B) 박물관에서 한 블록 더 가면 있어요.
(C) 저는 그 라디오 방송국을 좋아해요.

14 미국 ⇄ 미국

Could you help me find the mail room?
(A) Of course. Come with me.
(B) I already emailed it to you.
(C) That was very helpful. Thanks.

우편 실 찾는 걸 도와주실 수 있나요?
(A) 그럼요. 절 따라오세요.
(B) 제가 이미 이메일 드렸어요.
(C) 매우 도움이 되었어요. 감사해요.

15 미국 ⇄ 호주

Which candidate are you going to hire?
(A) I need to talk to the director first.
(B) A higher number of applications.
(C) I went to the café downstairs.

어느 지원자를 고용하실 건가요?
(A) 먼저 이사님께 말씀드려봐야 해요.
(B) 더 많은 수의 지원서들이요.
(C) 저는 아래층에 있는 카페에 갔어요.

16 미국 ⇄ 영국

I think Janelle will get promoted to account executive, don't you?
(A) An end-of-the-year sales promotion.
(B) I created a new user account.
(C) Most likely. She earned it.

제 생각에는 Janelle이 거래처 담당 임원으로 승진할 것 같아요, 안 그래요?
(A) 연말 판촉 행사요.
(B) 새 사용자 계정을 만들었어요.
(C) 그럴 것 같아요. 그녀라면 그럴만하죠.

17 미국 ⇄ 미국

When does the HR Department have its staff seminar?
(A) Last Friday of the month.
(B) The seminar room is on the sixth floor.
(C) Attendance is mandatory for all managers.

언제 인사팀에서 직원 세미나를 하나요?
(A) 월 마지막 금요일이에요.
(B) 세미나실은 6층이에요.
(C) 모든 관리자는 필수 참석이에요.

18 미국 ⇄ 영국

Please mind the gap when you exit the airplane.
(A) Thanks. I'll watch out.
(B) No, I don't mind.
(C) I took a cab to the airport.

비행기에서 내리실 때 틈새를 조심하세요.
(A) 고맙습니다. 주의할게요.
(B) 네, 상관없어요.
(C) 공항까지는 택시를 타고 갔어요.

19 미국 ⇄ 호주

We should come up with a new marketing channel.
(A) I'll turn on the channel.
(B) Around 8 weeks for the sales promotion.
(C) We're meeting about that tomorrow.

우린 새로운 마케팅 경로를 마련해야 해요.
(A) 제가 그 채널을 틀게요.
(B) 판촉 활동에 8주 정도요.
(C) 내일 그 건으로 회의를 할 거예요.

20 영국 ⇄ 미국

Aren't you organizing the trade convention?
(A) More than 50 attendees from overseas.
(B) That sounds quite stressful.
(C) No, Josie's responsible for it.

무역 컨벤션 준비하고 있지 않으세요?
(A) 해외 참석자가 50명이 넘어요.
(B) 엄청 스트레스일 것 같아요.
(C) 아니요, Josie가 맡고 있어요.

21 미국 ⇄ 미국

Why do you think customers will like this product?
(A) They're at the checkout counter.
(B) From an online store.
(C) That's what the survey said.

왜 고객들이 이 제품을 좋아할 것이라고 생각하세요?
(A) 그것들은 계산대에 있어요.
(B) 온라인 상점에서요.
(C) 설문 조사에 그렇게 나왔어요.

22 미국 ⇄ 미국

How would you like to pay for your clothes?
(A) In a medium size, please.
(B) Do you accept credit cards?
(C) We're having a sale.

옷 결제를 어떻게 하시겠어요?
(A) 미디엄 사이즈로 주세요.
(B) 신용 카드도 되나요?
(C) 저희가 지금 할인판매 중이에요.

23 영국 ⇄ 호주

Do we have to finish the promotional video by this week, or is next week OK?
(A) Sonya was set on the deadline.
(B) It still needs to be edited.
(C) He just got promoted last week.

홍보 영상을 이번 주에 완료해야 할까요, 아니면 다음 주도 괜찮은가요?
(A) Sonya는 마감일에 대해 의지가 확고했어요.
(B) 그건 아직 편집이 필요해요.
(C) 그는 지난주에 막 승진했어요.

24 호주 ⇄ 미국

You've had the annual employee review already, haven't you?
(A) I made a reservation for four people.
(B) The performance had wonderful reviews.
(C) Yes, this Monday.

연례 직원 평가 받으셨죠, 그렇죠?
(A) 네 명으로 예약했어요.
(B) 공연 후기가 아주 좋았어요.
(C) 네, 이번 주 월요일이에요.

25 영국 ⇄ 호주

How did the end-of-year sale turn out for us?
(A) I often take a few weeks off in December.
(B) I didn't have the time to review the report.
(C) No, he wasn't there last year.

연말 할인판매는 어떻게 됐어요?
(A) 저는 12월에 몇 주간 쉴 때가 종종 있어요.
(B) 보고서를 검토할 시간이 없었어요.
(C) 아니요, 그는 작년에 거기 없었어요.

26 미국 ⇄ 영국

Isn't Highway 46 currently closed for maintenance?
(A) The street sign.
(B) No, it reopened.
(C) I can spare 46 dollars.

46번 고속도로는 현재 보수로 폐쇄되지 않았어요?
(A) 도로 표지판요.
(B) 아니요, 재개통됐어요.
(C) 제가 46달러를 드릴 수 있어요.

27 미국 ⇄ 미국

Did you get a new coffee machine for the staff break room?
(A) The conference room is larger.
(B) I haven't purchased it yet.
(C) The paper is still being edited.

직원 휴게실에 커피 머신 새로 샀어요?
(A) 회의실이 더 넓어요.
(B) 아직 구입하지 않았어요.
(C) 논문이 아직 편집 중이에요.

28 미국 ⇄ 영국

Who is going to set up the projector?
(A) My phone number has changed.
(B) The marketing research project.
(C) Viola offered to help.

누가 프로젝터를 설치할 거예요?
(A) 제 전화번호가 바뀌었어요.
(B) 마케팅 리서치 프로젝트요.
(C) Viola가 도와주겠다고 했어요.

29 미국 ⇄ 호주

Would you like to schedule your personal training session with Vince in the afternoon or the evening?
(A) I've been training twice a week for two years.
(B) Brian is my regular trainer.
(C) That's a valid point.

Vince와의 개인 교육 일정을 오후로 잡으시겠어요, 아니면 저녁으로 잡으시겠어요?
(A) 전 2년 동안 일주일에 두 번씩 교육을 받고 있어요.
(B) 제 담당 트레이너는 Brian이에요.
(C) 일리가 있네요.

30 영국 ⇄ 미국

How much was the team budget reduced by?
(A) A 15% price increase.
(B) Please reduce the speaker volume.
(C) I haven't seen the number yet.

부서 예산이 얼마나 삭감됐어요?
(A) 15퍼센트 가격 인상요.
(B) 스피커 볼륨을 줄여 주세요.
(C) 아직 수치를 못 봤어요.

31 호주 ⇌ 영국

Our gallery's art exhibition received a favorable response.
(A) The impressionist paintings.
(B) We should arrange more tours.
(C) The brochure is on the reception desk.

저희 미술관의 전시회가 호평을 받았어요.
(A) 인상주의 그림요.
(B) 투어를 더 마련해야겠어요.
(C) 접수처에 안내 책자가 있어요.

PART 3

P. 119

호주 ⇌ 미국

Questions 32-34 refer to the following conversation.

M: Hey, Aubrey. **Do you have time to talk about the upcoming women's volleyball game?(32)**

W: Sure. I'm excited about the assignment, since I'm a huge fan. **I'm coming from a meeting with our network executive, and he let me know that we'd be using state-of-the-art cameras for the live broadcast.(33)** This is going to be great for our ratings.

M: Actually… **We've encountered a problem. We can't locate our slow-motion camera.(34)**

W: Oh, no. We still have some time. Let's see if we can purchase a new one before the event.

32-34번은 다음 대화에 관한 문제입니다.

남: 안녕하세요, Aubrey. **곧 있을 여자 배구 경기에 대해 이야기 나눌 시간 있으세요?(32)**

여: 그럼요. 그 작업 기대돼요. 완전 팬이거든요. **제가 지금 방송국 임원과 회의하고 오는 길인데, 저희가 생방송에 최신 카메라를 사용하게 될 거라고 알려주셨어요.(33)** 저희 시청률에 아주 좋을 거예요.

남: 실은… **문제가 생겼어요. 고속 촬영 카메라가 안 보여요.(34)**

여: 아, 안 돼요. 아직 시간이 좀 있잖아요. 경기 전에 새로 구입할 수 있는지 알아봅시다.

32 화자들은 어떤 종류의 행사에 관해 이야기하고 있는가?
(A) 스포츠 대회
(B) 뮤지컬 공연
(C) 공예 축제
(D) 지방 선거

33 화자들은 어디서 일하겠는가?
(A) 여행사에서
(B) 출판사에서
(C) 방송국에서
(D) 경찰서에서

34 남자는 어떤 문제를 언급하는가?
(A) 일부 장비를 찾을 수 없다.
(B) 좌석이 충분치 않다.
(C) 주문품이 배송되지 않았다.
(D) 직원이 없다.

미국 ⇌ 영국

Questions 35-37 refer to the following conversation.

M: Tabitha, I'd like to go over your annual performance evaluation. I'm sure you're aware of this, but **you wrote many of our newspaper's most popular articles this year.(35)** Your attention to detail is very impressive.

W: Thank you. **I believe producing high-quality materials is the most important thing.(36)**

M: **I agree.(36)** Anyway, I was thinking of making you a team manager. Would you be interested?

W: Really? This is a big surprise! Do I have to decide now?

M: No. Just tell me your decision by next Monday. Also, **I'll email you a document that lists the duties of the position.(37)**

W: All right. Thank you so much.

35-37번은 다음 대화에 관한 문제입니다.

남: Tabitha, 당신의 연례 고과를 좀 검토하고 싶은데요. 알고 있겠지만, **당신은 올해 우리 신문에서 가장 인기 있는 기사를 많이 썼어요.(35)** 세심한 주의력이 정말 인상적이에요.

여: 감사합니다. 저는 **고품질 자료를 생산하는 것이 가장 중요한 일이라고 생각합니다.(36)**

남: **동의해요.(36)** 그건 그렇고, 당신한테 팀장 자리를 맡길 생각인데요. 관심 있어요?

여: 정말이요? 생각지도 못한 일인데요! 지금 결정해야 하나요?

남: 아니에요. 다음 주 월요일까지 결정해서 알려주세요. 그리고 **제가 그 직책의 직무가 나와 있는 문서를 이메일로 보내줄게요.(37)**

여: 알겠습니다. 정말 감사합니다.

35 화자들은 어디에서 일하겠는가?
(A) 직물 매장에서
(B) 신문사에서
(C) 도서관에서
(D) 공장에서

36 화자들은 무엇이 가장 중요하다고 생각하는가?
(A) 해박한 직원을 고용하는 것
(B) 제품군을 확대하는 것
(C) 좋은 고객 관계를 유지하는 것
(D) 고품질의 자료를 만들어 내는 것

37 남자는 여자에게 무엇을 보낼 것인가?
(A) 보너스 급여
(B) 계약서 견본
(C) 업무 요약서
(D) 제품 목록

미국 ⇌ 호주

Questions 38-40 refer to the following conversation.

W: Hello, **I'm calling regarding a recent purchase I made from your website.(38)** The order number is XV7814.

M: Please give me a moment to check the system. All right, **it's the Sirka HD television,(38)** right?

W: Yeah, but when I reviewed my invoice, I discovered that **I chose the 50-inch one by accident. I actually wanted to purchase the 55-inch model.(39)** Is it possible to revise my order?

M: Yes. Fortunately, your item hasn't been sent out yet, so I can update the order. And just so you know, **this model is more expensive, so your credit card will be charged an additional $70.**(40)

38-40번은 다음 대화에 관한 문제입니다.

여: 안녕하세요, 제가 웹사이트에서 한 최근 주문 건과 관련해서 전화 드려요.(38) 주문 번호는 XV7814이에요.

남: 시스템을 확인하는 동안 잠시만 기다려 주세요. 네, **Sirka HD 텔레비전**이네요,(38) 맞으세요?

여: 네, 그런데 제가 청구서를 검토하다 발견했는데 제가 실수로 50인치 상품을 선택했어요. 실은 55인치 모델을 구매하고 싶었거든요.(39) 제 주문을 수정하는 것이 가능할까요?

남: 네. 다행히, 귀하의 물품이 아직 발송되지 않아서, 주문을 업데이트해 드릴 수 있습니다. 그리고 아시다시피, **이 모델이 더 비싸서, 귀하의 신용카드로 70달러가 추가 청구될 거예요.**(40)

---

38 여자는 온라인으로 무엇을 샀는가?
(A) 컴퓨터
(B) 텔레비전
(C) 카메라
(D) 전화기

39 여자는 어떤 실수를 했나?
(A) 잘못된 전화번호를 제공했다.
(B) 전액을 지불하지 않았다.
(C) 크기를 잘못 선택했다.
(D) 할인 적용하는 것을 깜박했다.

40 남자는 여자에게 무엇에 관해 알려주는가?
(A) 판촉 행사
(B) 제품 기능
(C) 배송 서비스
(D) 추가 요금

미국 ⇄ 미국

Questions 41-43 refer to the following conversation.

W: I'd like to welcome you all to today's managers' meeting. **This morning, Dan, our sales director, is going to go over the company's quarterly sales report.**(41) Dan, if you would...

M: Thank you. I'm sure most of you already know, but subscription numbers for our magazine's print edition have dropped considerably over the last few months. Nowadays, **people find it more convenient to read content online using new technological tools such as smartphones and tablets.**(42)

W: Hmm... **We should think about discontinuing our print edition service**(43) and just focus on promoting our online magazine.

M: Yeah, that would be a good idea. We'd also cut back on operating costs if we stopped printing the magazine.(43)

41-43번은 다음 대화에 관한 문제입니다.

여: 오늘 관리자 회의에 와 주신 여러분 모두 반갑습니다. 오늘 오전에는 영업부장이신 Dan이 자사 분기별 매출보고서를 검토하실 겁니다.(41) Dan, 진행 부탁드립니다...

남: 감사합니다. 대부분 이미 아시겠지만, 우리 잡지 인쇄판 구독자 수가 지난 몇 달간 크게 감소했습니다. 요즘에는 사람들이 스마트폰이나 태블릿 같은 새로운 기술 장비를 이용해서 온라인으로 콘텐츠를 읽는 걸 더 편한 것으로 보고 있습니다.(42)

여: 음... 인쇄판 서비스 중단을 고려하고,(43) 온라인 잡지 홍보에만 집중해야겠어요.

남: 네, 좋은 생각 같아요. 잡지 발행을 중단하면 운영비도 절감하게 될 겁니다.(43)

---

41 남자는 어느 부서에서 일하는가?
(A) 디자인
(B) 영업
(C) 재무
(D) 편집

42 남자는 소비행태 변화의 원인이 무엇이라고 말하는가?
(A) 더 좋은 기술의 이용 가능성
(B) 나아진 경제 상황
(C) 더 깨끗한 환경의 필요성
(D) 증가한 연료비

43 화자들은 무엇에 관하여 동의하는가?
(A) 온라인 워크숍을 진행하는 것
(B) 서비스를 중단하는 것
(C) 새 마케팅 대행사를 이용하는 것
(D) 사무실을 개조하는 것

영국 ⇄ 미국

Questions 44-46 refer to the following conversation.

W: Jerome, what's the latest on the new website we're building for the bank?(44)

M: Yes, I've just signed off on the latest version.(44) The security features we've added are absolutely fantastic.

W: I'm glad to hear it. Also, I've just received some fantastic news. **We have received a lot of requests for sites from other businesses based on how well this project is going.**(45)

M: That's going to be great for our business. **I reassigned our designer to handle the payments for this project.**(46) Afterward, I'll get him to process the incoming requests.

44-46번은 다음 대화에 관한 문제입니다.

여: Jerome, 저희가 만들고 있는 은행용 신규 웹사이트 관련 최신 소식은 무엇인가요?(44)

남: 네, 제가 방금 최신 버전을 승인했습니다.(44) 추가된 보안 기능이 아주 굉장해요.

여: 그 소식을 들으니 좋네요. 그리고 제가 방금 아주 좋은 소식을 들었어요. 이 프로젝트가 얼마나 잘 진행되는지를 보고 다른 업체에서 사이트 요청을 많이 받았어요.(45)

남: 저희 사업에 큰 도움이 될 거예요. 제가 이번 프로젝트 건 지불을 처리할 디자이너를 재배정했어요.(46) 나중에는 그분이 신규 요청을 처리하게 할게요.

---

44 남자는 최근에 무엇을 승인했는가?
(A) 웹사이트
(B) 설계도
(C) 사용 설명서
(D) 은행 안내 책자

45 여자는 어떤 좋은 소식을 공유하는가?
(A) 보안이 업그레이드되었다.
(B) 고객이 만족을 표했다.
(C) 사업체가 신규 주문을 받았다.
(D) 수익이 증가했다.

46 남자는 왜 직원을 재배치했는가?
(A) 고객과 만나기 위해
(B) 지급을 처리하기 위해
(C) 문제를 진단하기 위해
(D) 신규 프로젝트를 준비하기 위해

호주 ⇄ 미국

Questions 47-49 refer to the following conversation.

M: Ms. Kern, it's Matthew Weimer from Cyan Florist Co. calling about your recent order of white rose arrangements. We may not be able to deliver all 70 centerpieces to the wedding hall by this Saturday.[(47)]

W: Hmm... That's not good. I really need them to arrive then. The wedding is on Sunday, and the centerpieces have to be set on the tables the day before.

M: I see. The thing is, we're running very short of white roses at the moment. What if we use both pink and white roses for the centerpieces then?[(48)]

W: I'm afraid the client made a specific request for this.[(48)]

M: OK, here's what I'll do: I'll call some other flower shops in the city[(49)] and try to get some more white roses.

W: I'd appreciate that. Please keep me updated.

47-49번은 다음 대화에 관한 문제입니다.

남: Ms. Kern, 저는 Cyan 화훼회사의 Matthew Weimer라고 하는데요, 최근 주문하신 흰 장미 꽃장식 건과 관련하여 전화드립니다. 이번 토요일까지 웨딩홀로 센터피스 70개 전체를 배송해드리지 못할 수도 있어서요.[(47)]

여: 흠... 안 되는데요. 그때까지 꼭 도착해야 해요. 결혼식이 일요일이고, 그 전날 테이블에 센터피스가 세팅되어 있어야 해요.

남: 그렇군요. 문제는, 현재 흰 장미가 매우 부족하다는 건데요. 그러면 센터피스에 분홍 장미와 흰 장미를 함께 사용하는 건 어떨까요?[(48)]

여: 고객이 이걸 특별 요청한 거라서요.[(48)]

남: 네, 그럼 이렇게 할게요. 제가 시내 다른 꽃집에 전화해서[(49)] 흰 장미를 더 구해보겠습니다.

여: 그렇게 해주시면 감사합니다. 상황을 계속해서 알려주세요.

47 남자는 무엇 때문에 전화하는가?
(A) 주문을 완료하는 것
(B) 단기 직원을 채용하는 것
(C) 가구를 배열하는 것
(D) 더 큰 장소를 찾는 것

48 여자가 "고객이 이걸 특별 요청한 거라서요"라고 말할 때 무엇을 내비치는가?
(A) 남자가 고객에게 연락해야 한다.
(B) 가격이 이미 책정되어 있다.
(C) 변경을 할 수 없다.
(D) 남자가 오류를 수정해야 한다.

49 남자는 무엇을 하겠다고 제안하는가?
(A) 지역 업체들에 연락하겠다고
(B) 할인을 제공하겠다고
(C) 배송을 신속히 처리하겠다고
(D) 장비를 설치하겠다고

미국 ⇄ 영국

Questions 50-52 refer to the following conversation.

M: Good morning. I want to reserve a seat on a bus for Gwangju this Saturday.[(50)] I prefer to get on the one that departs at 1 P.M.

W: Hmm... Unfortunately, all the bus tickets to Gwangju that day are sold out.[(51)] Because of the special promotion we held this week, many people purchased tickets early. If you want, there are some open seats for Sunday.

M: That'll be too late. Maybe I should just take a train to Gwangju.

W: You can do that too. I recommend getting the train booking app. It's free and easy to use.[(52)]

50-52번은 다음 대화에 관한 문제입니다.

남: 안녕하세요. 이번 주 토요일 Gwangju행 버스 좌석을 예약하고 싶은데요.[(50)] 오후 1시에 출발하는 버스를 탈 수 있으면 좋겠어요.

여: 음... 죄송하지만, 그날 Gwangju행 버스표는 전석 매진이에요.[(51)] 이번 주에 연 특별 판촉 행사 때문에, 많은 분이 표를 일찍 구입하셨거든요. 원하신다면 일요일에 빈 좌석이 몇 개 있긴 합니다.

남: 그건 너무 늦어서요. 그냥 Gwangju행 기차를 타야겠어요.

여: 그렇게 하셔도 되고요. 열차예매 앱 이용을 추천 드려요. 무료인데다 사용하기도 쉽거든요.[(52)]

50 대화는 어디에서 일어나고 있는가?
(A) 기차역에서
(B) 버스 터미널에서
(C) 공항 게이트에서
(D) 연락선 부두에서

51 여자는 어떤 문제점을 언급하는가?
(A) 결제를 처리할 수 없다.
(B) 컴퓨터가 작동하지 않는다.
(C) 좌석을 이용할 수 없다.
(D) 문서가 분실되었다.

52 여자는 남자에게 무엇을 하라고 제안하는가?
(A) 애플리케이션을 다운받으라고
(B) 회원권을 구매하라고
(C) 식당에 가라고
(D) 쿠폰을 인쇄하라고

영국 ⇄ 호주

Questions 53-55 refer to the following conversation.

W: Welcome to Hive Studios.[(53)]

M: Hi. I'm interested in signing up for a shared office membership.[(53)]

W: You've come to the right place. We offer private offices, dedicated desks, as well as hot desks, all equipped with state-of-the-art equipment. Our members have access to a wellness room where they can take exercise classes, and a resting area furnished with massage chairs.

M: Wow, looking at this catalog, **the membership fee seems to be out of my price range.**(54)

W: You won't find many facilities that offer this many services.(54)

M: I see. Let me think about it.

W: Here's a free one-day guest pass for a hot desk.(55) Why don't you come in and try it out?

53-55번은 다음 대화에 관한 문제입니다.

여: Hive Studios입니다.(53)

남: 안녕하세요. 저는 공유 사무실 회원 등록을 하고 싶은데요.(53)

여: 제대로 찾아오셨네요. 저희는 최신 장비가 완비된 공용 책상뿐만 아니라 개인 사무실, 전용 책상을 제공합니다. 회원은 운동 수업을 들을 수 있는 웰니스 룸과 안마 의자가 구비된 휴게 공간을 이용할 수 있어요.

남: 와, 여기 카탈로그를 보니까, 회원권 요금이 제가 생각하는 가격대를 벗어난 것 같네요.(54)

여: 이렇게 많은 서비스를 제공하는 시설을 별로 찾지 못할 거예요.(54)

남: 그렇군요. 생각해 볼게요.

여: 공용 책상을 이용할 수 있는 일일 무료 이용권을 드릴게요.(55) 오셔서 체험해보시는 게 어떠세요?

53 대화는 어디서 일어나는가?
(A) 공립 도서관에서
(B) 공유 사무실에서
(C) 헬스장에서
(D) 미술관에서

54 여자는 왜 "이렇게 많은 서비스를 제공하는 시설을 별로 찾지 못할 거예요"라고 말하는가?
(A) 가격을 정당화하기 위해
(B) 시설에 대해 우려를 표하기 위해
(C) 창업을 권하기 위해
(D) 결정에 반대하기 위해

55 여자는 남자에게 무엇을 주는가?
(A) 명함
(B) 회원 아이디
(C) 일일 이용권
(D) 할인권

호주 ⇄ 영국 ⇄ 미국

Questions 56-58 refer to the following conversation with three speakers.

M: Sarah and Irene, our dairy cows are doing well, and milk production rates are on the rise. But **we should look for other sources of income.**(56) Do you have any ideas?

W1: How about selling products made from our milk? We could sell cheese, butter, and maybe even ice cream.

M: **Other dairy farms offer those products already.**(57) I'm not sure if that would be enough.

W2: How about one-day classes? We could hold classes for people interested in making cheese or yogurt from home.

M: Hmm... That sounds promising. **I'll try to see if workshops like that are being offered nearby.**(58)

56-58번은 다음 세 화자의 대화에 관한 문제입니다.

남: Sarah, Irene, 우리 젖소들이 잘하고 있고, 우유 생산율도 증가하고 있어요. 그런데 **다른 수입원을 찾아야 해요.**(56) 좋은 생각 있으세요?

여1: 우유로 만든 제품을 판매하는 건 어때요? 치즈, 버터, 어쩌면 아이스크림도 판매할 수 있어요.

남: 다른 낙농장에서 이미 그런 제품을 팔고 있어요.(57) 그걸로 충분할지 모르겠어요.

여2: 원데이 수업은 어때요? 집에서 치즈나 요거트를 만드는 데 관심 있는 사람들을 대상으로 수업을 마련할 수도 있어요.

남: 흠... 좋은 생각 같아요. **인근에 그런 워크숍이 제공되고 있는지 제가 알아볼게요.**(58)

56 화자들은 무엇에 관해 논의하고 있는가?
(A) 직원 유지 전략
(B) 고객 피드백 시행
(C) 추가 수입원
(D) 소셜 미디어 마케팅

57 남자는 유제품을 판매하는 아이디어에 관해 어떻게 생각하는가?
(A) 다른 곳에서 유사품이 판매된다.
(B) 그런 제품을 생산하려면 직원이 더 채용되어야 한다.
(C) 농장에 식품 제조 면허가 없다.
(D) 매장을 만들 공간이 충분치 않다.

58 남자는 무엇을 할 계획인가?
(A) 조사를 실시한다
(B) 조리법을 찾는다
(C) 온라인 광고를 게시한다
(D) 일부 공급업체와 이야기한다

영국 ⇄ 미국 ⇄ 미국

Questions 59-61 refer to the following conversation with three speakers.

W1: Hello, Mr. Almeda. I'm Rose Figueroa. **I'm the HR manager at Watscorp Publishers.**(59) And this is one of our senior editors, Nicole Lane.

W2: Thanks for coming in, Mr. Almeda. Why don't you start by talking about your previous work experience?(59)

M: Sure. I've been in the R&D field for many years. This is a list of my past projects.

W1: Oh, the list is quite extensive. **What would you say is your biggest accomplishment?**(60)

M: I'm proudest of my work on the South American history textbook series for local universities.(60)

W2: Why would you leave your current company? You've been there so long.

M: I enjoy the work, but the benefits aren't great. **Watscorp provides quarterly incentives, and that shows that you care about your staff. I really like that.**(61)

59-61번은 다음 세 화자의 대화에 관한 문제입니다.

여1: 안녕하세요, Mr. Almeda. Rose Figueroa예요. **저는 Watscorp 출판사의 인사 매니저입니다.**(59) 그리고 여기는 선임 편집자 중 한 명인 Nicole Lane이에요.

여2: 와주셔서 감사해요, Mr. Almeda. 이전 경력에 관한 얘기로 시작해 볼까요?(59)

남: 네. 저는 수년간 연구개발 업계에 종사했습니다. 이게 제가 몸 담았던 지난 프로젝트 목록입니다.

여1: 오, 이 목록은 꽤 광범위하네요. **가장 큰 업적은 무엇이라고 생각하세요?**(60)

남: **지역 대학용으로 작업한 남미 역사 교과서 시리즈가 제일 자랑스럽습니다.**(60)

여2: 왜 현재 회사를 그만두시려고 하시나요? 꽤 오래 계셨는데요.

남: 업무를 즐기지만, 복리후생이 그다지 좋지 않습니다. **Watscorp는 분기마다 인센티브를 제공해서 직원들에 대해 신경 쓴다는 걸 보여줍니다. 그 부분이 정말 마음에 듭니다.**(61)

59 남자는 왜 Watscorp 출판사에 있는가?
(A) 새로운 도서 프로젝트를 논의하기 위해
(B) 회사 워크숍을 진행하기 위해
(C) 점검을 실시하기 위해
(D) 일자리 면접을 보기 위해

60 남자에 따르면, 그의 가장 큰 업적은 무엇인가?
(A) 교육 자료를 만든 것
(B) 자영업을 시작한 것
(C) 국가상을 받은 것
(D) 연구개발 매니저가 된 것

61 남자는 Watscorp의 어떤 면을 마음에 들어 하는가?
(A) 유명한 소설을 출판한다.
(B) 직원들을 신경 쓴다.
(C) 업계 리더이다.
(D) 최근에 사옥을 확장했다.

미국 ⇄ 미국

Questions 62-64 refer to the following conversation and schedule.

M: Hey, Britney. You're at the station, right? **I'm stuck in traffic right now, so it'll take me another 20 minutes to get there.**(62) There's a chance I won't be able to board the train.

W: You'll be fine. **I just checked, and our train's departure has been delayed by 45 minutes.**(63) So don't worry.

M: Ah, OK. **But please message Mr. Riley.**(64) He needs to be aware that we won't be there for the opening speech of the company awards ceremony.

62-64번은 다음 대화와 일정표에 관한 문제입니다.

남: 안녕하세요, Britney. 지금 역에 계시죠, 그렇죠? **제가 지금 차가 막혀서, 도착하려면 20분이 더 걸릴 거예요.**(62) 제가 기차에 못 탈 수도 있어요.

여: 괜찮으실 거예요. 지금 막 확인해봤는데, 우리 기차가 출발이 45분 지연됐어요.(63) 그러니까 걱정하지 마세요.

남: 아, 그래요. 그래도 Mr. Riley에게 메시지를 보내주세요.(64) 우리가 회사 시상식 개회사에 참석하지 못할 거라는 걸 알고 계셔야 해요.

기차 번호	목적지	출발 시각/상태
230	Rochester	오전 8시 20분 정시 출발
231	Buffalo	오전 9시 15분 60분 지연
232	Albany	오전 10시 30분 정시 출발
233	Syracuse	오전 11시 45분 지연(63)

62 남자의 문제는 무엇인가?
(A) 늦게 도착할 것이다.
(B) 표를 예약하지 못했다.
(C) 노트를 집에 두고 왔다.
(D) 주차 공간을 못 찾고 있다.

63 시각 자료를 보시오. 화자들은 어떤 기차에 탑승할 것인가?
(A) 230
(B) 231
(C) 232
(D) 233

64 남자는 여자에게 무엇을 요청하는가?
(A) 연설하라고
(B) 메시지를 전송하라고
(C) 발표를 검토하라고
(D) 납부하라고

미국 ⇄ 영국

Questions 65-67 refer to the following conversation and event calendar.

M: OK, this is your gym membership ID and a list of our spring seminars.(65)

W: Great!

M: Since you're a member, you can participate in any seminar, free of charge.(65) But they fill up quickly, so register in advance!

W: In that case, can I sign up for the yoga seminar on March 29?

M: Ah, unfortunately, that session is already full. **But we still have a few spaces available at the one on a jogging program, if you're interested.**(66)

W: Sure, I'd like to check that out.(66)

M: OK, I've signed you up. And if you want, you can join tonight's special group fitness class. It's being led by Brianne Pyle, a local trainer. She's going to be introducing a special workout routine using a variety of gymnastics moves.(67)

65-67번은 다음 대화와 행사 일정표에 관한 문제입니다.

남: 자, 여기 체육관 회원증과 봄 세미나 목록입니다.(65)

여: 네!

남: 회원이시니까, 어떤 세미나든 무료로 참석하실 수 있습니다.(65) 하지만 자리가 빨리 차니 미리 등록하셔야 해요!

여: 그럼 3월 29일 요가 세미나에 등록할 수 있나요?

남: 아, 죄송하지만, 그 수업은 이미 다 찼어요. 하지만, 조깅 프로그램 수업은 아직 빈 자리가 몇 개 있어요, 혹시 관심 있으시면요.(66)

여: 네, 한번 참여해 보고 싶어요.(66)

남: 좋습니다, 등록해 드렸고요. 원하실 경우, 오늘 밤 그룹 피트니스 특별 수업에 참여하실 수 있어요. 이 지역 트레이너 Brianne Pyle이 진행합니다. 다양한 체조 동작을 활용한 특별한 운동법을 소개해 드릴 거예요.(67)

다가올 봄 세미나	
3월 12일	에너지를 위한 식사
3월 29일	요가 입문
4월 3일	**조깅 프로그램 짜기(66)**
4월 16일	훈련 일지 기록하기

65 여자는 왜 무료 세미나에 참석할 수 있는가?
(A) 지역 주민이다.
(B) 헬스 트레이너이다.
(C) 회원권을 구매했다.
(D) 조기 등록을 완료했다.

66 시각 자료를 보시오. 여자는 어느 날짜 행사에 참가할 것인가?
(A) 3월 12일
(B) 3월 29일
(C) 4월 3일
(D) 4월 16일

67 Brianne Pyle은 무엇을 소개할 것인가?
(A) 영양가 있는 식단 계획
(B) 운동 기계
(C) 운동법
(D) 건강 관련 도서

미국 ⇄ 호주

Questions 68-70 refer to the following conversation and supply cabinet.

W: Byeong-cheol. I'm arranging the refreshment desk outside the main event hall. It'll be used for a trade convention today.(68) According to the client's request form, **they want various baked goods.(69)** Which fridge are they in?

M: Ah, you'll have to look in the wall fridge, on the shelf above the fruit cups.(69)

W: Oh, here they are. Umm, did you know that we have cartons of orange juice just sitting in here?

M: Yeah. We miscalculated how much we really needed. Juice doesn't seem to be as popular with convention attendees lately.

W: I see. **Could you make a note on the inventory sheet so we won't order more juice next time?(70)**

68-70번은 다음 대화와 비품 캐비닛에 관한 문제입니다.

여: Byeong-cheol. 제가 지금 메인 행사장 밖에 있는 다과용 책상을 정리하고 있어요. 오늘 무역 컨벤션에서 사용될 거예요.(68) 고객 요청서에 따르면, 다양한 구운 제품을 원하세요.(69) 그게 어느 냉장고에 있죠?

남: 아, 벽장 냉장고 안을 살펴봐야 하는데, 과일컵 위 선반에 있어요.(69)

여: 아, 여기 있네요. 음, 오렌지주스 몇 상자가 여기 그대로 놓여 있는 거 알고 계셨어요?

남: 네. 저희가 실제로 필요한 수를 잘못 계산했어요. 요즘 주스는 컨벤션 참석자에게 인기가 별로 없는 것 같아요.

여: 그렇군요. 다음번에 주스를 더 주문하지 않도록 재고표에 메모해 주실래요?(70)

68 대화는 어디서 일어나고 있겠는가?
(A) 컨벤션 센터에서
(B) 식품점에서
(C) 커피숍에서
(D) 공항 라운지에서

69 시각 자료를 보시오. 남자는 여자에게 어떤 선반을 가리키는가?
(A) 선반 1
(B) 선반 2
(C) 선반 3
(D) 선반 4

70 여자는 남자에게 무엇을 해달라고 요청하는가?
(A) 메뉴를 업데이트하라고
(B) 주문에 대해 문의하라고
(C) 일부 제품을 교체하라고
(D) 재고 목록을 수정하라고

PART 4

P. 123

미국

Questions 71-73 refer to the following advertisement.

W: Are you looking to give your business a new look? If so, Olympus Interior is your answer. Our team of specialists will design your store to make it more appealing to customers.(71) The biggest advantage of hiring us is that we're willing to work around your schedule, even if it means coming on the weekend.(72) That way, you don't have to worry about us interrupting your daily operations. Go to our website to see some projects we've done in the past.(73) Give us a call anytime to schedule a consultation.

여: 당신의 사업체를 새롭게 단장하고 싶으신가요? 그러시다면 Olympus 인테리어가 답입니다. 전문가로 이루어진 저희 팀이 귀하의 매장을 고객에게 더 매력적으로 보일 수 있도록 디자인해 드립니다. (71) 저희에게 맡겨주실 경우 가장 큰 장점은 저희가 주말에 작업하는 일이 있더라도 기꺼이 귀하의 일정에 맞춰 드린다는 것입니다. (72) 그러면 저희가 정상영업에 지장을 주는 것을 염려하실 일이 없을 겁니다. 저희 웹사이트를 방문하셔서 저희가 이전에 한 작업들을 살펴봐 주시기 바랍니다. (73) 상담 일정을 잡으시려면 언제든지 전화주세요.

71 어떤 서비스가 광고되고 있는가?
(A) 행사 기획
(B) 인테리어 디자인
(C) 디지털 마케팅
(D) 제품 포장

72 광고는 어떤 장점을 언급하는가?
(A) 빠른 배송
(B) 고품질 상품
(C) 저렴한 가격
(D) 탄력적인 영업시간

73 청자들은 왜 웹사이트를 확인해야 하는가?
(A) 직원에게 연락하기 위해
(B) 이전 작업들을 살펴보기 위해
(C) 프로그램을 다운로드하기 위해
(D) 등록 양식을 작성하기 위해

호주

Questions 74-76 refer to the following excerpt from a meeting.

M: I want to focus on the way we store our data. Management likes that we can diligently help our customers with their problems, (74) and they're very pleased with our high satisfaction scores. However, we can minimize how long it takes to help by storing and using data. To that end, I've invited a renowned data consultant, Traci Soto, to give a workshop. (75) After the workshop, I want us to brainstorm how we can use her ideas in practice. (76)

74-76번은 다음 회의 발췌록에 관한 문제입니다.

남: 우리가 자료를 저장하는 방식에 집중하고자 합니다. 경영진은 우리가 고객의 문제를 도와주려고 애쓰는 것에 흡족해하며(74) 높은 만족도 점수에 아주 기뻐하십니다. 하지만, 우리는 자료를 저장하고 활용하는 방식으로 도와주는 데 걸리는 시간을 최소화할 수 있습니다. 이를 위해, 유명한 데이터 컨설턴트인 Traci Soto를 초청해 워크숍을 마련했습니다.(75) 워크숍이 끝난 후에는 그녀의 아이디어를 실제로 어떻게 활용할 수 있을지 브레인스토밍했으면 합니다.(76)

74 청자들은 누구겠는가?
(A) 경영 컨설턴트들
(B) **고객서비스 직원들**
(C) 컴퓨터 과학자들
(D) 기업 트레이너들

75 Traci Soto는 무엇에 관하여 말할 것인가?
(A) 고객 관리
(B) 시간 관리
(C) **자료 저장**
(D) 사업 기회

76 화자는 청자들에게 무엇을 해달라고 요청하는가?
(A) 이메일에 답장하라고
(B) 회의를 주최하라고
(C) 관리자와 만나라고
(D) 아이디어를 제안하라고

영국

Questions 77-79 refer to the following speech.

W: Today, I'd like to reveal the result of three years of research and development at Zephyr Tech. Here is the most advanced microwave you will find on the market. (77) To give you some background, when we started on this project, we knew that above all else, this should be simple to operate.(78) Then we sought to add in some features that would redefine the way you cook. For example, you can see that it has a built-in thermometer. That's so you know exactly what temperature your food has been heated to. Now, if you will turn your attention to this table here, I want to show you the microwave itself and show off some of the other features. (79)

77-79번은 다음 연설문에 관한 문제입니다.

여: 오늘 저는 Zephyr Tech에서 3년간의 연구 개발 결과를 발표하고자 합니다. 여러분이 시장에서 찾을 수 있는 가장 진보된 전자레인지가 여기 있습니다. (77) 여러분께 사전 정보를 드리자면, 저희는 이 프로젝트에 착수했을 때, 다른 무엇보다도 조작이 간단해야 한다는 것을 인지했습니다.(78) 그리고 여러분의 요리 방식을 재정의하는 몇 가지 기능을 추가하고자 노력했습니다. 예를 들어, 본 제품에 내장형 온도계가 있는 것을 확인하실 수 있습니다. 그러면 음식이 정확히 몇 도까지 데워졌는지 알 수 있습니다. 이제 관심을 여기 이 테이블에 돌리시면, 여러분께 이 전자레인지를 보여드리면서 그밖의 다른 기능들을 자랑해 보이겠습니다. (79)

77 화자의 회사가 개발한 제품은 무엇인가?
(A) 온도계
(B) 조리대
(C) **전자레인지**
(D) 냉장고

78 화자는 자신에게 무엇이 중요했다고 말하는가?
(A) 저렴함
(B) 미학
(C) 견고함
(D) **단순성**

79 화자는 다음에 무엇을 할 것인가?
(A) **시연을 할 것이다**
(B) 전단지를 돌릴 것이다
(C) 영상을 보여줄 것이다
(D) 어떤 자료를 참조할 것이다

호주

Questions 80-82 refer to the following telephone message.

M: Hello, this is John Moon from City Publishing, and this message is for Ms. Rivera. We are sorry to inform you that you were not selected for the position you applied for in our R&D Department. Although you have many years of experience, all of our researchers are required to work on a Saturday or a Sunday from time to time. (80) But we do feel that your knowledge of Spanish would be an asset to our Editing Department as we publish many books in Spanish. They also have an opening, and they've already started interviewing people.(81) The job is a little different from the R&D position, but if you're interested, I'll send them your résumé.(81)/(82) Call me back at 555-3849 if you have any questions.

80-82번은 다음 전화 메시지에 관한 문제입니다.

남: 안녕하세요, 저는 City 출판사의 John Moon이며, Ms. Rivera 께 메시지를 남깁니다. 지원하신 저희 연구 개발 부서 직무에 선발 되지 않았음을 알려드리게 되어 유감입니다. 수년간의 경력이 있으 시지만, 저희 연구원 모두 가끔 토요일이나 일요일에 근무해야 합니 다.(80) 하지만 저희가 스페인어로 된 책을 많이 출간하기 때문에 당신의 스페인어 지식이 편집부에서라면 장점이 되리라 생각합 니다. 거기도 공석이 있는데 벌써 지원자 면접을 시작했습니다.(81) 업무가 연구 개발직과 좀 다르기는 하지만 관심이 있으시다면 그쪽 에 당신의 이력서를 보내겠습니다.(81)/(82) 질문이 있으시면 555-3849로 다시 전화 주세요.

80 청자의 지원은 왜 거부되었겠는가?
(A) 업무 경력이 충분하지 않다.
(B) 특정 언어를 모른다.
(C) 주말에 일할 수 없다.
(D) 다른 도시로 이주할 수 없다.

81 화자가 "벌써 지원자 면접을 시작했습니다"라고 말할 때 무엇을 내비치 는가?
(A) 빨리 행동을 취해야 한다.
(B) 면접 일정을 다시 잡을 수 없다.
(C) 부서가 이미 누군가를 채용했다.
(D) 업무가 예상보다 더 어렵다.

82 화자는 무엇을 해주겠다고 제안하는가?
(A) 방을 예약해주겠다고
(B) 문서를 전달하겠다고
(C) 사무실을 방문하겠다고
(D) 지원자에게 전화하겠다고

호주 미국

Questions 83-85 refer to the following excerpt from a meeting.

M: Everyone, I need your attention up here. I have an important announcement to make. We need to expedite the development of our product. Our biggest rival's smartphone will be available in the market two weeks before ours.(83) This is a major issue. Our potential customers will purchase theirs since their product will come out first. Unless we release ours as soon as possible, we won't be able to sell as many units.(84) If we push ourselves, we will be able to meet the earlier deadline. To do this, I'll move some of our team members working on our laptop line to the smartphone team.(85)

83-85번은 다음 회의 발췌록에 관한 문제입니다.

남: 모두 주목해 주세요. 중요 공지 사항이 있습니다. 저희가 제품 개 발을 서둘러야 합니다. 최대 경쟁사의 스마트폰이 우리보다 2주 먼 저 시장에 나옵니다.(83) 중대한 문제예요. 잠재 고객들은 그쪽 제품

이 먼저 나와서 그쪽 제품을 구입할 겁니다. 우리가 제품을 최대한 빨 리 출시하지 않으면 많은 수량을 팔지 못할 겁니다.(84) 우리가 서두 른다면, 마감일을 더 빨리 당길 수 있게 됩니다. 이를 위해서, 노 트북 라인을 담당하는 우리 팀원 중 일부를 스마트폰 팀으로 이동시키 도록 하겠습니다.(85)

83 화자는 어디서 일하겠는가?
(A) 인터넷 회사에서
(B) 과학 연구소에서
(C) 전자제품 제조사에서
(D) 방송국에서

84 화자는 무엇에 관하여 염려하는가?
(A) 사업 손실
(B) 자재비 인상
(C) 운송 지연
(D) 안전 검사

85 화자는 무엇을 할 거라고 말하는가?
(A) 직원들에게 금전적 보상을 제공할 거라고
(B) 프로젝트에 더 많은 직원을 할당할 거라고
(C) 야근 요청서를 승인할 거라고
(D) 휴일에 근무할 거라고

호주

Questions 86-88 refer to the following excerpt from a talk.

M: Today, I have some great news in regard to our employee benefits package.(86) As you know, our company provides an extensive benefits package to all of its employees. Recently, our company has negotiated a deal with local pharmacies to give our employees a discount. Now, you can get 10 percent off all non-prescription drugs and vitamins.(87) Just show your business card along with a photo ID at the cash register to receive the discount. Details about the discounts and participating stores are on this list, which I'll distribute right now.(88)

86-88번은 다음 담화 발췌문에 관한 문제입니다.

남: 오늘은 우리의 복리후생제도와 관련된 아주 좋은 소식이 있습니 다.(86) 아시다시피 우리 회사는 모든 직원에게 폭넓은 복리후생 을 제공하고 있죠. 최근 우리 회사는 지역의 약국들과의 거래를 성사시켜 우리 직원에게 할인을 해주도록 했습니다. 이제 여러분 은 모든 일반의약품과 비타민 제품 가격의 10퍼센트를 할인받을 수 있습니다.(87) 할인을 받으시려면 계산대에서 사진이 포함된 신 분증과 함께 명함만 보여주시면 됩니다. 할인과 참여 매장들에 관 한 세부 사항은 지금 나눠드리는 이 목록에 있습니다.(88)

86 담화는 주로 무엇에 관한 것인가?
(A) 안전 절차
(B) 교육 일정
(C) 복리후생
(D) 휴가 정책

87 화자에 따르면, 청자들은 무엇에 대한 할인을 받을 수 있는가?
(A) 의약품
(B) 항공요금
(C) 전화요금
(D) 사무용품

88 화자는 다음에 무엇을 할 것인가?
(A) 질문에 대답할 것이다
(B) 정보를 나눠줄 것이다
(C) 손님들을 소개할 것이다
(D) 장비를 시연할 것이다

미국

Questions 89-91 refer to the following telephone message.

M: Hello, Katherine. This is Scott from the Administration Department. I'm calling regarding the company's anniversary celebration next month.(89) I know we were considering having it at the same place as last year, but the thing is, the employees from the overseas branch are also coming. They won't be having a separate event at their own branch this year.(90) So let's have a meeting to figure out how much money we have for the venue.(90)/(91) Then, we'll report to the CEO with some alternative options.(90) Call me back and let me know what time would be good for you.

89-91번은 다음 전화 메시지에 관한 문제입니다.

남: 안녕하세요, Katherine. 총무부의 Scott이에요. 다음 달에 있을 회사 창립기념행사 때문에 전화드렸어요.(89) 작년과 같은 장소에서 하는 걸 고려하고 있다고 알고 있는데요, 문제는 해외 지점의 직원들도 온다는 거예요. 올해는 자기들 지점에서 별도의 행사를 하지 않을 거라더군요.(90) 그러니까 회의를 해서 우리가 장소 마련에 쓸 돈이 얼마나 있는지 알아보도록 해요.(90)/(91) 그리고 나서 CEO께 대안들을 보고하기로 하죠.(90) 전화 주셔서 몇 시가 좋은지 알려주세요.

89 화자는 무엇을 준비하고 있는가?
(A) 기념일 행사
(B) 교육
(C) 영업 콘퍼런스
(D) 자선기금 마련

90 화자가 "해외 지점의 직원들도 온다는 거예요"라고 말할 때 무엇을 내비치는가?
(A) 음식을 더 주문해야 한다.
(B) 더 큰 장소가 필요할 것이다.
(C) 초대 손님 명단이 업데이트되어야 한다.
(D) 문서가 번역될 것이다.

91 화자는 왜 여자와 만나고 싶어 하는가?
(A) 메뉴 옵션을 선택하기 위해
(B) 예산에 관하여 의논하기 위해
(C) 계약을 검토하기 위해
(D) 발표자를 선발하기 위해

영국

Questions 92-94 refer to the following announcement.

W: We've talked about going above and beyond, and we've had several employees who did just that. The IT team volunteered to stay overnight to ensure the overseas teams could get their operations up and running. They're now ready to open for business next month.(92) We'll be hiring some photographers to capture the opening event, so keep an eye out for those.(93) We want to thank the IT team for the hard work and sacrifice. When we first started

the IT team, we only had two members. We're going to need a new office for the team at this rate.(94)

92-94번은 다음 공지에 관한 문제입니다.

여: 자신의 영역을 넘어서서 일하는 것에 대해 말한 적이 있었는데, 일부 직원들이 그것을 해냈습니다. IT팀에서 자원해 해외 부서에서 운영이 원활히 이뤄질 수 있도록 철야 근무를 해주셨습니다. 이제 다음 달 개장을 앞두고 있습니다.(92) 저희가 개장 행사의 모습을 담아낼 사진작가를 채용할 예정이니, 계속 지켜봐 주세요.(93) 노고와 희생에 대해 IT팀에 감사드리고 싶습니다. 저희가 IT팀을 처음 만들었을 때만 해도, 팀원이 두 명뿐이었습니다. 이런 속도라면 팀을 위한 새 사무실이 필요할 겁니다.(94)

92 화자는 무엇을 발표하는가?
(A) 회사가 수상했다.
(B) 곧 신규 지점이 개장한다.
(C) 프로젝트가 연기됐다.
(D) 제휴가 마무리됐다.

93 화자는 회사에서 누구를 채용할 거라고 말하는가?
(A) 사진작가들
(B) 웹디자이너들
(C) 음식 공급자들
(D) 기자들

94 화자가 "이런 속도라면 팀을 위한 새 사무실이 필요할 겁니다"라고 말할 때 무엇을 내비치는가?
(A) 장소가 이상적이다.
(B) 계약서를 수령했다.
(C) 제안이 주목받았다.
(D) 팀이 빠르게 성장했다.

미국

Questions 95-97 refer to the following talk and table.

M: Welcome to this week's sales team meeting, everyone. I'm sure you're all excited because today marks the end of the first month of our new sales incentive program. Remember, we are offering rewards to all staff members based on their clothing and accessories sales.(95) During this past month, nearly everyone sold between $2,000 and $3,000 worth of items.(96) If you were in this group, you may pick up your gift card after this meeting. Now, only one employee, Henry Manning, was able to sell over $3,000 worth of clothes. Henry is planning to take a week off next month to visit his parents in Vermont, so the flight tickets come at a good time.(97) Good work, Henry!

95-97번은 다음 담화와 표에 관한 문제입니다.

남: 모두 이번 주 영업팀 회의에 오신 것을 환영합니다. 오늘은 새 영업 인센티브 프로그램 시행 첫 달의 마지막 날이므로 여러분 모두 분명히 기대하고 있을 겁니다. 의류 및 액세서리 판매량에 근거하여 전 직원에게 포상이 이루어진다는 점을 기억하시기 바랍니다.(95) 지난 한 달 동안 거의 모든 분이 2,000달러에서 3,000달러 상당의 제품을 판매했습니다.(96) 이 그룹에 속하신다면 회의가 끝난 후에 상품권을 받아 가시면 됩니다. 자, 오직 한 명의 직원 Henry Manning만이 3,000달러 이상에 상당하는 의류를 판매했습니다. Henry는 Vermont에 계신 부모님을 뵈러 다음 달에 일주일간 휴가를 가는데요, 그러면 항공권이 적기에 나오는 것이군요.(97) 수고하셨습니다, Henry!

포상 단계	판매 금액	보상책
A 단계	3,000달러 이상	무료 왕복 항공료
B 단계	**2,000달러-3,000달러(96)**	300달러 상품권
C 단계	1,000달러-2,000달러	스테이크 나이프 세트
D 단계	1,000달러 미만	헤드폰

95 화자는 어떤 종류의 사업체에서 일하겠는가?
(A) 휴대전화 회사
(B) 자동차 대리점
(C) 의류 매장
(D) 광고 대행사

96 시각 자료를 보시오. 대부분의 직원들은 어느 포상 단계를 달성했는가?
(A) A 단계
(B) B 단계
(C) C 단계
(D) D 단계

97 화자는 Henry Manning이 왜 다음 달에 Vermont에 갈 거라고 말하는가?
(A) 가족을 만나기 위해
(B) 마케팅 세미나에 참석하기 위해
(C) 상을 받기 위해
(D) 대회에 참가하기 위해

98 화자는 지난주 월요일에 어떤 행사에 참석했는가?
(A) 요리 대회
(B) 회사 기념일 파티
(C) 신입사원 오찬
(D) 매장 개업식

99 시각 자료를 보시오. 화자는 어떤 양을 바꾸라고 제안하는가?
(A) 2
(B) 5
(C) 6
(D) 7

100 화자는 어디에서 조리법을 구했는가?
(A) 기사
(B) 친구
(C) TV 프로그램
(D) 요리책

Questions 98-100 refer to the following telephone message and recipe card.

W: Hello, Oscar. This is Whitney. **I really appreciate you giving me a hand in coordinating the celebration of our company's fifth year in business last Monday.(98)** I think everyone enjoyed it. Now, I forgot to mention this earlier, but **for the chili recipe I gave you, I only put in three red peppers, and it's just right for me. But if you like spicy foods, you can put in the full amount as the recipe card states.(99)** I just didn't want you to be surprised if it tastes different than what you had at the party. **A friend of mine gave me that recipe a little while back,(100)** and I didn't get around to changing it. Call me if you run into any problems!

98-100번은 다음 전화 메시지와 조리법 카드에 관한 문제입니다.

여: 안녕하세요, Oscar. Whitney예요. **지난주 월요일 회사 창립 5주년 기념행사 편성을 도와줘서 정말 고마워요.(98)** 모두 즐거운 시간을 보낸 것 같아요. 저, 미리 얘기한다는 걸 깜빡했는데, **제가 드린 칠리 조리법 말이에요, 저는 고추를 세 개만 넣는데, 그게 저한테는 딱 맞거든요. 그런데 매운 음식을 좋아하신다면 조리법 카드에 나와 있는 양대로 다 넣으셔도 돼요.(99)** 파티에서 드셨던 거랑 맛이 달라서 놀라실까 봐요. **제 친구가 오래전에 그 조리법을 줬는데,(100)** 미처 고쳐놓질 못했네요. 문제 있으면 전화 주세요!

매운 칠리 조리법
양파 2개
고추 5개(99)
토마토 6개
마늘 7쪽
슈레드 치즈 1컵
콩 1캔
소고기 500g

TEST 09

PART 1
P. 128

1 (A) **2** (A) **3** (B) **4** (C) **5** (A) **6** (C)

PART 2
P. 132

7 (C)   **8** (C)   **9** (B)   **10** (B) **11** (C) **12** (A)
13 (B) **14** (C) **15** (C) **16** (A) **17** (B) **18** (C)
19 (A) **20** (C) **21** (C) **22** (A) **23** (A) **24** (A)
25 (C) **26** (A) **27** (B) **28** (A) **29** (C) **30** (A)
31 (B)

PART 3
P. 133

32 (A) **33** (B) **34** (C) **35** (D) **36** (B) **37** (A)
38 (B) **39** (A) **40** (C) **41** (B) **42** (C) **43** (D)
44 (D) **45** (B) **46** (D) **47** (B) **48** (D) **49** (C)
50 (D) **51** (D) **52** (B) **53** (C) **54** (A) **55** (B)
56 (A) **57** (C) **58** (B) **59** (D) **60** (C) **61** (D)
62 (D) **63** (D) **64** (B) **65** (C) **66** (A) **67** (C)
68 (A) **69** (D) **70** (A)

PART 4
P. 137

71 (D) **72** (B) **73** (D) **74** (D) **75** (D) **76** (D)
77 (C) **78** (A) **79** (D) **80** (A) **81** (D) **82** (D)
83 (D) **84** (A) **85** (B) **86** (B) **87** (B) **88** (D)
89 (D) **90** (C) **91** (C) **92** (C) **93** (B) **94** (D)
95 (A) **96** (D) **97** (C) **98** (D) **99** (C) **100** (C)

PART 1
P. 128

1 영국
(A) A man is carrying a bag by the handle.
(B) A man is putting some documents in a briefcase.
(C) A woman is running down a street.
(D) A woman is sipping a beverage.

(A) 남자가 가방을 손잡이로 들고 있다.
(B) 남자가 서류 가방에 서류를 넣고 있다.
(C) 여자가 거리를 달리고 있다.
(D) 여자가 음료를 홀짝이고 있다.

2 미국
(A) She's loading some items into an automobile.
(B) She's inserting a coin into a shopping cart.
(C) She's handing some bags to a customer.
(D) She's parking a vehicle near a supermarket.

(A) 여자가 자동차에 물품들을 싣고 있다.
(B) 여자가 쇼핑 카트에 동전을 넣고 있다.
(C) 여자가 고객에게 가방들을 건네주고 있다.
(D) 여자가 슈퍼마켓 근처에 차를 주차하고 있다.

3 미국
(A) A woman is pointing at a door.
(B) A woman is holding some documents.
(C) A man is drawing a chart on a whiteboard.
(D) A man is distributing some handouts at a meeting.

(A) 여자가 문 쪽을 가리키고 있다.
(B) 여자가 서류를 들고 있다.
(C) 남자가 화이트보드에 도표를 그리고 있다.
(D) 남자가 회의에서 유인물을 나눠주고 있다.

4 호주
(A) One of the women is looking into a cabinet.
(B) One of the women is trying on some shoes.
(C) Some eyeglasses are on display.
(D) Some drawers are being closed.

(A) 여자들 중 한 명이 캐비닛을 들여다보고 있다.
(B) 여자들 중 한 명이 신발을 신어보고 있다.
(C) 몇몇 안경들이 진열되어 있다.
(D) 몇몇 서랍들이 닫히고 있다.

5 미국
(A) A man is loading some hay onto a cart.
(B) A man is fixing a broken wheelbarrow.
(C) A man is feeding a farm animal.
(D) A man is shoveling some dirt.

(A) 남자가 손수레 위에 건초를 싣고 있다.
(B) 남자가 부서진 외바퀴 손수레를 고치고 있다.
(C) 남자가 농장 동물에게 먹이를 주고 있다.
(D) 남자가 흙을 삽으로 파고 있다.

6 미국
(A) Some umbrellas are shading a balcony.
(B) A bridge leads to the ocean.
(C) Some chairs are facing a body of water.
(D) A cabin is located near the beach.

(A) 몇몇 파라솔들이 발코니에 그늘을 드리우고 있다.
(B) 다리가 바다로 이어져 있다.
(C) 몇몇 의자들이 수역을 향하고 있다.
(D) 오두막이 해변 근처에 위치해 있다.

PART 2
P. 132

7 미국 ⇄ 미국
How did you learn about this position?
(A) Put your seat in an upright position.
(B) How can I get to the meeting room?
(C) I heard about it from a former coworker.

이 일자리에 대해 어떻게 알게 되었나요?
(A) 좌석을 똑바로 세워 주기 바랍니다.
(B) 회의실에는 어떻게 갑니까?
(C) 예전에 함께 일했던 동료에게서 들었습니다.

8 영국 ⇄ 미국

Why is there a camera in the assembly hall?
(A) At the photography exhibit.
(B) Thanks. It's a new camera.
(C) To record the event.

회의장에 왜 카메라가 있죠?
(A) 사진 전시회에서요.
(B) 고마워요. 새 카메라에요.
(C) 행사를 녹화하려고요.

9 미국 ⇄ 호주

The project due date has been pushed back, hasn't it?
(A) On the projection screen.
(B) I'm done, actually.
(C) A little more to the left.

그 프로젝트 마감일이 미뤄졌죠, 그렇지 않나요?
(A) 영사 스크린에요.
(B) 사실, 저는 다 했어요.
(C) 왼쪽으로 조금 더요.

10 영국 ⇄ 호주

Who's going to drop Maria off at the train station?
(A) At platform 5.
(B) I'm planning to take her at 1 P.M.
(C) They're at a training session.

누가 Maria를 기차역에 내려줄 건가요?
(A) 5번 승강장에요.
(B) 제가 오후 1시에 그녀를 데려다주려고 해요.
(C) 그들은 연수 중이에요.

11 미국 ⇄ 미국

Aren't you managing the Parker account?
(A) Before 11 A.M.
(B) At the management office.
(C) Yes, Ashley and I are.

Parker 거래처를 관리하고 계시지 않으세요?
(A) 오전 11시 전에요.
(B) 관리 사무소에서요.
(C) 네, Ashley와 제가 하고 있어요.

12 미국 ⇄ 호주

What did you think of the training seminar?
(A) I thought it was very beneficial.
(B) During the orientation.
(C) Yes, it stopped raining.

교육 세미나는 어떠셨어요?
(A) 매우 유익했던 것 같아요.
(B) 오리엔테이션 기간 동안이요.
(C) 네, 비가 그쳤어요.

13 호주 ⇄ 영국

When are you planning to upgrade your computer?
(A) The latest computer software.
(B) By the end of the month.
(C) For the entire office.

언제 컴퓨터 업그레이드를 할 계획이세요?
(A) 최신 컴퓨터 소프트웨어요.
(B) 이달 말까지요.
(C) 전체 사무실에요.

14 영국 ⇄ 미국

Did you organize the office supplies in the storage closet?
(A) Some extra printer paper.
(B) They were purchased last month.
(C) No, Stanley sorted it out.

비품 창고에 있는 사무용품을 정리하셨어요?
(A) 여분의 인쇄용지요.
(B) 지난달에 구입한 거예요.
(C) 아니요, Stanley가 정리했어요.

15 호주 ⇄ 영국

How many employee workshops are we conducting this month?
(A) Fifty people per session.
(B) It was very informative.
(C) Check the schedule.

이번 달에는 직원 워크숍을 얼마나 많이 하나요?
(A) 세션당 50명이요.
(B) 아주 유익했어요.
(C) 일정을 확인해 보세요.

16 미국 ⇄ 미국

Where can I find women's sportswear?
(A) We don't sell any.
(B) OK. That's fine.
(C) I exercise three times a week.

여성용 운동복은 어디에 있나요?
(A) 저희는 안 팔아요.
(B) 알았어요. 괜찮습니다.
(C) 저는 주 3회 운동해요.

17 호주 ⇄ 미국

Could you look over the edited video clip?
(A) Ten minutes long.
(B) I'll be free tomorrow.
(C) A documentary film.

동영상 편집본 좀 봐주실래요?
(A) 10분짜리예요.
(B) 내일 시간이 될 거예요.
(C) 다큐멘터리 영화요.

18 미국 ⇄ 미국

Will you be paying with cash or with credit card?
(A) Here's my business card.
(B) We offer a 20-percent discount.
(C) I have some cash.

현금으로 지불하시겠어요, 신용카드로 지불하시겠어요?
(A) 여기 제 명함이에요.
(B) 20퍼센트 할인해 드려요.
(C) 현금 있어요.

19 미국 ⇄ 호주

When will the merger be announced?
(A) At the company-wide meeting next week.
(B) With the German automobile manufacturer.
(C) We purchased a new sound system.

합병은 언제 발표되나요?
(A) 다음 주 있을 전사 회의에서요.
(B) 독일 자동차 제조사하고요.
(C) 저희가 음향 장치를 새로 구입했어요.

20 미국 ⇄ 영국

Would you like to take a break now?
(A) I took care of it already.
(B) I repaired the ones that were broken.
(C) Andie wants this done in 30 minutes.

지금 잠시 쉬시겠어요?
(A) 제가 이미 처리했어요.
(B) 고장 난 것들은 제가 수리했어요.
(C) Andie가 30분 안에 끝내고 싶어 해요.

21 호주 ⇄ 미국

Which staff members are going to train the new interns?
(A) Did you finish your evaluation report?
(B) They are welcome to our company.
(C) Nora and Kyle volunteered.

어떤 직원들이 신입 인턴을 교육할 예정인가요?
(A) 평가 보고서 완료했어요?
(B) 우리 회사에서는 환영이에요.
(C) Nora와 Kyle이 자원했어요.

22 미국 ⇄ 미국

What kind of ink cartridge should I order for the photocopier?
(A) We're out of blue ink.
(B) Try the coffee.
(C) The current copier is perfectly fine.

제가 복사기에 어떤 잉크 카트리지를 주문해야 하나요?
(A) 파란색 잉크가 다 떨어졌어요.
(B) 커피 드셔보세요.
(C) 지금 복사기는 완전히 멀쩡해요.

23 미국 ⇄ 호주

This watch face is acrylic, isn't it?
(A) A glass one is available.
(B) That watch is set to Greenwich Standard Time.
(C) Give me a call when you're done.

이 시계판은 아크릴이죠, 그렇죠?
(A) 유리로 된 것도 있어요.
(B) 저 시계는 그리니치 표준시에 맞춰져 있어요.
(C) 마치면 전화 주세요.

24 영국 ⇄ 미국

Haven't you met the new employees?
(A) Yes, at the welcome dinner.
(B) We offer competitive employee benefits.
(C) I don't have any new ideas.

신입사원들을 만나보지 않았나요?
(A) 봤어요, 환영 식사 자리에서요.
(B) 저희는 경쟁력 있는 직원 복지 혜택을 제공해요.
(C) 새로운 아이디어가 없어요.

25 미국 ⇄ 미국

Should I send the package tomorrow morning?
(A) The brown box by the door.
(B) He's not available.
(C) That might be too late.

소포를 내일 아침에 보내야 할까요?
(A) 문 옆에 갈색 상자요.
(B) 그는 시간이 없어요.
(C) 그건 너무 늦을지도 몰라요.

26 미국 ⇄ 영국

This laptop is quite slow.
(A) Why don't you use mine?
(B) I work for a computer company.
(C) Can you slow down?

이 노트북은 꽤 느려요.
(A) 제 거 쓰실래요?
(B) 전 컴퓨터 회사에 근무해요.
(C) 속도 좀 줄여 주시겠어요?

27 미국 ⇄ 미국

You called the cab service, right?
(A) Use the promotional code.
(B) Their line's been busy.
(C) I need a lift to the airport.

택시 회사에 연락했죠, 그렇죠?
(A) 할인 코드를 사용하세요.
(B) 계속 통화 중이에요.
(C) 공항까지 태워 주세요.

28 미국 ⇄ 호주

Why aren't you going to the workshop with Joe and Bonnie?
(A) Because I will be away on holiday.
(B) They work in the shop next door.
(C) No, only for directors.

왜 Joe와 Bonnie와 함께 워크숍에 가지 않으세요?
(A) 제가 휴가 중일 거라서요.
(B) 그들은 옆 건물 상점에서 일해요.
(C) 아니요, 임원만 대상이에요.

29 영국 ⇄ 미국

Why don't you make photocopies of the report so we can go over it?
(A) A decision has been made.
(B) You should go sit over there.
(C) I've already done that.

검토할 수 있게 보고서를 복사하시는 게 어때요?
(A) 결정이 내려졌어요.
(B) 저쪽 가서 앉아 계세요.
(C) 제가 이미 했어요.

30 미국 ⇄ 호주

I'll contact the IT Department about the Internet issue.
(A) They need a written request.
(B) To update the software.
(C) For the wireless Internet connection.

인터넷 문제는 제가 IT 부서에 연락할게요.
(A) 서면 요청서가 필요해요.
(B) 소프트웨어 업데이트하려고요.
(C) 무선 인터넷 연결 때문에요.

31 영국 ⇄ 미국

Do you have time tomorrow afternoon to review the client presentation?
(A) I'm delighted to hear that.
(B) Does Thursday work?
(C) The directors were present.

내일 오후에 고객 프레젠테이션 검토할 시간 있으세요?
(A) 소식 들어서 기뻐요.
(B) 목요일도 괜찮나요?
(C) 임원진이 참석했어요.

PART 3

P. 133

호주 ⇄ 영국

Questions 32-34 refer to the following conversation.

M: Ms. Patel, all the passengers have boarded. We can close the gate doors and prepare for takeoff.(32)

W: How about the baggage? Are they properly stored in the cargo hold?

M: Yes.

W: Great. Please announce to the passengers that we're ready for departure,(33) and make sure they have properly fastened their seatbelts.

M: Sure, I can do that. And then I'll start the safety demonstration.

W: OK. While you take care of that, I'll be in the galley loading the carts for lunch.(34)

32-34번은 다음 대화에 관한 문제입니다.

남: Ms. Patel, 모든 승객이 탑승했어요. 게이트를 닫고 이륙 준비하면 돼요.(32)

여: 수하물은요? 화물칸에 제대로 놓여 있어요?

남: 네.

여: 좋습니다. 출발 준비가 되었다고 승객에게 안내하고,(33) 안전벨트를 제대로 맸는지 반드시 확인해 주세요.

남: 네, 알겠습니다. 그러면 제가 안전 설명을 시작할게요.

여: 알았어요. 당신이 그 일을 하는 동안, 저는 조리실에서 카트에 점심을 싣고 있을게요.(34)

32 대화는 어디서 이뤄지겠는가?
(A) 비행기에서
(B) 버스에서
(C) 열차에서
(D) 연락선에서

33 여자는 남자에게 무슨 작업을 해달라고 요청하는가?
(A) 승객을 도와주라고
(B) 공지를 하라고
(C) 안전 영상을 재생하라고
(D) 화물을 고정하라고

34 여자는 무엇을 할 예정이라고 말하는가?
(A) 탑승권을 확인하기
(B) 가방을 검사하기
(C) 식사를 준비하기
(D) 관제소에 연락하기

미국 ⇄ 미국

Questions 35-37 refer to the following conversation.

W: Thanks for suggesting moving to a screen golf center, James. I need to keep practicing my swing if I'm going to be ready for the tournament next month.(35)

M: Training's difficult in the wind and rain.(35)/(36) And there's going to be a storm for most of the week.

W: That's unfortunate. Do you have any tips for playing when it's raining like this? I'm quite nervous.

M: Well, the most important thing is to stay dry. Always bring the proper rain gear, like a jacket and shoes, if you expect it to rain.(37)

35-37번은 다음 대화에 관한 문제입니다.

여: 스크린 골프장으로 옮기자고 해서 고마워요, James. 다음 달 있을 경기를 준비하려면 스윙 연습을 계속 해야 하거든요.(35)

남: 비바람 속에서는 훈련하기 힘들어요.(35)/(36) 게다가 이번 주 내내 폭풍이 몰아칠 거예요.

여: 아쉽네요. 이렇게 비 올 때 치는 팁이 있나요? 너무 긴장돼요.

남: 음, 가장 중요한 건 젖지 않는 거예요. 비가 올 예정이면, 반드시 재킷이나 신발처럼 적절한 우천용 복장을 챙겨오세요.(37)

35 남자는 누구겠는가?
(A) 비즈니스 컨설턴트
(B) 공장 근로자
(C) 조수
(D) 골프 강사

36 화자들은 왜 다른 장소로 이동하는가?
(A) 다른 직원을 도와주기 위해
(B) 폭풍우 치는 날씨를 피하기 위해
(C) 프로젝트를 마무리하기 위해
(D) 고객을 응대하기 위해

37 남자는 무엇을 하라고 권장하는가?
(A) 적절한 장비를 착용하는 것
(B) 밖에서 뛰는 것
(C) 충분한 단백질을 섭취하는 것
(D) 여분의 가방을 가져가는 것

미국 ⇄ 영국

Questions 38-40 refer to the following conversation.

M: Welcome to the Crestfall Art Museum. I oversee this wing of the museum.(38)

W: Hi, I was interested in joining a guided tour of the Asian sculpture exhibits.(39) Do you know how long it usually takes? I have another appointment later.

M: It should take about two hours. Please be aware that you are not allowed to take photos or record videos of the exhibits.

W: OK. By the way, is there some place I can store my backpack?(40)

M: Yes, you can leave it here at the front desk.

38-40번은 다음 대화에 관한 문제입니다.

남: Crestfall 미술관에 오신 것을 환영합니다. 저는 이 미술관 별관을 관장하고 있습니다.(38)

여: 안녕하세요, 아시아 조각 전시회의 가이드 인솔 프로그램에 참여하고 싶은데요.(39) 보통 얼마나 걸리는지 아시나요? 이따 다른 약속이 있거든요.

남: 두 시간 정도 걸릴 겁니다. 전시물에 대한 사진이나 동영상 촬영은 허용되지 않으니 유의해 주세요.

여: 알겠습니다. 그런데 제 배낭을 보관할 수 있는 곳이 있나요?(40)

남: 네, 여기 안내데스크에 맡기시면 됩니다.

38 남자는 누구겠는가?
(A) 대학교수
(B) 박물관 관리자
(C) 유명 미술가
(D) 회의 주최자

TEST 09

39 대화의 주제는 무엇인가?

(A) 조각 전시회

(B) 교통 상황

(C) 회원 혜택

(D) 사진 제출물

40 여자는 무엇에 관하여 묻는가?

(A) 선물을 구매하는 것

(B) 장비를 대여하는 것

(C) 가방을 보관하는 것

(D) 요금을 납부하는 것

호주 ⇄ 영국

Questions 41-43 refer to the following conversation.

M: Welcome to the Bailey Theater. How may I be of service?

W: Good afternoon. It's our wedding anniversary today, and my husband and I wanted to celebrate it by watching a show here.[41] But it looks like *Take Me Away* is not on today's list of plays.

M: Oh, I'm afraid that play has been canceled for today[42] because the lead actor is not feeling well.

W: Ah, that's a shame. We really wanted to watch that play.[42]

M: I'm so sorry. If you'd like, I could give you a discount on tickets for another play tonight called *Sky Falling*.[43] It's quite popular.

41-43번은 다음 대화에 관한 문제입니다.

남: Bailey 극장에 오신 것을 환영합니다. 어떻게 도와드릴까요?

여: 안녕하세요. 오늘이 저희 결혼기념일이라서, 남편과 제가 여기서 공연을 보면서 축하하고 싶었어요.[41] 그런데 <Take Me Away>가 오늘의 연극 목록에 없는 것 같네요.

남: 아, 안타깝게도 주연 배우의 컨디션이 좋지 않아서 오늘 연극은 취소되었어요.[42]

여: 아, 아쉽네요. 그 연극을 정말 보고 싶었거든요.[42]

남: 정말 죄송합니다. 원하신다면, 오늘 밤에 하는 <Sky Falling>이라는 다른 연극 티켓을 할인해드릴 수 있어요.[43] 아주 인기 있어요.

41 여자는 왜 극장에 있는가?

(A) 배우를 면접하기 위해

(B) 기념일을 축하하기 위해

(C) 일자리에 지원하기 위해

(D) 점검을 실시하기 위해

42 여자는 왜 실망하는가?

(A) 입장료가 인상되었다.

(B) 주차할 곳을 찾을 수 없었다.

(C) 공연이 취소되었다.

(D) 주연 배우가 은퇴했다.

43 남자는 여자에게 무엇을 제공하는가?

(A) 헤드폰

(B) 프로그램 가이드

(C) 명함

(D) 할인 요금

영국 ⇄ 미국 ⇄ 호주

Questions 44-46 refer to the following conversation with three speakers.

W: Welcome to City Hall. Are you from Dea Construction Services?

M1: Yes. We've finished our evaluation of the mold on the building. We think that removing it would result in too much damage to the walls.[44] You may need to repaint them after the removal work.

W: How much would painting over it cost?

M1: Anthony here has the rough estimates.[45]

M2: As you can see, the total includes the cost of materials, labor, and some equipment we will need to rent. This is for your reference.[45]

W: Great. I will pass this over to the council, and we will be in touch. Once I have their approval, I will let you know.[46]

44-46번은 다음 세 화자의 대화에 관한 문제입니다.

여: 시청입니다. Dea 건설 서비스에서 오셨나요?

남1: 네. 저희가 건물의 곰팡이 감정 작업을 마쳤습니다. 저희가 보기엔 제거하면 벽에 손상이 아주 심할 것 같습니다.[44] 제거 작업 후에 다시 칠해야 할 거예요.

여: 덧칠하는 데 비용이 얼마나 들까요?

남1: 여기 Anthony가 견적을 대략 내봤어요.[45]

남2: 보시다시피, 총액에는 자재비, 인건비, 그리고 저희가 대여해야 할 일부 장비 사용료가 포함되어 있어요. 이건 참고용이에요.[45]

여: 좋네요. 제가 이걸 시의회에 전달하고, 연락드릴게요. 승인받으면, 제가 알려드릴게요.[46]

44 화자들은 무엇에 관해 논의하고 있는가?

(A) 벽화 그리기

(B) 장소 비우기

(C) 나무 보존하기

(D) 벽 닦아내기

45 Anthony는 여자에게 무엇을 주는가?

(A) 직원 목록

(B) 비용 견적서

(C) 사업 제안서

(D) 시 허가증

46 여자는 무엇을 해야 한다고 말하는가?

(A) 입찰해야 한다고

(B) 장비를 닦아야 한다고

(C) 예산을 평가해야 한다고

(D) 승인을 받아야 한다고

미국 ⇄ 미국

Questions 47-49 refer to the following conversation.

M: Good morning, Mimi. What is the current status of the grant that we're applying for at the Transportation Bureau?[47]

W: The one that will give us sufficient funds to get new buses?

M: Yes, that's the one. I was hoping to edit a couple of details in the application.[48]

W: Uh, I sent it in right before the final due date.(48)

M: I see. I hope we'll be able to get the approval either way. This would be great for our city. Our buses are too old, and they're not environmentally friendly.

W: I know. Getting enough funds for the electric vehicles will help reduce air pollution in the city as well.(49)

47-49번은 다음 대화에 관한 문제입니다.

남: 좋은 아침이에요, Mimi. 교통국에 신청한 보조금은 현재 상황이 어때요?(47)

여: 신규 버스를 마련할 충분한 자금을 얻는 거요?

남: 네, 그거요. 지원서에 몇 가지 세부내용을 수정할 수 있을까 해서요.(48)

여: 아, 제가 최종 마감일 직전에 제출했어요.(48)

남: 그렇군요. 어쨌든 승인받게 되면 좋겠네요. 우리 시에 아주 좋을 거예요. 우리 버스는 아주 낡은 데다, 환경친화적이지도 않아요.

여: 맞아요. 전기차용 자금을 충분히 받으면 시내 대기 오염을 줄이는 데도 도움이 될 거예요.(49)

47 화자들은 무엇을 신청했는가?
(A) 장학금
(B) 보조금
(C) 대출금
(D) 허가증

48 여자가 "제가 최종 마감일 직전에 제출했어요"라고 말할 때 무엇을 의미하는가?
(A) 연체료가 부과되지 않을 것이다.
(B) 절차가 업데이트되어야 한다.
(C) 동료가 외근 중이다.
(D) 업데이트를 할 수 없다.

49 화자들은 어떤 기술을 사용하기를 바라는가?
(A) 재생 에너지
(B) LED 조명
(C) 전기차
(D) 태양 전지판

영국 ⇄ 호주 ⇄ 미국

Questions 50-52 refer to the following conversation with three speakers.

W1: Welcome to Maxwell Laundry Cleaners.(50) How may I assist you?

M: Hi. I dropped off a suit here yesterday for dry cleaning. I was told that it would be done today by 2 P.M.(51) My name is Roman Park.

W1: OK, give me a moment to see if it's done. Corinna, did you take care of Mr. Park's request?

W2: Yes. Your suit is ready to go, Mr. Park.

M: Thanks for the speedy service!

W2: No problem. I'll grab it for you now.

W1: While she's doing that, I can process your payment. Also, if you have some time, do you mind filling out a comment card?(52) It'll help us improve our services.

M: Sure, I don't mind.(52)

50-52번은 다음 세 화자의 대화에 관한 문제입니다.

여1: Maxwell 세탁소에 오신 것을 환영합니다.(50) 어떻게 도와드릴까요?

남: 안녕하세요. 제가 어제 여기에 정장을 드라이클리닝 맡겼어요. 오늘 오후 2시까지 될 거라고 들었습니다.(51) 제 이름은 Roman Park이에요.

여1: 알겠습니다, 다 됐는지 알아볼 테니 잠깐만 기다려주세요. Corinna, Mr. Park께서 맡기신 것 처리했나요?

여2: 네. 정장 완료됐습니다, Mr. Park.

남: 빠른 서비스 고맙습니다!

여2: 별말씀을요. 지금 가져다드릴게요.

여1: 그녀가 가져다드리는 동안, 결제 도와드리겠습니다. 그리고 시간이 좀 있으시면, 의견 카드를 작성해주실 수 있으신가요?(52) 저희 서비스를 개선하는 데 도움이 될 겁니다.

남: 그럼요, 해드릴게요.(52)

50 여자들은 어디서 근무하는가?
(A) 정장 의류 소매점에서
(B) 직물 공장에서
(C) 패션 잡지 출판사에서
(D) 세탁 업체에서

51 남자는 왜 사업체를 방문하고 있는가?
(A) 계약서에 서명하기 위해
(B) 환불을 받기 위해
(C) 일자리에 지원하기 위해
(D) 물건을 찾기 위해

52 남자는 무엇을 하는 데 동의하는가?
(A) 다음에 다시 온다고
(B) 의견을 제공한다고
(C) 특별 방문을 한다고
(D) 현금으로 지불한다고

영국 ⇄ 호주

Questions 53-55 refer to the following conversation.

W: This is the event planning team. Allison Radnor speaking. How may I help you?

M: Hi, Allison. It's Josh Thornton. Thank you for inviting my jazz trio to perform at the music festival you are organizing.(53)

W: Hello, Josh. I'm looking forward to hearing your trio play. Did you have the chance to read through the contract we sent you?

M: I did. But I didn't find any clause about getting reimbursed for our travel expenses.(54)

W: Well, the music festival is a charity event to raise funds for a children's hospital. Other musicians are paying out of their own pockets, but you are the only group from out of state. I'll ask my supervisor and see what we can do for you.(55) Maybe we'll be able to make an exception.

53-55번은 다음 대화에 관한 문제입니다.

여: 이벤트 기획팀입니다. Allison Radnor입니다. 무엇을 도와드릴까요?

남: 안녕하세요, Allison. 저는 Josh Thornton입니다. 주최하시는 음악 축제에 저희 재즈 트리오를 초대해 주셔서 감사합니다.(53)

여: 안녕하세요, Josh. 당신의 트리오 공연을 기대하고 있어요. 저희가 보내드린 계약서는 읽어 보셨어요?

남: 네. 그런데 **저희 출장비 환급에 관한 조항이 안 보입니다.**(54)

여: 음, 음악제가 어린이 병원 기금을 마련하는 자선 행사예요. 다른 음악가는 자비로 지불하고 계시긴 한데, 유일하게 다른 주에서 참여하는 그룹이시네요. **제가 관리자께 여쭤봐서 저희가 해드릴 수 있는 부분을 알아볼게요.**(55) 아마도 예외로 적용해드릴 수 있을 것 같습니다.

53 남자는 누구겠는가?
(A) 여행사 직원
(B) 기자
(C) 연주자
(D) 행사 음식 공급자

54 남자는 어떤 문제를 언급하는가?
(A) 특정 비용이 포함되지 않는다.
(B) 일부 서류가 배송되지 않았다.
(C) 항공편이 취소되었다.
(D) 행사가 연기되었다.

55 여자는 다음에 무엇을 하겠는가?
(A) 추가 직원을 면접할 것이다
(B) 관리자와 의논할 것이다
(C) 호텔 방을 예약할 것이다
(D) 청구서를 재발행할 것이다

미국 ⇄ 미국

Questions 56-58 refer to the following conversation.

W: Glad I ran into you, Gerald. As you know, **we did a pretty good job with Haxwell Apparel's ad campaign.**(56) And apparently, they recommended us to other businesses.

M: That's wonderful! More people have been showing interest in our services recently. We just secured four new contracts last week.

W: With our company growing so rapidly, **we need to look into working with a corporate lawyer who can advise us on legal matters.**(57)

M: Well, I've read good things about Millerson & Associates. **Why don't I arrange a meeting with them?**(58) Does Friday work for you?

56-58번은 다음 대화에 관한 문제입니다.

여: 마침 잘 만났네요, Gerald. 아시다시피, **우리가 Haxwell 의류 광고 캠페인을 아주 잘 해냈어요.**(56) 그리고 듣자 하니, 그들이 다른 기업들에 우리를 추천해줬다고 해요.

남: 정말 잘됐네요! 최근에 더 많은 사람들이 우리가 제공하는 서비스에 관심을 보이고 있어요. 지난주에 신규 계약을 4건이나 땄어요.

여: 우리 회사가 빠르게 성장하고 있으니, **법적인 문제를 상담해줄 수 있는 법인 고문 변호사와 함께 일하는 것을 알아봐야 해요.**(57)

남: 음, 제가 Millerson & Associates에 대한 좋은 평가를 읽었어요. **제가 그들과 회의 자리를 마련해 볼까요?**(58) 금요일 괜찮으세요?

56 화자들은 어디에서 일하겠는가?
(A) 마케팅 회사에서
(B) 의류 소매점에서
(C) 법률사무소에서
(D) 제작사에서

57 여자는 무엇을 제안하는가?
(A) 더 큰 장소로 이전하는 것
(B) 세미나를 신청하는 것
(C) 변호사와 상담하는 것
(D) 추가 근무를 하는 것

58 남자는 무엇을 하겠다고 제안하는가?
(A) 납입금을 처리하겠다고
(B) 회의 일정을 잡겠다고
(C) 고객을 데리러 가겠다고
(D) 입사 지원서를 검토하겠다고

호주 ⇄ 미국

Questions 59-61 refer to the following conversation.

M: Hey, Liz. I see that we've received a new shipment of produce. Did you begin entering the data into the supermarket's database yet?(59)

W: I was just about to. **Are you free right now? If I do this alone, it'll take me the whole day.**(60)

M: I came at the right time, then.(60) Oh, these are the items that we purchased for our store's new organic produce section.(61)

W: Yeah, I'm looking forward to this new addition.(61) A lot of customers have been interested in healthier products lately. Anyway, let's get started.

M: OK. Why don't we unpack the shipment and take out the boxes first?

59-61번은 다음 대화에 관한 문제입니다.

남: 저기, Liz. 보니까 새로운 농산물 배송품을 받았네요. 슈퍼마켓 데이터베이스에 데이터 입력을 시작했나요?(59)

여: 막 하려던 참이었어요. 지금 시간 있으세요? 제가 이걸 혼자 하려면, 하루 종일 걸릴 거예요.(60)

남: 그렇다면 제가 제때 왔네요.(60) 아, 이것들은 우리 매장의 새로운 유기농 농산물 코너용으로 구입한 제품들이네요.(61)

여: 네, 저는 이 새로 추가되는 코너가 기대돼요.(61) 최근에 많은 고객들이 건강에 더 좋은 제품들에 관심이 있으셨거든요. 어쨌든, 시작합시다.

남: 좋아요. 배송품을 풀어서 상자 먼저 꺼내는 게 어떨까요?

59 대화는 어디에서 이루어지고 있는가?
(A) 제과점에서
(B) 식당에서
(C) 농장에서
(D) 슈퍼마켓에서

60 남자가 "그렇다면 제가 제때 왔네요"라고 말할 때 무엇을 내비치는가?
(A) 그는 행사에 제시간에 도착할 수 있었다.
(B) 그는 어떤 제품을 맛보고 싶어 한다.
(C) 그는 여자를 도와줄 시간이 있다.
(D) 그는 프로젝트 마감 기한을 맞출 수 있었다.

61 여자는 무엇을 고대하고 있는가?
(A) 수정된 포장 절차
(B) 더 많은 직원 채용
(C) 시즌 할인 행사
(D) 농산물 코너의 추가

미국 ⇄ 미국

Questions 62-64 refer to the following conversation and catalog page.

W: Hi. I'm looking through the furniture catalog on your website. I'm looking to order ten coffee tables for my new coffee shop. The shop will be opening in August,(62) and I need the tables to arrive before then.

M: That will work. We can guarantee your order will arrive within seven business days. Which style would you like?

W: I want the round table with a single leg.(63) Do you need me to read you the product number?

M: That won't be necessary. You're in luck. We're having a special promotion. **For every five tables you buy, you can get a complimentary one.**(64) If you'd like, we can send you the two extra tables with your order.

62-64번은 다음 대화와 카탈로그 페이지에 관한 문제입니다.

여: 안녕하세요. 제가 귀사 웹사이트에서 가구 카탈로그를 살펴보는 중인데요. 제 새 커피숍에 놓을 커피 테이블 10개를 주문하려고요. 가게는 8월에 문을 열 예정이고,(62) 테이블이 그 전에 도착해야 해요.

남: 가능합니다. 주문품은 영업일 7일 이내 도착하는 걸 보증해 드려요. 어떤 스타일로 원하세요?

여: 다리 하나짜리 원형 테이블을 원해요.(63) 제가 제품 번호를 읽어드릴까요?

남: 안 그러셔도 됩니다. 운이 좋으시네요. 저희가 특별 프로모션을 진행하고 있어요. 구입하시는 테이블 다섯 개당 한 개를 무료로 받으실 수 있어요.(64) 원하시면, 주문품과 함께 테이블을 두 개 더 보내드릴게요.

#1121 직사각형 철제 다리	**#1124** 원형 다리 3개
#1127 직사각형 교차 다리	**#1129** 원형 바 테이블(63)

62 여자에 따르면, 8월에 무슨 일이 일어나는가?
(A) 사무실을 개조할 것이다.
(B) 회식을 준비할 것이다.
(C) 다른 도시로 이사할 것이다.
(D) 새로운 사업체를 시작할 것이다.

63 시각 자료를 보시오. 여자는 어떤 제품을 주문할 것인가?
(A) #1121
(B) #1124
(C) #1127
(D) #1129

64 남자는 여자에게 어떤 제공에 대해 말하는가?
(A) 제품이 빠른 배송으로 발송될 수 있다.
(B) 구매에 경품이 포함된다.
(C) 제품 보증이 연장될 수 있다.
(D) 할부로 결제될 수 있다.

호주 ⇄ 미국

Questions 65-67 refer to the following conversation and trail information.

M: It feels great to finally get out for some fresh air. We really needed this nice, relaxing break after all the work we've done this week.

W: You're right. We've been working overtime this entire week. **I was surprised at all the financial documents we needed to review for our client's merger and acquisition.**(65)

M: Yeah, it's been a stressful week. We should probably check the time, though. **I have to get back in time for a meeting with our client at 2.**(66)

W: That shouldn't be a problem. **We're on the shortest trail anyway.**(67) You'll get back to the office with plenty of time to spare.

65-67번은 다음 대화와 산책로 정보에 관한 문제입니다.

남: 드디어 신선한 공기를 쐬러 나오니 너무 좋네요. 이번 주에 업무에 시달렸더니 이런 쾌적하고 느긋한 휴식이 정말 간절했어요.

여: 맞아요. 이번 주 내내 야근했잖아요. 저는 고객 인수합병에 검토해야 할 전체 금융 서류를 보고 깜짝 놀랐어요.(65)

남: 맞아요, 스트레스받는 일주일이었어요. 근데 우리 시간을 확인해야 해요. 저는 2시 고객 회의에 늦지 않게 복귀해야 해요.(66)

여: 문제없어요. 우린 가장 짧은 산책로에 있거든요.(67) 아주 여유롭게 사무실에 복귀하게 될 거예요.

산책로 명	산책로 길이
Housatonic 산책로	10마일
Naugatuck 산책로	4마일
Pistapaug 산책로	**2.5마일(67)**
Pattaconk 산책로	5마일

65 화자들은 어디서 일하겠는가?
(A) 부동산에서
(B) 정부 기관에서
(C) 회계사무소에서
(D) 홍보대행사에서

66 남자는 왜 걱정하는가?
(A) 행사에 일찍 도착하고 싶어한다.
(B) 급한 이메일에 답변해줘야 한다.
(C) 문서를 마무리하지 못했다.
(D) 매니저에게 잘못된 정보를 줬을지도 모른다.

67 시각 자료를 보시오. 화자들은 어느 산책로를 걷고 있는가?
(A) Housatonic 산책로
(B) Naugatuck 산책로
(C) Pistapaug 산책로
(D) Pattaconk 산책로

TEST 09

Questions 68-70 refer to the following conversation and bar graph.

W: Hey Mark, I wanted to talk about how solar panel sales have been going for the past few months.**(68)** Are we reaching more consumers?

M: Yes, much more than expected. A lot of interest has risen since coal and gas prices have gone up. People are more willing to invest in something they know will save money in the long run. One month, we even sold 800 panels.**(69)**

W: That's great. We should discuss our plans for the next quarter. How can we maintain this growth?

M: Well, a drop in sales could be expected in colder months. But I think if we make a TV commercial, we could reach more potential buyers.**(70)**

68-70번은 다음 대화와 막대그래프에 관한 문제입니다.

여: Mark, 안녕하세요. 지난 몇 달간 태양열 전지판 판매량 추이가 어땠는지 얘기 나누고 싶었어요.**(68)** 소비자가 더 늘고 있나요?

남: 네, 예상보다 훨씬 많아요. 석탄 및 가솔린 가격이 오르면서 관심이 아주 많아졌어요. 사람들이 장기적으로 보면 돈을 절약하게 될 걸 아는 것에 더 투자하려고 하고 있어요. 심지어 어떤 달에는 전지판을 800개 팔았어요.**(69)**

여: 잘됐네요. 저희는 다음 분기 계획에 대해 논의해야 해요. 이 성장세를 어떻게 유지할 수 있을까요?

남: 글쎄요, 추운 달에는 판매량 감소를 예상할 수 있어요. 그런데 제 생각에 저희가 TV 광고를 만들면, 더 많은 잠재 구매자들에게 다가갈 수 있을 것 같아요.**(70)**

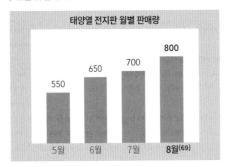

68 대화의 목적은 무엇인가?
(A) 제품 판매량에 대해 논의하기 위해
(B) 새로운 안전 규칙을 검토하기 위해
(C) 문제를 강조하기 위해
(D) 예산안을 제시하기 위해

69 시각 자료를 보시오. 남자는 어느 달을 언급하는가?
(A) 5월
(B) 6월
(C) 7월
(D) 8월

70 남자는 무엇을 하는 것을 제안하는가?
(A) 텔레비전에서 광고하는 것
(B) 컨설턴트를 고용하는 것
(C) 예산을 축소하는 것
(D) 방문 판매를 하는 것

PART 4

호주

Questions 71-73 refer to the following tour information.

M: Welcome to Ranger Views Village. This village is known for its iconic pottery that has been part of its history dating back centuries. While taking photographs is allowed, touching anything is strictly prohibited.**(71)** Our artists work hard on their pieces, so we try to respect their hard work. You may have actually heard about the artists who reside here. They were featured in a documentary that aired last month on television.**(72)** They've also started hosting pottery classes on weekends. If you're interested, I have some flyers.**(73)**

71-73번은 다음 여행 정보에 관한 문제입니다.

남: Ranger Views 마을에 오신 것을 환영합니다. 이 마을은 수 세기 전부터 역사의 한 켠을 차지해온 상징적인 도자기로 유명합니다. 사진 촬영은 허용되지만, 만지는 행위는 엄격히 금지됩니다.**(71)** 저희 예술가들이 작품을 만드는 데 헌신하기에, 그분들의 노고를 존중해 주세요. 이곳에 사는 예술가에 대해 들어보셨을 겁니다. 지난달 텔레비전에 방송된 다큐멘터리에 특별 출연했습니다.**(72)** 게다가 주말에는 도자기 수업 진행도 시작했습니다. 관심 있으시면, 저에게 광고지가 있습니다.**(73)**

71 화자는 투어에서 무엇이 금지되어 있다고 말하는가?
(A) 뛰어다니는 것
(B) 사진을 찍는 것
(C) 큰 소리로 말하는 것
(D) 도자기를 만지는 것

72 화자는 지난달에 무슨 일이 있었다고 말하는가?
(A) 한 지역단체에서 행사에 자원했다.
(B) 몇몇 예술가들이 다큐멘터리에 출연했다.
(C) 예술 작품이 거액에 판매되었다.
(D) 몇몇 신규 시설이 대중에 공개되었다.

73 화자는 청자들에게 주말에 무엇을 할 수 있다고 말하는가?
(A) 새로운 투어에 합류할 수 있다고
(B) 예술가들과 소통할 수 있다고
(C) 선물을 구입할 수 있다고
(D) 몇몇 수업에 참석할 수 있다고

미국

Questions 74-76 refer to the following telephone message.

M: Hi, it's Victor O'Brien at Riptide Publishing. I appreciate you sending over the cover design of Mr. Wong's novel.**(74)** My manager, Ms. Yoon, was impressed with how quick you were. She has looked over the details and really liked the font and colors you have chosen. However, she is worried about the total cost you quoted for creating all of the illustrations.**(75)** Do you mind emailing me a detailed pricing chart? Ms. Yoon needs to review it by the end of the day.**(76)** Let me know if you have any other inquiries.

74-76번은 다음 전화 메시지에 관한 문제입니다.

남: 안녕하세요, Riptide 출판사의 Victor O'Brien입니다. Mr. Wong의 소설 표지 디자인을 보내주셔서 감사합니다.**(74)** 빨리해 주셔서 저희 Ms. Yoon 부장님이 감탄하셨어요. 세부 사항들을 살펴보

시고선 골라 주신 서체와 색상을 정말 마음에 들어 하셨어요. 그런데 뽑아 주신 전체 삽화 견적에 대해서는 염려하고 계십니다.**(75)** 상세 가격표를 이메일로 보내주시겠어요? Ms. Yoon이 오늘까지 검토하셔야 하거든요.**(76)** 다른 문의 사항 있으시면 연락주세요.

74 청자는 어디에서 일하겠는가?
(A) 소프트웨어 개발업체에서
(B) 서점에서
(C) 출판사에서
(D) 그래픽 디자인 대행사에서

75 화자의 상사는 무엇에 대하여 염려하는가?
(A) 출간 마감일
(B) 배송 날짜
(C) 현지 법규
(D) 가격 견적

76 화자가 "Ms. Yoon이 오늘까지 검토하셔야 하거든요"라고 말할 때 무엇을 내비치는가?
(A) 문서에 몇 가지 오류가 있다.
(B) 상사가 휴가를 갈 것이다.
(C) 혼자서는 업무를 완료할 수 없다.
(D) 요청 사항이 빨리 처리되어야 한다.

미국

Questions 77-79 refer to the following excerpt from a meeting.

W: Today is a new chapter for ShopSharp as we introduce our very own customer rewards program.**(77)** I'm very excited about this as it will finally give us a way to reward our loyal customers with great gifts. I always envisioned ShopSharp being a place where busy workers can pick up whatever supplies they need for the office in an instant.**(78)** With this new program in place, I want to focus on building on that vision. Our customers have now come to expect the lowest prices from us, and I'm glad to have developed that good reputation.**(79)** Let's see what we can do to keep building on that.

77-79번은 다음 회의 발췌록에 관한 문제입니다.

여: 오늘은 저희가 자체 고객 보상 프로그램을 도입하면서 ShopSharp의 새로운 장이 열리는 날입니다.**(77)** 이제야 단골 고객에게 훌륭한 선물로 보답하는 방법을 갖게 되어 저는 아주 기쁩니다. 저는 ShopSharp이 바쁜 직장인이 사무실에 필요한 어떤 물품이든 재빨리 사 갈 수 있는 곳이 되길 꿈꿔왔습니다.**(78)** 이 새로운 프로그램의 시행으로 저는 그 비전을 키워가는 데 주력하고 싶습니다. 이제 고객은 저희에게 최저가를 기대하게 되었고, 저는 그러한 좋은 평판을 키워온 것에 기쁘게 생각합니다.**(79)** 계속해서 그 기대를 구축할 방법이 뭐가 있을지 알아봅시다.

77 화자는 오늘 무슨 일이 있을 거라고 말하는가?
(A) 시즌 할인판매가 시작된다.
(B) 신제품이 도착한다.
(C) 보상 프로그램이 시작된다.
(D) 새 매니저가 일을 시작한다.

78 사업체에서는 어떤 제품군을 판매하는가?
(A) 사무용품
(B) 실내용 가구
(C) 운동기구
(D) 전자제품

79 사업체의 평판이 좋은 이유는 무엇인가?
(A) 위치
(B) 노련한 직원
(C) 제품 종류
(D) 낮은 가격

호주

Questions 80-82 refer to the following announcement.

M: Attention Mythic Theatre attendees. **We are offering half-price tickets for the seven o'clock showing of the new movie,** *Channel on the Mountain.***(80)/(81)** This is part of our campaign to promote locally made movies. If you have already purchased a ticket, we will provide you with free snacks. **We will be offering the same for the 1 P.M. showing tomorrow.(81)** Support our local movie industry by bringing your family and friends. Additionally, we have officially launched our online ticketing service. **If you purchase your ticket online, we can offer some additional goodies such as a poster.(82)** Thank you for choosing Mythic Theatre.

80-82번은 다음 안내에 관한 문제입니다.

남: Mythic 극장에 계신 분들께 알려드립니다. 새 영화 <Channel on the Mountain> 7시 상영 티켓을 절반 가격에 제공해 드리고 있습니다.**(80)/(81)** 이는 현지 제작 영화를 홍보하는 저희 캠페인의 일환입니다. 티켓을 이미 구입하신 경우, 무료 스낵을 제공해 드립니다. 내일 오후 1시 상영에 대해서도 동일하게 제공해 드릴 예정입니다.**(81)** 가족과 친구를 데려오셔서 저희 지역 영화 산업을 지원해 주세요. 또한, 저희는 온라인 티켓팅 서비스를 정식으로 시작했습니다. 티켓을 온라인으로 구입하시면, 포스터 같은 추가 물품을 제공해 드립니다.**(82)** Mythic 극장을 선택해 주셔서 감사합니다.

80 안내의 주요 목적은 무엇인가?
(A) 상영에 대한 최신 정보를 알려주기 위해
(B) 매점의 새로운 제품을 광고하기 위해
(C) 관객에게 일반 에티켓을 상기시켜주기 위해
(D) 신규 제한사항을 소개하기 위해

81 화자는 내일 오후 1시 영화에 관하여 뭐라고 말하는가?
(A) 당일에 취소될 수 있다.
(B) 첫 상영이 될 것이다.
(C) 감독이 참석할 것이다.
(D) 가격이 인하될 것이다.

82 청자들은 티켓을 온라인으로 구입하면 무엇을 받을 것인가?
(A) 사운드트랙
(B) 무료 음료
(C) 경품권
(D) 영화 관련 기념품

미국

Questions 83-85 refer to the following telephone message.

M: Hi, Erica. This is Daniel. **I just got off the phone with a client who's using the payroll program that our IT Department is in charge of.**(83) It looks like there are a few issues regarding the way overtime is being calculated. **Tony referred me to you since you have extensive experience with this kind of application and would probably know how to deal with this problem.**(84) This needs to get fixed by next week, and... Most of my teammates are at a seminar until Friday.(85) Let's talk when you have a moment. Thanks in advance!

83-85번은 다음 전화 메시지에 관한 문제입니다.

남: 안녕하세요, Erica. Daniel이에요. **방금 우리 IT 부서가 담당하는 급여 관리 프로그램을 사용하고 있는 고객과 통화했는데요.**(83) 초과 근무가 계산되는 방식에 관여해서 몇 가지 문제가 있는 것 같아요. **Tony가 당신이 이런 종류의 응용 프로그램에 대한 경험이 풍부하고 이런 문제를 처리하는 방법을 아마 알 거라고 당신과 얘기해보라고 하더군요.**(84) 이게 다음 주까지는 해결되어야 하거든요, 그런데... 우리 팀원들 대부분이 금요일까지 세미나에 참석해요.(85) 당신이 시간 있을 때 이야기 나눠요. 미리 고마워요!

83 화자의 부서는 무슨 작업을 맡고 있는가?
(A) 고객 설문조사 응답
(B) 고객 서비스 절차
(C) 신규 휴대전화
(D) 컴퓨터 소프트웨어

84 Tony는 왜 청자를 추천했는가?
(A) 그녀에게 기술 지식이 있다.
(B) 그녀가 전에 회사와 일해본 적이 있다.
(C) 그녀가 교육 워크숍을 맡을 수 있다.
(D) 그녀가 외부 업체를 추천할 수 있다.

85 화자는 왜 "우리 팀원들 대부분이 금요일까지 세미나에 참석해요"라고 말하는가?
(A) 행사를 연기해달라고 요청하기 위해
(B) 도움을 요청하는 이유를 설명하기 위해
(C) 마감 기한 연장을 제안하기 위해
(D) 물품을 더 주문하기 위해

호주

Questions 86-88 refer to the following broadcast.

M: Thanks for tuning into Stranger Stories, a radio program about everything strange and unusual in our world. **Today we'll discuss the strawberry which, believe it or not, is not a berry.**(86) Why is this the case? **Leave that for Jodi Ray, a botanist who specializes in fruit.**(86) She will be discussing the history of strawberries and why they're not berries. **She'll also be letting us know the benefits of adding more strawberries to our diets.**(87) But before we get to that, let's discuss the answer to last week's riddle. If you think you know the answer, call us on 555-7399 and let us know.(88)

86-88번은 다음 방송에 관한 문제입니다.

남: 이 세상에 있는 이상하고 특이한 모든 것을 다루는 라디오 프로그램 Stranger Stories를 청취해주셔서 감사합니다. 오늘은 믿기지 않으시겠지만 베리가 아닌 딸기에 대해 이야기를 나눌 예정입니다.(86) 왜 그럴까요? 과일 전문 식물학자 Jodi Ray께 맡겨주세요.(86) 그녀는 딸기의 역사와 왜 딸기가 베리에 속하지 않는지 이야기를 들려주실 겁니다. 또한 우리의 식단에 딸기를 늘리는 것의 이점을 알려주실 겁니다.(87) 하지만 모시기 전에, 지난주 수수께끼 정답에 대한 이야기부터 나눠봅시다. 정답을 안다고 생각하시는 분은 555-7399번으로 전화 주셔서 알려주세요.(88)

86 라디오 프로그램에서는 어떤 종류의 음식에 집중하는가?
(A) 고기
(B) 과일
(C) 야채
(D) 견과

87 Jodi Ray는 음식의 어떤 면에 관해 이야기할 것인가?
(A) 계절성
(B) 건강상 이점
(C) 다양한 용도
(D) 가용성

88 청자들은 왜 방송국으로 전화해야 하는가?
(A) 상품을 타기 위해
(B) 게스트와 이야기하기 위해
(C) 제안하기 위해
(D) 질문에 답하기 위해

영국

Questions 89-91 refer to the following talk.

W: Hello, and welcome to Tung Hing Chinese Buffet. Before you're seated, **let me tell you about our buffet layout. Along the wall over here is where the appetizers are. The main dishes are on the middle tables there, and desserts and beverages are on the right side by the window.**(89) And **to celebrate the opening of our restaurant, we're offering special lobster and steak dishes this weekend!**(90) You'll find those on the middle tables. Umm... By the way, **I think a private room might be more comfortable for your group as there are quite a few of you. Let me quickly check to see if there is an unoccupied one.**(91)

89-91번은 다음 담화에 관한 문제입니다.

여: 안녕하세요, Tung Hing 중식 뷔페에 오신 것을 환영합니다. 자리로 안내해 드리기 전에 뷔페 배치에 대해 말씀드리겠습니다. 애피타이저는 이쪽 벽을 따라 있습니다. 주요리들은 저쪽 중앙 테이블에 있으며, 디저트와 음료는 오른쪽 창가에 있습니다.(89) 그리고 저희 식당 개업 기념으로, 이번 주말에는 특별 랍스터와 스테이크 요리를 제공하고 있습니다!(90) 중앙 테이블에서 찾아보실 수 있습니다. 음... 그런데, 제 생각엔 일행이 꽤 많으셔서 개인 방이 더 편리하실 것 같습니다. 빈방이 있는지 얼른 확인해 보겠습니다.(91)

89 담화의 주제는 무엇인가?
(A) 요리 재료
(B) 메뉴 변경
(C) 식당 개조
(D) 음식 위치

90 어떤 특별 행사가 열리고 있겠는가?
    (A) 환영회
    (B) 시상식 만찬
    (C) 개업
    (D) 은퇴 파티

91 화자는 무엇을 확인할 것인가?
    (A) 테이블의 크기
    (B) 예약의 세부 사항
    (C) 방의 이용 가능 여부
    (D) 제품의 가격

미국

Questions 92-94 refer to the following broadcast.

W: Thanks for tuning in to the local evening news. Tonight, we're going to take a look at Kensington's new subway line,(92) which was constructed in just under one year. Having lived in this town for over 30 years, I know that this kind of thing takes a lot of time.(93) Quite a few people are already using the new line, and the reviews have been very positive. With me tonight is Mr. Rodney Rames, Kensington's Transportation Director. He will go over some helpful tips on how you can use this line to travel efficiently throughout the town.(94)

92-94번은 다음 방송에 관한 문제입니다.

여: 저녁 지역 뉴스를 청취해 주셔서 감사드립니다. 오늘은 Kensington의 지하철 신규 노선에 대해 알아보겠습니다.(92) 짓는 데 일 년도 안 걸렸는데요. 저는 이 도시에서 30년 넘게 살면서 이런 일은 긴 시간이 걸린다고 알고 있습니다.(93) 이미 꽤 많은 사람들이 새 노선을 이용하고 있으며 평가도 매우 긍정적입니다. 오늘 제 옆에는 Kensington 교통국장이신 Mr. Rodney Rames가 나와 계십니다. 이 노선을 이용하여 도시 이곳저곳을 효율적으로 이동하는 방법에 관한 몇 가지 유용한 팁을 알려주실 겁니다.(94)

92 프로그램의 주제는 무엇인가?
    (A) 시내 퍼레이드
    (B) 도로공사 프로젝트
    (C) 대중교통 서비스
    (D) 취업 기회

93 그녀는 "이런 일은 긴 시간이 걸립니다"라고 말할 때 무엇을 의미하는가?
    (A) 마감 기한을 지키기 어렵다.
    (B) 프로젝트의 결과가 인상적이다.
    (C) 예산이 증액되어야 한다.
    (D) 업무를 위해 자원봉사자들이 더 필요하다.

94 화자에 따르면, Mr. Rames는 무엇을 할 것인가?
    (A) 후기를 읽을 것이다
    (B) 주민을 인터뷰할 것이다
    (C) 책임자를 소개할 것이다
    (D) 조언을 해줄 것이다

미국

Questions 95-97 refer to the following talk and map.

M: I'd like to welcome everybody to the opening of Kokhanok's Community Garden. We would first like to extend our deepest gratitude to DMG Partners for their part in helping us raise the necessary funds.(95) This garden would not have been possible without their support. Currently, there are only empty plots around us. Today, we're going to put in some vegetables, set up a strawberry patch, and also put in our lemon tree in the middle. We also have some flowers that would look great right next to the entrance.(96) Before we get started, why don't we spend a few minutes exploring the garden?(97) Then we'll start putting in the soil.

95-97번은 다음 담화와 지도에 관한 문제입니다.

남: Kokhanok의 커뮤니티 정원의 개장에 오신 모든 분을 환영합니다. 우선 저희가 필요 자금을 모으는 데 도움을 주신 DMG Partners에 깊은 감사를 표하고 싶습니다.(95) 그들의 지원이 없었더라면 이 정원은 가능하지 않았을 겁니다. 현재, 저희 주변으로만 빈 구역이 있습니다. 오늘은 몇 가지 채소를 심고, 딸기밭을 만들고, 중앙에는 레몬 나무를 심을 예정입니다. 입구 바로 옆에서 아주 멋져 보일 꽃도 가지고 있습니다.(96) 시작하기 전에 잠시 정원을 둘러보는 건 어떠세요?(97) 그런 다음 흙 넣는 작업을 시작하겠습니다.

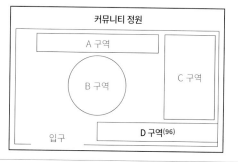

95 화자는 DMG Partners에 무엇을 감사하는가?
    (A) 자금을 제공한 것
    (B) 행사를 촬영한 것
    (C) 안내 책자를 제작한 것
    (D) 정원을 설계한 것

96 시각 자료를 보시오. 화자에 따르면, 꽃은 어디에서 자랄 것인가?
    (A) 정원 A 구역에서
    (B) 정원 B 구역에서
    (C) 정원 C 구역에서
    (D) 정원 D 구역에서

97 다음에 무슨 일이 일어날 것인가?
    (A) 몇몇 나무가 심어질 것이다.
    (B) 도구가 배분될 것이다.
    (C) 청자들이 정원을 구경할 것이다.
    (D) 시 공무원이 연설을 할 것이다.

Questions 98-100 refer to the following excerpt from a conference and diagram.

W: So far, we've discussed identifying your target market, researching the competition, and determining the prices of your services and products. As you know, finding success in any industry is difficult, so **as new entrepreneurs in the tourism sector,**(98) you must find ways to differentiate and make your business stand out. Before we move on to discuss launching your business, there is an important stage that we need to cover. **We have a guest speaker today, a renowned Web designer, who will talk about building your website and the essential elements it should contain.**(99) Before we invite our guest speaker to the stage, I'd like to remind everyone that **there is a site builder program that you can try out in the computer lab on the first floor, so please check it out at the end of the conference.**(100)

98-100번은 다음 회의 발췌록과 도표에 관한 문제입니다.

여: 지금까지 우리는 목표 시장 확인하기, 경쟁업체 조사하기, 그리고 서비스와 제품의 가격 결정하기에 대해 논했습니다. 아시다시피, 어떤 업계에서든 성공하기란 어렵습니다, 따라서 **관광업 분야의 새내기 사업자로서,**(98) 여러분은 자신의 사업체를 차별화하고 눈에 띄게 할 방법을 찾아내야 합니다. 이어서 사업체 설립을 논하기 전에 다루어야 할 중요한 단계가 하나 있습니다. **오늘 웹사이트 제작 및 필수 포함 요소에 대해 알려주실 유명 웹 디자이너를 연사로 모셨습니다.**(99) 연사분을 무대로 모시기 전에 다시 한 번 알려드리면, **1층 컴퓨터실에 사용해보실 수 있는 사이트 제작 프로그램이 있으니 학회가 끝나면 가서 확인해 보시기 바랍니다.**(100)

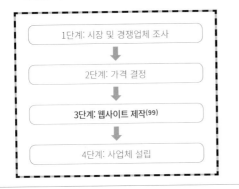

98 청자들은 어떤 업계에 일하는가?
  (A) 정보 기술
  (B) 식품 산업
  (C) 건강 관리
  (D) 관광업

99 시각 자료를 보시오. 연사는 어느 단계에 관해 논할 것인가?
  (A) 1단계
  (B) 2단계
  (C) 3단계
  (D) 4단계

100 화자에 따르면, 청자들은 1층에서 무엇을 할 수 있는가?
  (A) 다른 세미나에 참석할 수 있다
  (B) 우려를 표할 수 있다
  (C) 컴퓨터 프로그램을 이용할 수 있다
  (D) 지도를 확인할 수 있다

TEST 10

PART 1
P. 142

1 (B) 2 (C) 3 (A) 4 (B) 5 (C) 6 (A)

PART 2
P. 146

7 (A)   8 (A)   9 (B)   10 (A) 11 (A) 12 (B)
13 (C) 14 (A) 15 (A) 16 (B) 17 (A) 18 (B)
19 (B) 20 (A) 21 (C) 22 (B) 23 (A) 24 (B)
25 (A) 26 (C) 27 (B) 28 (A) 29 (A) 30 (B)
31 (A)

PART 3
P. 147

32 (A) 33 (C) 34 (C) 35 (C) 36 (D) 37 (B)
38 (D) 39 (A) 40 (B) 41 (B) 42 (D) 43 (A)
44 (C) 45 (C) 46 (B) 47 (D) 48 (C) 49 (A)
50 (D) 51 (B) 52 (A) 53 (C) 54 (D) 55 (D)
56 (D) 57 (A) 58 (C) 59 (A) 60 (A) 61 (C)
62 (D) 63 (B) 64 (B) 65 (B) 66 (B) 67 (A)
68 (C) 69 (B) 70 (B)

PART 4
P. 151

71 (D) 72 (B) 73 (A) 74 (A) 75 (D) 76 (C)
77 (A) 78 (D) 79 (C) 80 (B) 81 (D) 82 (C)
83 (A) 84 (D) 85 (D) 86 (D) 87 (C) 88 (A)
89 (B) 90 (B) 91 (A) 92 (C) 93 (C) 94 (A)
95 (A) 96 (B) 97 (D) 98 (D) 99 (C) 100 (A)

PART 1
P. 142

1 미국
(A) She's lifting the hood of a car.
(B) She's opening a toolbox.
(C) She's replacing a car engine.
(D) She's inspecting a vehicle.

(A) 여자가 자동차 덮개를 들어 올리고 있다.
(B) 여자가 공구함을 열고 있다.
(C) 여자가 자동차 엔진을 교체하고 있다.
(D) 여자가 자동차를 점검하고 있다.

2 영국
(A) He's raking some leaves.
(B) He's watering some plants.
(C) He's picking up some wood.
(D) He's cutting some tree branches.

(A) 남자가 갈퀴로 나뭇잎들을 긁어모으고 있다.
(B) 남자가 화초에 물을 주고 있다.
(C) 남자가 나무를 집어 들고 있다.
(D) 남자가 나뭇가지를 자르고 있다.

3 미국
(A) Some papers are posted on a board.
(B) Some potted plants are arranged on a table.
(C) One of the women is pointing at a picture.
(D) One of the men is handing over a document.

(A) 문서가 게시판에 붙어 있다.
(B) 몇몇 화분들이 탁자 위에 놓여 있다.
(C) 여자들 중 한 명이 그림을 가리키고 있다.
(D) 남자들 중 한 명이 서류를 건네고 있다.

4 호주
(A) He's using a power tool.
(B) He's removing some carpet from the floor.
(C) He's fastening a safety mask.
(D) He's installing some cables in a room.

(A) 남자가 전동공구를 사용하고 있다.
(B) 남자가 바닥에서 카펫을 제거하고 있다.
(C) 남자가 방독면을 잡아매고 있다.
(D) 남자가 방에 케이블을 설치하고 있다.

5 영국
(A) A vehicle is being manufactured.
(B) A vehicle door is being opened.
(C) Some vehicles are in a row.
(D) Some vehicles are stopped at a traffic light.

(A) 한 차량이 제조되고 있다.
(B) 한 차량의 문이 열리고 있다.
(C) 몇몇 차량들이 일렬로 줄지어 있다.
(D) 몇몇 차량들이 신호등에 멈춰 있다.

6 미국
(A) One of the men is being photographed by the other.
(B) One of the men is pushing his bicycle down a path.
(C) The men are mowing some tall grass.
(D) The men are hiking in the mountains.

(A) 남자들 중 한 명이 다른 남자에게 사진 찍히고 있다.
(B) 남자들 중 한 명이 길을 따라 자전거를 밀며 나아가고 있다.
(C) 남자들이 길게 자란 풀을 베고 있다.
(D) 남자들이 산에서 하이킹하고 있다.

PART 2
P. 146

7 미국 ↔ 영국
Where's the bus terminal?
(A) Across the street from the hospital.
(B) A short-term lease.
(C) No, I usually take the subway.

버스 터미널이 어디에 있나요?
(A) 병원길 건너예요.
(B) 단기 임대요.
(C) 아니요, 저는 주로 지하철을 이용해요.

8 영국 ⇄ 호주

When will the computer parts be shipped out?
(A) By the end of the week.
(B) Through a shipping company.
(C) For a new computer monitor.

컴퓨터 부품은 언제 발송될까요?
(A) 이번 주말까지는 될 거예요.
(B) 운송회사를 통해서요.
(C) 새 컴퓨터 모니터용이에요.

9 미국 ⇄ 미국

Why did you take a day off yesterday?
(A) Not until I speak with Annie.
(B) Because I had to go see my dentist.
(C) I'll probably be back on Friday.

어제 왜 휴가를 내셨어요?
(A) Annie와 먼저 얘기해 봐야 해요.
(B) 치과 진료를 받아야 했거든요.
(C) 저는 아마 금요일에 돌아올 거예요.

10 호주 ⇄ 영국

Did you like the product demonstration this morning?
(A) Yes, it was helpful.
(B) The new breakfast cereal.
(C) I'd love to join you.

오늘 오전 제품 설명회 좋았어요?
(A) 네, 유익했어요.
(B) 새로운 아침 식사용 시리얼이요.
(C) 저도 함께하고 싶어요.

11 미국 ⇄ 미국

Would you like to tour our manufacturing plant?
(A) I don't have enough time.
(B) The product has been returned to the manufacturer.
(C) Sure, I can water the plants.

저희 제조 공장을 둘러보시겠어요?
(A) 시간이 별로 없어요.
(B) 제품이 제조사로 반송됐어요.
(C) 그럼요, 제가 식물에 물 줄 수 있어요.

12 미국 ⇄ 영국

When did you make your dentist appointment?
(A) The annual checkup.
(B) I booked in November.
(C) Dr. Chang will be with you shortly.

언제로 치과 예약했어요?
(A) 연간 검진이요.
(B) 11월로 예약했어요.
(C) Dr. Chang이 곧 오실 거예요.

13 호주 ⇄ 미국

How often is the carpet cleaned?
(A) I'll be traveling by car.
(B) The multi-purpose room is on the third floor.
(C) Every six months.

얼마나 자주 카펫을 청소하시나요?
(A) 저는 자동차로 여행할 거예요.
(B) 다목적실은 3층에 있어요.
(C) 6개월에 한 번이요.

14 미국 ⇄ 호주

I have to pick up the clients from the airport tomorrow afternoon.
(A) I see. Then I'll lead the meeting for you.
(B) Thursday's delivery.
(C) Thank you for putting it up.

내일 오후에 공항에 가서 고객들을 모셔 와야 해요.
(A) 그렇군요. 그럼 제가 대신 회의를 주재할게요.
(B) 목요일 배송이요.
(C) 게시해 줘서 고마워요.

15 영국 ⇄ 미국

Have the interns attended the orientation yet?
(A) That's scheduled for this afternoon.
(B) You should wait for your turn.
(C) Thank you for the orientation.

인턴들은 오리엔테이션에 참석했나요?
(A) 그건 오늘 오후로 예정되어 있어요.
(B) 차례를 기다려 주세요.
(C) 오리엔테이션 해주셔서 감사합니다.

16 미국 ⇄ 호주

What kind of cuisine does the restaurant serve?
(A) We're open from 11 A.M. to 10 P.M.
(B) Let me bring you the menu.
(C) Please wait here to be seated.

이 식당에서는 어떤 종류의 음식을 제공하나요?
(A) 오전 11시에서 오후 10시까지 영업합니다.
(B) 메뉴를 가져다드릴게요.
(C) 여기서 기다리시면 자리로 안내해 드릴게요.

17 미국 ⇄ 미국

Which of these wallpaper patterns do you prefer?
(A) The floral one, for sure.
(B) That picture should be moved.
(C) Sorry, I missed that one.

여기 벽지들 중에 어떤 게 마음에 드세요?
(A) 확실히 꽃무늬요.
(B) 저 사진은 옮겨야 해요.
(C) 죄송해요, 제가 그걸 빠트렸어요.

18 미국 ⇄ 영국

The museum will be closed this weekend.
(A) Actually, it's not that close.
(B) Let's reschedule our trip then.
(C) You're always on time.

이번 주말에는 박물관이 폐장합니다.
(A) 실은 그렇게 가깝지는 않아요.
(B) 그러면 일정을 다시 잡읍시다.
(C) 항상 시간 맞춰 오시네요.

19 영국 ⇄ 미국

Shouldn't Amira have arrived at the office by now?
(A) At the new office building.
(B) Yes, she's here.
(C) The order number is 250.

지금쯤이면 Amira가 사무실에 도착했어야 하지 않아요?
(A) 새로운 사무실 건물에요.
(B) 네, 여기 있어요.
(C) 주문 번호가 250이에요.

20 호주 ⇄ 미국

The lead vocalist gave an impressive performance, didn't he?
(A) He's my favorite.
(B) I've been taking singing classes.
(C) The movie tickets are sold out.

리드 보컬 무대가 인상적이었죠, 그렇지 않았나요?
(A) 제가 제일 좋아하는 가수예요.
(B) 제가 노래 수업을 듣고 있어요.
(C) 영화표가 매진됐어요.

21 미국 ⇄ 영국

Which vendor does your company use?
(A) Would 9 A.M. work for you?
(B) Thank you, but that won't be necessary.
(C) We went with Hardin Productions.

당신 회사에서는 어떤 협력업체를 이용하세요?
(A) 오전 9시 괜찮으세요?
(B) 감사합니다만, 필요 없어요.
(C) Hardin Productions로 선택했어요.

22 미국 ⇄ 미국

Are you interested in ordering some cake or ice cream?
(A) The movie was really interesting.
(B) I just want the bill.
(C) The items are in alphabetical order.

케이크를 주문하실래요, 아니면 아이스크림을 하실래요?
(A) 영화가 정말 재미있었어요.
(B) 계산서만 주세요.
(C) 항목은 알파벳 순으로 나와 있어요.

23 호주 ⇄ 미국

When are the delivery trucks scheduled to arrive at our facility?
(A) The date is in Jocelyn's e-mail.
(B) No, but we should rent the facility.
(C) Around 20 trucks.

배송 트럭이 저희 시설에 언제 도착 예정인가요?
(A) Jocelyn의 이메일에 날짜가 나와 있어요.
(B) 아니요, 하지만 저희가 시설을 빌려야 해요.
(C) 트럭 20대 정도요.

24 미국 ⇄ 호주

What are we publishing on the front page of our newspaper tomorrow?
(A) No, Dylan is the editor.
(B) Let's figure it out after lunch.
(C) It will be published next month.

내일 우리 신문 1면에는 뭘 실을 건가요?
(A) 아니요, Dylan이 편집장이에요.
(B) 점심식사 후에 생각해봐요.
(C) 다음 달에 출간될 거예요.

25 호주 ⇄ 미국

I didn't see you at the team dinner last night.
(A) Oh, I had to work overtime.
(B) I'd like the steak and a side salad.
(C) At the restaurant downtown.

어젯밤 회식 자리에서 안 보이던데요.
(A) 아, 저는 야근해야 했어요.
(B) 스테이크에 사이드로 샐러드 주세요.
(C) 시내 식당에서요.

26 미국 ⇄ 미국

Do you mind if I take the afternoon off?
(A) Sorry, I had to take yours.
(B) Try turning it on instead.
(C) Have you completed your article?

제가 오후에 휴가를 내도 될까요?
(A) 죄송해요, 제가 당신 걸 가져가야 했어요.
(B) 대신 그걸 켜 보세요.
(C) 기사 작성은 다 하셨어요?

27 미국 ⇄ 영국

Should we tour the manufacturing plant this week or next week?
(A) The factory manufactures glass.
(B) Let's get it over with.
(C) You can use a tourist visa.

제조 공장 견학을 이번 주에 할까요, 아니면 다음 주에 할까요?
(A) 공장은 유리를 생산합니다.
(B) 빨리 해치웁시다.
(C) 관광 비자로 가능하세요.

28 미국 ⇄ 미국

Frida, could you give me a lift to the office supplies store?
(A) I do need some binders.
(B) Sorry, he already left the office.
(C) We keep those stored in the kitchen.

Frida, 사무용품점까지 태워줄 수 있어요?
(A) 저 바인더가 꼭 필요하긴 해요.
(B) 죄송해요, 그분은 이미 퇴근하셨어요.
(C) 저희는 그것들을 주방에 보관해요.

29 미국 ⇄ 호주

Why hasn't the team moved into the new office yet?
(A) Renovations are time-consuming.
(B) I'll email it to you this afternoon.
(C) We bought some new furniture.

왜 부서가 아직 새로운 사무실로 이사하지 않았어요?
(A) 수리에 시간이 오래 걸려요.
(B) 오늘 오후에 이메일 보내드릴게요.
(C) 가구를 새로 샀어요.

30 미국 ⇄ 미국

How long does it take to walk to the subway station?
(A) It doesn't stop at this station.
(B) I ride the bus there.
(C) Usually by 8 A.M.

지하철역까지 걸어가는 데 얼마나 걸리나요?
(A) 이 역에는 정차하지 않아요.
(B) 저는 거기까지 버스로 가요.
(C) 보통 오전 8시까지요.

31 미국 ⇄ 호주

We've made the cake too sweet, haven't we?
(A) Our customers like that.
(B) We have some empty seats.
(C) Dark chocolate, not milk.

케이크를 너무 달게 만들었어요, 그렇지 않아요?
(A) 손님들이 그걸 좋아해요.
(B) 빈자리가 좀 있네요.
(C) 다크 초콜릿이요, 밀크 초콜릿 말고요.

PART 3

P. 147

미국 ⇄ 영국

Questions 32-34 refer to the following conversation.

M: Hello, this is Jean Carlos from Smiles Dentist Clinic. **I'm calling to confirm your wisdom tooth extraction for Wednesday at 9 A.M.**(32)

W: Yes, thank you. By the way, I'm allergic to certain medications, and **I was wondering if you received my medical history forms that were faxed to your office.**(33)

M: Let me check... Yes, we received your medical forms. One more thing, we encourage our patients not to drive after surgery. **So I'll send you the phone number of a cab service.**(34) They provide a discount for our patients.

32-34번은 다음 대화에 관한 문제입니다.

남: 안녕하세요, Smiles 치과의 Jean Carlos입니다. **수요일 오전 9시 사랑니 발치 건 확인차 전화 드립니다.**(32)

여: 네, 감사합니다. 참, 제가 특정 약물에 알레르기가 있어서요, **혹시 제 진료기록 서류를 팩스로 받아보셨는지 궁금해서요.**(33)

남: 확인해볼게요... 네, 진료 서류를 받았습니다. 한 가지 더 있는데요, 저희는 환자분께 수술 후 운전하지 않는 것을 권장 드립니다. **그래서 제가 택시회사 전화번호를 보내드릴게요.**(34) 저희 환자분들께는 할인을 해줍니다.

32 남자는 왜 여자에게 전화하는가?
(A) 예약을 확인하기 위해
(B) 과정을 설명하기 위해
(C) 결제 방법을 논의하기 위해
(D) 서명을 요청하기 위해

33 여자는 무엇을 알고 싶어 하는가?
(A) 더 많은 정보를 찾을 장소
(B) 시험 등록 시기
(C) 서류 수령 여부
(D) 불만 제기 방법

34 남자는 무엇을 제공하겠다고 말하는가?
(A) 할인 코드
(B) 주차증
(C) 전화번호
(D) 보증서

미국 ⇄ 미국

Questions 35-37 refer to the following conversation.

W: Hey, Lester. **It's fascinating to watch you operate that drone. I'm thinking about learning how to do that as well.**(35)

M: That's a great idea. **Since it's the football playoffs, the broadcasting station wanted me to use this drone to get an aerial shot of the game.**(36) We'd be able to see all the action from up high.

W: You're right. **Can you tell me more about how you received the certificate to fly the drone?**(37) Was it difficult?

M: It was quite easy, actually. **I just had to study the operating requirements and safety procedures. And then I took a two-hour test.**(37)

35-37번은 다음 대화에 관한 문제입니다.

여: 저기, Lester. 당신이 드론 조종하는 걸 보니 굉장히 끌리네요. **저도 작동법을 배울까 싶어요.**(35)

남: 좋은 생각이에요. **축구 플레이오프라서, 방송국에서 제가 이 드론으로 경기를 항공 촬영해 주길 원했어요.**(36) 높은 곳에서 모든 행동을 볼 수 있을 거예요.

여: 맞아요. **드론 조종 자격증을 어떻게 땄는지 좀 더 알려줄 수 있으세요?**(37) 어려웠나요?

남: 실은, 꽤 쉬웠어요. **조작 요건과 안전 절차를 공부하면 됐어요. 그러고 나서 두 시간짜리 시험을 봤어요.**(37)

35 여자는 무엇을 하고 싶다고 말하는가?
(A) 몇몇 동료들을 만나고 싶다고
(B) 해외로 여행을 가고 싶다고
(C) 새로운 기술을 배우고 싶다고
(D) 새로운 언어를 배우고 싶다고

36 남자는 어떤 종류의 행사를 언급하는가?
(A) 연극 공연
(B) 밴드 투어
(C) 영화제
(D) 스포츠 경기

37 남자는 여자에게 무엇을 설명하는가?
(A) 어느 사무실을 방문하는지
(B) 자격을 어떻게 취득하는지
(C) 어디서 등록하는지
(D) 몇몇 장비를 어떻게 설치하는지

호주 ⇄ 미국

Questions 38-40 refer to the following conversation.

M: Tanya, **we just got a radio transmission from the air traffic control tower. They won't clear our flight for touchdown yet.**(38)

W: Our passengers will be disappointed about that since a lot of them have connecting flights to catch once we land. Why won't they clear us?

M: **The controller said the airport is congested because of the influx of flights for the holidays.**(39) We probably won't be able to prepare for landing for another 10 minutes.

W: All right. **I'll use the intercom system and inform our passengers about the delay.**(40) I'll ask our flight attendants to serve some snacks and beverages as well.

38-40번은 다음 대화에 관한 문제입니다.

남: Tanya, **방금 항공 관제탑에서 무선을 받았어요. 우리 항공기 착륙 허가를 아직 내리지 않겠대요.**(38)

여: 탑승객 중에 착륙하면 연결 항공편을 탈 분들이 많아서 승객들이 실망하겠어요. 왜 허가를 안 할 거예요?

남: **관제관 말로는 휴가철이라 항공기가 몰려서 공항이 혼잡하다고 해요.**(39) 앞으로 10분 정도 착륙 준비를 할 수 없을 것 같아요.

여: 알았어요. **제가 기내 방송으로 승객에게 지연 공지를 할게요.**(40) 또한 승무원에게 스낵과 음료를 제공하라고 요청할게요.

38 화자들은 누구겠는가?
(A) 공항 엔지니어
(B) 화물 감독관
(C) 출입국 직원
(D) 항공기 조종사

39 무엇이 지연을 유발하고 있는가?
(A) 교통 혼잡
(B) 악천후
(C) 보안 확인
(D) 기술적 문제

40 여자는 다음에 무엇을 할 것인가?
(A) 탑승객 정보를 확인할 것이다
(B) 방송을 할 것이다
(C) 안전 절차를 살펴볼 것이다
(D) 공항 직원에게 연락할 것이다

미국 ⇄ 영국

Questions 41-43 refer to the following conversation.

M: Hey, Fatima. I really like your idea about creating a new mobile application for our users.

W: Thanks. A productivity app would help improve user experience.(41) We've received many requests for one as well.

M: You're right. Well, we'd probably need to hire three to four full-time app developers for the project.(42)

W: Did you see our annual budget?(42)

M: Ah. How about hiring just two then? It may take longer, but it would be cost-efficient.

W: Maybe we should work with an agency instead. Let me look up some agencies that can help us develop the app.(43)

41-43번은 다음 대화에 관한 문제입니다.

남: 안녕하세요, Fatima. 이용자용 신규 모바일 앱을 만든다는 당신의 아이디어가 아주 마음에 들어요.

여: 고마워요. 생산성 앱이 이용자 경험을 개선하는 데 도움이 될 거예요.(41) 요청을 많이 받기도 했어요.

남: 맞아요. 음, 그 프로젝트를 하려면 정규직 앱 개발자를 세, 네 명 채용해야 할 거예요.(42)

여: 우리 연간 예산 보셨어요?(42)

남: 아. 그러면 두 명만 채용하는 건 어때요? 시간이 좀 더 걸리겠지만, 비용 면에서 효율적일 거예요.

여: 그 대신 에이전시를 끼고 일하는 게 좋겠어요. 제가 앱 개발을 도와줄 에이전시를 몇 군데 알아볼게요.(43)

41 화자들은 주로 무엇을 논하고 있는가?
(A) 웹사이트 개발하기
(B) 이용자 경험 개선하기
(C) 고객과 소통하기
(D) 사무실 장비 구입하기

42 여자가 "우리 연간 예산 보셨어요"라고 말할 때 무엇을 내비치는가?
(A) 재무 보고서를 수정하고 싶어 한다.
(B) 연기된 마감일에 대해 남자에게 주의를 준다.
(C) 기밀문서에 접근할 수 있다.
(D) 제안에 대해 주저하는 마음이 있다.

43 여자는 다음에 무엇을 할 것인가?
(A) 몇몇 회사에 관해 알아볼 것이다
(B) 이메일을 재발송할 것이다
(C) 자신의 업무공간을 청소할 것이다
(D) 작업 일정을 업데이트할 것이다

미국 ⇄ 호주 ⇄ 미국

Questions 44-46 refer to the following conversation with three speakers.

W: Brad, Tyler, I'm excited about our vacation next month. (44) I heard Seoul has a lot of great restaurants and entertainment options.

M1: I'm looking forward to it, too! Have you booked the accommodations yet, Brad?(45)

M2: Umm... No. I've made a list of affordable hotels, but I want you two to review them before I choose.(45) Also, should we rent a car to get around there?

M1: I'm not sure. Celia, you've been there before, right?

W: Yeah, the public transportation system there is really great. I can install the mobile app for it on both of your phones.(46)

M2: I'd appreciate that!

44-46번은 다음 세 화자의 대화에 관한 문제입니다.

여: Brad, Tyler, 저는 다음 달 휴가 갈 생각에 신나요.(44) Seoul에 훌륭한 식당들과 즐길 거리들이 많다고 들었거든요.

남1: 저도 기대하고 있어요! 숙박은 예약했나요, Brad?(45)

남2: 음... 아니요. 가격이 적당한 호텔 목록을 만들었는데, 제가 고르기 전에 두 분이 검토해 주셨으면 해요.(45) 그리고, 거기서 돌아다니려면 렌터카를 이용해야 할까요?

남1: 잘 모르겠어요. Celia, 거기 가본 적 있잖아요, 그렇죠?

여: 네, 거기 대중교통 시스템이 아주 훌륭해요. 제가 두 분 핸드폰에 모바일 앱을 설치해 드릴 수 있어요.(46)

남2: 감사해요!

44 화자들은 다음 달에 무엇을 하려고 계획 중인가?
(A) 고객을 방문하려고
(B) 신규 프로젝트를 시작하려고
(C) 휴가를 가려고
(D) 회의에 참석하려고

45 Brad는 왜 아직 숙소를 예약하지 않았는가?
(A) 적당한 가격대의 예약 가능한 호텔들이 없다.
(B) 법인 신용카드를 사용해야만 한다.
(C) 의견을 받고 싶어 한다.
(D) 다음 주에 판촉 행사가 시작된다.

46 여자는 무엇을 하겠다고 제안하는가?
(A) 렌터카 대리점에 전화하겠다고
(B) 애플리케이션을 설치하겠다고
(C) 식당 메뉴를 인쇄하겠다고
(D) 티켓을 주문하겠다고

Questions 47-49 refer to the following conversation.

W: Brody, it's so nice to see you. **I can't believe it's been four years since our graduation. What have you been up to since college?**[47]

M: Yeah, well I did some volunteer work abroad for a year. That's how I discovered my passion for public service. **And after that I decided to go to law school.**[48]

W: Wow, that's great! How's it been?

M: It's been eye opening. I've learned a lot about contracts and civil procedures. I even interned at the National Law Association.

W: I'm so glad we met up then! **I need some advice on whether I should sign this new contract.**[49]

M: **I haven't passed the bar yet.**[49]

47-49번은 다음 대화에 관한 문제입니다.

여: Brody, 만나서 정말 반가워요. 졸업한 지 4년이 지났다니 믿겨지지가 않네요. 졸업하고 어떻게 지냈어요?[47]

남: 그렇네요, 음, 일 년 동안 해외에서 봉사활동을 했어요. 그 덕에 공익사업을 향한 열정을 찾았어요. 그 후에는 로스쿨에 진학하기로 했어요.[48]

여: 와, 잘됐네요! 어땠어요?

남: 눈이 번쩍 뜨였어요. 계약이랑 민사소송에 대해 많이 배웠어요. 전국법률협회에서 인턴도 했어요.

여: 우리가 만나서 다행이네요! 제가 이 신규 계약서에 서명해야 할지 조언이 필요하거든요.[49]

남: 제가 아직 변호사 시험을 통과하진 못했어요.[49]

47 화자들은 서로 어떻게 아는가?
(A) 서로 친척관계다.
(B) 같은 동네에 산다.
(C) 같은 사무실에서 일한다.
(D) 같은 대학을 나왔다.

48 남자는 어떤 직업에 종사하는가?
(A) 지도교사
(B) 은행원
(C) 변호사
(D) 교수

49 남자는 "제가 아직 변호사 시험을 통과하진 못했어요"라고 말할 때 무엇을 의미하는가?
(A) 여자에게 조언을 해줄 만한 자격을 아직 갖추지 못했다.
(B) 새로운 장비를 구매해야 한다.
(C) 대회를 위해 훈련하고 있지 않다.
(D) 관리자에게 물어봐야 할 것이다.

Questions 50-52 refer to the following conversation.

W: Randy, I had a meeting with an officer from the National Organic Food Department last week. **We discussed the steps our dairy farm could take to be eligible for organic certification.**[50]

M: I see. Well, **something we should do immediately is start letting our cows graze on pastures outdoors. That way most of their diet would come from grass, not feed.**[51]

W: That would be a great start. Next, **we should probably look into hiring a consultant who can help us with the rest of the certification process. I got a referral already, so I'll make a phone call later today.**[52]

50-52번은 다음 대화에 관한 문제입니다.

여: Randy, 제가 지난주에 국립 유기농 식품 부서 관계자와 회의를 했어요. 우리 낙농장이 유기농 인증을 받을 수 있는 단계에 대해 논의했어요.[50]

남: 그렇군요. 음, 우리가 당장 해야 할 일은 소를 야외 목초지에 방목하는 일이겠네요. 그렇게 하면 주식이 여물이 아니라 풀이 될 테니까요.[51]

여: 아주 좋은 출발이 되겠어요. 이제, 남은 인증 과정을 도와줄 컨설턴트 고용을 알아봐야 할 거예요. 제가 이미 추천을 받아 놓았으니, 이따 전화해 볼게요.[52]

50 화자들은 어디서 일하겠는가?
(A) 정부 기관에서
(B) 지역 식당에서
(C) 식품점에서
(D) 낙농장에서

51 남자는 무엇을 하고 싶어 하는가?
(A) 경력 노동자를 채용하고 싶어 한다
(B) 기법을 변경하고 싶어 한다
(C) 규정을 따르고 싶어 한다
(D) 장비를 더 구입하고 싶어 한다

52 여자는 오늘 무엇을 하겠다고 말하는가?
(A) 업계 전문가와 이야기하겠다고
(B) 가능 고객 목록을 작성하겠다고
(C) 연례 점검 일정을 마련하겠다고
(D) 사업 제안서를 제출하겠다고

Questions 53-55 refer to the following conversation.

M: Hey, Rosie. **You're covering the story on the IT Trade Show**[53] next week, right?

W: Yeah, I am. Why?

M: **One of my old colleagues develops his own mobile applications, and he's going to be revealing a new kind of camera app at the convention.**[54] I know you were looking to interview exhibitors, and I think he'd be a perfect candidate.

W: Ah, that sounds good. I'm actually meeting with the lead event planner tomorrow, so I'll try to arrange an interview with your colleague sometime after that.

M: OK, **let me give you his e-mail address.**[55] I'll tell him to expect your message.

53-55번은 다음 대화에 관한 문제입니다.

남: 저기, Rosie. 다음 주 있는 IT 무역 박람회에 대한 취재하시죠,[53] 맞죠?

여: 네, 맞아요. 왜요?

남: 제 예전 동료 중 한 명이 직접 모바일 앱을 개발하는데, 박람회에서 새로운 종류의 카메라 앱을 공개할 거예요.[54] 당신이 출품자들을 인터뷰하려고 한 걸로 알고 있는데, 제 생각에 그러면 아주 훌륭한 후보자가 될 것 같아요.

여: 아, 그거 좋죠. 실은 내일 행사 총 기획자와 만나기로 했는데, 그 후에 당신 동료와 인터뷰 자리를 마련해볼게요.

남: 알았어요, **그 친구 이메일 주소를 알려드릴게요.**(55) 그 친구에게는 당신이 메시지를 보낼 거라고 말해둘게요.

53 여자는 누구겠는가?
(A) 행사 준비위원
(B) 전문 사진작가
(C) 뉴스 기자
(D) 컴퓨터 기술자

54 남자의 친구는 무엇을 만드는가?
(A) 스피커
(B) 노트북 컴퓨터
(C) 디지털카메라
(D) 모바일 프로그램

55 남자는 여자에게 무엇을 주는가?
(A) 콘퍼런스 일정표
(B) 방문자 출입증
(C) 신청서
(D) 연락처

호주 ⇄ 미국 ⇄ 영국

Questions 56-58 refer to the following conversation with three speakers.

M: Tricia, are the arrangements for Anthony's retirement party going all right?(56) I know you haven't planned something like this before.

W1: It's going great. I've already got a venue reserved.

M: Oh, good. And you've ordered food?

W1: Well, Chelsea's actually taking care of that. Let's check. Hey, Chelsea, have we ordered food for the retirement party yet?

W2: Actually, I'm still waiting for a list of foods that people prefer.(57)

M: Hmm. We need to make sure there is a catering service available to make enough food for us that night. I really think you should order something right away.(58) We can change the menu later if it's necessary.

56-58번은 다음 세 화자의 대화에 관한 문제입니다.

남: Tricia, Anthony의 은퇴식 준비는 잘 돼가고 있어요?(56) 전에 이런 일을 계획해보지 않은 걸로 알고 있어서요.

여1: 잘 돼가고 있어요. 이미 장소도 예약했고요.

남: 오, 좋아요. 음식은 주문하셨어요?

여1: 어, 그건 Chelsea가 할 거예요. 확인해보죠. Chelsea, 은퇴식을 위해 음식을 주문했어요?

여2: 실은, 사람들이 선호하는 음식 명단을 아직 기다리고 있어요.(57)

남: 흠. 그날 저녁에 우리에게 충분한 음식을 제공할 수 있는 케이터링 서비스가 있는지 확실히 알아봐야 해요. **지금 바로 주문을 하셔야 할 것 같아요.**(58) 메뉴는 필요하면 나중에 바꿀 수 있어요.

56 화자들은 무엇에 관해 논의하고 있는가?
(A) 재무 계획을 짜는 일
(B) 회사 합병을 완료하는 일
(C) 음악 공연에 참석하는 일
(D) 은퇴식을 준비하는 일

57 Chelsea는 어떤 정보를 필요로 하는가?
(A) 음식 선호 명단
(B) 예산안 승인
(C) 공급업체 연락처
(D) 발표 안건

58 남자는 가급적 빨리 무엇을 하라고 제안하는가?
(A) 예약을 변경하라고
(B) 응답을 확인하라고
(C) 주문을 하라고
(D) 대금을 보내라고

영국 ⇄ 호주

Questions 59-61 refer to the following conversation.

W: Will, I need to speak to you since you're the floor supervisor.(59)

M: What's wrong? Do we have a problem with the assembly machines? Are we falling behind on our production?(59)

W: The machines are OK, but we can't start producing our water bottles right now. The shipment of plastic polymers scheduled for this morning has been delayed, which is a huge problem.(60) I'm not sure if we'll be able to meet the deadline.

M: Did you let Robyn know? She's the supplies manager.

W: I did. She's on a call with the supplier.(61)

M: Ah, thanks. Let me see if I can join them now.(61)

59-61번은 다음 대화에 관한 문제입니다.

여: Will, 총 감독관이시니 드릴 말씀이 있어요.(59)

남: 무슨 일이죠? 조립 기계에 문제 있으세요? 생산이 지연되고 있나요?(59)

여: 기계에는 문제 없는데요, 지금 바로 생수병 생산을 시작할 수 없어요. 오늘 아침으로 예정된 플라스틱 폴리머 배송이 지연돼서, 큰 문제가 되고 있어요.(60) 저희가 마감일에 맞출 수 있을지 모르겠어요.

남: Robyn에게 알려줬어요? 그녀가 물품 관리자예요.

여: 알렸어요. 공급업체와 통화하는 중이에요.(61)

남: 아, 고마워요. 제가 지금 합류할 수 있는지 알아볼게요.(61)

59 화자들은 어디서 일하겠는가?
(A) 제조 공장에서
(B) 수송 창고에서
(C) 기계 정비소에서
(D) 고객 서비스 센터에서

60 여자는 어떤 문제점을 언급하는가?
(A) 배송이 도착하지 않았다.
(B) 직원이 아프다.
(C) 일부 기계가 작동하지 않는다.
(D) 일부 문서가 제자리에 없다.

61 남자는 다음에 무엇을 하겠는가?
(A) 송장을 재발급할 것이다
(B) 새로운 공급업체를 찾을 것이다
(C) 전화 회의에 참여할 것이다
(D) 항의 편지를 작성할 것이다

Questions 62-64 refer to the following conversation and list.

W: Hey, Richard. Did you hear the news? **To celebrate our TV station's anniversary, the director of programming wants to rebroadcast some newsclips from 70 years ago.** (62)

M: Wow, what a wonderful way to showcase our seven decades in the business!

W: I know, right? I've been watching the old newsclips and compiled this list of possible segments we could air. **How do you feel about broadcasting this video from March 22?**(63)

M: **Our viewers will enjoy that.**(63) We should also show them what the location looks like now. **Let me talk to our camera crew.** (64)

62-64번은 다음 대화와 목록에 관한 문제입니다.

여: 안녕하세요, Richard. 그 소식 들었어요? **저희 TV 방송국 창립 기념일을 축하하기 위해, 프로그램 감독이 70년 전의 뉴스 클립을 재방영하고 싶어 하네요.**(62)

남: 우와, 우리의 70년 사업을 소개할 수 있는 정말 멋진 방법이네요!

여: 네, 그렇죠? 제가 오래된 뉴스 클립을 보면서 우리가 방송할 수 있는 가능한 부분들을 목록으로 정리했습니다. **3월 22일 이 영상부터 방송하는 게 어떨까요?**(63)

남: **시청자들이 즐겁게 볼 거예요.**(63) 그분들께 그곳이 지금은 어떤 모습인지도 보여드려야 할 것 같아요. **저희 카메라 팀과 얘기해 볼게요.**(64)

방송 날짜	클립
3월 21일	관광객이 지역 동물원에 방문하다
3월 22일	**Reyes 극장의 대개장**(63)
3월 23일	미술관의 새 전시회
3월 24일	Westville 도시공원의 음악 공연

62 TV 방송국에서 왜 뉴스 클립을 방송할 것인가?
(A) 지역 행사를 홍보하기 위해
(B) 지역 업체의 프로필을 알려주기 위해
(C) 도시의 건축양식을 선보이기 위해
(D) 기념일을 축하하기 위해

63 시각 자료를 보시오. 여자가 어떤 클립을 언급하는가?
(A) 관광객이 지역 동물원에 방문하다
(B) Reyes 극장의 대개장
(C) 미술관의 새 전시회
(D) Westville 도시공원의 음악 공연

64 남자는 무엇을 하겠다고 말하는가?
(A) 정보를 확인하겠다고
(B) 동료들에게 연락하겠다고
(C) 영상 클립을 보겠다고
(D) 주민들을 인터뷰하겠다고

Questions 65-67 refer to the following conversation and storage racks.

M: Cindy, have you checked out the canned foods section? **We're all out of the beans and corn. So we'll have to get some more from this storage room.**(65)

W: OK. I'll get to that once I finish unpacking these crates of oranges.(66) By the way, do you have another scanning device I can use? This one is running low on battery power.

M: Yeah, I'll grab you one from the office. Also, once you've finished both tasks, **please pick up any unused boxes and put them in the recycling bin.**(67)

65-67번은 다음 대화와 저장고에 관한 문제입니다.

남: Cindy, 통조림식품 구역을 확인하셨나요? 콩과 옥수수가 다 떨어졌어요. 그래서 이 창고에서 좀 가져가야 해요.(65)

여: 네. 오렌지 상자들을 풀고 난 후 바로 시작할게요.(66) 그런데, 혹시 제가 사용할 수 있는 다른 스캐너가 있나요? 이건 배터리가 거의 없어요.

남: 네, 사무실에서 하나 가져다드릴게요. 그리고, 두 가지 업무를 끝내면, 사용하지 않는 상자를 가져다가 재활용품 통에 넣어주세요.(67)

선반 1	사과
선반 2	오렌지(66)
선반 3	복숭아
선반 4	딸기

65 남자는 어떤 문제를 보고하는가?
(A) 창고가 청소되어야 한다.
(B) 물품을 다시 채워야 한다.
(C) 식품의 유통기한이 만료되었다.
(D) 배송품이 파손되었다.

66 시각 자료를 보시오. 여자는 어떤 선반에서 작업하고 있는가?
(A) 선반 1
(B) 선반 2
(C) 선반 3
(D) 선반 4

67 남자는 여자에게 무엇을 하라고 지시하는가?
(A) 상자를 폐기하라고
(B) 장치를 수리하라고
(C) 업체에 전화하라고
(D) 고객 문의에 대응하라고

Questions 68-70 refer to the following conversation and poster.

W: Hey, Jerome. Are you looking forward to the cooking contest?

M: I am! I heard all the contestants are famous local chefs.

W: **How about riding to the fair together?**(68) John from Purchasing has a van, and he says he's got room for a couple more people.

M: Ah, I have some errands to run early afternoon. **But I should arrive in time to watch my favorite cuisine being prepared at 3 o'clock.**(69) I'll see you all in front of Elk Arena.

W: All right. Also, **remember to wear a thick jacket.**(70) It's going to be cloudy and chilly all day.

68-70번은 다음 대화와 포스터에 관한 문제입니다.

여: Jerome. 요리 경연대회를 기대하고 있나요?

남: 네! 모든 경연자들이 지역에서 유명한 요리사들이라고 들었어요.

여: 행사장까지 함께 차를 타고 가시는 건 어떠세요?(68) 구매부의 John에게 밴이 있는데, 몇 사람 더 탈 자리가 있다고 하네요.

남: 아, 제가 오후 일찍 급히 해야 할 일이 좀 있어서요. 하지만 3시에 제가 가장 좋아하는 요리가 준비되는 걸 보러 시간에 맞춰 갈 순 있을 거예요.(69) 여러분 모두 Elk 아레나 앞에서 뵐게요.

여: 알겠어요. 그리고, 잊지 말고 두꺼운 재킷을 입고 오세요.(70) 하루 종일 흐리고 쌀쌀할 거라고 하네요.

Mayertown 요리 경연대회	
5월 25일 일정	
시간 / 장소	요리
오후 2시 / Elk 아레나	중식
오후 3시 / Elk 아레나	**이탈리아식(69)**
오후 4시 / Remo 아레나	멕시코식
오후 5시 / Remo 아레나	그리스식

68 여자는 무엇을 하자고 제안하는가?
(A) 자리를 바꾸자고
(B) 일찍 만나자고
(C) 차를 같이 타고 가자고
(D) 음식을 주문하자고

69 시각 자료를 보시오. 남자가 가장 좋아하는 음식은 무엇인가?
(A) 중식
(B) 이탈리아식
(C) 멕시코식
(D) 그리스식

70 여자는 남자에게 무엇을 하라고 상기하는가?
(A) 테이블을 예약하라고
(B) 따뜻한 옷을 입으라고
(C) 서식을 제출하라고
(D) 우산을 가져하라고

PART 4

호주

Questions 71-73 refer to the following telephone message.

M: Hello there, Tiffany. Ivan Flores here. **I'm calling to ask about the property that our development firm recently acquired.**(71) I realize we don't have any concrete plans for the property at the moment, so I'd like to make a suggestion. **It's a great location, with easy access to the expressway.**(72) I was thinking maybe we could develop it into a shopping mall. **I want to talk to you about this before our board meeting next Friday. I won't be able to attend because I'll be traveling for my sister's wedding.** (73) Could you call me back as soon as possible?

71-73번은 다음 전화 메시지에 관한 문제입니다.

남: Tiffany, 안녕하세요. Ivan Flores예요. **저희 개발 회사에서 최근에 취득한 부동산 관련 문제로 전화 드려요.**(71) 저희가 현재 부동산에 대한 구체적인 계획이 없다는 걸 알게 돼서, 제안을 하나 드리려고요. **그곳이 위치가 아주 좋은데다, 고속도로 접근이 용이하죠.**(72) 쇼핑몰로 개발하면 어떨까 싶어요. 다음 주 금요일 이사회 전에 이 문제에 대해 논의하고 싶어요. 제가 여동생 결혼식에 가야 해서 참석하지 못하거든요.(73) 최대한 빨리 회신해 주시겠어요?

71 화자는 누구겠는가?
(A) 건설 노동자
(B) 시 공무원
(C) 건물 관리자
(D) 부동산 개발자

72 화자는 위치의 어떤 면을 마음에 들어 하는가?
(A) 주요 주거 지역에 있다.
(B) 편리한 곳에 위치한다.
(C) 해변에 가기 용이하다.
(D) 주차 공간이 많다.

73 화자는 왜 회의에 못 가는가?
(A) 예식에 참석할 예정이다.
(B) 구경하는 집을 안내할 예정이다.
(C) 차가 고장 났다.
(D) 열차가 지연됐다.

미국

Questions 74-76 refer to the following advertisement.

M: Are you looking for your next superstar to lead a new project? Perhaps you are in need of someone with very specialized skills? **WeCrewt.com is here to help.**(74) We are a top-tier headhunting firm with a diverse network of contacts. Whatever your needs are, WeCrewt can find the right person for you. **Sign up for a consultation today at www.wecrewt.com and find out how we can help you.** (75) As a bonus for this week only, if you are a new client, you will receive a $50 gift certificate to Ethereal, the trendiest office furniture store in the city.(76)

TEST 10

74-76번은 다음 광고에 관한 문제입니다.

남: 새로운 프로젝트를 이끌 차기 슈퍼스타를 찾고 계시나요? 고도의 전문 기술을 가진 사람이 필요한 것 같으세요? WeCrewt.com에서 도와드립니다.(74) 저희는 다양한 인적 네트워크를 구축한 일류 헤드헌팅 회사입니다. 무엇을 필요로 하시든 WeCrewt에서 당신에게 딱 맞는 사람을 찾아드립니다. 오늘 www.wecrewt.com에서 상담을 등록하셔서 저희가 어떻게 도와드릴 수 있는지 알아보세요.(75) 신규 고객이시라면 이번 주에만 보너스로 시내에서 가장 핫한 사무용 가구점인 Ethereal에서 이용 가능한 50달러짜리 상품권을 받게 됩니다.(76)

74 무엇이 광고되고 있겠는가?
(A) 직업 알선 업체
(B) 인테리어 디자인 회사
(C) 보관 창고
(D) 온라인 광고 서비스

75 화자는 청자들에게 무엇을 하라고 권하는가?
(A) 서류를 읽어보라고
(B) 지원자 면접을 보라고
(C) 고객 후기를 작성하라고
(D) 상담을 신청하라고

76 첫 이용 고객은 이번 주에 무엇을 받게 되는가?
(A) 콘서트 티켓
(B) 맞춤 머그잔
(C) 매장용 상품권
(D) 잡지 구독권

Questions 77-79 refer to the following excerpt from a meeting.

W: I called this meeting because I'm concerned about our turnover rate. We're having to recruit checkout staff every month because someone is always leaving.(77) I think there are ways we can retain the employees we already have. Starting next month, we're going to start running leadership workshops with the purpose of providing pathways into higher roles here.(78) I want everyone here to submit some ideas for skills a manager or leader should have. I understand many of you do not have experience in management, and that's perfectly fine. Submit your ideas anyway. In fact, some of the best feedback actually comes from the users.(79)

77-79번은 다음 회의 발췌록에 관한 문제입니다.

여: 오늘 회의를 소집한 건 이직률이 걱정돼서예요. 끊임없이 누군가가 나가니 매달 계산대 직원을 채용해야 하는 상황입니다.(77) 저희가 기존 직원을 유지할 수 있는 방법이 있다고 봅니다. 다음 달부터 이곳에서 고위직으로 나아가는 방향을 제공하려는 목적으로 리더십 워크숍을 실시할 예정입니다.(78) 저는 여기 계신 모든 분께서 관리자나 지도자가 가져야 하는 기술에 대한 아이디어를 내주셨으면 합니다. 많은 분들이 관리직에의 경험이 없다는 건 알고 있으며, 그 부분은 완전히 괜찮습니다. 개의치 말고 의견을 내주세요. 사실, 최고의 피드백은 실제 사용자에게서 나오는 법이죠.(79)

77 화자는 무엇이 걱정된다고 말하는가?
(A) 직원 이직률
(B) 예상 매출액
(C) 상점 보안
(D) 배송 지연

78 다음 달에 어떤 프로젝트가 시작되는가?
(A) 보상 시스템
(B) 해외 진출
(C) 매장 개조
(D) 리더십 워크숍

79 화자는 왜 "최고의 피드백은 실제 사용자에게서 나오는 법이죠"라고 말하는가?
(A) 요점에 동의하지 않기 위해
(B) 문제를 강조하기 위해
(C) 직원들을 독려하기 위해
(D) 다른 아이디어를 제안하기 위해

Questions 80-82 refer to the following announcement.

M: May I have your attention, please? I've just received notice that there is some road construction ahead that is causing delays on the highway.(80)/(81) As a result, we will be arriving at the terminal about an hour later than originally scheduled. We'll be pulling into a rest area shortly to fill up on gas. You may use this time to purchase snacks and use the restroom. Please make sure to take your belongings with you when you get off the bus.(82) We are not responsible for any lost items. We apologize for the inconvenience.

80-82번은 다음 안내 방송에 관한 문제입니다.

남: 승객 여러분께 안내 말씀드립니다. 방금 전방에 고속도로 정체를 유발하고 있는 도로공사가 있다는 통보를 받았습니다.(80)/(81) 따라서 터미널에는 원래 예정보다 한 시간 늦게 도착할 것입니다. 곧 주유를 위해 휴게소에 도착합니다. 이 시간을 이용하여 간식을 구매하시거나 화장실을 이용하실 수 있습니다. 버스에서 내리실 때는 반드시 소지품을 챙기시기 바랍니다.(82) 저희는 분실물에 대한 책임을 지지 않습니다. 불편을 끼쳐드리는 점 사과드립니다.

80 안내방송이 어디서 나오겠는가?
(A) 기차 안에서
(B) 버스 안에서
(C) 비행기 안에서
(D) 연락선 안에서

81 화자는 어떤 문제점을 언급하는가?
(A) 험한 날씨
(B) 인력 부족
(C) 시스템 결함
(D) 도로공사

82 청자들은 무엇을 하라고 안내받는가?
(A) 자리에 계속 앉아있으라고
(B) 할인 쿠폰을 가져가라고
(C) 소지품을 챙기라고
(D) 가족들에게 연락하라고

Questions 83-85 refer to the following telephone message.

M: Hello. I'm calling for Barbara Loggins. I was driving through the Glenmoore community because I'm looking to buy a house there, and I came across your real estate ad. I really like the fact that there is a recreation center nearby, as health and fitness are very important to me.(83) Concerning the kind of house I want, I need a place with a basement that has enough room for my music equipment—I have quite a lot.(84) I'm leaving the country tonight to do some business overseas, so I'll give you another call when I get back.(85)

83-85번은 다음 전화 메시지에 관한 문제입니다.

남: 안녕하세요. Barbara Loggins께 메시지 남깁니다. Glenmoore 지역에 집을 사려고 알아보기 위해, 차를 타고 지나가다 당신의 부동산 광고를 우연히 발견했어요. 저에게는 건강과 운동이 매우 중요해서 인근에 레크리에이션 센터가 있다는 사실이 정말 마음에 들어요.(83) 원하는 집의 종류에 관해 말씀드리자면, 음악 장비를 위한 공간이 충분한 지하실이 있는 곳이 필요합니다–꽤 많거든요.(84) 제가 오늘 밤 업무차 해외로 출국해서요, 돌아와서 다시 전화 드리겠습니다.(85)

83 화자는 왜 Glenmoore 지역에 관심이 있는가?
(A) 레크리에이션 센터 근처에 있다.
(B) 보안 출입문이 있다.
(C) 학군이 좋다.
(D) 가격이 알맞다.

84 화자는 자신의 집에 무엇을 원하는가?
(A) 홈 시어터
(B) 정원
(C) 가구가 비치된 거실
(D) 넓은 지하실

85 화자는 오늘 저녁에 무엇을 할 거라고 말하는가?
(A) 악기를 구매한다
(B) 밴드와 만난다
(C) 집주인과 이야기한다
(D) 출장을 간다

Questions 86-88 refer to the following telephone message.

W: Hi, Dwight. This is Belinda Lane from Barfoot Partners. I'm calling to give you an update on our new location. Yesterday, the management team reported that it is our most successful opening yet, and the feedback from customers has been fantastic.(86) To show our gratitude for helping us with this, we'd like to invite you and your staff to a celebration event. We're hoping that you can take the stage to explain the ideation process that went into the construction of the store.(87) I think our staff would love that. If that sounds good, I'd like to organize a suitable time and date for the event. The first week of July is looking quite good. After that is generally when we expect things to pick up dramatically.(88)

86-88번은 다음 전화 메시지에 관한 문제입니다.

여: 안녕하세요, Dwight. 저는 Barfoot Partners의 Belinda Lane 입니다. 저희 신규 지점에 대한 소식을 알려드리고자 전화 드립니다. 어제, 역대 가장 성공적인 개장이었고, 고객의 반응이 엄청났다는 경영진의 발표가 있었습니다.(86) 저희를 도와주신 데 감사를 표하고자, 귀하와 귀하의 직원들을 축하 행사에 초대하고 싶습니다. 저희는 귀하께서 무대에 올라 매장 건설을 시작하게 된 아이디어화 과정을 설명해주셨으면 합니다.(87) 저희 직원들이 아주 좋아할 것 같습니다. 괜찮으시다면, 적합한 행사 날짜 및 시간을 정하고자 합니다. 7월 첫째 주가 아주 좋아 보입니다. 그 이후에는 보통 저희가 일이 급격히 많아지는 시기로 보거든요.(88)

86 화자는 무엇을 알리게 되어 흥분하는가?
(A) 협찬 계약이 확정됐다.
(B) 시설 관리자가 새로 채용됐다.
(C) 프로젝트가 예정보다 일찍 마무리됐다.
(D) 매장 개장이 성공적이었다.

87 화자는 청자가 행사에서 무엇을 하기를 바라는가?
(A) 의견을 수렴하기를 바란다
(B) 명함을 나눠주기를 바란다
(C) 발표하기를 바란다
(D) 경영진을 만나기를 바란다

88 화자는 왜 "그 이후에는 보통 저희가 일이 급격히 많아지는 시기로 보거든요"라고 말하는가?
(A) 시간이 나지 않을 수 있음을 내비치기 위해
(B) 지원을 요청하기 위해
(C) 좌절을 표현하기 위해
(D) 제안에 반대하기 위해

Questions 89-91 refer to the following excerpt from a meeting.

W: Let's begin by taking a look at last month's production numbers. As you can see, we saw a seven-percent decline in output, which means we'll need to raise our manufacturing rate in the factory. We, as managers,(89) are aware that a few of our packaging machines on the production line have been malfunctioning and that has been the cause of the decline. So we've decided to install new ones this Friday.(90) These machines function a lot quicker and won't require frequent repairs. We have scheduled several training workshops next week, so please sign up for one as soon as possible.(91) A list will be posted in the staff room.

89-91번은 다음 회의 발췌록에 관한 문제입니다.

여: 지난달 생산 수치를 보면서 시작합시다. 보시다시피 생산량이 7 퍼센트 감소했는데, 이는 공장 생산율을 높여야 한다는 것을 의미합니다. 저희 관리자들은(89) 생산 라인의 포장기계 몇 대가 오작동을 일으키고 있으며 이것이 감소의 원인이라는 걸 알고 있는 바입니다. 따라서 이번 주 금요일에 새 기계를 설치하기로 했습니다.(90) 이 기계는 훨씬 더 빠르게 가동되며 잦은 수리도 필요하지 않을 것입니다. 다음 주에 교육 워크숍 일정을 잡아 놓았으니 되도록 빨리 신청하시기 바랍니다.(91) 목록은 직원 사무실에 게시하겠습니다.

89 화자는 누구겠는가?
(A) 수리 기사
(B) 공장 감독관
(C) 프로그램 개발자
(D) 자동차 판매사원

90 화자에 따르면, 이번 주에 무엇이 교체될 것인가?
(A) 소프트웨어
(B) 기계
(C) 이름표
(D) 보관시설

91 청자들은 무엇을 하라고 요청받는가?
(A) 교육에 등록하라고
(B) 안전 장비를 착용하라고
(C) 다가오는 점검에 대비하라고
(D) 아이디어를 제안하라고

미국

Questions 92-94 refer to the following tour information.

W: Good afternoon. I'll be your guide today here at the Fremont Museum. **This museum is one of the largest in California.** In fact, it covers an area of nearly 70,000 square meters. (92) **We are proud to offer free admission, but the museum does rely on financial donations from our guests.**(93) All right, let's start with the Ancient Egypt exhibit. **We ask that you not use your cameras in this exhibit.** Thank you in advance for your kind understanding.(94)

92-94번은 다음 여행 정보에 관한 문제입니다.

여: 안녕하세요. 저는 오늘 여러분께 이곳 Fremont 박물관을 소개해 드릴 가이드입니다. 이 박물관은 California에서 가장 큰 박물관 중 하나인데요. 실은 거의 7만제곱미터 면적을 차지하고 있습니다.(92) 저희는 무료입장 시행을 자랑스럽게 생각하고 있습니다만, 박물관이 방문객의 재정 기부에 의존하는 것도 사실입니다.(93) 그럼, 고대 이집트 전시관부터 시작하죠. 이 전시관에서는 카메라 사용을 삼가시길 바랍니다. 양해에 미리 감사드립니다.(94)

92 화자는 박물관에 관하여 무엇을 강조하는가?
(A) 직원
(B) 역사
(C) 규모
(D) 위치

93 화자는 왜 "박물관이 방문객의 재정 기부에 의존하는 것도 사실입니다"라고 말하는가?
(A) 방문객의 불만 사항에 대응하기 위해
(B) 회원제에 관해 설명하기 위해
(C) 기부금을 요청하기 위해
(D) 개정된 정책을 발표하기 위해

94 화자에 따르면, 무엇이 금지되는가?
(A) 사진을 찍는 것
(B) 그룹을 이탈하는 것
(C) 가방을 소지하는 것
(D) 유물을 만지는 것

미국

Questions 95-97 refer to the following announcement and schedule.

M: I am excited to announce that our company will soon begin its month-long Productivity Challenge. As you can see by this schedule, for each week in March, we'll hold daily sessions on one aspect of becoming a more effective employee. **Teams with 100-percent participation will be rewarded with generous prize money.**(95) In addition, the company will be holding a health seminar at the local recreation center. **This event will be held at the end of the week that is dedicated to physical activity.**(96) This will give you a chance to learn how to eat right and adopt a healthy lifestyle. **For those of you who'd like to participate in the special seminar, complete a registration form online.**(97)

95-97번은 다음 공지와 일정표에 관한 문제입니다.

남: 우리 회사가 한 달간 생산성 증진 프로그램을 시작할 예정임을 알려드리게 되어 기쁩니다. 이 일정표에서 보실 수 있는 것처럼, 3월 한 달간 매주 더욱 유능한 직원이 되는 한 가지 방법에 관해 매일 교육을 진행할 예정입니다. 참석률이 100퍼센트인 팀은 후한 상금을 포상으로 받게 됩니다.(95) 뿐만 아니라 우리 회사는 이 지역 레크리에이션 센터에서 건강 세미나를 주최합니다. 이 행사는 주로 운동을 많이 하는 주말에 열릴 예정입니다.(96) 이 세미나를 통해 여러분은 올바른 식습관을 갖고 건강한 생활방식으로 바꿀 수 있는 기회를 얻게 될 것입니다. 특별 세미나에 참석하시고 싶은 분들은 온라인 등록양식을 작성하시기 바랍니다.(97)

생산성 증진 프로그램	
1주 차	삶과 일을 정리하라
2주 차	신체 활동으로 활기를 얻어라(96)
3주 차	기술 역량을 개발하라
4주 차	발표력을 향상시켜라

95 일부 직원들은 어떤 보상을 받을 것인가?
(A) 상금
(B) 1일 휴가
(C) 할인 쿠폰
(D) 무료 식사

96 시각 자료를 보시오. 세미나는 언제 있을 것인가?
(A) 1주 차
(B) 2주 차
(C) 3주 차
(D) 4주 차

97 세미나에 참석하고 싶은 청자들은 무엇을 해야 하는가?
(A) 행사 주최 측에 연락해야 한다
(B) 설명회에 가야 한다
(C) 보증금을 지불해야 한다
(D) 신청서를 작성해야 한다

Questions 98-100 refer to the following talk and graph.

M: Thank you for attending this talk on promoting sustainability in cities. While I'm here, I'd also like to congratulate Mayor Wagner for her recent efforts on reducing unemployment in the city.(98) To build on the success of that project, becoming greener is sure to make our city the most livable city in the world. First, I want to start with the data. A recent survey showed that only 11% of our car owners have electric vehicles.(99) Some cities measure 30% on this metric. Clearly, this is an area we can improve on. I have information on the initiatives these other cities took to promote electric vehicles. Let me pass these around, and you can take a look before I continue.(100)

98-100번은 다음 담화와 그래프에 관한 문제입니다.

남: 도시 내 지속 가능성 증진을 주제로 한 오늘 강연에 참석해 주셔서 감사합니다. 이 자리에 선 김에, 최근 도시 실업률을 낮추느라 애써주신 데 대해 Wagner 시장님께 축하의 말씀을 드리고 싶습니다.(98) 그 프로젝트의 성공에 더해, 친환경을 실천하면 우리 도시를 세계에서 가장 살기 좋은 도시로 만들게 될 거라 확신합니다. 우선, 자료부터 살펴보겠습니다. 최근 조사에 따르면, 저희는 자동차를 소유한 사람들 중 11퍼센트만이 전기차를 소유하고 있습니다.(99) 몇몇 도시에서는 이 측정 기준을 기준으로 30퍼센트를 기록했습니다. 확실히 개선의 여지가 있는 부분입니다. 다른 도시들에서 전기차를 홍보하기 위해 취했던 계획에 관한 정보를 가지고 있습니다. 제가 나눠 드릴 테니, 계속 진행하기 전에 살펴봐 주세요.(100)

98 화자는 왜 Wagner 시장에게 축하하는가?
   (A) 시장이 사비로 새로운 계획에 투자하고 있다.
   (B) 시장이 현재 전기차를 소유하고 있다.
   (C) 시장이 최근 재선됐다.
   (D) 시장이 중요한 프로젝트에 착수했다.

99 시각 자료를 보시오. 강연은 어디서 이루어지는가?
   (A) Potwin에서
   (B) Canterbury에서
   (C) Saginaw에서
   (D) Mountain Brook에서

100 화자는 다음에 무엇을 할 것인가?
   (A) 자료를 나눠줄 것이다
   (B) 다음 강연자를 소개할 것이다
   (C) 질문에 답할 것이다
   (D) 다양한 제품을 보여줄 것이다

파고다
토익 LC

실전 1000제 | 정답·해석